Lecture N
Computer

Lecture Notes in Computer Science

Lecture Notes in Computer Science

Edited by G. Goos and J. Hartmanis

54

Design and Implementation of Programming Languages

Proceedings of a DoD Sponsored Workshop
Ithaca, October 1976

Edited by
John H. Williams and David A. Fisher

Springer-Verlag
Berlin Heidelberg New York 1977

Editors

Prof. John H. Williams
Dept. of Computer Science
Cornell University
Ithaca, N.Y. 14850/USA

Dr. David A. Fisher
Research Staff
Sciences and Technology Division
Institute for Defense Analyses
400 Army-Navy Drive
Arlington, Virginia 22202/USA

Library of Congress Cataloging in Publication Data
Main entry under title:

Design and implementation of programming languages.

    (Lecture notes in computer science ; v. 54)
    Bibliography: p.
    Includes index.
    1. Programming languages (Electronic computers)--
Congresses. I. Williams, John H., 1939-
II. Fisher, David A., 1942-   III. United
States. Dept. of Defense. IV. Series.
QA76.7.D47   001.6'424   77-21344

AMS Subject Classifications (1970): 68-02, 68 A 05
CR Subject Classifications (1974): 4.2

ISBN 3-540-08360-X Springer-Verlag Berlin Heidelberg New York
ISBN 0-387-08360-X Springer-Verlag New York Heidelberg Berlin

Printing and binding: Beltz Offsetdruck, Hemsbach/Bergstr.
2145/3140-543210

PREFACE

Since the Department of Defense began its common high order programming language effort in 1974, there have been many discussions
about the features that such a language should include.   One of the
frequently recurring questions has been the extent to which the various
features proposed for inclusion are within the present capabilities of
language designers and implementors.   Therefore it was thought that it
might be useful to organize a workshop for the purpose of identifying
the current state of the art of programming language design and implementation.

This report contains the proceedings of the resulting workshop.
It was held on September 30 and October 1, 1976 at Cornell University
in Ithaca, New York.   During those two days, 62 people from academe,
industry and the services met to present position papers and to discuss the design and implementation of programming languages.   The
workshop was conducted in four sessions, the first three being technical sessions and the fourth a general discussion of the common language
effort.   Each technical session consisted of brief presentations of
the position papers followed by a panel discussion of the topics presented in the papers.

This report is organized into five sections.   The first is a
brief review by David Fisher of the DoD's common programming language
effort.   Section II is a transcript of the discussion of data types
that followed the presentations by C. Earnest, B. Brosgol, J. Nestor,
J. Donahue and R. LeBlanc.   Section III is the discussion of parallel
processing, machine dependence and program verification that followed
the presentations by J. Dennis, G. Andrews, J. Ichbiah, L. Weissman
and R. London.   Section IV is the discussion of specifications, optimization and run time support systems that followed the presentations
by P. Cohen, J. Goodenough, F. Richard, A. Evans and T. Cheatham.

Rather than interspersing the papers throughout the transcripts
of the discussions, they have been collected and appear in Section V.
Also, in Section V is a copy of Jim Horning's semi-extemporaneous
after dinner speech, a rough draft of which was sketched on the back
of an envelope during the first morning's coffee break.

Finally, to permit a ready reference source for some of the dis-
cussions, the needed characteristics section of the "Tinman" document,
"Department of Defense Requirements for High Order Computer Programming
Languages", July 1976, has been included as an appendix to this report.

We wish to thank CENTACS, U.S. Army Electronics Command at Fort Monmouth and the U.S. Army Computer Systems Command at Fort Belvoir for funding the workshop and all of the participants for making the workshop a success, and we gratefully acknowledge the excellent work of Pauline Cameron and Geri Pinkham who transcribed the discussions and typed this manuscript.

John H. Williams
David A. Fisher

PROGRAM COMMITTEE

Major Benjamin Blood
    U.S. Army Computer Systems Command

Serafino Amoroso
    U.S. Army Electronics Command

Douglas White
    Rome Air Development Center

David A. Fisher
    Institute for Defense Analyses

Robert I. Kahane
    Naval Electronic Systems Command

John H. Williams
    Cornell University

WORKSHOP SPONSORS

U.S. Army Computer Systems Command

U.S. Army Research Office

U.S. Army Electronics Command

U.S. Air Force Rome Air Development Center

U.S. Naval Electronic Systems Command

WORKSHOP PARTICIPANTS

Serafino Amoroso
U.S. Army Electronics Command

Gregory R. Andrews
Cornell University

Benjamin Blood
Computer Systems Command

Benjamin M. Brosgol
Intermetrics

Robert S. Cartwright
Cornell University

Steven Chappell
Bell Telephone Laboratories

Thomas E. Cheatham, Jr.
Harvard University

Lori Clarke
University of Massachusetts

Paul M. Cohen
Defense Communication Agency

Joseph Cointment
Texas Instruments

Richard W. Conway
Cornell University

Alan J. Demers
Cornell University

Jack B. Dennis
M.I.T.

Sam DiNitto
Rome Air Development Center

James E. Donahue
Cornell University

Christopher P. Earnest
Computer Sciences Corporation

Peter Elzer
Universitat Erlangen-Nurnberg

Arthur Evans, Jr.
Bolt Beranek & Newman

Clem Falzarano
Rome Air Development Center

Charles N. Fischer
University of Wisconsin

David A. Fisher
Institute for Defense Analyses

John B. Goodenough
Softech

Robert M. Graham
University of Massachusetts

David J. Gries
Cornell University

James J. Horning
University of Toronto

Jean D. Ichbiah
Cii Honeywell Bull

Mel Kanner
Computer Sciences Corporation

Gray Kinnie
IBM

Walter Klaus
Computer Systems Command

Richard J. LeBlanc
University of Wisconsin

Henry F. Ledgard
University of Massachusetts

Barbara H. Liskov
M.I.T.

Ralph L. London
Information Sciences Institute

Paula Loring
MITRE

David Madison
Texas Instruments

Nick Martellotto
Bell Telephone Laboratories

Raghubir N. Mathur
Computer Sciences Corporation

Stuart McDonald
RLG Associates

James R. McGraw
Cornell University

James S. Miller
Intermetrics

Charles G. Moore III
ADP Network Services

C. Robert Morgan
Bolt Beranek & Newman

John R. Nestor
Intermetrics

J. Gregory Noel
NELC

Frederic Richard
University of Massachusetts

Charles Sampson
Computer Sciences Corporation

Stephen L. Sauires
Department of Defense

John Shore
Naval Research Laboratory

Jay Spitzen
Stanford Research Institute

Ray T. Teitelbaum
Cornell University

William M. Waite
University of Colorado

Yuan-rean Wang
Computer Systems Command

Eberhard Wegner
GMD Bonn

Peter Wegner
Brown University

Larry Weissman
Intermetrics

Charles S. Wetherell
Lawrence Livermore Laboratory

Phillip R. Wetherall
British Ministry of Defence

William A. Whitaker
ARPA

Douglas White
Rome Air Development Center

John H. Williams
Cornell University

William A. Wulf
Carnegie-Mellon University

Richard G. Zwakenberg
Lawrence Livermore Laboratory

CONTENTS

*The latest version of the technical requirements are
available from members of the High Order Language Working
Group as DoD document Department of Defense Requirements
for High Order Computer Programming Languages - Revised
"IRONMAN", dated July 1977.

SECTION I The Common Programming Language
Effort of the Department of Defense

As you know the DoD is attempting to establish a minimal number of
programming languages for use in military software. This effort has
been underway for nearly two years now and has been built on independent efforts in the Services during 1974.

Software is becoming increasingly costly to the DoD. Digital
computer software costs in the DoD in 1973 were estimated at $3 billion
to $3.5 billion annually. Between 1968 and 1973 there was a 51 percent
increase in the reported cost of DoD computer systems (including both
hardware and software). These increases occurred even though there
were drastic reductions in both unit and total costs of computer hardware and fewer systems were reported in 1973. The increased costs of
computer software may reflect a combination of factors, including (a)
the trend toward more automation and increased use of computers, (b)
the greater complexity of software resulting from increased expectations and expanded requirements generated by improved hardware and
software technology, and (c) rising personnel costs.

Software costs are about equal among the Services but vary widely
among application areas. Scientific applications use the largest,
fastest and most expensive digital computer in the DoD but constitute
only about 5% of the software costs. Data processing applications
represent about 20% of DoD software costs. The majority (56%) of
software costs, however, are associated with what are called embedded
computer systems. The remainder are primarily indirect costs that cannot be attributed to a particular application.

Embedded computer systems are integral to larger systems whose
primary function is not computation. They include support software
for the system design, development, and maintenance. The larger systems include electromechanical devices, combat weapon systems, tactical
systems, aircraft, ships, missiles, spacecraft, command and control
systems, and communication systems. Data processing, scientific, and
research computers are not normally included among embedded computer
systems.

Embedded computer systems are often large (50,000 to 100,000 lines
of code and greater), long-lived (10 to 15 years), and subject to continuous change (annual revisions often of the same magnitude as the
original software development). They must conform to the physical and
real-time constraints of the associated system hardware and application

requirements. Software for embedded computer systems generally include control signals and computer data in their output.

Computer software shares many of the problems of other electronic equipment, but unlike them has no inherent physical constraints to limit expectations. This has led to a variety of complex and poorly understood software problems. Some of the most frequently mentioned symptoms of software problems in the DoD are that software is nonresponsive to user needs, unreliable, excessively expensive, untimely, inflexible, difficult to maintain, not reusable, and inefficient.

As can be seen these symptoms are not unique to the military. They may, however, be more pressing in the DoD because the critical need for systems to operate correctly when called upon, and because resources available to individual projects are often more restricted then in civilian systems. For a variety of reasons, limitations on dollars, development time, computer hardware capability and capacity, competent personnel, and useful programming tools are unusually constraining in embedded computer systems.

A primary reason is the lack of programming language commonality. Within the DoD all data processing applications are programmed in COBOL and most scientific applications are programmed in FORTRAN. There are, however, over 500 different general-purpose programming languages used for DoD embedded computer applications. This lack of programming language commonality in embedded computer applications has had many ill effects:

- It has led to excessive duplication in the programming and maintenance for the languages, their translators, and their associated software support.
- It slows communication and technology transfer among software practitioners in the DoD.
- It impedes system growth by forcing continued redevelopment of software for systems that have similar requirements.
- It scatters and dilutes research on the problems of embedded computer software, obscures the problems, and impedes experimentation when problems are recognized.
- It unnecessarily ties the maintenance of software to its original developer.
- It diffuses expenditures for support and maintenance software so that only the most primitive aids can be afforded by forcing their repeated development.
- It diverts effort from the important tasks of the application software to the design, implementation and maintenance of project unique languages.
- It limits the applicability of support software to the users of

the associated language, usually a single project.
- It creates a situation in which it is often risky but more cost effective to develop a new language than to adopt an existing language for a new project.
- It unnecessarily increases the cost of software to the DoD.

Although the above perceptions about the ill effects of the lack of programming language commonality in the DoD can be substantiated only by examples, and their true extent is unknown, they have provided much of the incentive for the common language effort. The continued proliferation of programming languages for embedded computer software may reflect an unfounded optimism that software problems would disappear if only there were a language better suited for the task at hand. However, the little available evidence indicates that the major payoffs will come from better programming methods and techniques, more software commonality, and more useful and easily accessible software tools and aids.

During 1974 elements in each of the Military Departments independently proposed the concept of a common programming language for use in the development of major defense systems within their own departments and undertook efforts to achieve that goal. Those efforts included the Army "Implementation Languages for Real-Time Systems" study, the Navy CS-4 effort, and the Air Force "High Order Language Standardization for the Air Force" study.

In January 1975 the Director, Defense Research and Engineering (DDR&E), in a memo to the Assistant Secretaries of the Military Departments for R&D, suggested that the benefits would be multiplied if there were a single common language for military applications. He requested immediate formulation of a joint Service program to assure maximum useful software commonality in the DoD. A working group (HOLWG) was formed with members from the Army, Navy, Air Force, Marine Corps, DCA, NSA, and DARPA and chaired by DDR&E. Representatives from OASD-I&L, OASD-COMP, and NASA have also participated. I have acted as technical advisor.

The purpose of the Common Programming Language Effort is to assure maximum useful software commonality in the DoD through adoption of a minimal number of common programming languages. Specifically it is attempting to reduce the number of general-purpose programming languages used in embedded computer systems of the DoD.

On the other hand, programming languages are the primary means of introducing new programming methods, tools, techniques, and greater automation into software development and maintenance processes.

Consequently, there should be periodic reviews of any common language
for possible replacement to accommodate demonstrable and useful advances in software technology. Because there are few practical ways
to reimplement existing software, any attempt to create greater language commonality can be fully effective only after 10 to 15 years
when current systems have expired.

Programming languages are neither the cause of nor the solution
to software problems, but because of the central role they play in all
software activity, they can either aggravate existing problems or
simplify their solution. Adoption of a single common language alone,
will not make software more responsive to user needs, reduce software
design or programming errors, make software more reliable, reduce
software costs, simplify test and maintenance, increase programmer
productivity, improve object efficiency, or reduce untimely delivery
of software. However, adoption of an appropriate common programming
language may remove many of the barriers to solving these software
problems. It may lessen the communications barriers which prevent new
systems from using the experiences of earlier, similar systems to full
advantage. It may reduce the burden and delay of designing, building,
and maintaining languages, compilers, support software, and software
tools for each new project and permit them to be concentrated on the
needs of their applications. It may reduce the dependence on initial
software vendors and increase competition. It may encourage development of better tools, both through pooling of costs within the DoD and
by creating a larger market for independently developed software tools
and aids.

Several steps have been taken to reduce the number of languages
used in the DoD. In January 1975 a prohibition was placed on further
development of production compilers for new programming languages for
major defense systems. Another is the establishment of an interim
list of approved languages. Each of the Military Departments has
nominated two or three of its currently used languages. New DoD embedded software system development efforts will be required to use an
approved language unless it can be conclusively demonstrated that an
unapproved language is more cost effective on a life cycle basis. The
interim approved list will likely consist of: CMS-2, SPL-1, TACPOL,
J3 Jovial, J73 Jovial, 1974 ANSI COBOL, and 1966 ANSI Fortran. [Edi-
tor's note: This list was issued as DoD Instruction 5000.31 on
26 November 1976].

The major effort to date, however, has been to identify an appropriate set of technical requirements for a common language. The scope
of this effort has been limited to applications subsumed by embedded

computer systems because there are several software problems unique to embedded computer systems, because such systems represent the majority of software costs in the DoD, because they are the major application areas in which there is no widely used language currently, because they represent the applications with the most pressing software problems, and because they are the only area in which most programming is currently done in assembly or machine languages. The diversity of functions performed by embedded computer systems, however, guarantees that most characteristics needed in data processing and scientific programming will be supported by languages for embedded computer systems.

Particular care has been taken in the requirement's generation process to ensure that they incorporate the specialized needs of embedded computer system applications, that a programming language satisfying them would be suitable as a common language, and that such a language could incorporate the most useful existing computer software and programming language technology.

The technical requirements are intended as criteria for measuring the appropriateness of candidate languages. They attempt to address the major issues associated with selection of a common language. For some issues they prescribe the desired resolution of a design decision, in other cases they provide only guidelines. They do not specify specific language features and are not intended as a language specification.

The requirements were developed through a feedback process involving the HOLWG, IDA, many commands and offices within the Military Departments, and military contractors. The first year of the effort was characterized by interactions with potential users. The HOLWG solicited inputs from users. A task at IDA analyzed, interpreted, and resolved conflicts among the inputs to produce a trial set of technical requirements together with the considerations, implications and trade-offs that led to their choice. The HOLWG distributed the trial requirements among the Services and their contractors for further comment. This process was continued through a total of four iterations and resulted in a preliminary set of requirements that were approved by the Military Departments in January 1976.

During 1976 the effort has been primarily to test and refine the requirements for improved clarity and consistency, for appropriateness to the applications, and for feasibility. We are concerned with the feasibility and practicality of achieving the requirements individually and in combination using existing technology.

This workshop is intended as a major input to this revision

process. This is a workshop on alternatives in the design and implementation of languages satisfying the established technical requirements. We are particularly concerned with those aspects of programming languages which reflect the special needs of embedded computer systems that are not normally needed in data processing and scientific applications. These include real-time control, parallel processing, input-output interfacing mechanisms, exception handling, and user definable data types.

It is hoped that the discussions here will give us a better understanding of the feasibility and practicality of achieving the requirements. The requirements are intended as realistic goals that are currently achievable. If requirements are found to conflict with one another, to be infeasible, inappropriate, or too expensive, appropriate changes will be made.

This is a workshop and as such we expect the greatest value to the DoD common programming language effort to come from the discussions rather than the papers. The papers are intended to stimulate the discussions, but the discussions should be directed to the session topics rather than the specifics of the papers. Let me again remind you that in addition to the needs for real-time, parallel processing, input-output interfacing, and exception handling capability, we are concerned about languages for applications in which reliability, modifiability, and execution efficiency are very important. For example this means that an acceptable language will be compilable, will be very static in execution, will be strongly typed, and will permit encapsulated type definitions but only to the extent that they can be processed entirely during compilation.

SECTION II DATA TYPES

Williams: Having heard the brief overviews by Earnest, Brosgol,
Nestor, Donahue, and LeBlanc, we will turn now to a discussion of the
current status of data types in high level languages. The panelists
who will lead this discussion are David Gries from Cornell University,
Jim Horning from the University of Toronto, and Barbara Liskov from
the Massachusetts Institute of Technology.

Gries: This DoD language project, which has been going on for several
years now, has a lot of goals--the final language is supposed to be
reliable, maintainable, pedagogical, transportable, readable, writable,
speedable, acceptable, and because of the pollution involved, also
returnable and biodegradable. Not only that, looking at the main languages in use currently, it should probably self-destruct in fifteen
years.

    It is supposed to be a state of the art language; that is, it
should include features that we really understand, both as implementors
and as programmers. The main feature we are discussing in this session
is data types -- what are they, and how we should implement them. I
suggest that DoD be very conservative about what is included in the
language regarding data types, because I don't really feel we know
what they are. Many problems involving data types have been brought
up. Thus we have heard discussions about how to hide and export names,
how to implement the primitive operations, and so on. We have thought
about how to allow a primitive operation that takes as arguments variables from two different types, and is able to look at the representations of both of them. We have discussed whether an operation belongs
to a type, or whether it belongs to a variable of that type (that is,
for a variable C do we refer to operation S by C.S or   S(C) ?).

    All sorts of problems have been brought up, and none of them have
been answered. So I really think DoD should be very conservative. It
is better to include a simple, conservative idea of data type even
though it is not as flexible and powerful as what we would like, rather
than something that is flexible and powerful, but not thought out properly.

    The problem with the questions concerning data types, as I see it
so far, is that they have been asked and answered on the wrong level.
Our discussions of data types (and other features, for that matter)
always seems to be in terms of implementation: how do we implement

the construct, how is it supposed to be represented on the machine, how does it get executed? And I think this is the wrong level. Machines should inspire our languages -- they have done that -- but when we begin talking about the language we should talk about it more in terms of how we communicate algorithms to people, rather than how we execute them on the machine.

Let me give you three examples of this. Ben Brosgol, when talking about whether arrays a[1:10] and b[1:20] with different bounds should have the same type, said perhaps they should, because they're represented in the machine the same way. Secondly, Nestor talked about the object as an abstract model of memory. Well, a programmer, when looking at a program, need not know about memory at all; that is purely an implementation characteristic which varies from machine to machine. Even my colleague Donahue, when discussing a data type as a set of objects together with operations on them, discussed storage allocation as an operation which helps define the particular data type. But storage allocation has nothing to do with the data type. In terms of correctness, of understanding a program, how storage gets allocated is totally irrelevant and does not help me understand what a data type is.

If I were to try designing a data type facility (which I probably won't, because it probably won't work), I would attempt to look at these questions from a much higher viewpoint, instead of down at the bits. It's okay at times to go down to the bit level to gain understanding, but there is a limit to how much understanding the process can yield.

When we begin thinking of programming constructs not in terms of executing, but in terms of having a sound theory for designing a language to communicate algorithms to people, when we forget about the ideas that have been forced on us by the machine, we can begin to address questions like the following.

(1) Is an array a function, or is it an independent set of variables which just happen to be referenced with the same name? That's a very simple question which has deep implications for how our language is going to look. (2) Is a function or an array with bounds 1 to 10 the same as an array with bounds 1 to 20? If we looked upon an array as a function, irrespective of efficiency (we have to take that into account at times) we might very well say that the bound information has nothing to do with the type itself. The reason we have to talk about bounds is solely for efficiency, for management of resources. The bound information could then be considered solely as instructions to

the compiler; it can use this information (it is under no obligation to) in order to allocate storage efficiently. So it's a comment for the compiler in the sense that it's not needed for correctness or understanding, but only for efficiency on our current machines. (3) What is a data type? A set of objects, a set of values -- what's that? What kind of objects do you allow? Integers, reals, procedure bodies? What structure should these particular sets of objects have? Should a data type be a heterogeneous algebra, or something like that?

Other questions, like should we have implicit conversion or even programmer-defined implicit conversion, should be answered at a higher level. You might conclude that general implicit conversion promotes misunderstanding, but that implicit conversion from a subtype to a higher type makes sense. The next question to answer would then be: What is a subtype? Are integers a subtype of the reals? Because, mathematically the reals are defined in terms of the integers, one would say yes. However, the problem here (and you see the machine coming in) is that the machine doesn't really implement reals, it implements what we might call unrationals. Each floating point number defines a range of reals, but the range really is dependent upon the particular number; around zero the range is very small, and around large numbers the range is very big.

Comment from floor: Perhaps they are really unreals.

Gries: They are really unreals. And if you look at it from this view-point, then you see that integers are perhaps not a subset of the reals because they have a totally different interpretation. An integer is an exact quantity; an unrational, or unreal, is not an exact quantity.

These are in a sense philosophical questions, but they are questions which, if we answer them at a high level, can have profound impact on what the final language will look like.

Wirth, in designing PASCAL, tried to design his language this way (I think). Wirth said array [1:10] is different from array [1:20] -- they have different types. Secondly, he said, when I call a procedure, for understandability the actual parameter type has to match exactly the formal parameter type. This implies -- and it has to, based upon these premises -- that a procedure may not sort an array a[1:10] one time and an array b[1:20] another time. You may not disagree with this particular implication; you have to disagree with the original statements that he made, that array [1:10] is different from array [1:20] , or that actual parameters should match formal parameters. Forcing ourselves to address these questions at a much higher level, away from the machine, is (I think) very important. I think our first speaker talked about having variables which can contain procedure bodies as objects. The question is not can you implement this, but whether or not it is a reasonable thing to have in the language. And my answer would be no, because then the program becomes un-understandable; the proof of correctness of the program is much more difficult. So my plea here is to address things not at the machine level, but to forget about the machine (keep it in the back of your mind, because efficiency is always necessary) and begin thinking of these more important questions -- principles behind your idea of programming which indicate to you what the programming language has to have in it. From there, once you've got these principles, the design of the programming language has to follow those principles, and you are much more restricted. I think that's the way to go.

Ledgard: I disagree with your statements that array bounds are machine dependent characteristics. I believe the order of the algorithm is important, but if you view an array as a function from one domain to another, the two things that make an array unique are that the domain is finite, as distinct from certain types of functions, and that the mapping is generally static. For example, if you take an array representation of state names into their abbreviations, the range of elements is not a machine characteristic, but in fact a property of the array.

Gries: Dijkstra, in his book Discipline in Programming, introduces a totally different kind of array where you may add elements to either end of it. He doesn't discuss implementation. It's a different view of arrays, which may or may not be better for understanding. But the point is that he developed a new concept based on his ideas of how programmers should use and understand arrays, and not on how an array should be implemented on the machine.

Donahue: Lest I be characterized as a semantic bit pusher, I think I could recast one of the statements you made in terms that you would be willing to agree are at a higher level and yet are asking exactly the same questions about data types.

Gries: That's fine, I wish you would. In the paper you wrote, many of the things are in terms of the machine, and I don't understand that. I want it at a higher level.

Donahue: All right, I'll try this one on you. Let's look at the question of handling subrange types in a language. Let's say I declare a variable X to be of subrange 1 to 10 and inside my program I have the assignment X gets 15. The post-condition I would like to prove is X = 15 . Depending on the characterization of assignment, the

proper pre-condition is either true or false. Now I think we are
talking at the sort of level you are interested in. But the questions
about what data type means have simply been recast, not fundamentally
changed.

Gries: That's right. This is really unfair for him to ask this,
because he asked me yesterday and he knew I didn't have an answer.

Donahue: I asked you about differing possibilities, but the point is
that that decision has got to be based on what we consider types to be.
Once that decision is made, we have said an awful lot about how we've
characterized types in our language.

Gries: Exactly. You have to worry then about what plus means on the
subrange [1...n] . In general, you have to wonder about what a subtype is. These are the questions to address first, and once you've
come to your decision, as you say, then you can start going lower and
look at assignment and the rest of the things. I agree whole-heartedly
but get the questions at the right level, not down in terms of the
machine. I agree with you.

Horning: Just to add to this interchange, I'd like to accuse David of
having taken one of his examples from the wrong semantic level, when
he talked about floating point as the representation on particular
machines, rather than addressing the issue of what numbers we should
be manipulating in our programming languages.

Gries: Fine. I submit.

Ichbiah: Sometimes I get the impression that time is flowing backwards. I heard both Gries and Nestor say that encapsulated data types
were not yet state of the art. Well, there used to be a language (it
is so old that probably you've forgotten it) called SIMULA 67; as the
name indicates, it was designed in '67.

Anon.: 1867?

Ichbiah: Actually, I spent some time implementing a SIMULA compiler;
our compiler was delivered in '71 -- it was the second one on the
market. It seems to me that the implementation issues of classes and
other forms of abstract data types are now quite well-known. We know
what makes the SIMULA classes too complex, and what has to be removed
from them to make them work efficiently. So I terribly disagree with
Gries and Nestor when they say that encapsulated data types are not
yet within the state of the art.

Liskov: I agree with Jean Ichbiah that we have some experience with
encapsulated data types, because SIMULA has been implemented, and so
has CLU. However, both of these languages are heap oriented languages,
which I believe is not what is needed for DoD-1. In addition, CLU

differs substantially from SIMULA, and ALPHARD differs substantially from CLU, and we don't understand the significance of these differences. Finally, the work on CLU and ALPHARD has been going on for three years, and I know there are many problems in CLU that have not yet been resolved. So I believe that you can't say, in spite of SIMULA, that encapsulated data types are something you can put into DoD-1 today.

Ichbiah: It is clear that if you are looking for the ultimate form of abstract data types some issues are still open. However, we can certainly define a model of abstract data types which just retains that subset of their properties which is now well understood. Obviously, this would include functional attributes. It is clear that we can already get a significant part of the advantages of abstract data types with such a simple model. Hence, any decent language should contain it.

P. Wegner: Is, in fact, DoD-1 going to be a non-heap language? If so, you can throw out a lot of things. Clearly, most notions of encapsulated data types presuppose that you have retention and require something like a heap.

Wulf: I absolutely disagree! The notion of heap is not implicit in the notion of encapsulated data type at all. It may be the case that for clarity a heap is a good idea -- I think Barbara Liskov would argue that -- but I don't think so. But that's an issue we can discuss at many levels. I don't believe there are any inherent inefficiencies in the notion of encapsulation at all.

What I really did want to address, however, was the issue that David Gries raised about being conservative. I find a certain amount of inconsistency in first saying "be conservative" and then suggesting that Dijkstra's "rubber ducky" arrays are a serious thing to consider. By the way, that notion of an array is also the notion used in CLU and was there considerably before Dijkstra advocated it. But anyway, I also believe very strongly that DoD-1 ought to be conservative. I just want to point out that any new language design is an inherently risky business, and you can use the argument to be conservative on either side of a rather high fence. In particular, if one chooses to not provide an abstraction mechanism (it's been called an encapsulation mechanism here, I would prefer to call it an abstraction mechanism) on the grounds that that might be dangerous, you will probably be driven in the direction of adding a larger number of features to the language. The whole point of having an abstract data type mechanism is to allow one to smoothly extend the language to incorporate program-specific features, features that are needed in a particular program, and specialize it to that particular program. One can replace many relatively ad hoc features by a nice, consistent encapsulated mechanism. I agree with Jean Ichbiah that at least some parts of encapsulation are well enough understood at this point that they are relatively safe. I think the language EUCLID has walked a fine line between what is well understood and what is not, and by including an encapsulation mechanism which is well understood has managed to avoid a proliferation of ad hoc constructs which are just as potentially dangerous, just as non-conservative, as the encapsulation mechanism. So, be careful when you argue for conservatism.

Gries: I agree with you that if we are conservative about what we try to implement with data types, that we can certainly do it and do it well. I brought up the point about the arrays only because Henry Ledgard said that he disagreed violently, that arrays had to be static. Now I would like to view the language definition, or my attempt to design the language, on two levels. First, how do I write algorithms effectively and communicate them to others? To me, that implies that I need a formal definition which shows how to prove programs correct; that says nothing about whether arrays have to be static or not.

The second point, however, is efficiency; you do have to worry about how the language is implemented. But these are two separate questions which should be addressed separately.

Williams: Are there any other opinions?

Earnest: Just a brief comment, it's really a question. I don't understand why encapsulation has to be for just one data type. Why can't you have a capsule which includes as many data types as the "authorized person" is allowed to define, so you don't have the problem of crossing data types?

Liskov: Permitting a module to contain definitions of several data types will probably provide a good solution to this problem of wanting to do conversions from one type to another.

Spitzen: I think it's easy to lose track of the fact that we're talking about two different things here. Data abstraction is really a specification; it's a requirement of how a program should behave. And it's possible to specify data abstractions without ever going into the issue of what language facilities are necessary to implement them. To take an extreme example, at SRI we've managed to specify some things that would appear to require abstraction at the level where CLU or EUCLID would provide it. It is possible to implement these in a graceful way with FORTRAN, which one might have thought very unsuited. By choosing a suitable programming discipline it's possible to overcome what appear to be insuperable difficulties in the language used.

Liskov: It's certainly true that you can do data abstractions in any programming language, including Assembly language (it's been used there, for example, in building operating systems). However, I believe that establishing conventions on the use of an unsuitable language is not a good substitute for a language that enforces constraints. The problem with conventions is that as the group of programmers grows, and as the life of the program grows, the chances of the conventions being violated grow, and after a while, you have nothing left to stand on.

Spitzen: I agree in general, but it turns out in the case of FORTRAN that it was possible to describe a preprocessor that was quite capable of checking on the conventions.

Wulf: So you did have a language!

Liskov: That's right! You have a language!

Spitzen: A language which was very inexpensive to build on top of something already existing in that case.

Graham: I'd like to ask Barbara Liskov what are the problems that she was alluding to that are unsolved that would cause her to feel that data encapsulation shouldn't be included in the DoD language.

Liskov: Well, one problem involves storage allocation. CLU and SIMULA have been implemented, but both depend on a heap. ALPHARD has a stack oriented semantics, but ALPHARD hasn't been implemented yet, and therefore the difficulty of obtaining an efficient implementation is not known. For example, I am uncertain about what happens when you create an object down many levels of procedure calls; you may end up with lots of copying. Bill Wulf says no, but I'm not convinced.

Another problem is the following. Bill also said that he thought maybe heap oriented semantics makes the concepts cleaner and that I would argue that, and I do argue that. In CLU we model objects of data abstractions, whereas in ALPHARD we model variables containing objects of data abstractions, and I believe that the former is closer to the way programmers would like to think about things than the latter. Now, these two points of view have various implications. For example, in CLU the parameters of a type need not include information about the bounds of arrays, but in ALPHARD this information must be included because it is needed to create space to hold an array variable. The point is that issues arising from the different points of view are not yet well understood.

Horning: I have a couple of things that have come up in various points in the conversation. One of them is that there was the question of why not use an encapsulation to encapsulate more than one data type. That is exactly the approach taken in Wirth's new language MODULA, and one can get that effect in EUCLID by only a slight perversion of what is in the language. I would like to briefly discuss data abstraction versus EUCLID; I say the "versus" advisedly. We did not feel that within our charter (doing something that was within the state of the art) that we could build in a data abstraction facility of the sort being attempted in CLU and ALPHARD and other successors to SIMULA. What we did feel we could build in was a simple name protection mechanism, or visibility mechanism, that would be of considerable assistance to a disciplined programmer and enforce some part of the discipline of data abstraction, but by no means the whole of it. One thing that we did not do and do not feel is within the state of the art, is to meet the requirement that user-defined abstract data types be indistinguishable from built-in types. The only ways that we know to do that involve making all built-in types as inefficient as data abstraction, so we did not feel that was acceptable.

Liskov: Jim Horning just slipped into David Gries' trap and talked about implementation.

I think the issue here is not one of efficiency. I think that neither CLU nor ALPHARD is going to treat user-defined types just the same as built-in types, because we don't know how to make a powerful enough definition facility. For example, it's very difficult to allow literals for user-defined types, and I believe such an ability is not even very important. I feel that the goal that user-defined types and the built-in types be indistinguishable is not a reasonable one.

Shore: I would like to support Jay Spitzen's comments. We built a medium-sized FORTRAN system at NRL using a preprocessor together with a set of conventions that permitted us to implement a certain form of type abstractions including run-time checking that could be turned on and off. We were delighted with the results in every respect, except that the program took much longer to write than it would have if we had had a strongly typed extensible language. The point is not that preprocessors provide a better solution than designing a new language with all the features that are being discussed here; the point is that preprocessors provide an alternative that permits you to solve the technical problems later and then impose the solutions by means of the preprocessor. This avoids the severe risks of thinking that you've solved the problems now, building a compiler now, and standardizing on it now only to discover enormous problems later on.

Ledgard: Anyone who's tried to define some data types for some interesting subjects will find that it's very difficult. For instance, if you want to write a program to play poker, then you have to develop a data type that knows about cards, shuffling, wild cards, flushes, and such things like jacks and aces. Unlike procedure abstractions, which I think everyone here knows how to use and has been using for many years, I've always questioned whether we really know how to use such a facility. Have any of you who have had the pleasure of using encapsulated data types found that they really are used? That is, are they actually developed and used by people? I've never seen any evidence that we really know how to use them effectively.

Spitzen: SIMULA is the obvious example of the language that has some form of data encapsulation that's actually been out in the field for many years, and I think its users can even claim that that was a superbly helpful facility.

Dennis: How much of the SIMULA experience is relevant to the question we're attacking? The class concept in SIMULA was introduced as a tool for constructing simulation programs; it wasn't conceived originally as a tool for abstraction. So I wonder how much programming experience there is in using SIMULA where the programmers have thought in terms of data abstraction.

Wetherall: We, that is, the Royal Radar & Signals Establishment, at Malvern, England, put most of the SIMULA facilities into an ALGOL 68 real-time package which is now widely used both in simulations and straight forward 68 programming.

Anon.: Straightforward 68 programming?

LeBlanc: I wish to answer Jack Dennis' question concerning the relevance of experience with SIMULA 67. I've had the opportunity to use it during the last year, not at all for simulation, and have found that the encapsulation facility makes it quite easy to slip into a very different design mode, actually thinking in terms of abstract data types. I've mainly used SIMULA for a graphics program for which it was found to be quite useful for producing a modular program while making the total development time amazingly short. There is one thing that I've found that may be considered a problem -- it seems that SIMULA sometimes encourages the development of very elegant programs that are very inefficient. That may be a characteristic of the implementation. Hopefully we can overcome it, because I think the encapsulation facility has a very significant effect on how you think about programming.

Ichbiah: I first want to comment on the relevance of the SIMULA user
experience. We have an extensive experience with the SIMULA compiler
which we have developed. Most applications are actually in non-simu-
lation situations, and most of them have been using classes as an
abstraction tool.

My second comment addresses the implementation of SIMULA classes:
One example which shows both the advantage and the limit of SIMULA is
the treatment of input/output. In SIMULA, input/output is defined by
extension in terms of classes -- that's the advantage. However the
code produced by the compilation of these classes is not efficient
enough, and hence most SIMULA compilers have used a direct implementation of the input/output classes.

Nevertheless I want to reiterate what I said earlier, that you
can define a simpler form of class with no inefficiency at all. We
have done this in the LIS language. In some situations, the compiler
is able to expand the body of short functional attributes at the place
of the call. With this straightforward optimization you get the notational advantages at no cost at all. In general, the treatment of
abstract data types does not depend on whether the objects are statically allocated or heap allocated. I see the issues of abstract data
types and of allocation as being totally disconnected.

Williams: Would one of the panelists like to make a short summary of
encapsulation -- whether it is state of the art or is well understood?

Horning: I think it's generally agreed that what is well understood
is the notion of tying certain procedures to certain data structures
and treating that as a unit and hiding at least part of the detail of
the data structure from the ordinary users. What is not well understood is the way to promote that into a genuine, first-class type
definition facility in which you can implement all the basic quantities
of your language, such as integers and booleans and real and input/
output and so on, using exactly the same mechanism without paying an
inordinate penalty, either notationally or computationally. If you'll
accept that as a summary --

Wulf (interrupting): No, there's more that's not understood. We
don't really understand what the word "type" means, or at least we
don't agree. I think there are a large number of issues. I guess I
very strongly agree with Jean Ichbiah, however, that there is a subset,
which is essentially the subset you enumerated, of the notions which is
well understood and is probably useful.

Horning: I'd like to direct your attention to a few other topics that
were raised by the various talks. First, the potential conflict

between the points of view taken by Earnest and LeBlanc on the subject
of pointers. In the one case, the plea for a much greater amount of
flexibility and power than is given by the PASCAL notion of pointers;
in the other case, the explanation of the large number of problems that
seem to be raised even by the restrictive PASCAL notion of pointers.
Now, I view the last paper as a collection of really quite clever
solutions to what, on the scale of the problems you're talking about
in this meeting, are really small problems with PASCAL. But they're
small problems with really very nontrivial consequences, both to the
implementer and to the user, to the user primarily because of the
efficiency penalty as small as is reasonable. Most of the problems
that were discussed in that paper, I believe, spring from two sources;
I believe the Tinman shares both of these sources and therefore will
necessarily acquire all of these problems unless modified. One of
them is the ability of functions, and therefore expression, to have
side effects; this causes tremendous problems, both in optimizing
programs and producing efficient code and also in the specific area
that was being discussed. The other is the possibility of "aliasing",
where you can have multiple names for the same object. This particularly becomes a problem when you use one of the names to change the
type of an object which you then refer to by another name, or to free
an object which you then refer to by another name, and so on. I believe these are problems in language design, that is, they are small
mistakes in PASCAL that should be corrected, rather than being dealt
with by the implementer. We have, in fact, succeeded in eliminating
at least those two problems in EUCLID. Some of the other problems
that were less central, and dealt with peripherally by LeBlanc, are
properly dealt with, I believe, in at least some applications, by
verification rather than by run-time checks. (Of course there is a
continuous spectrum in which you leave in the run-time checks for only
those things you can't verify.) I strongly agree with the point of
view taken in that paper that all language restrictions must be enforced. It is certainly not acceptable to, on the one hand, have a
formal definition that describes a nice, clean language with clean
semantics and, on the other hand, have a compiler which accepts a much
larger language without complaint and that has hideously ugly semantics
for the parts not described in the formal description. And that's a
problem that we have in certain areas of PASCAL.

On the other hand, it seemed to me that Dennis' paper was a plea
for flexibility at the cost of both verifiability and understandability; there may well be situations in which this is called for, but

I'm not sure that DoD is one of them. Most of the additional problems
beyond those of PASCAL seem to spring from the notion of modifiable
connectors, in which one can, for example, have sharing between storage in nodes by pointer and non-pointer variables. The verification
problems come when by changing something using one name, you also
change something that has quite a different name. The techniques for
verifying these programs are just horrendous, as London, for example,
will be telling you later. This gets even worse when the connection
that you can change is that between a procedure name and its body,
which means that at some point in the program you're invoking a procedure whose identity you don't even know, and whose body you don't have
any direct access to. That's a tremendous complication.

A comment on Nestor's talk, in particular on the last section,
which I perhaps enjoyed the most, on guidelines for languages; they
were, unfortunately, all on a feature-by-feature basis. One of the
serious dangers of language design is the assumption that by selecting
the right set of features you will get a good language. That's very
hard to do. There was a suggestion with a double negative that we
design a language that will not be incompatible with later additions,
in other words, will be compatible with later additions. It's really
very hard to do that. If the features are well enough understood that
you know what is not going to interfere with it, they're probably well
enough understood to be considered. It's precisely the ones that are
deferred because they aren't well understood whose interactions with
the rest of the language can't be anticipated. Because the primary
problem is not that the feature itself is not understood, it's that
the interactions of that feature with all the other features that are
(or may be) in the language aren't understood, and you can't anticipate
that.

Brosgol's talk I found very illuminating, in particular his mention of the large number of minor issues. Each of these minor issues
is of about the magnitude (and some of them are bigger) of the ones
that caused so much problem in the run-time checking. Brosgol is
leading us to a very real agony of choice. The fact that I think I
have answers, or have made choices, for most of these for myself,
merely means that I have made a choice among the problems. Some of
the problems he mentions are ones I'm more willing to live with than
others. Most of the issues he raised are ones for which there are no
universally acceptable answers. For example, he mentions safe discriminated unions. That is done in ALGOL 68, it's done in EUCLID, it's
done in various other languages, but at a cost in language complexity,

perhaps an unacceptable cost for many applications. And then, just to reinforce a point: There is no general agreement on extension facilities; there have been conferences for close to ten years, I guess, on extensible languages, but there has not been convergence.

Earnest: I'd like to rebut a couple things -- what you just said, and also what Gries said earlier. In the first place, I agree with you about where the problems lie with pointers, that is, in the sharing of -- I don't like the term "aliases", but I'll come back to that -- the sharing of something via two paths. I don't think that's avoidable, but I do think it's controllable, and we already have had it for years. We have procedure reference parameters which share their value with the real variable, the actual parameter outside, and the reason that's not so bad is that within the scope of the procedure...

Horning: It is so bad if you try to axiomatize procedures.

Earnest: It's not too bad if you say that you can only get to it by one name inside the procedure, which FORTRAN does, and that seems like a reasonable rule.

Wulf: But FORTRAN does not -- there is an interaction through common and parameters.

Earnest: I'm sorry; okay, FORTRAN doesn't really, but it should. And that's where the problem lies, and I tried to point out that I think we have to decide where the problems lie instead of trying to outlaw shared objects. I don't think you can do that.

Horning: I agree.

Earnest: Let me say one more thing. I don't think "alias" is the right term; it can be used that way, but I don't particularly like to use it that way. If I have a data object which really is a property of two other data objects -- is a component of two other data objects -- those are not two aliases for the data object. Two people have the same bank account, for example, and those are real people, those are not aliases. That's the use, I think, that you can't get around and that you need, so I think "alias" is the wrong term.

Going back to something Gries said earlier as to whether procedure bodies should be pointed to or should be connectors; it seems to me that you do want to define -- to be able to define -- the way assignment and reference works for some variables; they need not be of a new type, but they might be. You might even want to define the way assignment and reference works, to define a different representation for that variable, for the type. Okay, we've been able to do that for years for reference, using functions, and I happen to believe that the way to define assignment is to allow functions on the left in the way

AED does it, not in the way ALGOL 68 does it. Once you start doing that, then a function is just like a variable, for that use at least. To say arbitrarily that you can't point to those things or use them as connectors seems to me to be artificial and wrong; that's an arbitrary distinction which you're making. You are saying that if I want to define my own representation or my own assignment/reference operations, now there are certain other things that I can't do, and as I think Gries said, it's not that hard to implement and I think provides a useful consistency of thought.

Gries: The question is not whether it's hard to implement, the question is whether it's understandable. You have to make sure that any time you define assignment that it satisfies the axiom of assignment that you have in your language. If you do that, fine. But you have to be very careful. The point is that the operation of assignment is not a property of the data type itself; the properties of the data type are the operations which, when given values, produce new values essentially. Assignment is a totally different thing which combines variables and objects together. So it's not the same kind of an operation, it doesn't really belong, it's a "panmorphic" operator, I guess.

Earnest: But it's something you want to define, don't you agree?

Gries: You may have to, yes. Whether we know how to design a language in which we can do that nicely now, I doubt.

Liskov: I thought I'd better talk quickly, before everything I was going to say was said. I have several points that I want to make.

My first point concerns the use of optimization techniques to improve the efficiency of structured programs. One simple and well understood technique is inline substitution, in which a procedure invocation is replaced by the body of the invoked procedure. Not only does this technique remove the penalty for using small procedures, but it serves to unify the semantics of built-in and user-defined operations. Expressions can be viewed as operation calls, which are optimized by inline substitution. For example, Ichbiah commented that abstract I/O in SIMULA was too expensive and had to be replaced by built in functions, so that it appeared that the abstraction was nice in principle, but not in practice. I suspect that what happened was simply the optimization of the abstract I/O operations via in-line substitution, and that the abstraction was still there. So in-line substitution is a nice optimization technique; it gets rid of a kind of overhead the arises with abstract data types, where you tend to have very small procedures that just call other procedures; it also seems to unify the language.

My second point concerns the semantics of data abstractions. I agree with Spitzen that a type is an algebra. One of the benefits of taking this point of view is that then you can manipulate type definitions mathematically to discover properties such as whether one type is a subtype of another. I think when we understand the mathematics better, we will be able to say what conversions make sense. On the other hand, of course, a compiler is not a program verifier, and therefore it's not going to be able to analyze algebraic descriptions to tell whether two types are equivalent. All it's going to be able to do is to believe what you tell it. So in a programming language you develop a declarative mechanism to inform the compiler about new types. Different declarative mechanisms are possible. For example, in PASCAL the mechanism is the type definition in which you introduce a new type identifier on the left hand side of an equal sign. In CLU new types are not introduced by definitions in programs. Rather, we introduce new abstractions in the CLU system. We view an abstraction as a kind of behavior, and a CLU module is not considered to be an abstraction, but merely an implementation of an abstraction. For example, a cluster is an implementation of a data abstraction. An advantage of this approach over the PASCAL approach is that it permits you to change the implementation of a data abstraction without recompiling any of the procedures using that type. One of the earlier speakers said something like "in the behavioral definition when you reimplemented a type it was necessary only to recompile, but not reprogram". Actually, it is not necessary to recompile. All that's necessary is to rebind things.

Waite: This assumes though that you are not doing in-line substitution.

Liskov: That is correct. I believe that in-line substitution is done only after you are certain that the implementation is what you want. There's a trade-off to be made between efficiency and ease of changing the implementation.

My third point concerns type-checking: I believe that complete type checking should be done at compile time, so that a compiled program is known to contain no statements in which an object of one type is treated as if it were of some other type. A result of the requirement for compile-time checking is that certain constructs must be included in the language. For example, a union mechanism must be accompanied by a control construct for discriminating on the various cases. In CLU we have a tagged union mechanism; an example is:

<u>oneof</u> [value: int, empty: null]

A variable of this type can either hold an integer or the single null value, <u>nil</u>. In order to use such a variable in a program, the <u>tagcase</u> control construct must be used; e.g.,

```
tagcase x
   case value (y : int) : z:=z + y; %y has the integer value
                                     %currently associated with x
   case null            : z:=0;
   end
```

Note that the choice of which line of the <u>tagcase</u> to execute is made at runtime, but at compile time each line can be checked to ensure that there are no type errors within it. By the way, I believe such a construct should not be a special use of the <u>case</u> statement, but rather a distinct construct, because the compiler interprets it very differently from the <u>case</u> statement.

My reason for bringing up the <u>tagcase</u> example is that the question of whether such a construct should be included in the language has been raised several times. I believe the complexity of such a mechanism is small, much smaller than the complexity that is introduced when you don't have it. Complexity both in building correct programs, and in implementing the programming language, as was descibed by one of the earlier speakers. I think the inclusion of such a mechanism is a pretty small price to pay to get rid of some of the problems that arise otherwise.

<u>Gries</u>: If I could make a point on that? I disagree with the terminology being used here, with the use of the word "tag" which refers to implementation. I as the programmer don't know whether or not a tag is implemented, and I really don't care. I should be able to differentiate between the various possibilities for x based on its current type, or on the identifier currently in use. For example, I would rather see your above statement written as

```
caseoneof x
      case value : z=z + x.value
      case null  : z=o
      end
```

To force the programmer to think in terms of "tags", and perhaps to allow him to change them explicitly, is thinking too much in terms of implementation.

<u>Liskov</u>: I disagree with you. The tag usually has an abstract meaning, and the fact that the tag can be implemented by a small integer is not of interest. In designing CLU we investigated both tagged unions and unions in which the discrimination is one type alone. These two unions

have different uses: the tagged union is useful for building data structures, while the type union is useful for writing polymorphic procedures. We decided on the tagged union because we use another method for polymorphic procedures, which I will discuss below.

E. Wegner: Isn't that exactly the conformity case clause of ALGOL 68?

Liskov: Not exactly, because the discrimination is on the tag rather than on the type.

My next point concerns the interpretation of type parameters. I believe with the people from Cornell that when you introduce type parameters, every distinct set of parameters defines a new type. I think that is a necessary conclusion. However, distinguishing types on the basis of the type parameters doesn't limit the power of a language, you can't fault the definition on this basis. But it does imply that you have to have a lot of polymorphic procedures around. And I believe that this is an area that has been fairly well worked out by now, although some questions about efficiency of implementation remain. Note that the need for polymorphic procedures is independent of the data abstraction issue. The idea is that we'd like to be able to define a procedure that works on many types; for example, all arrays with different bounds. Such a procedure is called polymorphic because it doesn't work on just one type, it works on many types.

For example it would be convenient to have a sort procedure that works on arrays of integers and arrays of characters and so forth. In order to support the definition of such a procedure, the language must provide a syntax for the procedure heading that states clearly what sort of polymorphism is involved. For example, in CLU you would write the following:

sort = <u>proc</u> [T: type] (a:array[T])
        <u>where</u> T <u>has</u> equal, lt: <u>proctype</u> (T,T) returns (bool);
which states that the sort procedure will work for arrays of different element types. Note first of all the absence of any information about the size of the arrays. Nothing tricky is going on here; this information is not a parameter to the CLU array type. Secondly, note that the sort procedure doesn't make sense for all arrays, but only for arrays whose elements have an ordering on them. The way to express this so that the compiler can make some sense out of it is to talk in terms of the operations that the element type provides. This information is contained in the <u>where</u> clause: The sort procedure only works for types providing an operation named equal and an operation named lt (less than); both these operations take in two objects of type T and return a boolean.

The information in the where clause is used by the compiler to do checking. Every use of a polymorphic procedure can be checked to ensure that the type parameter provides the required operations. And within the procedure the only operations of type T that can be used are those described in the where clause.

Note that the where clause does not describe all the information that is required for the polymorphic procedure to operate correctly. For example, the sort procedure requires a total ordering on the elements of T and there is no guarantee that the operation names lt and equal provide this if T is a user-defined type. However, in order to do more checking on the properties of T a program verifier is required.

My next point involves implicit conversions. I believe that implicit conversions should almost never be permitted, even if we understand mathematically that the conversion makes sense. The reason is that implicit conversions make a program more difficult to understand; in general, the more clever a compiler is in ascribing a meaning to a program, the more understandability suffers.

Finally, the issue has been raised of using multiple implementations of a type within a single program. I'm not convinced that this is an important issue, except that a packed representation may be viewed a second implementation of a type, so it may be important in this one sense. If multiple implementations of a type are desired, the view of types taken in the language can make things easy or difficult. In SIMULA, where the type's operations are considered part of the object, it's easy to have different implementations of different objects. In CLU and ALPHARD, the operations are considered part of the type, so multiple implementations are difficult. However, binary operations, like, for example, "plus", which take in two objects of the type that the binary operation belongs to, are handled well in CLU and ALPHARD and not so well in SIMULA. If multiple implementations are desired in a language like CLU or ALPHARD, there are a couple of approaches that can be pursued. One of them was mentioned today: The idea that there is a distinguished representation of the abstract objects, and every implementation using a different representation defines conversions between the two representations. Another approach is what I call the "abstract representation" approach, in which you introduce an intermediate abstraction with only unary operations (that is, operations taking as parameters at most one object of the type to which they belong). Then every implementation of the type must provide implementations for the operations of the intermediate abstraction, and these operations can be used to manipulate objects whose representation is not known.

It is fair to say that solutions to providing both multiple implementations of a type, and efficient implementations of binary operations, have not been studied. I believe that multiple implementations of a type should not be a requirement for DoD-1, especially since I am doubtful of the utility of such a feature.

In closing I want to say that I've always been confused about the timing of DoD-1. It appears that a language is needed soon, for example, with a running compiler by 1978. But many of the requirements, for example, data abstractions, would necessitate a much longer development. It would be helpful to pin down the time span. For a short term effort, a conservative approach to data abstractions must be taken; perhaps something like EUCLID is a possibility. For a longer term project, I agree with Wulf that data abstractions provide many benefits and that they should definitely be part of the language.

Graham: That will appear in the Sixty Million Dollar Man!

Liskov: That's the gold man, is that it?

Shore: Barbara, a specific question: You said that you believe that types are algebras, and I wondered if you meant that in the formal way that mathematicians mean, or if that's just your informal way of saying that types can be given a notation that permits derivations.

Liskov: No, I mean it formally. I mean that a data abstraction should be defined by some axiomatic or other description that actually describes an algebra. It is true that such a description is not too useful for compiling, but eventually when we combine compilation and verification, then we will be using descriptions of algebras.

Waite: I'd like two clarifications from Horning; let me state the two questions I have and then you can answer them separately, because I think they are quite separate. First, you say that you want to prohibit the possibility of changing the name of a procedure. How does this relate to procedure parameters? Do you wish to completely avoid procedure parameters? Secondly, you say that you don't want any side effects in functions. I'd like to know just how far you want to go with that. For instance, am I permitted to have a random number generating function, or am I allowed to use a random number generating procedure within a function? Secondly, if I have a data type, presumably that data type has local hidden storage, as, for example, a stack would. Would I be able to use such a data type in a function?

Horning: I suppose I should really wear my "EUCLID hat", rather than my "arbitrary language designer hat", in answering these, since the answers would be somewhat different. In the long term, there are a

lot of research issues where I would like to be able to generalize
from what we've considered acceptable in EUCLID. EUCLID does not permit procedures to be passed in as parameters. Functions, procedures,
and types are not acceptable parameters, not because we believe that
in general those are not useful constructs, but because we are not
prepared to verify programs containing them, and because we did believe they added some complexity to the language. Certain things for
which such parameters would be used in other languages have been
covered by special cases, such as having function and procedure attributes of modules, where module variables can be passed as parameters.
This does not violate the restriction, because it is always the same
function or procedure that you get inside. All module variables of a
given type have the same functions and procedures.

Liskov: I wanted to ask for a clarification on a point that has been
confusing me. What do you object to about procedures as parameters?
Is it because they have free variables that are bound in a different
context?

Horning: That would be part of it.

Liskov: Okay, suppose you didn't have that problem. Then what is the
objection?

Horning: The one of calling something whose name you don't know.

Anon.: But what does the name have to do with it?

Horning: When we have more adequate specification techniques for procedures so we know something about what calling F is going to do,
then I'm prepared to reconsider the issue, but as long as we only know
that F takes two reals and produces a boolean, ...

E. Wegner: You can provide more information, just as ALGOL 68 provides more information than ALGOL 60.

Horning: Yes, I'm saying that is an interesting research topic --
what additional information should we provide to make this a reasonable thing. Let's go to Waite's second question.

Conway: But this is an important question.

Horning: Yes, but the two are not unrelated. Second, side effects in
functions. The rule in EUCLID is that you can't have them. That is,
a function cannot change its environment. There can be effects within
the function, because you can have assignments there. You can call
procedures, but you can only call procedures that modify things local
to the function, not procedures that modify anything not local to it.
For example, you can't do I/O in a function, even if the square root
routine gets a negative argument; it can't scream "negative argument".
Our answer to that, of course, is that you should have verified the

program and established that there are no calls with negative arguments. It is a very restrictive notion, but it does happen to be safe, and it greatly facilitates verfication.

Conway: You can't have a random number generator?

Horning: You can have a procedure which generates random numbers; you can have a random variable which has an attribute which is "set it to the next"; but you can't have a random function.

Waite: Yes, but wait a minute. When you call a random number generator you change its internal state, and therefore when you call it the next time you are going to get a different number than you would had you not called it.

Horning: No, in EUCLID you can have a random variable whose state you change; you can't change the state of a function. A function doesn't have any internal state.

Waite: Yes, but you say you can call a random variable inside a function. But the random variable must have a state. I don't understand that. I don't understand how with that definition you can use a random number inside a function.

Horning: I think you are correct.

Graham: Although its a little bit off this topic, I would like to make my "anti-efficiency" speech. This applies to a number of the sessions, but it particularly applies to some of the statements made with respect to data abstraction and encapsulation being inefficient and therefore should not be included in the language. I was involved in the MULTICS project from beginning to end and a number of things became clear from that project; one is that efficiency should really come from understanding the problem and from redoing the algorithm in a major way, rather than turning up little parts of it. Thus, understandability is extremely important with respect to efficiency in the global sense. Secondly, bottlenecks are never where you expect them to be, and the parts of the program that cause the bottlenecks usually are an extremely small percentage of the code, and the rest of it is irrelevant. Budget figures that I hear from people with respect to the problems in large DoD software developments are that testing and other operations of that nature are 50 to 90% of the cost depending on whether you include maintenance and "enhancements" after the product is delivered. Therefore, I think anything that can help understandability and thus decrease testing time and all the other related aspects is very important, and data abstraction and encapsulation is probably the most powerful thing that I know of today in terms of understanding the problem and proving it correct and other things that will drastically decrease the time and cost for developing the program,

testing it out, and maintaining it after it is delivered. Therefore I
don't really understand this concern about efficiency with respect to
including some of these concepts in the language; I think if we can
possibly include data abstraction and encapsulation ideas in this
language the payoff is probably immeasurable in the long run; efficiency you can worry about in other ways at some later stage in the
process.

Williams: Before we get too far with efficiency, did anybody want to
continue to talk about procedures?

Gries: I just wanted to make a point about the function business.
You have to state right in the beginning what you think a function
should be, and if you think it should be a mathematical thing which
for each pair of arguments or set of argument values produces a unique
result, then you just can't have functions which change other variables. They can't have side effects from that particular point,
because then you might call this function twice with the same arguments but get different results. Consider functions also from the
standpoint of understandability of programs, in terms of proving programs correct. If you allow side effects in functions, then the
definition of what an expression, assignment or just about anything
else means becomes very complicated, and those who believe in proofs
of correctness then say that the program is not understandable
because the proof rules are less understandable.

Dennis: I'd just like to point out that when you regard procedures as
implementing mathematical functions, then there is no difficulty in
passing a function in, or a procedure in, as a parameter.

Gries: Yes, function we'll define as arguments.

Waite: Except for the specification problem

Dennis: The specification is no more difficult than specification of
data abstractions.

Horning: Your specification now is a second order thing, because
this function can only be defined in terms of what it does as a function of the other function that is given as an argument.

Liskov: No, you specify in the function what the argument function
does, and then for every invocation you have to verify that the function you are passing in does what the invoked function expects.

Wulf: You now have a new type-checking problem, right? You have to
verify some assertions as well.

E. Wegner: I think the random example is not a counter-example against
the restriction to functions without side effects, since it's relevant
only if you depend on the sequence of numbers you get; if you have

really random numbers, then the problem of Waite's will not arise.
Just consider the random function as a hardware random number generator for which you really don't know what it produces; say a geiger
counter or something like that.

Gries: I can't do that, because two different executions of the same
program with the same input would produce different results.

Dennis: A very interesting way of looking at a random number generator is to consider it as a function which takes no input, but produces as output a stream, then it is in fact a mathematical function.

Ledgard: Will all those who have written a program in the last five
years that has passed functions or procedures as a parameter please
raise their hand? (Laughter....)

Gries: You should ask how many have written a program.

Earnest: I have a comment on the random number generator. In
Dijkstra's new book, he points out that it is sometimes better to have
indeterminate programs, if you don't care about which way it goes. As
long as all the results are acceptable to you, then it can be indeterminate, and that is certainly true of a random number generator. In
other words, you are not counting on it to produce the same result
every time; you are counting on the fact that it will produce some
random number. And that's what you base your proof on. I don't see
the problem.

Dennis: That is actually wrong, because in simulations you are often
counting on getting the same result if you run the program twice.

Miller: I'd like to ask Horning something and then ask the audience
something. Jim, in the XPL compiler, to which I understand you made
some contribution, there was a pragmatic device which was typical of a
kind of innocent side-effect which in DoD programs is a relevant thing
to consider using; that is, there are a number of procedures in the
XPL compiler which increment a global variable every time they are
called, so that at some other place you can print out the number of
times these procedures were invoked. That's an "innocent" side effect
-- it doesn't really in any way affect the semantics, and it provides
instrumentation of the use of the program. You apparently disallow
this technique in EUCLID. I think EUCLID's restriction makes instrumentation of programs in the language itself a rather difficult
problem.

I could stop here, but I have another question.

Horning: Why don't you let me reply to that, because the answer is
yes. That is an innocent way of using side effects -- what you would
have to guarantee in order to make that safe in a language (now XPL
was a totally unsafe language and so the fact that those were used in

carefully controlled ways was purely self-discipline). In order to
insure that you were using this in a safe way, what you would like to
have is a class of "harmless" variables and allow side effects on
harmless variables, but not allow any programs to depend on harmless
variables except the class of "harmless" programs. And then one could
build up a hierarchy of "harmlessness".

I've done this as a mental exercise, and I think it would all go
through. But it would take a rather large change in the language
structure to get this kind of instrumentation, and perhaps it should
really be coming from modifying the compiler or having an instrumentation tool. Again, one could say that putting out error messages or
diagnositcs, or whatever, to a separate output stream was a "harmless"
activity, so you might have harmless I/O devices and so on. It could
be done, but I don't know how to do it simply.

Gries: On that point, these harmless variables, or instrumentation
variables, are totally different from the variables of the program.
We look at the program and we prove it correct; then, because of our
other main concern for efficiency, when we execute the program we have
to instrument it and find out how a lot of things are executed, but in
a sense they are totally different -- they are a separate class of
variables. Perhaps our languages of the future should deal with these,
as different parts of the program, in a sense.

Mathur: I would like to ask a question on uniform referent notation
at this point, since this subject has been touched by many people here
and yet has not been dealt with thoroughly. I disagree that DoD
should use uniform referent notation in this language because, number
one, use of functions in the same way as variables is undesirable
because of side effects in functions, as so many people have mentioned.
The array notations do not have similar side effects. Secondly, the
use and execution of a function takes a longer time than the use of
arrays, and that's a fact a programmer may want to know before he
designs a program. Thirdly, I think it reduces the readability and
understandability of programs if you mix the two things together.

Williams: Jim, you had a second question, didn't you?

Miller: Yes, I did. In attempting to design a language in which, for
example, data abstractions are included, we have run into the problem
that, although we have a semantic model that leads us to believe that
we understand the concepts we are working on and that we know semantically how to describe them and how to use them, nonetheless the implementation for this semantics on the hardware architectures that are
available today makes that implementation unacceptable from an efficiency point of view. As a result, we are led to think about hardware

architectures that might be invented to support what seem to be the
semantically desirable programming language components. (I shy away
from calling this easy.) I wonder if the others here who have designed
languages with these kinds of features in them have been led to the
same conclusion, and whether we agree that the DoD should be thinking
of the common HOL effort in connection with a common high-order language architecture which could efficiently support such a language.
Then the language could contain the things it really ought to have
without failing to satisfy the efficiency requirements, as it might
if only existing computer architectures were considered. In other
words, can we afford the language we want without better hardware to
run it on?

Dennis: Jim, I have felt that way for a long time, so you know you
have my support.

Goodenough: I have a question, but I would first like to discuss the
uniform referent concept which was mentioned earlier. This concept
is often considered to imply only that arrays and functions should be
referenced using the same notation in a language, and that functions
should be permitted on the left side of assignments. But the principle is much deeper than that. Doug Ross used the term "referent"
because it means either the object referred to or the means of referring to an object. Hence, uniform referents implies uniformity among
objects referred to as well as uniformity of notation. The essence of
the idea is that a notation should reflect semantic uniformities, i.e.,
given several ways of realizing some abstract object, the notation for
referring to that object should not depend on how the object is realized, i.e., how it is implemented. So the issue is not whether arrays
can be realized efficiently as functions, but whether arrays and functions can be viewed as different ways of realizing the same abstract
object, and if so, how to provide a notation that reflects this
similarity.

The uniform referent concept applies to more than just array and
function notation. For example, to what extent can you rearrange the
components of a data structure and then operate on it without changing
how the components are referred to in a program? Can you change it
from a packed to an unpacked structure and still use it in the same
way? To the extent the answer is "Yes", your language supports the
uniform referent principle.

The uniform referent principle also only requires abstract notational uniformity. For example, array and function references do not
have to have the same syntax as long as the notation for array references can also be used to invoke a function, and vice versa. And such

a capability is required only to the extent you feel it is reasonable to consider arrays and functions different methods of realizing the same abstract object.

As an operational definition, you can ask this question: To what extent can I change just declarations in a program and still compile it without changing the logical effect. To the extent this is possible, the language supports the uniform referent concept. So its not a question of having uniform referents or not having them; its a question of to what extent does a language support the uniform referent concept, i.e., what kinds of objects does a language consider to be alternate implementations of the same abstract semantic object, and in what contexts can these alternate implementations be referenced interchangeable.

The other thing that I wanted to say was that I wasn't sure what the resolution of passing procedures as parameters was. If you have enough information about how a procedure passed as a parameter is going to be used, that is, all the arguments it is going to take, the results it's going to produce, and its side effects if it has any -- is there then any objection to passing them, or is it a question of how to provide all that information and use it effectively. Is that why you don't want to pass them?

Horning: I think it is, in my own mind, primarily a problem of specification and understanding, and secondarily an issue of acceptable implementation. I think if we know how to specify these things adequately, we will also by that time know how to implement them with perfectly acceptable ....

Goodenough: But if you have the same information about the parameter as you do when you are calling it directly, since you can verify the actual procedure call, why can't you verify it when it is passed as a parameter?

Horning: Okay, the same issue comes in when you are talking about passing types as parameters. Should a type generator take types as parameters, and so on. I believe that ultimately we will have languages that don't allow any of the three to be passed as parameters -- function, procedures, or types -- and we will have languages that will allow all three, but that it will be very hard to justify languages that allow one or two out of the three.

Shore: I'd like to ask Goodenough whether you consider the need to pass procedures as parameters as another support for uniform referents?

Goodenough: I am torn by another view that you don't need to pass procedures as parameters because you can usually deal with them as exception conditions and get the effect that you want that way. That

is, if the exception condition takes parameters at the point of the
call, then when the exception is raised, the effect can be similar to
invoking a procedure passed as a parameter. I'm not sure that I really
want to defend using exceptions as a substitute for passing procedures
as parameters. I'm just suggesting that as a possible alternative.
Mathur: If we implement this, should we or should we not support the
uniform referent notation, that is the question.
Goodenough: I think we should support uniform referents, if you have
any belief in modularity as a desirable concept.
Shore: But one of the consequences of that is that you have to be
able to pass procedures.
Goodenough: I see what you are getting at. If you have a function,
F(A) , where A is an array, and if you consider arrays and functions
to be alternate implementations of the same abstract object, then you
should be able to implement A as a function and still call F(A) .
Well, I think this illustrates why you may decline to support the
uniform referent concept uniformly, i.e., in all contexts. In this
case, permitting F to be called with either an array or function
argument might pose more implementation complexity than is considered
desirable. A compromise solution might be to permit F to be declared with a formal parameter that is the union of suitable function and
array modes.

What this example points out is that the uniform referent concept is a design principle (like all design principles) which is to be
followed only as long as it pays off. When it causes conflicts with
other goals, e.g., simplicity or efficiency, then a compromise must be
made or more effort must be spent in finding an acceptable solution.

So although the uniform referent concept does seem to suggest
that it should be possible to pass functions as parameters, this
decision cannot be justified without considering its effect in terms
of other design principles as well.

SECTION III PARALLEL PROCESSING, MACHINE
DEPENDENCY AND PROGRAM VERIFICATION

<u>Williams</u>: The panelists for this discussion are Bill Waite from the
University of Colorado, Eberhard Wegner from GMD Birlinghoven, and
Bill Wulf from Carnegie-Mellon University.

<u>Wulf</u>: We are supposed to be provocative, so I'll try to be provoca-
tive -- maybe I shouldn't say that. I want to reinforce one thing that
London was saying. I personally am very, very tired of having discussions (or arguments) about language design. They tend to have the
character, "Gee, look at this nifty new feature in my language; it
lets me write this thing in one line instead of two." Someone else
will say, "Well, perhaps so, but look at the way that you write it in
my language -- you see, I get it in two less characters" or "I only
have to turn this inside out in order to make that happen." The problem is that we have tended to come at a discussion of language features with different preconceived notions about what the frequency of
use of constructs is, and thus how important various things are. We
don't have any objective criteria for evaluating languages. Well, the
specification of verification conditions for a language is one such
objective criterion!

   I started out three years ago or so believing that verification
was sort of a pie-in-the-sky idea, but it might be coming along one of
these days. I've turned around one hundred and eighty degrees. I've
certainly turned around in the sense that I now am, on the basis of a
fair amount of experience, I think, absolutely convinced that there is
a high correlation between understandability and verifiability. If I
can understand what a construct means, I can write down the verification conditions for it. Conversely, if I can't state the verification
conditions rather concisely, I probably can't understand the construct
either. I don't know that that is universally true, it is simply true
in all the cases I have examined, which is a fairly large number. So,
independent of whether you ever verify programs, stating the verification conditions as you design the language is a worthwhile endeavor.

   I happen to also believe that the encapsulation mechanisms, if
they are reasonable at all, will allow us to really do verifications.
I believe that ten years from now we will routinely verify programs.
I know there are a lot of people who don't agree with that, and I
didn't three years ago. But the issue is that encapsulation mechanisms tend to reduce the size of the program that you have to verify

and verification of small programs is relatively routine.

Enough on verification. Let me comment just briefly on parallelism, which is a major topic of this session. I think Dennis in his
opening remarks said something to the effect that we've been doing
quasi-parallel programming for quite a few years. We have been using
constructs like semaphores and message buffering systems for quite a
few years, and therefore he concluded that that was a safer notion, a
more conservative notion, to include in DoD-I than encapsulation. I
wish I believe that. I have tried to make a list of what we know
about parallel or quasi-parallel programming. The first thing that I
wrote down, after I thought about it a little while, was "damn little."

One of the things that we know is that there are lots of possibilities for synchronization mechanisms (or communication mechanisms)
which will work. One can express a large class of interesting parallel programs using only message buffers, or using only semaphores, or
using critical regions, or conditional critical regions, or monitors.
But, in fact, most of the experience that we have is in building
things like operating systems, which use relatively low-level constructs; we have relatively little experience using the high-level
notions that are being kicked around, like monitors, conditional
critical regions and the like. In particular, we have very little
practical experience -- there are quite a number of experimental
systems. Again, let me expose a little bit of dirty laundry; London
already exposed some of our dirty laundry, in the sense that he had
page long verification conditions in ALPHARD for a while. Let me
expose some dirty laundry about HYDRA. We started out by providing a
message buffering system, semaphores, and an encapsulation mechanism
to the users. We had quite a number of users come to us and beat us
about the head and shoulders and tell us that we ought to have interrupts. We said, "No, no, no, no -- that is a bad idea; you don't want
to structure programs that way. Tsk, tsk, bad, bad."

Well, in fact, we have not put in a sort of high-level image of
interrupts. I deeply regret that -- I feel very badly about it, but,
in point of fact, neither message buffering systems nor PV synchronization (and I consider PV to be a very low-level mechanism, a very
unsafe mechanism) were adequate for expressing a set of things that I
could not argue were unreasonable. In particular, all of those mechanisms tend to have a sort of polling characteristic: you don't know
whether there is a message there unless you ask. You don't know
whether the semaphore is positive or negative until you peek. There
are things like handling user terminals, where a guy wants to sit and
hit some special control character and say, "Wait a minute! My

program's running away! Stop it!" Where, in fact, the only thing we
can think of to do is to send an interrupt, because the program is not
about to poll; the trouble is it's in an infinite loop doing nothing
interesting.

Dennis (stage whisper): He's not about to poll either.

Anon.: Interrupt!

Wulf: I'm not advocating interrupts -- don't misunderstand me. All
I was trying to say was that I don't think, unfortunately, that we
know very much about parallel processing mechanisms. I certainly
would like to advocate very high level constructs which we can verify;
that is the whole thrust of the ALPHARD effort. I'm just saying that
the situation is not so clear.

There are also a set of interactions between parallel processing
constructs and exception conditions; Larry Weissman suggested that.
Here again, in the particular case of HYDRA we have an exception mechanism in BLISS which is not super elegant, but it can be used to
simulate the kinds of things that Goodenough is talking about in his
paper. Unfortunately, it is simply not adequate in the parallel processing context. In particular, if you want to use that mechanism to
deal with hardware malfunctions (and that's one of the kinds of things
that we need to cope with if we are going to build fail-soft software),
and the hardware malfunction relates to a shared variable, it may
become necessary to broadcast the exception to all processes which
have access to the variable. In particular (you should pardon the
word), it may be necessary to interrupt; it may be unsafe to let them
proceed, because if they go any further they may just make the situation worse.

Dennis: I object;

Wulf: You can object, and I'm going to quit. I had another point to
make, but I'll quit. So, there are interactions between the parallel
processing facilities and the exception handling mechanisms that I
think we know very little about, and it makes me feel queasy to talk
about including some of these things in a "conservatively designed"
programming language. All right, I'll quit -- I said I was going to
be provocative; I hope I was.

Dennis: I would take issue with two statements that Wulf made. On
the question of interrupts, I think when we argue that interrupt's are
necessary it is a consequence of thinking about systems in which processes are expensive and process switching is expensive. If there is
a part of a program which needs to respond to some possible event,
then the natural arrangement is to set up a process which is in an
idle state waiting for that event to happen. This does away with any

need for an interrupt. The reason that we are generally unwilling to
use that technique is because processes are expensive; if we build
systems in which processes are not so expensive then perhaps that need
will go way.

Wulf: Interrupt!

Dennis: I won't accept your interrupt. I'll go on then and make the
point about exceptions, because I am bothered with the notion that an
exception mechanism should deal with hardware malfunction, particularly where the hardware malfunction is in the central processing units
or main memory of the computer system, because a failure in the CPU
or central memory is a failure of the basic mechanism which is interpreting programs, so there is simply no way that a program can count
on that mechanism to always respond to the malfunction in a sensible
way. So I don't think that an exception mechanism for programming
languages will be able to deal adequately with hardware malfunction.

Wetherell: Why did you state that "the CPU, the memory", as if there
were only one of each?

Dennis: Oh, I'm sorry. A CPU, a memory.

Wetherell: In which case, exceptions may still be reasonable because
they then may except to other processors which could handle the first
processor's failures.

Dennis: But the programmer does not know which processor his program
is running on. I would like to see a convincing argument as to what
kinds of hardware failures an exception mechanism is intended to deal
with and what the recovery mechanism is going to be, before I would
accept it as part of a language.

Liskov: I would like to agree with Wulf that we don't know how to
entirely do away with interrupts. I can offer some more evidence to
Wulf's favor. In the VENUS system semaphores were implemented in the
microprogram, and interrupts were turned automatically into V operations. Nevertheless, we had a break interrupt, and it was for precisely the reason that you discussed: To capture the attention of a
process that was not listening. Furthermore, we had a terrible time
using the break interrupt correctly. It clearly is a bad way to do
things, but we didn't know a better way.

Anon.: Is that an argument for or against it?

Liskov: It is both. It's a bad solution, but it was the only one we
could think of to solve a real problem that exists in real systems.

Wulf: But that is exactly my point. I was not advocating interrupts.
I was simply asserting that I had some dirty laundry; the dirty laundry
results from the fact that the mechanisms which have been proposed, PV
and the whole nicely structured set of things above that, do not

suffice for all of the things that you have to face in real systems, unfortunately.

Dennis: I don't think you have answered my point though. One can handle these situations conceptually by having a process waiting for the break event.

Wulf: That does not abort the process which is still in the infinite loop, and I care about that process, because it is spinning the tape off at the end, or grinding the disk surface.

Dennis: There is an alternative mechanism, which is very attractive here. And that is to have the concept of one process being superior, or the monitor of another one. And, one capability the superior process should have is the ability to stop the processing activity which is going on beneath it.

Liskov: That sounds like an interrupt to me.

Dennis: Well, it is not really an interrupt, because it is not a signal coming from some unknown outside place and stopping an arbitrary ongoing activity.

Liskov: I think perhaps it is correct to say that although you can imagine ways of looking at these problems that might be conceptually superior to interrupts, in fact, we have no practical experience with such mechanisms.

Earnest: That is not really true. Data base management systems do not typically have an interrupt orientation; when they start a transaction, it is not exactly interrupted, but can be set back, in Dennis' sense, to a previous statement. That is an example of a way to handle a particular exception condition which is getting a lot of use these days.

Fisher: In response to Dennis' question about hardware failures, there are many existing military systems that do self diagnostics and automatic recovery from hardware failures. The methods are old and well tested, if not well understood. Many applications have real-time or environmental constraints that preclude human intervention when errors occur. Just as these applications require modularity and redundancy in their hardware, they require programming languages in which the diagnostic and recovery processes can be described.

Wulf: Could I comment on that? I think Dennis is being sort of fundamentally unrealistic. If the program that you are executing happens to be landing a 747, it is not an acceptable thing to say, "Whoops! I got an arithmetic error, or I got an overflow, obviously I can't continue." It is just not an acceptable answer.

Dennis: I did not say that that was what should be done. The question is where are the exception conditions handled? Is it going to be handled in the application programmer's program?

Fisher: Embedded computer systems seldom run under general purpose operating systems. Instead they have integral special purpose executives. Thus, almost by definition, exception processing must be done by the application programs.

Elzer: I would like to bring up a very provocative point in this elaborate circle here. It is not especially on interrupts; it is on parallel processing in general, and it is on the general use of such a language, what we are doing here, and that is why I said it was a very provocative point. This morning a gentleman said that we must regard the overall efficiency of the language for programming. Now, what kind of language shall come out of this effort? A language for programming real-time systems. These real-time systems depend on time, depend on the outer world; the programs have to respond to the outer world. That is one thing which I did not hear about the whole day today. Another problem is that we must do something to improve the quality of programs; we must reduce the error rate. There are fine and good thoughts about program proving, but what you can prove by such methods only concerns the internal logic of the program; you never can prove the external logic -- does the program really solve the problem? Therefore there is one thing that I want to emphasize here: Though we must not forget how programs are to be written properly, we must be aware that there are other and maybe more important interfaces involved in the design process. That one main interface is the interface between the programmer and the man who understands the problem, the engineer or technician. Shouldn't we, instead of trying to solve internal problems of the programs and of the languages, try to solve this problem of the interface between the engineer and the programmer? That means, shouldn't we try more to design languages which are understandable for the engineer. This would reduce the rate of errors in producing the program, I think, to a great extent, because the problem-oriented logic of the program would be more correct than it might be today. So why don't people try (or why don't they dare) to include features in languages (which, maybe, are not proven very well in the sense which is discussed here) like e.g., start activities, stop activities, wait for other activities. Okay, this was discussed. But what was not discussed today here at all is I/O. But the program does have to communicate with the outer world in some way. There is not a single paper on this. Now, my impression is, that this DoD language does not intend to have I/O in it. There is a little paragraph dealing with it, okay, but it is only one paragraph.

There are languages around -- I just mention some from Europe because
I know these more, than I know the languages here -- let me quote two
French developments, PROCOL and LTR, and a German development, PEARL,
and a newer English development, a system that is called MASCOT --
languages which attempt to solve these problems; maybe they use constructs which are not pure, and so on, but that is why I would like
to hear the opinion of this group here. Wouldn't it be better to use
constructs which are, from a theoretical standpoint, not so pure and
not so perfect, but which would reduce the error rate of programs to a
much greater extent and allow global optimization of the development
process of programs. Because they are also understood by other
people than the expert programmers.

Well, that is one of my questions. I had a lot more, of course,
but I don't want to hold up this discussion too long. I just want to
ask one other thing -- about the style -- for whom will this language
be? What class of problems shall it solve?

E. Wegner: I have made some notes on the lectures this morning, and
I'll proceed with them in the order of the talks this morning. Professor Williams extended the title of the session this afternoon, and
I propose to extend it once more, by the word real-time; it is a different thing from parallel processing and we shall have to talk on
proofs for real-time programs. Dennis talked about concurrency, and
during his lecture I asked myself how he would handle asynchronous
interrupts; perhaps they could be realized as a system module which
sends only, a module with no incoming stream, with one of the outgoing
streams of messages called interrupts, I don't know, it is just an
idea.

Dennis: The answer is yes; the messages called interrupts would be
merged with messages representing the ongoing activity of a system,
and in that way, the module which is processing this stream of messages would simply interleave its responses to the interrupts among
the steps of the regular computation.

E. Wegner: Another point which I don't want to treat deeply: Dennis
says that the outside has no knowledge of internal states. I have
heard about some students who killed the THE system by getting some
information from inside out by using the common time scale. The
system inside which looked at whether a required portion of code was
loaded. In this case, it responded immediately but otherwise, if not
loaded, it took some time to load, and after that, it said okay and
the outside module exploited this response time to get information
from inside out, and so some students succeeded in killing the system.
I don't want to do this deeper, but there is a problem in prohibiting

getting information inside out.

Another point here has the notion of a resource. It is just an
idea which is being processed in Germany in distributed systems in
process control to handle a computer as a resource so that at the
time the problem is written, it is not known on which computer a program or fresh process will be executed, so that the computers in the
systems may be handled under the concept of a resource, just as other
resources.

In the lecture of Ichbiah, he said that some objects are shown;
the data are shown. I always thought they were shown to everyone who
wants to see them. And I think that this is no longer state-of-the-
art; it is now someone who offers them and others who explicitly say
that they want to see them; not only exports must be indicated explicitly, but also any import, and piece of code which imports external
data must indicate explicitly which data it intends to import.

On the point of garbage collection, another idea seems to have
been forgotten; it comes from the working papers of the IFIP Working
Group 2.1 (Manchester M5, 1972) in the paper of Hodgson -- the idea
that a heap may be segmented into heaps owned by blocks or modules so
that a segment of the heap may be released at the time the owning process is abandoned. I never found this idea again anywhere in the
literature and this working paper is rather old, four years or so.

Another point of Weissman is that machine dependency must be
parameterized. There is a research area of computer hardware description language as commenced in the book of Bell and Newell, and I was a
bit disappointed that one could not succeed in formalizing more perfectly the computer hardware. It is only half formal, and up to now
there have been, to my knowledge, only a few attempts at formalizing
the computer hardware -- I think someone formalized the 360. As soon
as one had a proper computer hardware description language, the things
which are not called compiler compilers, which in reality are only
analyzer compilers, could be supplemented and complemented by a code
generator generator.

The topic of London's seems to be related to formalizing semantics , and this is one of the remarks I made on the Tinman, to Fisher
directly -- can we now devise a language without having formalized the
semantics? There are a lot of different approaches for programming
languages fit to describe computable functions.

Programming languages in which asynchronous interrupts occur
pose new problems, and there are few methods for describing this, apart
from the parallel program schemata (I don't see the use of them). One
approach is that of Peter Lauer in the University of Newcastle upon

Tyne, and myself, and my colleague, Cornelius Hopmann, in the GMD are
doing some work on formalizing the semantics of the real-time language
PEARL by a method similar to that used by Peter Lauer, and I am perfectly ready to talk ten minutes or so tomorrow afternoon on a discussion of this.

For my other point, I offer some ideas of Cornelius Hopmann on
input/output; I'll just give a sketch. The programming language
allows describing of devices, albeit physical devices or functional
devices, and interfaces, and the programmer may then by programming
an interface create a functional device on one or more physical or
functional devices.

Wetherall: There is just one point which I was going to raise. The
requirements specify access to variables, to channels, the explicit
export and import of data. In the British Ministry of Defence, we
have been working on a language called MORAL. This is one of the
PASCAL derivatives, influenced by ALGOL 68, but the main aim was to
introduce some of the concepts of MASCOT. I know that some of you
here have already heard about MASCOT, which is an approach to real-
time system construction and operation. One of the things we have
put into the language is a concept of locking. You can specify in
your encapsulation mechanism the key or keys that are to be associated
with the different components. The user must then specify, at an
appropriate point, just one key to gain access to the permitted components. We have found this invaluable in restraining the eagerness
and lack of control of the average programmers by whom most existing
systems have been written. All of you here are experienced, sensible
and never make mistakes, but I have a feeling that programmers of the
military system with which we are concerned need more control, more
discipline, and so I would certainly commend this concept. It and
other features of MORAL and MASCOT and expanded more fully in the MOD
paper,, "Parallel Processing and Modular Software Construction" by
Ken Jackson, of RSRE, Malvern, England in these proceedings.

Gries: I would like to address the problem of interrupts again. The
interrupt is a mechanistic device which we have in our machines and
which we need there. The problem is to design the parallel language
without them because they are difficult to understand, to design the
parallel language in such a way that it is understandable and clear,
but so that the interrupts can be used in order to implement the
language. That is the problem.

Wulf: I agree. I feel I opened up a bigger can of worms that I
intended to, and that I am being misinterpreted. I was not advocating
the interrupt, all right?

Gries: Yes, I know.

Anon.: You said you can't ignore them though.

Wulf: That you can't ignore them is only part of it; the other part
is that the other set of proposals which exist do not seem to be a
complete system. They are not sufficiently rich to deal with the
class ...

Gries: (interrupting) Which just shows we don't really understand
the whole parallelism problem yet.

Wulf: Precisely.

Anon.: Or the goto.

Wulf: Well, I would not agree with that.

Gries: Secondly, on this question that Elzer raised about why don't
we just design a language that the engineer can understand and program
in: The problem is that we ourselves don't understand completely how
to program, and the average programmer understands even less. Our
purpose here is to learn more about programming and how to design
languages. Let him reply to that and then I'll ask my second question.

Elzer: I understand this concept, but I am listening into the scene
of the user. To be correct, I am not thinking of the 'end user' who
just wants to see a pushbutton, I am thinking of engineers who have to
design application systems, who understand the process technology and
requirements. Such people keep telling me and I have good reasons to
believe that they mean it: "If you computer people don't come up with
a simple (to use!), maybe not perfect, solution soon, we will use
Process-FORTRAN forever and we will construct real-time BASIC, and
that's it." I think that surely you don't want to develop things in
this direction.

Gries: Well, I think Fisher wants exactly that -- a simple language.
Right? Simple in that people understand programs written in it.

Fisher: Absolutely. Language simplicity is critical to developing
reliable and understandable programs, to achieving commonality among
separate implementations, to attracting users within the DoD community,
and to the producing of reliable and effective translators, diagnostic
aids and optimizers.

Gries: And what we are saying is that this idea of simplicity hangs
very much on problems of verifying programs. How we understand them
depends very much on how we prove them correct at a theoretical level.
That is at least brought out by Wulf and London.

Williams: I think Ichbiah had a comment on that same remark that you
just addressed.

Ichbiah: I'd like also to address the comment made by Elzer. He
complained that practical issues have not been addressed at all. One

way to answer his remark is to say that if a language offers the following items:

(1) mechanisms for separate definition,

(2) mechanisms for separate compilation, and

(3) an encapsulated form for machine code insertions,

then input/output may be defined by semantic extension. This is what we have done in LIS. The language itself does not contain special primitives for input/output; these facilities are provided in the form of standard "partitions". The main advantage of this approach is that the base language is kept much simpler than if you introduce special primitives.

Gries: Is there any difference between these partitions you speak of and the abstract data types we have been discussing this morning? For example, the view that a data type is a heterogeneous algebra?

Ichbiah: There are differences between partitions and abstract data types both from a conceptual and from an implementation viewpoint.

From a conceptual viewpoint, a partition will most of the time appear as a group of several semantically closely related data types, and not just one data type. Typically a partition will be used to describe a given sphere of knowledge such as topology, graphs, structures in the examples which I presented. As a consequence, it does not make sense to have more than one instance of a given partition in a given context. On the other hand, for encapsulated data types we think more of objects, of which you have many different instances. It is true that in SIMULA the two notions are fused in the unique concept of class: If a class is used as prefix of a block, the knowledge defined in the class becomes available in the block. This use of a class thus corresponds to partitions and, obviously, classes may also be used as abstract data types.

In terms of the implementation, however, this overloading of the class concept plays against efficiency. In the partition case, because we have a unique instance of each partition, the compiler is able to perform an optimal allocation of resources (registers,...) to the different partitions. As a consequence, accesses to information defined within a partition may be implemented with the highest degree of efficiency. On the other hand, more anonymous conventions have to be applied for the treatment of dynamically created instances of abstract data types and this results in less efficiency. This justifies the introduction of two different concepts here.

Waite: When I was at Columbia, Ken King, who was then director of the computer center, used to say that everybody has a pushcart that he pushes through life. I have the feeling that (at least in the view of

the world) my pushcart is portability. So I am supposed to say something about machine independence, and I think that the comment that
Ichbiah made just before his last response gives me an opening. He
said that if you have primitive facilities for separate compilation
and encapsulation and so on, you can define operations such as input/
output. I would like to call your attention to the fact that ALGOL 60
had mechanisms for procedural extension and therefore did not require
any input/output specification. The result was that everybody developed their own, and they were all different. One of the things that
I have seen in the Tinman specification is the desire to avoid exactly
that sort of thing; to specify the facilities which people feel are
necessary for a wide variety of programs.

If you wish to have a language which has some modicum of machine
independence then you need a model for each thing that you do, each
thing which is supposed to be machine independent. There must be
some general agreement in the field on just what constitutes that
model, because if there isn't any agreement, then people will want to
implement the model in different ways. Now it turns out that we have
our intuition and experience most highly developed in the area of
mathematics. We have been schooled in mathematics ever since the
first grade, we know all there is to know, and consequently definitions of languages have a highly uniform structure, at least as far as
the mathematics is concerned. At least we think that this is the case.

In the course of developing some techniques for moving programs
from one place to another, we came upon the question of integer division. What is the meaning of three divided by two using integer
division? Well, everybody seems to agree that three divided by two is
one. But how about minus three divided by two? Is that minus one, or
is it minus two?

Horning: It would be minus one/half in PL/I, I think.

Waite: We did a survey among a number of languages, and we found some
(such as BCPL) which simply said that they did not define the result
for integer division with operands of different sign. Others (such as
ALGOL 60) made straightforward definitions. LISP, however, said that
the result would be "the number theoretic quotient". That definition
intrigued me, so I went to a mathematician down the hall and asked
"What's the number theoretic quotient?" "Well, I am not a number
theorist" he replied, and he reached up and picked out a book (I think
it was Birkhoff and MacLane). He paged through it until he came to
EUCLID's algorithm. "Well", he said "obviously it means this." "What
happens if we have minus three divided by two?" I asked. He looked at
the book, scratched his head for a while and then ventured "Since the

remainder has to be positive, the result <u>must</u> be minus two." But you see, he could not give me a definition of the number theoretic quotient. I went to the next mathematician down the hall, and he said, "Well, I am not a number theorist." But he grabbed a book from his shelf, and he paged through it, came up with an algorithm and said, "According to this algorithm, the answer is <u>obviously</u> minus one." Then I went to the head of the department, and he said, "Well, I am not a number theorist, but I know where our number theorist is. He is at home writing a paper, but I think I can disturb him." So he called the guy up, asked the questions, and then sat for a long time nodding his head and making noncommittal noises. Finally, he handed the phone to me. "You know, you have an interesting problem there" the voice at the other end explained. "There are two algorithms for doing division and number theorists can not agree on which is the right one."

So you see, even in mathematics, we have some problems with machine independence. It turns out, however, that that problem is not very severe. If we want to make a decision as to which version of divison to use, we will almost certainly choose the version which truncates towards zero. The reason for that is that in our survey of twenty machines we found only one whose hardware truncated away from zero. Does anybody know what that might be?

Anon. guesses: CDC? The 360?

Waite: No, the ICL KDF9.

Anon.: Of course, one nobody's ever heard of.

Waite: Now, there is another interesting question that we come across when we look at machine hardware, and that is the question of truncation. Suppose that we truncate a negative number, using an arithmetic right shift. If you have a machine that uses sign magnitude or one's complement representation of negative numbers, this operation truncates toward zero. On the other hand, if you have a machine which uses two's complement representation and in which the hardware has not been specially altered, an arithmetic right shift will truncate toward minus infinity.

Another question which comes up from time to time is the question of the meaning of the components of a multi-dimensional array. Supposing I have an array that is subscripted by i and j. Do I interpret this as an array of arrays with the rows being the subarrays, or with the columns being the subarrays? Well, it varies from language to language. Some of them say, some of them don't; ALGOL 60 does not and makes no bones about it. That is all right, theoretically, but when you sit down to write a program, the efficiency of your solution may depend critically on how the array is structured. If you sequence through the array by row and the implementation is paging by column, then you may get a page fault on every access, and your program may run one or two orders of magnitude slower than a program which goes through the array the other way. Some measurements in this area have been given in a paper by Cleve Moler.

All right, so here we have an area, mathematics, in which we thought our experience and intuition were well developed, but it turns out that there are still some holes in it. Consider the questions of I/O, exception handling, and so on, and so on. I don't think we have any experience or intuition to speak of that at all. There does not seem to be much hope for achieving machine independence, because everybody has a different idea of how these things should be done. They will be done differently in different hardware, and if the mechanism which is chosen in the language does not reflect the hardware, then the efficiency may be just unacceptable.

E. Wegner: Environment inquiry.

Waite: There are limits to environment inquiry, I am afraid. It is a question in most cases not of just small fix-ups, but of changing the entire algorithm.

E. Wegner: That is right, you read both algorithms and make an environment inquiry to decide which one to apply.

Waite: Okay, that is a possibility if you only have two or three mechanisms, but unfortunately, I don't think that is the case. 2^n algorithms might be a bit too many to handle that way!

Let me say, though, that even though I am somewhat pessimistic on this point, I think that the designers of the language must take a position, even if it is wrong. They must take a position, and they must enforce that position in the way that the Tinman document enforces the positions which it takes: It simply says "This is the way it is going to be." There are no exceptions, no freedom for the implementer, no hedging.

Ledgard: I have heard something different in your story. I think what your story really says is that we should not have an integer division operator at all. When you divide three by two, the answer is three halves, a rational number. If you keep rounding or truncating or leaving it up to the program, you do get problems. But, if you get rid of that operation, then the whole thing is solved. Why isn't that, in fact, the moral of your story?

Waite: Well, that may be a moral of the story. The point of the story was that if you speak to almost anyone that person will unhesitatingly tell you what the answer should be, because on the basis of his intuition and experience he knows. Now in a language definition,

of course, you have to make a choice as to whether you are going to
rely on the intuition and experience of the implementer or not. I
think that most language definitions do, in fact, rely on the intuition and experience of the implementer. The result is that maybe here
-3+2 results in minus one and over at the other installation it
results in minus two. Your point is a good one, however. I think
that the language designers should formalize and fix everything. If
they decide to simply eliminate that operation, that is okay, or if
they fix the result, that is okay too.

E. Wegner: I strongly object to this. I think there is a necessity
that the language designer does not fix everything and a reason for
the ALGOL 68 people who in many places of the report say "the further
elaboration is undefined".

The Tinman says something about the short circuit mode. It says
in the boolean expression if there is a boolean OR and the first
operand is true, then the second one need not be elaborated, must not
be elaborated. Must not or need not, I don't know, but it does not
matter.

Anon.: But it does matter!

E. Wegner: Yes, but for my point it does not matter. Of course it
does matter for the semantics of the language. My point is that you
require an overspecification. The programmer should be allowed to say
"don't care". If you want to specify short circuit mode, you write
the ALGOL 68 "ELIF", but if you don't care, you write boolean expressions. I would definitely prefer if the programmer has the choice of
leaving something open so that an optimizer may use the feature which
is explicitly left open for the optimizer or the programmer fixes and
specifies, but don't force the programmer to overspecify.

Elzer: I would like to draw another moral out of this story which
Professor Waite told us. You can draw two consequences: One is to
say that you don't understand enough of I/O, that there are millions
of solutions, etc. and so you better choose no one. So you get incom-
patability forever or people will use other languages, such as FORTRAN.
I would prefer the other consequence, and that is not to look at the
computer science side of the thing, but at the problem side of the
thing!

There are not very many capabilities an engineer wants from, e.g.,
a process I/O mechanism. He wants to set registers, to reset registers, to read registers -- that is one thing he wants. He wants to
set I/O values, read I/O values, to convert from engineering units to
bit representation and vice versa. Well, there may be some more, I am

oversimplifying now, but anyway. Some more, but he will be happy with
nearly every solution you give him, as long as it is on a higher
level, instead of forcing him to go back to assembly coding or constructing this encapsulated procedure or whatever it is. I would like
to illustrate this by an example from my experience: CAMAC is a very
powerful and nearly tricky means to interface processes to computers.
Now, in our institute this was interfaced to a certain computer and
this computer had a very difficult way of handling I/O. You had to
set up channel programs, etc., etc., in order to include process I/O
in a compiler for a higher level language. We did it in a very
general way, and so we got a lot of overhead, too. In the first
moment, the CAMAC specialists screamed and said: "you are ruining our
nice CAMAC features" etc. But half a year later the CAMAC man is just
interested in using the features that I described before and not
everything and this and that and he forgets about all the overhead.
He is just happy being able to write his CAMAC-commands in his higher-
level program and that is all he wants.

And, if you are not happy with the overhead, improve the machine!
Waite: I just wanted to correct a possible misinterpretation -- I did
not say throw up your hands! Make a decision, even if it is the wrong
decision, make it on some grounds, but don't sit there making no
decision. Definitely make it.
Graham: I would like to suggest that maybe we are approaching this a
little bit wrong. I agree with Waite that we should make a decision;
I think we should even be more forceful than that and perhaps be mean.
For years we have tried to put features in languages and worry about
particular statements and things to get around the "features" that the
hardware designers give us to work with. I think we ought, in future
languages -- particularly ones like this language -- to go whole-
heartedly in the way several people have suggest, particularly Gries
this morning. Let us look at what kind of things you need to do the
problem right, to get correct programs in the easiest most understandable way to solve the kinds of problems we want to solve, and
then we will design a language that expresses that well and we will
make decisions on everything, like whether division rounds up or down
and becomes minus or negative and all these things. We will define
the language completely and say, "that is the way it is going to be."
Then, if you, Mr. Manufacturer, want to sell us a machine, it better
run that language well. And the manufacturers, I am sure, will figure
out how to build a machine so it will run that language well. We have
not done that up 'til now. They offer us some piece of junk, and then
we bend over backwards and spend a lot of money trying to make -- warp,

our languages so we can use the hardware well, without telling them
to get off their something or other and give us some good stuff.
(Laughter and applause)

Horning: I, of course, agree wholeheartedly with that. I would like
to return to the issue of whether complete specification is in fact
overspecification. I think it is a terrible mistake in a language
definition to say that we would like to have an optimizing compiler,
therefore let us make our semantics as fuzzy as we can to leave the
optimizer as much room as possible to rearrange. For example, in the
order of evaluation of expressions or the order of execution of the
statements, if we do this to the extent that we have no longer specified a meaning to a program, then the optimization itself becomes
meaningless. Or we can be in a situtation where it is the programmer's responsibility to consider every possible permutation of the
operands, and if all of them give the same result, then he is free to
write the expression. What we must do instead is to say there is a
meaning, it is defined in some straightforward way, like, for example,
evaluation from left to right, or execution of statements in the order
in which they appear in the program. If the optimizer can determine
that there is another order which is more efficient, but equivalent
in its effect....

E. Wegner: In some sense.

Horning: Then you must define the sense of equivalence. But it must
be the responsibility of the optimizer to verify that it has preserved
equivalence, not the responsibility of the programmer to ensure that
any permutation the optimizer might attempt will result in equivalence.
Now that principle is accepted at the statement level. We allow
optimizers to change the order of statements, but only if the optimizer does the checking. In most language definition efforts, that
has not been accepted at the expression level, but it should be.

Wetherell: I support the position that we should specify everything.
I am a little disturbed by some things I heard, particularly throwing
out integer division, but I suspect that was slightly facetious. I am
disturbed by the attitude that if there are several different interpretations and you want to specify some one of them, and if half the
people want one interpretation and the other half want another, and
the other half don't really care....

Anon.: But you have got three halves there! (Lots of comments about
three halves being relevant to the problem at hand!)

Wetherell: Then you should not specify anything. Integer division,
in fact, is a good example. Integer division is used in many programs,

but I think the reason that the programming language manuals do not specify what it does with negative numbers is because hardly ever does anybody use it that way. Almost always, it is used only involving the integers. Now, it does not argue you should define it only for the positive integers, though I think somebody this morning said that there was a language in which that was true. In fact, it argues that it really doesn't matter how you specify it in that rather unusual case, half the people will be happier, half the people will be unhappier, and the half that are unhappy can probably use one of our magic encapsulation techniques or something like that to replace it. You should not throw out the whole problem, and you <u>do</u> have to specify. Think back about the specific topics talked about today -- that issue has come up several times.

E. Wegner: Defining the language completely, that means defining the word length and what happens with overflow, defining rounding, range and precision of reals -- this is the only way of defining a language completely. That is, then you have the machine and the operating system and everything. I do not think that is what you want.

Wetherell: That is quite possibly true for real numbers -- I notice that the Tinman requires that you specify a procedure and how you are going to round it.

E. Wegner: In Tinman, you specify equivalence of reals by some precision and then require that the result of a long floating point computation is not changed by an optimization in the order of the evaluation. Within this precision, I think this is not fulfillable.

Earnest: I have a couple of comments. You mentioned that you did not want to warp the language to suit the hardware, but you have to warp it to suit the users sometimes. Wulf mentioned an example of that, where the interrupt had to be in even though he did not know how to put it in well.

Just to tell another story here: I used to be a horn player, and in one lesson I thought I was playing pretty well, but I was missing notes, and my teacher stopped me and said, "How come you're missing so many notes?" I gave this little explanation that I thought it was not too bad because I was playing beautifully, and he looked at me and said, "Well, just because you are missing notes does not mean you are playing beautifully." In other words, I agree with the notion that elegance in axioms is an extremely valuable goal to strive for, in fact, I have been impressed by some of the concrete improvements resulting from, for instance, PASCAL's axiomatization. Still, at some point in the development you must say, okay, that is as elegant as we

can get for now, then you stick in all the other features that you
don't really know how to do and do them as unobtrusively as possible.
Gries: Rather than warp the language to fit the user, maybe it would
be better to unwarp the user.
Wulf: I would really like to agree with the sort of thing that Graham
said, both in this session and in the previous one, about efficiency
and the structure of the machines. I really agree with him, nevertheless, I would like to disagree for just a minute. If I can, I will
quickly paraphrase what he said. In the last session, he said that
we should first get programs correct; then we should go measure and
tune them. That is the way we should get efficiency. Because, in
fact, the big gains come from changing algorithms, data structures,
and so on. Just now he said we should not warp language features by
the nature of the underlying machines. In other contexts, I would be
saying exactly that same thing. However, I have the feeling that now
there is a tendency to swing a little too far in that direction. I
think five years ago we desperately needed to be saying that. I have
the feeling now I am being backed against the wall. I tell my students
that I think programming ought to be an engineering discipline; I do
not think it is, but I think it ought to be.

I would like to draw an analogy. In particular, when I am telling
them what it is that gets good grades, I say, "Hey, look. Suppose
that you were a civil engineer and you were asked to design a bridge.
Nobody is going to consider your design -- you are trying to sell it,
right -- if it is not functionally correct. If it does not reach all
the way across the river, I don't care about anything else." That is
the first condition; its clearly got to be correct. But, there are
important engineering differences between correct bridges. Even
though it reaches all the way across the river, I would consider it a
totally unacceptable if it cost more than the gross national product.
Efficiency does matter. Given functionally correct programs, efficiency matters a great deal. It is one of the primary characteristics
on which you judge the quality of two functionally correct alternatives.

There are situations, and we have got to be intellectually honest
about all this, where ten percent matters -- ten percent in size, ten
percent in speed, the size usually being particularly critical. Where
large numbers of replications of systems are involved, literally an
instruction can cost thousands or even millions of dollars, as it
keeps getting replicated. If we sit here and say that efficiency does
not matter, or that we should not warp the languages to the machines,
I do not think we are being completely honest. Yeah, sure, in the
past the pressure was the other way and that should be turned around

to some extent. But let us not be ridiculous on the other side either.

Graham: I did not intend to imply that efficiency did not matter. In fact, I have a great interest in that area and tomorrow I intend to say something to the effect the efficiency should be considered from the very beginning, but I am going to indicate that I think it should be done considerably differently than anyone does it now and should not be done by not putting desirable language features in because they might be inherently inefficient. I will also make comments about efficiency and hardware in the context of the languages that we are talking about now. I do not quite believe the optimism I have heard around here, and I would guess that it will be about five years before it bears fruit. Five years from now we will be able to buy micro-processors with a better memory for $1.25 a piece, and not for half a million. I can make a ten thousand dollar computer with nearly ten thousand of those things in it, and I am going to have so much compu-tation power coming out of my ears that I need to look at the whole thing completely differently than we are looking at it now, and there-fore I would like to say, look at the language -- what we want in languages -- first, then try to put some pressure (or do it myself) to look at how you would build machines to do that kind of thing correct-ly. We have ten thousand little computers sitting there churning away doing all sorts of little things in parallel; I do not need to worry about a lot of the problems that are being worried about, I don't think.

Miller; I would like to agree with what Graham said about looking at things differently. I would first like to bridge the gap a little bit by reminding people about a session on the high cost of software which Wulf chaired two years ago at Monterey. This session concluded that there are a number of items after correctness that are very important measures of the quality of a program. One thing that has always bothered me is that the specification of programs, deficient as it usually is in a number of ways, is most markedly deficient in specify-ing those other ("quality)" attributes: Robustness, maintainability, efficiency and the other properties by which programs are customarily measured. When those items are not mentioned in the specification, the programmer whose responsibility it is to implement the software in accordance with the specification is left on his own with respect to making these tradeoffs without guidance from the original specifier of the product. Thus, the specification of a program needs a great deal of improvement in this respect, as well as the most visible ones of completeness and accuracy.

Dennis: Graham's remark reminded me of a point I would like to make about the form of computer system that programs written in a language will be running on. In the tactical domain especially, I think we will be seeing systems gradually taking the form of multi-computer systems -- distributed multi-computer systems. This is in contrast to our current languages, designed to express programs intended to run on single processors, or to express multi-process computations in a form that requires shared memory among multiple processors for efficient operation. I am pretty much convinced that the era of microprocessors will introduce us to system configurations that are more distributed; that is, numbers of processors, each with local memory, which are communicating with each other through some kind of communication network. I think the languages in which programs have to be written to run naturally on these systems must make use of concepts which do not imply communication through shared memory. This is a fundamental reason why I suggested the form of language in my paper -- one in which the structure of programs expressed in the language can readily be mapped onto a distributed configuration of micro-computers.

Wulf: Isn't that the antithesis of what Graham was just saying? He was saying that language should dictate machine structure rather than the other way around.

Dennis: That is true. My fondest goal is to have a machine which truly responded to the needs of a language which is based on concepts of verification, but I simply do not see such a machine arising in the near future. Instead, I see our present day machines, the conventional multi-processors, being superceded in the near future by the distributed multi-computer systems, because we do not know how to build any better configuration of familiar types of hardware modules. Even though the distributed multi-computer systems are not ideal from the point of view of supporting a good language, I think they are the kind of system which we are going to have to learn how to use, how to write programs for, and how to gain confidence in writing reliable and correct programs. These systems are going to support highly concurrent operation; we must learn how to deal with concurrency in a form which is applicable to that kind of computer configuration.

The ability of the language in which we write programs to match the character of these hardware systems is going to be crucial to our ability to write reliable systems and to overcome the programming difficulties in the systems we are trying to build today. So I am still dismayed by the lack of attention to the question of parallel processing, and I am dismayed by the attitude: "Oh well, what do we do for

parallel processing? That is up to the operating system designer.
We will take whatever primitives he provides us and we will somehow
make them do."

That is absolutely the wrong attitude. The facilities for concurrent processing must be considered as part of the language design
and must be fixed and completely specified by the language designer,
otherwise we simply will not make any progress in being able to write
correct programs.

Morgan: I agree with the concept that the concurrent processing
primitives should not be built into the language but for different
reasons. I belive that concurrent processing primitives should not
be included in standard languages. Not only are such primitives
operating system dependent, these primitives can affect the efficiency of certain applications.

Certain applications are very sensitive to the concurrency primitives available. As an example, if the processes involved in the
application are very short, a complex implementation of concurrency
primitives can swamp the actual computation. We at Bolt Beranek and
Newman Inc., have been faced with this exact problem. Our multi-
processing switch for the ARPANET consists of about 60 small processes,
averaging 400 μsec in length. If the concurrency scheduling primitives were complex, the throughput of this system could be seriously
affected.

Dennis: Let us go back to the days when floating point arithmetic was
not built into the machine. The first thing one did on receiving the
machine from the manufacturer was write an interpretive package to do
his floating point arithmetic for him. When the suggestion came that
floating point arithmetic should be built into the machine, there
obviously was the cry, "Well, it wouldn't be right for my problem, my
problem is special, it needs this particular precision, or this particular algorithm or truncation rules or whatever." However, we accepted the fact that there was so much advantage to having a particular
solution to the problem built into the hardware; from the point of view
of efficiency we accepted it.

Waite: Have you talked to any numerical analysts lately?

Dennis: Okay, they did not make some of the right decisions.

Weatherall: Can I just reinforce Dennis' previous point about the
need for the operating system. Unfortunately, the Tinman says in section K that we will not consider an operating system -- the language
must work without one. I think one of the problems we have got is
that we are now going the other way and saying that no programs will
have operating systems.

However, we must decide upon a set of good concurrency mechanisms during the language definition stage. There are several proposals -- at the operating system level -- around which ought to be seriously considered before determining the language priorities. We cannot go very much further in designing the more esoteric constructs of the language until we fully understand the different parallel processing schemes.

Dennis: I did not understand your point. What is your position on the operating system? Are you saying that an operating system is necessary to have parallel processing primitives?

Wetherall: I believe that is the proper level. In the long term, DoD needs some specified operating system for its "real-time" systems.

Wulf: What is the difference between an operating system in that sense, and a run-time system as we know it for I/O and allocating resources? I think you are using the word operating system in a kind of arbitrary sense.

Wetherall: I may be, but otherwise I think we will go too far the other way.

Goodenough: I have been giving some thought to these issues recently. It is nice to have certain concurrency and parallelism primitives in a language, but the issue really is, how do they get implemented in the system that you are actually running on? Does the compiler builder implement them, or does the application programmer have control over how the primitives are implemented? Within DoD systems, it seems essential that some application programmers of the system have the ability to implement those primitives in a way that satisfies system-specific requirements for efficiency as well as the semantics that are defined in the language for the primitives. I am not sure how that should be done from one application to another and I am going to have people saying that that is not the case -- I would be happy to see that it is not, but it appears to be. So the question really comes down to what do you gain by putting primitives into the language? I think the answer has to be in terms of what kinds of program errors you are going to detect at compile time because the primitives are in the langauge (rather than if the primitives are defined by procedural extension), and what kinds of optimizations you are going to be able to make because the primitives provide information to the compiler that would not be available if the primitives were realized by procedural extension.

Cartwright: While we are talking about omissions in Tinman, there is an obvious one which we have completely overlooked up to this point.

We pay a lot of lip service to the idea of verification (by verification I mean, and I assume everyone else means, proving a program is consistent with some set of formal specifications). We have totally ignored the issue of how to state these formal specifications. For trivial programs like greatest common divisor (and that seems to be the canonical example for papers that are published on program verification) first order number theory is an adequate specification language, but for more complex programs a simple first order theory of the program data is not sufficient. For non-trivial programs you must have some mechanism for defining new assertion language primitives. As an illustration, consider a simple sorting program. To state its formal specifications, you need the concept of permutation, and every treatment of the permutation predicate that I have seen in the literature introduces it as an ad hoc primitive indirectly specified by an entirely new set of axioms provided by the programmer. The question is: Are we going to have to invent an axiomatic description for every new assertion language predicate that we need to describe the behavior of a program verification?

Anon.: (chorus of "yes".)

Cartwright: I am surprised at your willingness to blindly accept systems of axioms. How does one know what a new predicate symbol appearing in a new set of axioms means? I can read and understand programs much more easily than axioms. In fact, I would rather trust my ability to determine whether a program is correct than whether a set of axioms is consistent with the interpretations I think that programmer intends. There are more disciplined, specific, and intelligible methods for defining new assertion language primitives than by ad hoc axiomatizations. A specification language should provide such a mechanism.

E. Wegner: A question to Dennis. What is an operating system becoming in the case of a multi-computer system? I talked previously about operating systems. We share a lot of computers, and I suppose an operating system must turn into a set of conventions between the operating systems of the many constituent computers and multi-computer systems, where any computer may replace any other one in case of failure. I think we need completely new terms, instead of the term operating system.

Dennis: Rather than think of each of these distributed computers having their own little operating system and saying that the operating system is the convention by which those kernels communicate, I would rather simply say that the language implementation involves conventions as to how programs running in these machines will interact with one another, that is, the means they will use to send and receive messages. Now, as to the fault tolerance, I think that the distributed multi-computer has an advantage in fault tolerance because of the absence of shared memory; that is, any failure can only affect local information, rather than affect information contained in a shared memory, which is almost necessarily at least more of a global character, and it is easier to detect and recover from local failures than a global failure.

Wulf: The great Northest power failure is an example -- you all know about that, perhaps you were here. It was caused by the failure of a single, local component in a distributed network.

Dennis: What conclusions do you draw from that?

Wulf: You cannot deduce that just because the components are physically remote from each other that you have implicitly got fault tolerance. As long as there is an electrical or information path between them, the problem exists.

Dennis: But my point is that the distributed multi-computer is a more convenient configuration to deal with fault tolerance than the one in which we have.....

Wulf: That is not clear. What prevents the following situation? Consider a mini-processor system. One processor has a faulty interconnection to the next; it happens to drop some bits which are not discovered by the detection mechanism.

Dennis: How can you hope to detect failures when your failure detection mechanism has failed?

Wulf: But that is precisely the issue. Detection mechanisms are themselves hardware, they can fail too. No matter what you do in hardware, there is a non-zero probability of failure.

Dennis: So the only thing you can hope is to have a mechanism which survives single failures.

Wulf: That is why the Northeast power failure was so bad, you are right.

Dennis: You said that it did not survive a single failure -- it was the failure of a single component that caused the Northeast blackout. That is what you said.

Wulf: It was an unanticipated failure.

Dennis: I would like to complete my statement, which is that I feel that a distributed multi-computer has the possiblity of being designed so it is strictly tolerant of single failures; for shared-memory multi-processor systems, no satisfactory scheme has been devised that can tolerate all single failures.

Mathur: In the Strawman set of requirements -- which was a predecessor to the Tinman set of requirements -- one of the requirements was to attempt to standardize the language/ operating system interface. And, I think that a lot of things that have been said here bear on the point that perhaps that interface should be defined and standardized. Features such as multi-processing, multi-programming, input/output, storage allocation, etc., should be defined, and they should be defined by the language. I think that for too long the compilers have depended upon the idiosyncracies of the operating systems. Up to this time, as a rule, the operating systems were defined or implemented first, before the compiler design and/or implementation was undertaken. The functions and characteristics of the compilers were thus always dependent upon the functions being performed by the operating systems. This pattern should change. I think that a half-way path should be established between these two critical pieces of software, and the interfaces and the functions of each piece of software should be properly identified and standardized. Some of the functions, or parts thereof, traditionally being assigned to the operating system should be delegated to the compiler, while the others should be continued to be performed by the operating system, and vice versa. The functions to be performed by the interface and the language and operating system features necessary to support them, should be standardized.

Horning: If we are to attempt a conservative language design, we should make sure that those things which fall within the area of the language are very well defined indeed. We should make sure there are as few things as possible within the area of language design and therefore have to be very well defined. Anything that we suspect is going to have to change drastically from application to application should be rigidly excluded from our language definition. And that is the problem -- that we really do not, I think, anticipate that a common operating system will cover all the applications that the common language is supposed to. (Or a common scheduling algorithm, or a common method of parallel programming.) If we define those things, and we are wrong in only half the cases, or say a third of the cases, although we picked the thing that covers the majority, we have still excluded a third of the things. If we exclude one third of the possible applications in each of six different decisions, we have drastically narrowed the scope of the language. Now maybe that is a good thing, but I don't think it is the intent of Tinman.

Dennis: I would like to make the point that if it does not provide adequate support for concurrent processing, then you cannot think of Tinman, the language, as being of long term interest to the Department of Defense.

Wulf: But maybe that is a good idea.

(incredible laughter...)

Dennis: But we are now looking at it as something that might come
into practice five years from now and probably will stick with us for
ten years after that, or more.

Horning: Yes, but assembly language does not deal with the problems
of parallel processing, and you can still write the individual modules
of a concurrent system in assembly language. And you can still write
individual pieces and couple them by whatever mechanism is appropriate
to the application.

Dennis: Provided, Horning, that the language or operating system
provides the pieces, the mechanism, for coupling these modules together. But it does not.

Fisher: I would envision the DoD common language effort taking two
to three years from the current point until production compilers are
available.

Graham: I think I heard, but do you know anybody who can implement a
language in two years?

Gries: Do you know anybody who can define a language in two years?

Fisher: Two years is not unusual for the design of programming languages particularly if they are not unduly complex. The time should
be considerably shorter in this case because many of the most difficult and time consuming language design decisions have been completed
already through the requirements-generation process and because we are
willing to live with what is achievable without extending the state-
of-the-art. Complete prototype translators might be available at
essentially the same time as the language definition. An additional
year should be sufficient for production of a quality compiler. Much
of the compiler development can be done in parallel with testing and
refining of the language definitions.

Williams: Well, that is certainly a topic for Session IV, and it is
now five o'clock.

<u>Williams</u>: The panelists for this session are Lori Clarke and Bob
Graham from the University of Massachusetts and Peter Wegner from
Brown University.

<u>P. Wegner</u>: I would like to start by raising some global issues con-
cerning the management of the DoD-1 project, and relate these global
issues to specific technical issues in yesterday's and today's discussions.

First, the matter of developing a complete requirements specification before doing specific language design. This is a classical
life-cycle approach to the solution of complex problems in applications
areas. I would like to give some reasons why this may not be an
appropriate approach in the language design area; the language design
may be different in certain, very specific, technical respects. Programming language development differs from the development of applications programs in that requirements cannot be given by concrete
behavioral performance specifications. They could in principle be
defined in terms of a combination of machine independent principles of
concept modelling and machine dependent principles of efficiency.
Such principles tend to be so abstract and general that they are difficult and perhaps impossible to enunciate in a form that is useful to
the language designer. The Tinman report is a capable attempt to
express polished concepts, such as reliability, maintainability, and
efficiency, in terms of concrete programming language features. However, it is not really a requirements specification, but rather a
shopping list of desirable programming language features. Such a
shopping list is a useful guide to the programming language designer,
but should not be confused with, or given the status of, a complete
requirements specification. It is a qualitatively different kind of
document, and I think this is very important and also has important
practical repercussions. I feel that the attempt to give a complete
requirements specification before starting on the concrete design of a
language is unrealistic and that the language should be developed by
iterating and overlapping the processes of requirements monitoring,
design, and implementation, particularly if the objective is a short
time frame for completion of a project. We can argue endlessly about
the role of specific language design issues relating to modularity,

pointers, control structures, parallelism, and philosophical issues relating to whether optimization should be part of the language, but these issues can be resolved only on the basis of specific complete language design proposals. If I were running the DoD-1 project, I would immediately fund several intensive pilot language design efforts and let these designs compete against each other in much the same way that important architectural designs are chosen by competition. In the case of DoD-1, several iterations of design evaluation and partial implementation might be needed, and supporting documentation and justification of the design might play an important role. It has been mentioned that readability is an important issue in applications programming; it is also vitally important in language design, definition, and standardization.

Yesterday I detected a polarization of points of view between Gries, who felt that we should express concepts and requirements in machine independent, people oriented terms, and programming language implementers who use the machine dependent terms like abstract model of memory, heap language, and separate compilation to describe concepts and goals in language design. Williams characterized this in terms of idealists and realists. It seems to me that the successful programming language designer must be able to think in terms of both points of view simultaneously. A good language feature, such as a data type or data abstraction mechanism, must help the user in thinking about and formulating problems, but also have a simple and efficient implementation. The fact that language designers must be able to view a construct from many different points of view simultaneously is probably one of the factors that makes language design so difficult. Cheatham said there is a great deal more to a programming language than syntax and semantics -- programming analysis tools, optimization features, performance evaluation, operating system hooks, verification and synthesis, potential, and this sort of thing. Some of these require the machine independent view, some the machine dependent point of view, and most require both points of view simultaneously.

When we talk about the language concept, we cannot always verbally express the multiple viewpoints simultaneously, and must sometimes choose the people oriented or the machine oriented shorthand for characterizing a language concept. In such circumstances I personally often choose the machine oriented shorthand, simply because it is often more concrete. Thus the term "heap languages" may sound like an implementation oriented term; it is really a shorthand for something that involves people oriented concepts, in the sense that it is a shorthand for languages having features such as pointer variables,

potentially recursive data abstraction modules, and other features
that require heaps to implement them.

Now we have a people oriented, and a machine oriented aspect to
this, but the detailed reasoning in terms of what a heap oriented
language really is does effectively put the machine oriented model
first and the people oriented model second, and this is, in fact (it
turns out from the point of view of simplicity and understandability)
often the way we have to look at these matters, although from an
idealistic point of view we might prefer to look at it the other way.
So there are many contexts in which an implementation oriented point
of view is a greater aid to understanding and simplicity than a people
oriented point of view. And I feel that over-emphasis of the people
oriented point of view in thinking about programming concepts can lead
to losing touch with reality.

One rather important example, for purposes of this conference,
is the emphasis on developing a complete requirements specification
before embarking on concrete language designs. This, I think, is an
example of emphasizing the idealists' view, the way we would really
like to develop the language, at the expense of pragmatism. Another
example is Goodenough's suggestion that implementation oriented optimization standards should be part of the language. Here, again,
machine independent things predominate.

Now, another way of dealing with this is that top-down development, from a "what" specification to a "how" specification, is what
the idealist wants, while bottom-up implementation, from lower level
to higher level concepts, is what is often pragmatically possible. In
a really difficult project we cannot rely exclusively on bottom-up or
top-down development but must iterate by performing both kinds of
development simultaneously. And DoD-1 is an example of precisely the
kind of project where such iteration is necessary.

Now I would like to make some remarks about program verification,
which will turn out to be related to this point about machine independence and dependence as well. A knowledge of proof rules for
individual language constructs is an important tool in identifying
simple language constructs and sources of complexity in language
design. The work of program verification, similarly, plays an important role in suggesting how applications programs should be organized
to maintain simplicity and understandability. But I disagree with
Wulf's remark yesterday that automatic or semi-automatic program verification will be state-of-the-art in production programming in ten or
even twenty years from now. The problem is not so much that of

automatically verifying programs whose specification is given, but
rather that of developing a sufficiently rich specification language.
It was pointed out yesterday that almost every new program required
the introduction of new primitives with their own proof rules such as
permutations in the case of sorting. There is also the problem that
many practical problems have large, three or four hundred page, semi-
formal requirements specifications. It is clearly important to use
rigorous management disciplines, such as structured design, to control
the complexity and reliability of such large programs, but it is
unlikely that we will be able to develop formal specification techniques or formal verification for such programs. I feel that formal
verification technology will reach a plateau similar to the plateau
reached by artificial intelligence technology and for much the same
reason, namely combinatorial complexity of reasoning about programs
and difficulty of formal specification of practical parts in the
production environment.

Difficulty in specification or verification reflects the enormous
difference between mathematical and computational ways of looking at a
problem. It is important to realize that both views are valid and
both views are important, both at the level of language design and at
the level of application programs. Some things are more easily said
and understood by mathematical formalisms, but there are tasks that
can be specified more simply and concisely by computational algorithm
than by mathematical specification, and that is precisely why computation of programming languages were invented.

One further important point about specification is that the set
of computable functions, specifiable by programs, is richer than the
set of recursive functions specifiable by input/output specifications.
This implies, among other things, that axiomatic semantics does not
provide a complete semantics for programming languages, since a complete semantics is a mapping of all programs of a programming language
into meanings. Input/output, or behavioral semantics, provides a
meaning only for a subset of denotations, and it requires a much
subtler domain of denotation, such as that proposed by Scott, to serve
as a realistic denotation domain for all programs. Axiomatic semantics
allows us to handle programs that can easily be specified in terms of
a subset, in terms of a simple specification language, but not all
programs.

Now, this question is not as academic as it seems, because one of
the classes of programs with no behavioral specifications is the class
of programming language interpreters. This implies, among other
things, that operational definitions of programming languages by

interpreters have no associated behavioral definition. Now this in turn implies that it is theoretically impossible to give a complete behavioral specification of a programming language, such as that being attempted for DoD-1. So no wonder this talk is so difficult.

So basically I have made several points that relate to the issue of machine dependence and machine independence in viewing programming design and programming applications. Now this is perhaps a slightly more general topic than we have discussed before, but in terms of Williams' issue-oriented view of things, that is the issue I have mentioned, and I wonder if there is any discussion on it.

Gries: I agree wholeheartedly with Wegner that we have to deal with the issues of programming languages on all levels; the problem is that I feel that in general the machine level has been most emphasized in most language developments, and I am glad to see mostly here that people seem to agree that we do have to consider things like verification on a different level, on a people oriented level. But, we do have to approach it on all levels. It is important that each question be addressed at the right level.

As an example of being able to put things on the right level, so far we have seen the following words in relation to data types: partitions, packages, forms, clusters, encapsulated data types, capsules, modules, and classes. If you look at these just on the level of the machine and try to compare these you just can not do it, because they are only defined in terms of the machine. I don't know how to say this exactly, but if you try first of all to determine what a data type is at a higher level, to give some kind of a formal definition, then you have a better basis for comparing these things.

Spitzen: I quite disagree with Wegner's claim that specification is so primitive today, and even more so with the suggestion that that is going to be the bottleneck in ten or twenty years to verification. There is a good deal of work going on on specification that is far beyond the level of say, using first order predicate calculus to describe a GCD program. For example, there is the work on algebraic specification that has appeared in the literature. At SRI we have written a formal specification for a full-scale operating system; we have developed a specification language called SPECIAL which is an elaboration of Parnas' methodology and attends to the ideas of specifying something hierarchically. I think this is a wide open area, and I do not see it plateauing out.

Wulf: Can I strike an intermediate point between those two things? When I talked yesterday about verification and what I thought would happen in ten years, I was making a number of assumptions which I did not state explicitly. First of all, I was assuming that we were only talking about verifying the functional properties of a program; there are many other very important characteristics in programs: The performance, the ease with which it can be modified, its robustness to errors either in the underlying hardware or errors that may crop up because of the way the system is used, and so on. All of those things need to be specified.

I think, in large part, the reason why the specifications of real systems are so large and complex is that they try to attend to all of these issues. I don't see any breakthroughs on the horizon, for example, in the simple business of formally specifying performance. I do not know anybody who has tried to formally specify what it means for a program to be modifiable. All those things are extremely important, and I do not see that in ten years we are going to be able to deal with those issues and prove, for example, that a program is modifiable. I do not even know if I could state what it means to be modifiable, much less talk about proving it.

So, I disagree with Wegner; I think that we are making good progress on specification, and I think we are making good progress on verification -- both with respect to functional properties. But, there are all these other things which are just crucially important to large systems that we have not attended to yet.

London: Wegner had four points, and Spitzen and Wulf have disposed of three of them. All I want to do is talk about the last one, which is the analogy to artificial intelligence. It seems to me verification has an important notion going for it, namely all the systems are designed to keep people in the loop. If the combinatorial explosion blows up in the machine alone and the person can cut it, that is just fine. If the person can not cut it, which I think will not happen, well then we are in trouble. In AI, the name of the game was do it all by machine, with no human interaction. The machine was asked to work on a problem, and people observed how well it did. That is not the way we plan to do verification -- we will stay in the loop.

Shore: Two comments -- one on specifications and one on the role of requirements. First of all, I also have been a little surprised at the apparent success or rate of improvement of some of the verification work. But I do feel strongly that the problem is going to be in writing specifications, not in processing them by machine. While some progress is being made, I see the problems as being quite immense. At NRL this past summer, together with Dave Parnas, John Guttag, and a few others, we spent considerable time writing formal specifications for about five rather different problems. The problems ranged from trivial ones, such as specifications for a stack, to specifications for pieces of a real system that we had actually written. (In effect, we went back and said, "Suppose we wanted to specify some of these modules formally -- how would it have worked out?") We had a "hell" of a time getting the specifications "right". Among the problems were surprising cases in which a small change in the semantics of the problem would cause a complete change in the specifications. For example, in the stack problem, a minor change to what happens when the stack overflows resulted in the entire specification having to be rewritten in a different form with considerable debate as to whether or not the new specification was correct.

On the question of requirements, I too feel quite strongly that requirements of the form that are in the Tinman are dangerous if used as anything more than a means for comparing two or more existing designs that have been created in an attempt to meet those require- ments. If those requirements are used as a specification, then I believe that the result would be very bad. I want to mention that NRL has taken an official position that the Tinman, if used as a procure- ment specification for a new standard language, would lead to a rather large disaster.

Williams: Perhaps we can focus on this issue for a while -- the ques- tion that Peter Wegner raised about the relative merits of a "life- cycle" approach to this project compared to a concurrent development and specification approach. Does anyone have any comments?

Horning: Yes, I have a five minute speech, if you will bear with that.

Anon.: Yes, Mr. Lincoln.

Williams: Do I have to start my watch?

Horning: My general title is "Why DoD should be looking for uncommon HOL's." In the first place, I think it has become quite apparent from the discussion in the last two days that it would be exceedingly uncommon for a language to meet the goals that are set in Section III of the Tinman. Now that is a play on words, perhaps, but it raises a very serious issue: If we first agree on the goals and sell the goals, and later discover that the best we can do is 75% of them, then, even though that may be substantially better than what is being done now, there is still a possible backlash. I think there are a number of languages already demonstrated -- two that come to mind are LIS and BLISS -- that meet a large number of the goals, not all of them, but a large number, and would be an improvement. So that proves that it is possible to improve; it does not prove that it is possible to do the whole thing. Finally, even if I am wrong, and we can design an

Absolutely Lovely Common Higher Order Language, ALCOHOL, there is still going to be an "alcoholism" problem. I base that remark on DoD's previous sponsorship of a common language, COBOL, which (regardless of its success as a language) has been very destructive of research in business oriented languages within the computer science community; essentially there has been little or no research in that area since a common language was adopted, and I think that is largely because a common language was adopted.

The second point is that it has become clear during our discussion that the commonality requirement is going to extend any common language into several controversial areas; the ones that have received the most attention here have been parallelism and abstract data types. And this puts the language designer into a double bind. On the one hand, he can not eliminate that area from his language without apparently eliminating a large number of the intended application areas, which would be unacceptable. On the other hand, any particular choice he makes in that language area is also going to eliminate application areas, which is why there has been no consensus among this group about what we ought to do about, say, parallelism. There are a variety of choices being advocated, and there are reasons against adopting any one of them for all applications. And the compromise position of taking the union of all proposals leads to well-known disasters -- it would be very destructive of the language. However, if we allowed some limited degree of flexibility, we could have a few languages, each of which was more efficient for some area of application than any conceivable language could be for all of them. In summary, I think we should take our motto not from J.R.R. Tolkien, "One language to rule them all," but rather from one of the services (this may cause jealousy among the others, but that can be dealt with), "The DoD is looking for a few good languages."

Klaus: I would like to comment on the implications of COBOL. First of all, I disagree that it is wrong to standardize a language. On the other hand, I have to agree that very little progress has been made in COBOL, but I have to blame the academic community for the fact that it has never attempted to improve COBOL. There is very little, if any, research that deals with COBOL as a language. In fact, when I talk with some universities in terms of research projects using COBOL as a development tool, it is totally shunned.

Horning: That is exactly my point. If you adopt a common language, academic research in the area will be stunted by the requirement of compatibility.

Klaus: I don't understand that.

Williams: I think we may have strayed a bit from the question of a life-cycle approach versus one of concurrent development and specification.

P. Wegner: On the particular issue that Williams is trying to get back on the rails, I do think that one of the dangers of the requirements specifications is that requirements may be inconsistent, and if the language does not satisfy these requirements, it is most probably the case that this particular requirements specification and the problem of trying to satisfy too many masters at the same time is something that.... Well, one might have the illusion that one is accomplishing it, if one writes requirements, but when you come right down to actually doing the language, you find that in fact you can not satisfy all those masters.

Klaus: That is actually true, but the point that I am trying to get at is that as you develop a language, since you cannot satisfy all the requirements from the beginning and probably never, you have to define the language and develop the language in such a way that it can be modified as time goes on, particularly in respect to deletion of features. One of the basic problems with COBOL, and this is why I want to come back to COBOL, is the fact that you have a tremendous economic stake and therefore there is literally no way of deleting anything form the language. The absence of conversion tools is, of course, a major factor here. I think it is very important to develop a language, consider these points right from the beginning and to make it a critical design goal.

Whitaker: If you will allow me, I think I may be able to clear up a couple of points here. We have some very specific and I think very well pointed out guidelines. The Tinman document that now exists is used for evaluation of languages; it is not a specification. Very specifically, and it has been said over and over again, there may someday be a specification, but it won't be called Tinman. We are not, at this time, dependent on what may happen in the future or committed to a single language. All the documentation, very carefully points out, very carefully points out, that we are searching for the minimal number of higher order languages that will satisfy the DoD requirements. What that number is, I don't know. It may be one, two, or seventeen, but we will get them. There obviously will be a number of them -- call them designs, attempts at implementation, iterations, or what have you. If there are those here who are concerned with the matter, I would appreciate your getting in contact with me. This can be done through the ARPA-net facilities which I think are familiar to

most of the group here. We do take these things into account, but
this is not the appropriate place.

Elzer: I would like to comment on this question of the design process,
if I may. We have a similar task in front of us at this LTPL-E group
which we have in Europe, and I am strongly in favor of an interative
design. But this also tends to be a sort of academic question, because it turns out that this is an extremely difficult idea to sell to
management people who are responsible for money. They just think you
want to do several implementations to enrich yourself or to keep yourself busy. So it is very difficult to get the money for iterative
design; they want to see something straightforward. So I think what
should be done and what we ought to do is a kind of compromise. We
have observed that during the development of former programming languages, (lots of them) accepted by the user and accepted by the
programmers, have never really been tested before actually coming into
use. And so what we propose, and what we will do, is to formulate
test problems, to formulate a kind of evidence, or to get evidence for
the usability of the language, before starting implementation, before
finalizing the specification. And I think that is extremely necessary,
and that is a good compromise between the wishful thinking of having a
totally iterative design and the more straightforward thoughts of
management people who say, "Well, you can get the money for one thing,
but not for more."

Clarke: I want to discuss a few of the points mentioned today. First,
I want to pick up on two points that Cheatham mentioned in his list
of things to be considered. They are testing and maintaining programs.
It is important to consider these areas, particularly when you realize
that a major part of the programming cost is spent in testing and
maintaining code. If you are going to talk about efficiency, you have
to consider the efficiency gained if you reduce testing costs while
increasing program reliability.

One often suggested way of doing this is by verifying programs.
There has been quite a bit of discussion on this topic, and P. Wegner
pointed out some of the limitations. I agree with him. To verify a
program, you have to create assertions and axioms, and then prove the
assertions, using the axioms and program statements. This is a complicated process and, as Waite pointed out in his example about integer division, incorrect assumptions are often made. So I would
strongly disagree with those that say verification is all that is
needed.

Since verification introduces another level of abstraction to the programming process, another problem arises in that the majority of programmers are not comfortable or trained to deal with this level of abstraction. Does this mean programmers have to change or does this mean our ideas on verification have to change? I do not know the answer.

Verification does not solve all our problems; we have to consider a wide range of tools, and we need to test programs in a real environment. Testing is an area we have been very lax about. Studies have found that about 60% of the code has never been tested at the time a program is released as a tested product. No wonder maintaining programs is so expensive. In general, our testing needs fall into the following categories: First, to test each module in a stand alone environment; second, to test groups of modules as they are developed, hopefully in a top-down environment; third, to test complete systems; and fourth, to test modified areas of code as changes are needed.

It is inappropriate to discuss testing needs in more detail at this time, but we should discuss testing in terms of how it affects language design. On this point, I feel the needs for testing and program validation are the same as those for verification and probably optimization, as well. Some of these needs London discussed, such as avoiding side effects and aliasing, well-defined program constructs, and languages that aid in developing well structured program modules. Also, it would be advantageous if the programmer could supply information that is not necessarily apparent in the code. For instance, information on the legal range of a variable or stating a variable is monotonically increasing, would aid in testing. Assertions are one way of handling this. We need to address how to include this type of information in the language.

Finally, I want to discuss optimization. I am skeptical about Goodenough's statements about optimization affecting the way programmers code. I feel that in the majority of cases programmers know very little about the optimization that is done nor do I feel they should, since the compiler may change. Programmers should be concerned with reliability and readability and not the implementation. There was an example given earlier about arrays and the importance of a programmer knowing if it is stored in column order or row order. I disagree; arrays are just another data structure and you would like the programmer to handle an array in the way that best fits the problem, be that column order or row order. A smart optimizing compiler could determine the order an array is referenced and generate code accordingly.

Another alternative is for the programmer to state explicitly row or column order. I would hesitate to include optimization at this point in the language design.

DiNitto: I would like to get just one thing clear on this confusing testing cost. I think at least the general emphasis we are giving this in the Air Force is not so much to reduce the testing cost, where I think we are in line at this workshop, but what we are talking about in the Air Force is getting more testing for the dollar (i.e., more thoroughly tested software for the same dollars). You pointed out that 60% of the code is not tested, and it is our goal to change that to 0%. I think with what we call path testing nowadays we just are not going to reach it. You can mathematically prove that you can not possibly test all the possible paths, and this is why we are also leaning towards formal verification.

A point of contention I have has to do with Clarke's remarks on optimization; it has been our experience in watching DoD programmers and from some of the comments that come out of these people, that they do know how the compiler produces code, and they do take advantage of it.

Even in a university environment, and maybe Graham can back me up on this, I remember seeing some of the MULTICS system development notes, or whatever they called them at that time, issuing edicts: "Don't use this feature". I guess it was for the EL1, early PL/I compiler, or something, that produced very inefficient code for some features. I really think I have to agree with Goodenough, that optimization issues should be reflected in language design. People do take advantage of the compiler's code generation idiosyncrasies.

Graham: I would like to make a brief comment in connection with that. The document you are referring to is the set of guidelines on how to use the PL/I compiler that was in use at that time for MULTICS development, and the guidelines were put out because the programmers didn't know what code the compiler generated and didn't know what optimizations it did or didn't do, and therefore they paid no attention whatsoever to the way they wrote code and invoked horrendous inefficient mechanisms which a good optimizing compiler, which was later built, would have taken care of for them. I think the problem largely went away once the full optimizing compiler was developed and put into use, but in the early stages the compiler did relatively little optimization and the programmers really went gung-ho on a higher level language and used all the features without knowing the cost of them.

DiNitto: Some programmer had to identify those features initially.

Many times in DoD systems, the system is developed almost concurrently
with the development of the compiler, when the compiler might be in a
poor state and you know damned well the code is not going to be re-
coded when the optimized version comes out.

Graham: My point is that if the optimizing compiler is a good optimizing compiler, it should not need to be re-coded because it will suddenly become efficient when it is compiled in the new compiler.

Williams: Clarke raised two specific points: First, the notion of
the impact of verification and testing on language design; and second,
the notion of optimization issues and how they are reflected in language design. Let's try to address these things one at a time and
begin with optimization.

Ichbiah: I agree with the premise of Goodenough, but not with the
conclusion. It is clear that optimization increases the distance between the source text and the object text, and hence provides you with
much more freedom at the source level, and it is clear that you can
use this freedom to adopt a better style of programming. Now, where I
think he is going too far is in saying that you should set up optimization standards in the hope that a standardized style will result. I
think one must disagree with this on two accounts. First of all, what
we know about style now is very little and is going to vary a lot in
the coming years, so it won't help to do any style standardization at
this date.

The second is what he said about optimization standards. I
looked very carefully at the examples he gave us, and many of the
optimization specifications given in this report turn out to be just
special cases of code motion techniques. Now, I would hate to see
specification of code motion by individual cases; it might mean that
if you ever have a more general code motion algorithm you would have
to explicitly disallow the additional cases which were not anticipated
by the designers of the optimization specification. Hence, setting
optimization standards now would create the danger of freezing optimization techniques to the present level of knowledge -- that is certainly not the thing to do.

One example I want to give is the issue of exception handling.
It is clear that unless you define exception handling with enormous
care, you are going to make that become an optimization killer, you
are going to deny any possible optimization anywhere in your programs.

Goodenough: Although the problems you point out are valid, I disagree
with the overall implications of your comments. I think the effect of
optimizations on language use needs to be given more consideration
than is currently the case. Since not all optimizations that can be

performed in theory can be performed within practical lengths of time, it is important to decide what optimizations the programmer is to perform (through appropriate use of a language) and what optimizations a compiler is to perform. To leave the boundary undefined causes problems. The boundary does not have to be totally defined, but we should go at least part way toward defining a boundary. How far you go before other considerations become overriding and the definition becomes counterproductive is something yet to be determined. Certainly it is true that we don't know enough about good programming style to constrain it totally through appropriate optimization standards (even if this were possible). But we do know some things about programming style and some things that are destructive of understandability. Optimization standards can at least encourage what we are pretty sure about. The ideas I presented today are really intended to point to a neglected aspect of factors affecting language use. There needs to be much more done to understand how far these ideas can be pushed, and that is really the spirit in which I put them forth.

Wulf: A couple of comments. First, there are a couple of undercurrents here, which have not been explicitly stated, but I would like to get them on the table and express my opinion on them. One is that somehow optimization relates to individual language features, which, by their presence or absence in a particular language, affect the degree to which it can be optimized. That is true, but it is not nearly as important as the interaction between features. When you are designing a language there are frequently a set of issues related to whether you have both X and Y in the language. You can have either one at essentially zero cost in execution time, but if you try and have them both, there is a big conflict. My favorite example is recursion and ALGOL block scope rules which permit nested procedure declarations. Recursion has a very bad name. In fact, if you do not allow nested procedure declarations, recursion has essentially zero cost; it need not cost any more than non-recursive procedures. You can decide, at language design time, that you think that recursion is worth more than nested procedure declarations or the other way around. Given either choice you can get efficiency. Or, you can decide that the conjunction of the two features is so important that you will pay the price. But, you must look at the cost of the interaction of features, not just at individual ones.

There is a second undercurrent in what Clarke just mentioned, namely that somehow optimization produces very much more complicated compilers that are very much slower. I do not think either one of those things is true. Yes, optimizing compilers are a bit more complicated; yes, they are a bit slower. But an awful lot of that feeling comes from folklore which was probably true five or ten years ago, but I don't believe it is true anymore. Generally speaking, as fields become more formalized, you can improve speed and reduce errors. A tremendous amount has been done to formalize optimization in the past few years. It is just not the case that optimizing compilers are that much more complicated, or that much slower than non-optimizing compilers.

Williams: Are there any other comments about the optimization issue? Lets turn then to the question of the impact of verification and testing on language design.

Spitzen: I would like to respond to Clarke's remarks. First, I don't think that very many people in the verification community would claim either that verification is now an omnipotent technique for achieving reliability or even that in the day of UTOPIA 1984 verification will be omnipotent. On the contrary, there are wide spectrums of sophisticated tools that one can bring to bear, or envision bringing to bear, on the reliability problem. Conventional testing sits on that spectrum, formal verficiation sits there, and there are things in between. Cheatham mentioned a number of other program analysis techniques. Any particular user who has a particular program and a particular number of dollars he is willing to spend on achieving reliability can make a decision about what is the best way to combine these techniques; presumably as our technology improves, the result of that decision will change somewhat. Fortunately, we do not have to decide who the ultimate winner is going to be. Many of the tools we are developing bear equally well at different points on the spectrum. Second, I would like to remark on the observation that to develop programs using such sophisticated tools as verifiers will require a more specialized kind of programmer than presently available. I think that is very true, but I do not conclude from that that we should not go in that direction. One would not suggest that if physicians did not need to know biochemistry or biology we could have more physicians and therefore conclude that we should drop those requirements for medical school. By the same token programmers who have the sophistication to bring to bear good design technique and mathematical abstraction in building their programs will be able to produce more reliable programs. In a future technology, with powerful verification techniques, the cost effectiveness of having a job done by people of that background will be much greater than that of having it done by teams of eighth-grade-educated programmers.

Cartwright: I would like to talk once more about the problem of writing formal specifications for programs. This problem is a fundamental issue in program testing as well as in program verification. For a trivial program you can examine the output to determine if it is correct, but for more interesting programs like compilers, you need a formal specification of what that program is supposed to do before you can determine if the program has produced the correct result. I certainly think that computer scientists have ignored the specification problem. However, I disagree with P. Wegner when he says that the problem is intractable. The truth of the matter is that we just have not devoted much attention to it. A specification language is very much like a programming language. In fact, it is possible (and probably desirable) to use a LISP-like programming language as a specification language. Unfortunately we have not applied our experience in developing programming languages (like LISP) to the problem of designing specification languages. Currently, specification languages are defined with much less precision than the programming languages that they document. Frequently, it is not clear what a particular set of specifications means (formally or informally). No wonder many computer scientists are skeptical of verification. In many cases, we are not even sure what, if anything, we have proven. By developing rigorous specification languages, we can make program specifications easier to write and to understand and greatly improve the credibility of program verification.

P. Wegner: Just a technical point concerning this particular issue. It is the case that theoretically we can not specify all possible programs that we can write by input/output specifications. Now this may not be too relevant to many of the practical programs that we have to specify in detail, but this is a theoretical point, and this is definitely the case.

Dennis: I disagree with your theoretical point. I believe the inadequacy of input/output specification that you are referring to is that the present way we write input/output assertions does not apply to programs which accept inputs during their operation. I think that is perhaps what you had in mind.

P. Wegner: Languages which have a non-halting and possibly undecidable domain of input for halting.

London: In the whole area of verification, you are always flirting with undecidability. If you really take your dictum seriously, you would never prove a theorem, because you would be scared to death of the undecidability. So, yes, we take account of those things; we do

not have our heads in the sand, but we also do not get overly dis-
couraged by the difficulty of the task. We just do not claim that we
are about to solve the halting problem.

P. Wegner: I agree with you completely.

London: On the other hand, we do often prove that programs terminate,
because in fact they terminate for good reasons, for example, people
intended them to terminate. I often hear a comment that somehow says
verification should be a very trivial, easy task. I do not know where
that came from; perhaps we have had some bad salesmen. Maybe it was
some early optimism in the beginning days of verification that suggested that it would all be done automatically. We all thought very early,
"Wouldn't that be nice, and it sure looks encouraging", but we have
learned better than that. Nobody now claims they are going to do
everything automatically. Similarly, programming is a difficult task,
and I am not sure why people think verification will be the panacea to
remove all the problems. Moreover, specification is about as difficult
as programming. Let's face it. It is going to take time. My eleven-
year-old daughter is not going to write the specifications for an
operating system.

Spitzen: But given the specifications, she will implement it, right?

Williams: Cheatham had a point -- did you want to speak to verification and testing?

Cheatham: Yes, if I could include maintenance in that. I think we
have not said enough about maintenance here. I am very happy Clarke
raised it. I meant to say something about that, but in my haste to
finish my talk, I did not get that said. Let me make a couple of
comments. Maintenance, I think a lot of us realize, is an extremely
important cost element, particularly of embedded long-lived systems;
you have maintenance costs ranging up to 80 to 90% of the total cost
of some systems. Maintenance is done carelessly. Why? I think it is
because we have a maintenance crew who are usually not our most gifted
programmers, who are given this huge box of cards I spoke of. That is,
a compile module and told, "Fix it. We've got a new kind of radar,
we've got a new kind of disc, we've got some other new possibility,
and you've got to modify the program to reflect this new thing."

     Now, if we had developed the program in a structured way, with
the tools I spoke of with the many levels, and could get back into the
context where we made some decision, make it a different way (this is
called maintenance) and follow the ramifications of that, the verification ramifications, the refinement ramifications, the choice of data
structure ramifications, all within the context of the facts we

employed when we first made the decision (there now being different facts because we are making it a different way), the whole maintenance scheme might be able to be an entirely different ball game. I think we have got to think about what it means to maintain, what tools we need, as we devise a language. That is something we have always forgotten.

Klaus: I would like to talk about maintenance, too. I think, first of all, there is too much under the label of maintenance that is not maintenance at all. There is true maintenance, of course, but introducing major new functions in a system and calling that maintenance, is misleading.

Graham: At the risk of sounding like a broken record, I want to repeat quite a few things that have been said and interject some new things. The gist of what I am going to talk about is my contention that program development methodology, that is, the use of a programming language in the development of a program, should be a major factor in the design of a programming language, and I feel this is perhaps even more important than many of the specific features of the language. Influences of this type on the design would be, for example, the decision to include abstract data types within the language because that supports very strongly a good programming methodology and the design and development of programs. I include also in this the compiler and other programming language processors. I think they are an integral part of the design, too, and we have had some discussion about optimizers in that context. I want to reiterate this again and give you an example, because there does seem to be, maybe not deliberate, but there does seem to be a neglect of the program development process and the use of the language in the design considerations for the language. I think perhaps that may be the most important aspect of the whole business for DoD-1.

Let me talk about performance and efficiency. I got accused yesterday of making statements that indicated that I did not think it was important. I do think efficiency is very important. How should efficiency be achieved though? I differ with many people on that. I think your intuition is unreliable in predicting the bottlenecks in a system or program; the bottlenecks include only a small percentage of the code; it is not cost effective to spend much on the optimizing of the other code segments, the ones that don't figure into the bottlenecks, and one should not sacrifice other extremely important gains for the purpose of efficiency, particularly when efficiency is only concerned with a very small percentage of the code. In other words, one should not sacrifice low implementation cost, understandability, modifiability, etc., etc., etc., in the name of efficiency. How can one get efficiency then, if it is important, which I maintain it is? I think the solution is in analysis and/or simulation prior to implementation. Efficiency is attacked nowadays in two directions: One, you say, well, we won't put things in the language that allow me to write inefficient code; two, we will let you have escape hatches in the language so that you can get to machine language so that you can write efficient code. And if that does not work, then we put in a lot of probes and we measure the performance of the thing once it is on the machine, and then we try to fix up the efficiencies.

By focusing on locating the bottlenecks early in the process, prior to the completed implementation, you can correct them before the cost is excessively high. And you then need to apply the expensive optimization only where the payoff is high. And if you want to get right down to it, then say you would only have to write machine code if you were going to go to machine code as an ultimate solution in those areas where the bottlenecks occur, which are not very predictable. We did not predict them in MULTICS, they were never where we thought they were going to be, and we did not discover them until the system was put on the machine. Believe it or not, when the system was attempted to be loaded for the first time, for the first test session, it would not fit in memory. Now, it would have worked all right once the paging got going because the system paged itself, but you could not get it in to get the paging going, because it was too big.

Another example was the very sophisticated algorithm for determining where on the drum to read out pages, and the computation time to make this decision amounted to one and a half drum revolutions. If you picked a place at random, you would have a 75% improvement over the original algorithm.

How can you, prior to implementation, achieve this process of getting information about the performance? I mentioned analysis and simulation. Analysis rests strongly on symbolic execution in which one derives, from the source description of the program, formulas for execution time as a function of the data parameters. Symbolic execution is also used to do other nice things, like generate test data that will guarantee testing all the paths in the program -- not all combinations, but all branches at least once, and so forth. That is certainly some of the things Cheatham had in mind in his talk. For complex systems, especially asynchronous systems, I think simulation has to be invoked, but this has not worked very well in many instances, because the simulation is done in a different language, it is done by

a separate group, and it is done as a side effort. The simulation
model drifts away from the main system, and by the time the simulation
model works, the system is doing something else. So I think the model
has to be automatically derived, and it can be automatically derived
by coupling it with the analysis and using the symbolic execution to
generate the formulas that are needed to do the simulation. This is,
I think, an extremely important example, but nonetheless simply another example of the development tools that can be and should be used
in developing programs and particularly large programs that Cheatham
was talking about.

I think that all of these things are coupled together very
closely; if you have a language that supports things like top-down
development, verification, and so forth, then you will also support
this performance analysis and many other goodies too, for example,
verification coupled with top-down analysis based on the concept of
abstract machines. You postulate an abstract machine and sketch out
your algorithm, the major control flow, using the operations of that
machine. If you have data abstractions in the language, you formulate
the major data abstractions. Then you assume these things are correct,
and you verify the correctness of the major control flow part of the
program. Then you plunge down in and attempt to work on the correctness of the abstractions you have formulated, and so forth. So you
refine this in a top-down method.

If you assume that the abstract machine has certain performance
characteristics, you can also analyze the performance of the higher
level programs in the abstract machine, and then as you plunge down
and refine the abstract machine you can refine the performance characteristics of the abstract machine and get increasingly more and more
realistic performance measures. The point at which your assumption
begins to deviate drastically from the reality as you refine it, gives
you the clues as to where the bottlenecks are. I think, certainly,
that the direction of the future with respect to the development of
large programs is a program development system that is interactive,
involving the designer and the programmer interactively exploring the
properties of the program, and exploring the implications of the decisions he makes along the way, exploring alternate representations of
the data abstraction, perhaps even the compiler doing it automatically
for him, trying to induce the correct or the most efficient representation, given the way he uses it in the program, but allowing the programmer to interact with this.

So, the implications of all of this on language design are that
the same kinds of considerations that are good for verification are

good for performance analysis prediction and for many other things.
In fact, the assertions that would be needed for verification can be
of use in establishing the performance. Additional assertions that
are useful are things like the probability of branches and tighter
bounds on the domains of types (like PASCAL does). For example, if
you limit the domain of definition of a variable to a small number of
values, then the symbolic execution and therefore the analysis of
loops and other things is perhaps easier, or at least has a higher
probability of being easier. Anything that gives you more knowledge
as to what is being done, as opposed to just general loops, such as
characterizing data structures as tables or queues or other kinds of
common structures in which you have search operations, insert operations, and so forth, give more information to the language processor,
and the performance. Whether this comes about from enriching the
language by a large number of permanent additions, or whether it comes
about by some kind of clustering encapsulation mechanism to define
abstract data types is, I think, still open, and perhaps either way
gives you a valid solution.

All of the features that the language has for supporting these
things I think are very important, and a number of them have been
mentioned. I'm sure we are unaware yet of the full range of these
things, but I guess my pitch would be that I think much more consideration of the program development process and the use of the language
needs to be considered in the design of this language than seems to
have been up to this point.

Morgan: I agree with what Graham had to say, to a large extent, but
I find that he has not made some distinctions that I find necessary.
When he talks about efficiency, I see several kinds of efficiency.

One I would call algorithmic efficiency; basically, you have this
program, it is a logical entity, it does something, and you want to
know where the bottlenecks are and eliminate them. That is a perfectly valid thing -- you just need that. But that is completely
different from what I would call implementation efficiency. Once you,
and I'll grant this is an iterative process, once you run it on the
machine to find the bottlenecks, you still have a certain efficiency
problem. How well does the compiler generate code? How well does it
implement what you have said? Certain choices of language constructs,
certain choices of compiler forms can improve the implementation efficiency without decreasing the algorithmic efficiency. You can still
find your bottlenecks and have things in a structured, maintainable
form and not lose implementation efficiency.

So I think that we at BBN (Bolt, Beranek, and Newman) have tried
to take the middle point of view, between the idealism and the complete
pragmatism of the machine efficiency. We have tried to design a
system (we have not implemented it) which you could compile very efficiently. If we lose 20% on our code generation, first of all we lose
20% of memory; this is one of the things Graham missed. There are
certain kinds of efficiency that are not controlled by the bottlenecks; if you generate 20% worse code, you have lost 20% of memory;
if you are using 90% of memory already, and lose 20% more, you are not
going to run. On small machines, like real-time systems, that is very
criticial.

So I would like to argue for a compromise between the poles; we
can have both. I think Wulf's BLISS language shows that. It lacks
some necessary features, but it does give you both the efficiency of
expressibility and the ability to get your bottlenecks and eliminate
them. And I think we can have this in the Tinman as well. I guess
what I am saying is that the arguments are hitting against each other
and they are not arguments at all; you can say both.

Graham: I don't know. It seems to me we have a semantic problem.
In my dictionary, "bottleneck" means the location of the worst inefficiency, so I really can not quite see the distinction you are making.
I certainly did not imply that eliminating bottlenecks implied inefficient code.

Goodenough: What is a space bottleneck?

Graham: That is a bottleneck.

Goodenough: I mean, 10% of the code may account for 90% of the
execution time, but not for 90% of the space, i.e., space efficiency
cannot usually be achieved by local modifications; to me, "bottleneck"
implies an inefficiency that can be removed by a local change.

Graham: That is your decision. I mean a bottleneck to one person is
not to another. I hope I have not said anything that implied that I
am going to force on every user of this tool my idea of what is efficient or inefficient for their particular situation. What I was suggesting is a tool that will give you an analysis of the performance
early in the game, allowing you to make the decision of what you consider to be your bottleneck and to take the appropriate action as
early as possible to modify your algorithm or whatever else you need
to do to eliminate the things that you think are bottlenecks. That
was all I said. This is a tool, like verification, that is involved
in the program development process that I think is important.

Cheatham: I would like to argue once again -- I will probably be
doing this in 1990 -- about the idea that if you have got one source

on one level and you have got to compress everything into that, then
you are bound to have problems understanding, verifying, and maintaining a program. After all, there exists a LIS language, which is implemented, that is a two-level language, where you deal at one level with
getting things going and deal at another with the crucial questions of
efficiency. One can generalize that -- even in 1976.

SECTION V

The following papers were prepared to stimulate discussion at the Workshop and were presented in the appropriate sessions.

A Note on "Pointers"

C. P. Earnest

September 1, 1976

1. INTRODUCTION

One of the key issues in data structural models, and therefore in programming

language design, is the way in which parts of dynamically constructed structures

are interconnected. In programming languages, some sort of "pointer" mechan-

ism is normally used for the purpose. No two languages have the same mechanisms,

and the Tin Man D6 requirement[2] calls for one not in any existing language. Some

of the best-known computer scientists disagree with each other on the desirability

of explicit pointers -- Knuth, as might be expected, likes them[7, p. 263]; Hoare

doesn't[3].

The issue is closely related to a number of others -- for example, the way in

which a variable is connected to its value, a structure to its components, a formal

parameter to an actual parameter. The issue is also related to the structural

models used in database management systems, but these are mentioned only briefly

in this paper.

I believe that all these aspects should be treated within a single general framework,

and a possible one is outlined later in the paper. First, the problems to be solved

are described, and a brief discussion is given of leading current mechanisms, and

of the Tin Man requirement.

2. DESIDERATA

I believe the chief requirements for a "pointer" mechanism are:

a.)   The data structures must provide for the representation of any directed graph, including recursive graphs, and it must be possible in general to change structural connections or values in any part of the graph dynamically.

b.) It must be possible to build, or to copy, any structure piece by piece. (For example, it must be possible to copy a recursive list structure member by member -- whether or not the list can be copied as a whole).

c.) For at least some variables, it must be possible either to (1) assign a copy of a new value without changing any sharing relationships, or (2) to assign the value of another variable such that both come to share the same instance of the value. These types of assignment will be referred to henceforth as (1) copy, and (2) remap. The variables x and y share their value, in this sense, if a change to the value changes both x and y.

d.) The notations for remap and copy assignment must be clearly different. The distinction cannot depend only on properties of the variables. Similarly, reference to the mapping information (i.e., the pointer part) for a variable must be written clearly differently from that to the value of the variable.

e.) A single conceptual mechanism should handle the connections from:
- a variable to its value, for either a shared or a non-shared value.
- a structure instance to its components
- a formal parameter to an actual parameter, including the case of procedure parameters.

f.) Dynamic binding of procedure names to procedure bodies must be supported, not only in the parameter context.

g.)   The mechanism must respect the idea of "type". That is, for any variable
        x, the operators applicable to its value must be known at compile time.

h.)   Physical pointers must be inaccessible to the user (except perhaps in
        assembly code sections).

Note that unless c.) is met, the mechanism cannot handle the connections from
formal to actual parameters. For a normal call-by-reference parameter (as in
FORTRAN, Algol 68, Pascal, etc., but not Algol 60), the connection between formal and actual is established on procedure entry by a remap (Algol 68 identity declaration), and thereafter normal assignment to the formal parameter changes both
it and the actual parameter.

3.   SOME EXISTING MECHANISMS

Pascal[4, 5]

Directed graphs, including recursive ones, can be represented using pointer variables. Both remap and copy assignment are provided for such a variable; the
first is "p := ", the second "p↑ :=". This is clean, but only partially meets requirement d, because for a non-pointer variable, the notation is reversed:
"x := " is a copy assignment. Reference is just like assignment, with no automatic
dereferencing. That is, the value of a pointer variable is p↑ , its pointer part is
p. Pointer variables are typed. Copying stops at a pointer; that is, only the
pointer part, not the value, is copied.

The mechanism does not handle parameters, because a pointer variable may share its value only with another pointer variable. There are no pointers to procedures.

Because the "warning flag" ↑ goes with a reference to the value rather than to the pointer part, a reference to a structure component looks different from a reference to a component of a pointed-to object. If p is a pointer whose value comprises components (x, y, z), then p↑.x refers to the x component, but if R is a record with components (x, y, z), then R.x refers to the x component. The Pascal mechanism thus meets all the above requirements except f, part of d and part of e.

Algol 68[8]

The Algol 68 pointer mechanism is rather similar to that of Pascal, but with some important differences. Directed graphs can be represented by using _ref_ variables. Both remap and copy assignment are provided for these; if x is _ref ref real_, the first is "x :=", the second is "_ref real_ (x) := ", using the new notation. Note that, unlike Pascal, the latter requires mentioning the type name; like Pascal, whether "x :=y" is a remap or a copy depends on the declaration of x. A major difference is that in Algol 68, it is possible to have _ref ref's_, etc., and reference to such a variable can mean the pointer part at any level or the value, depending on context. This doesn't seem very useful, and it causes quite a bit of extra complexity and makes programs harder to read. Algol 68 ref variables are typed, and copying stops at a ref, just as in Pascal.

The mechanism does not handle parameters, but there are pointers to procedures. Furthermore, the same notation is used for reference to components, whether they are constituents or are pointed-to (e.g., x of p).

In summary, the Algol 68 mechanism meets all the above requirements except d and part of e. It comes closer to meeting e than Pascal, but in my opinion, the confusion caused by automatic dereferencing more than overbalances this.

4. THE TIN MAN REQUIREMENT (D6)

The Tin Man requirement was apparently motivated by a desire to have a simple mechanism which makes pointers as implicit as possible. The result, insofar as I understand it, is a combination of the weakest features of the Pascal and Algol 68 capabilities.

Directed graphs would be represented by using pointer variables. Assignment to a pointer is always a remap; to a non-pointer, always a copy. Hence there are no variables for which both remap and copy assignment are possible, and local context never betrays which is meant. Reference to a pointer variable apparently would mean either the value or the pointer part, depending on context -- a sort of mini-dereferencing feature. For example, if x is a non-pointer, and p and q are pointers, then "p := q" is a remap assignment, and "q" refers to the pointer part, while "x := q" is a copy assignment, and "q" refers to the value. (There is in any case no restriction against this in the Tin Man requirement, no indication that different notation for pointer parts and values is foreseen, and certainly it is necessary to be able to copy the value of a pointer into a non-pointer). Tin Man pointer variables are typed.

The Tin Man required mechanism cannot handle parameters, because the value of a pointer can be shared only with another pointer (else the restriction against scalar-valued pointers makes no sense). Nothing is said about pointers to procedure bodies, about reference to components of pointed-to objects, or about copying of recursive structures, so these could at least be handled in a way which meets the above requirements. There are some additional restrictions: certain values (e.g., scalars) cannot be the value of pointers, while others (e.g., certain dynamically allocated values) can never be the value of a non-pointer.

In short, the Tin Man requirement includes the above requirements a, g, and h; it is inconsistent with requirements c, d, and e; and it leaves open whether b and f are to be met. Its only advantage appears to be that no additional notation is needed for referring to pointer parts, but exactly this will make programs hard to read, and limits the mechanism -- pointer parts and values should appear different.

5. A SUGGESTED MECHANISM

The above discussion has probably already betrayed the main features of a pointer mechanism meeting our requirements. Establish the convention that in general, a variable has both a value and a connector. For at least some variables, both are modifiable. A constant has only a value -- no connector. To refer to the value of a variable, use its name; to refer to its connector, use its name followed by the symbol @. The key relationship linking connectors and values is $x@ = y@ \supset x = y$; the reverse does not hold, in general.

Copy assignment is then "x := "; it does not change x@. Remap assignment is "x@ := y@" ; it changes both x and x@. The component(s) of a variable is (are) treated as its value, whether or not the value is sharable.   If c is a component of x, its value is referred to as x.c, its connector as x.c@. The connector for an element of an array is A(i)@. The following are meaningless: x@@ and x@.c@. Connectors and values are never of the same type, so x@ := y and x := y@ are illegal. The only operations permitted with connectors are assignment, equivalence comparison, and use as a parameter. The declaration of a variable specifies whether its connector is modifiable; a possible notation, similar to Pascal, is "x, y: @integer".

The @ notation is a compromise with current usage and brevity. The value of a variable is a function of its connector, but not vice versa, so it would be more logical to use x to refer to the connector, and x@ or x.@ to refer to the value, much as for Pascal pointers. This notation would make the assignment axioms easier to write   (but note that even in Pascal,   the axiom $x = y \supset x\uparrow = y\uparrow$ for all pointers x and y is needed, although it does not appear in (4)). However, this notation becomes quite unwieldy if extended to non-pointers, for which I believe the syntax should be consistent (unlike Pascal). I also prefer putting the "warning flag" on those assignments which can change structure, rather than those which can change possibly shared values. The Pascal $\uparrow$ is preferable to @, but the latter is used to avoid confusion.

The connection between a formal and an actual parameter is established by normal assignment, executed on procedure entry. For call-by-reference, the formal parameter must carry the @; if it does not, the call is by value. (The latter is not permitted by the Tin Man, but is clearly useful). A formal parameter has a connector just like any other variable, and if it is called-by-reference, the connector must be modifiable, in general throughout the procedure. It should be possible to specify that the connector and/or the value for a formal parameter is modifiable only once at entry, if that is the case. Note that if the formal parameter definition has the @, the actual must also, and if the formal has no @, the actual cannot either; otherwise the initial assignment would be illegal. If the actual parameter has no @, its value cannot be changed by the procedure, unless result parameters are also provided (e.g., JOVIAL output parameters).

The connector for functions and procedures is very interesting: it is the procedure body! The same procedure name can have different connectors, or procedure bodies, at different times--a remap assignment accomplishes the change. A procedure of course might not have a value; for a function, the value is the result of the function. Functions and arrays are consistent. For either, the set of all values has the name, e.g., H, a particular value has the name H(a1, a2, ... an), the connector (if any) for a particular value has the name H(a1, a2, ..., an)@, and the connector for the entire set of values--i.e., for the function, the procedure body--has the name H@. A function may or may not be able to supply connectors for individual values; in any case, they are of interest only if the function values can be modified. If f is a function and A is an array, then f@ and A@ are never of the same type, so that an array can be substituted for a function, or vice versa, only by a change in declarations. The reasons for making the procedure body the connector, rather than the value, are (1) the connection from a function name to the value is in fact established by the code, and (2) the notation then allows reference to either the function body (f@) or the result (f) even for a parameterless function.

Recursive structures are supported by allowing any structure to be a component of itself, of a component of itself, or etc. For copying dynamic structures, there are two alternative possibilities which would be compatible with the remainder of the mechanism. The cleanest is to provide that copying of a value copies all levels, so that to copy a single recursive level, remap assignment would be necessary for some components. For example, given the following declarations, in a Pascal-like notation:

list = @record x, list end

x: integer

L1, L2: list

the assignment "L1:= L2" would cause a copy of the entire list, and the multiple assignment "L1.(x, list@) :=L2.(x, list@)" would cause a copy of just the first member, leaving L1 and L2 sharing any subsequent list members.

Alternatively, a variable with modifiable connector could be treated like a Pascal pointer or an Algol 68 ref, in that copying would stop at such a variable, and copying of an entire recursive structure would require more than a single assignment statement. The first alternative seems much better because the assignment state-

ment alone shows what is meant: moreover, one may wish to change a substructure from sharable to non-sharable or vice versa without changing the program.
The first alternative also allows recursive structures without explicit connectors
or pointers. For example, the following adds a new element to L1:

L1.(x, list) := (47, L1)

and this removes it again:

L1 := L1.list

Both are copy assignments; neither depends on the ability to modify L1.list@.
Clearly, explicit connectors of some sort are needed only for sharing of parts of
structures -- not for recursive structures without shared parts. Of course, even
just a cursor shares its value, hence requires explicit connectors. In practice,
explicit connectors can also lead to better code and simpler compilers.

6.   A COMPARATIVE EVALUATION

The chief advantages of the suggested mechanism, in comparison with that of Pascal,
are:

- The same notation is used for reference to a component of either a constituent
  or a pointed-to structure. This advantage is shared with Algol 68.

- A connector may be a procedure body, which permits the association between
  a procedure name and the procedure body to be changed dynamically in any
  context.

- The notation for reference to a connector is clearly different from that for reference to a value, in several contexts. In Pascal, this is true only for pointer variables.

- A "pointer" (variable with modifiable connector) can share its value with a non-pointer. That is, the connector for a variable may be accessible even if it is not modifiable, so the call-by-reference parameter mechanism is available in other contexts.

- For a recursive structure, it is possible to copy either one level or the entire structure (with the preferred mechanism).

The last could equally well be listed as a disadvantage, because it makes the compiler more expensive; note however that some of the same tools are necessary for copying dynamically allocated arrays (also not in Pascal). The only other disadvantage, vis a vis Pascal, appears to be that optimization may suffer slightly if non-pointers can share their values with pointers. This can be avoided by the addition of equivalence class declarations, such that two variables could share the same value only if they were in the same equivalence class, and such declarations are valuable for pointers alone, independent of non-pointers.

The last three advantages listed above also apply to a comparison with Algol 68. In this connection, the suggested mechanism also has the advantage, shared with Pascal, that no automatic dereferencing occurs. The comparative disadvantages are the same as for Pascal.

7.   MUST CONNECTORS BE EXPLICIT?

It may be necessary to point out that shared data objects -- shared in the sense

that modification changes the object for all sharers -- are indispensable if n:m

interrelationships are to be represented (e.g., students vis a vis classes). This

has long been obvious in the database context, but it is not always recognized in

the context of programming languages (see for example (6)). If shared objects

are supported, and the sharing relationships are to be constructed dynamically,

then some kind of explicit, modifiable connectors are unavoidable. The value of

the connector need not always be kept from the user -- for example, in Codd's

relational data model (1), two tuples can be effectively connected by including an

identifying value from one (e.g., a social security number) in the other. In the

programming language context, it is often inefficient to establish connectors which

a user may safely access directly, and in any environment, it can be inconvenient

for the user.

In short, I maintain that some sort of user-inaccessible, explicit, modifiable

connectors are necessary in a modern programming language. Wirth regards such

connectors as similar to goto's, and equally as dangerous, because they can be used

to build any kind of structure, even a circular one (9, p. 169). This seems to me

misleading. A reference via a connector to a value or a component is essentially

like a call on a possibly re-entrant procedure. Modification of a connector is like,

or is, the substitution of a different procedure body for a given procedure name.

The essential point is that when one refers to or modifies a pointed-to object, the context does not change, as it can upon execution of a goto. With connectors, different contexts may overlap, but only one should be pertinent at a time for each object. Implicit run-time checks or explicit interlocks can be used if desired to enforce this uniqueness of reference rule.

This paper has outlined one way to realize the required connectors, which has some advantages over current mechanisms, which in turn are better than what the Tin Man requires.

REFERENCES

1. Codd, E. F. A relational model of data for large shared data banks. CACM 13/6 (June 1970), pp. 377-387.

2. Department of Defense Requirements for High Order Computer Programming Languages: "Tinman" (June 1976).

3. Hoare, C. A. R. Recursive data structures Stanford Artificial Intelligence Laboratory Memo STAN-CS-73-400 (Oct. 1973).

4. Hoare, C. A. R. and Wirth, Niklaus. An axiomatic description of the programming language PASCAL. Acta Informatica 2, pp. 335-355 (1973).

5. Jensen, Kathleen and Wirth, Niklaus. Pascal User Manual and Report, Second Edition. Springer Verlag, New York (1975).

6. Kieburtz, Richard B. Programming without pointer variables. Proceedings of Conference on Data, March 22-24, 1976. SIGPLAN Notices Volume 8, No. 2 (1976), pp. 95-107.

7. Knuth, D. E. Structured programming with go to statements. ACM Computing Surveys, Vol. 6, No. 4 (December 1974), pp. 261-301.

8. Van Wijngaarden, ed. Revised report on the algorithmic language Algol 68. Acta Informatica 5, pp. 1-236 (1975).

9.   Wirth, Niklaus.   <u>Algorithms + Data Structures = Programs.</u>

      Prentice-Hall, Inc., Englewood Cliffs, N. J. (1976)

SOME ISSUES IN DATA TYPES AND TYPE CHECKING

Benjamin M. Brosgol

Intermetrics, Inc.
701 Concord Avenue
Cambridge, Massachusetts   02138

Abstract

   This paper presents a survey of issues which arise in contemporary
High Order Languages in conjunction with the implementation of data types
and type checking. Attention is paid to alternatives and tradeoffs in
language features which realize various desirable goals regarding data
types. Interactions between features are pointed out, and implementation
techniques are discussed.

   This work was supported by Contract N00123-76-C-1688, Naval
Electronics Laboratory Center, San Diego, California.

1. INTRODUCTION

In this paper we attempt to summarize a number of issues which arise in contemporary high-order languages (HOLs) in the area of data types and type checking. Our motivation is that, despite the widespread attention currently devoted to the concept of data type, language-specific problems tend to be covered only sketchily. It is directly relevant, to those designing, selecting, or using a HOL, to be aware of these issues and appreciate how they are handled.

In Section 2, we attempt to provide a framework for later discussion by considering the variety of interpretations of the basic notion of a "data type." Section 3 presents a classification of data definition facilities into three categories, here termed "data structuring", "type definition", and "data abstraction." Section 4, the main portion of this paper, discusses type safety issues. In Section 4.1 we look at implicit conversions; Section 4.2 treats the type identity question from the perspective of the three categories of data definition facilities; Section 4.3 views the type safety issue with respect to separate compilations and file I/O; in Section 4.4 we consider the problem of dealing with "typeless" data. Section 5 summarizes the conclusions of this study.

2.   WHAT IS A "DATA TYPE"?

Although the issue of type safety revolves critically around the notion of a data type, the precise meaning of this latter concept has proved to be quite slippery to pin down. Indeed, a number of approaches are possible and profitable, depending on one's viewpoint. A mathematician might look at data "as a mapping from a set of names to a set of values" [No 76, p. 1] and regard a data type as a set of values. A hardware designer might view a data type primarily in terms of its efficient hardware representation. A researcher in the field of programming languages might attempt to unify a variety of useful viewpoints into a single concept of "data type" -- witness the framework proposed by [PSW 76], in which a data type is regarded as a class of variables whose members can be substituted for each other in certain contexts.

A somewhat more prevalent view, which is the basis for much of the work in data abstraction, holds that a data type is essentially defined by two properties: a specification[1] of the behavior of instances of the type, and a structural description which defines the representation of the type's instances. Other approaches include the set of instances of a data type as an essential part of the type's definition; e.g. as asserted in [DD 76, p. 19]: "By the type of a data object is meant the set of objects themselves, the essential properties [viz. the representation] of those objects and the set of operations which give access to and take advantage of those properties." One reason for including the set of instances of a type as an essential ingredient in the type concept is to account for useful applications, such as data bases, where the lifetime of the data objects is of direct concern. As stated by [Ha 76, p. 59]: "The definition of a shared data base is principally determined by the data which it contains, rather than by one particular set of operations which may be applied to it."

It is perhaps not surprising that such differences of interpretation as described above should surround the notion of "data type." The problem is

---

[1] This specification is typically algorithmic, but there has been some work on algebraic, axiomatic approaches (e.g. [St 71],[Gu 76]).

that "data type" is essentially an imprecise concept, especially when compared with such relatively concrete entities as variables (which have lifetimes) and procedures (which can be executed). A data type is basically an
attribute, and attributes are considerably less tractable and scrutinizable
than the objects which possess them.

When considered in this light, however, the problem suggests an approach
to its own solution: viz., to regard a data type as a special kind of object
in existence at compile-time. (In the ECL language [Hw 74] this idea is
carried even further; a data type there can be a run-time object.)
Essentially, a data type is denoted by means of some (language-dependent)
type-specification; the latter may be regarded as a compile-time analog of
a procedure invocation. Viewing data types in this framework offers
several advantages. First, it reminds us that the (compile-time) representation of a data type, derived from the type-specification, has critical
implications regarding the (compile-time) efficiency of type checking.
Second, it establishes a convenient basis for classifying data type
mechanisms in HOLs, as shown in the next section.

3.   CATEGORIES OF DATA DEFINITION FACILITIES

Despite the wide variety of data definition facilities available in
HOLs, the basic means for providing such facilities can be divided into three
general categories. The first category, which we will call data structuring,
is illustrated by such languages as FORTRAN, COBOL, PL/I, ALGOL 60, JOVIAL,
and TACPOL. Each of these languages supplies a set of built-in data types
and provides a means of structuring composite objects. Typical built-in
types include integer, real (fixed and/or floating point), character, and
boolean. The structuring facilities permit the creation of objects representing homogeneous sequences of components (arrays) and may also allow the
generation of heterogeneous objects (records), overlaid objects (unions),
and references to other objects (pointers).

In a language which provides data structuring, the notions of data type
and type safety tend to be relatively diffuse. Although the representation
of structured objects is apparent, the behavior is not. The key issue --
when do two objects have the same type -- can be quite complex, especially
when the language provides records. This is true in PL/I, where an elaborate set of rules is used to determine compatibility of STRUCTUREs. An
alternative approach is provided in COBOL in the CALL...USING statement:
type checking is absent, and the only requirement for matching is that
actual and formal parameters have the same storage size.

The second category of data definition method will be called type
definition and is illustrated by languages such as ALGOL 68, ECL, and
PASCAL. These HOLs allow the user to associate a name with the invocation
of a data structuring operation. Thus, structuring facilities can be regarded as type generators which, when provided with types as parameters,
produce new data types. A programmer-supplied name for the type can be
used for checking purposes, since this name may be used (instead of the data
structuring operation) in the declaration of variables or parameters.

The provision of type definition facilities offers several advantages
over the data structuring approach described earlier. For example, the
name of a type is a convenient shorthand notation in declarations. Also,
if the language defines that the name denotes a different type than that

yielded by the invocation of the type generator, then the user has a means for creating different types whose instances have identical representations.

The third category of data definition method will be called <u>data abstraction</u> and is realized to varying degrees by such languages as CLU, ALPHARD, CS-4, and SIMULA 67. The main features of this approach are <u>encapsulation</u> of the specification of the representation of a type's instances, together with the specification of the behavior of the instances; and <u>protection</u> of this encapsulated information so that representational details are unavailable outside the abstract type's definition. The basic concept underlying data abstraction is similar to that behind procedure abstraction; as stated in [Ho 76, pp. 60-61]: "When we try to understand a large program, it is essential that we be able to understand <u>what</u> the procedures do without worrying about <u>how</u> they do it and to separately understand <u>how</u> they work without worrying about <u>why</u> they are invoked. Similarly, it will be necessary to understand programs in terms of <u>what</u> [abstract data types] represent, without worrying about <u>how</u> they do it, and to separately understand <u>how</u> they represent abstract objects without worrying about <u>why</u> they were created."

4. TYPE SAFETY ISSUES

The purpose of type checking is to guarantee that the actual uses of data objects are consistent with the stated behavior associated with the objects' types. Such checking is useful and necessary in the interests of program reliability and maintainability, but the enforcement of type safety raises a number of practical issues which merit discussion. In the following subsections we will explore some of these issues.

4.1 IMPLICIT CONVERSIONS

Implicit conversions appear in several guises, and it is worthwhile to examine these in order to reveal the interactions with type safety. One kind of implicit conversion, which is currently surrounded by a certain amount of controversy, is illustrated by "mixed-mode" arithmetic. Under this scheme a procedure or operation which expects an argument of type T1 will also accept an argument of type T2; in general, run-time code is produced so that the T2 object is transformed into a T1 object. Although from one perspective such an arrangement appears to defeat type-checking, in fact this behavior may be regarded as a specialized kind of generic facility. That is, the procedure name may be considered to be associated with two bodies: one which accepts a T1 argument, and another which accepts a T2 argument but which first transforms this to a local T1 value and then carries out the same operations as the first body. With this view of the semantics of the conversion, there is no conflict with type checking.

The main advantage of this kind of implicit conversion is notational convenience. For example, since mathematically the integers are a subset of the reals, many programmers expect to be able to use an integer wherever a real is required. There are, however, certain disadvantages to this kind of implicit conversion. Probably the largest, from the viewpoint of both reliability and efficiency, is that the behavior is implicit. An incorrect program may have a legitimate but non-obvious interpretation via rules for implicit conversion and thus be difficult to debug -- e.g. in PL/I the expressions 1<2<3 and 3<2<1 are both legal, and each yields the result <u>true</u> ('1'B) via conversions between bit and arithmetic values. With respect to

efficiency, the fact that the conversion is implicit means that the programmer may not be aware of the run-time expense which is involved. Another
disadvantage is language complexity. Certainly the presence of implicit
conversions, especially if user-definable, implies extra work (and thus
size) for the compiler; also, the interactions between implicit conversions
and "By reference" parameter passage can be tricky. In short, the provision
of an implicit conversion from type T2 to type T1 in effect extends the
behavior of T2 to incorporate that of T1. The test of the utility of the
conversion is how well the notational convenience and the benefits of so
extending the type behavior weigh against the disadvantages mentioned above.

A second variety of implicit conversion, involving no run-time overhead,
consists of interpreting the storage area representing an object of one type
as though it represented an object of another type. This kind of behavior
is always possible with "free union" (i.e. overlaid) data; here the representations may be quite different, the effects of the "conversion" may be
implementation-dependent, and type safety is thus completely subverted.
However, there are contexts outside of free union where such an implicit
conversion may be necessary -- in particular, when the representations of
the types in question are identical. A case in point is an object of some
abstract data type T. If P is a procedure which is part of the behavior of
the abstract type, then presumably P expects an object whose type is T.
Within the body of P, however, this object should be interpreted as though
its type were that of the representation specified in T. (This situation is
handled in the CLU language by an explicit conversion, denoted by the
reserved word cvt, which is used in parameter specifications [Li 74, p. 13].)

Another example of a similar kind of implicit conversion occurs in
languages which allow type definition. Suppose that a user defines type T1
as an array of integers, and then defines type T2 as T1, where the language
rules imply that T2, T1, and array of integers are distinct types. (This
situation is illustrated by the ECL language [Hw 74].) In such a case
implicit conversions occur from T1 (and from T2) to the array type, for the
purpose of such operations as subscripting and object creation. Thus, some
of the behavior of the source type is inherited by the type being defined.

4.2 TYPE IDENTITY

Underlying the notion of type safety is the question of when two objects
have the same type. For a variety of reasons, this is a complex question
in many languages. First, the ultimate test of type identity is the set of

rules governing parameter passing, but owing to the different bindings
possible for parameters, there may in fact be several varieties of type
identity. (For example, binding by copy only requires that the argument be
assignable to the formal parameter, perhaps via implicit conversion, but
binding by reference requires identity of representations.) Second, the
rules for type identity must be geared to a variety of sometimes-conflicting
goals, such as intuitive appeal, ease of implementation, and run-time
efficiency. Third, the same facilities which add power to the language in
terms of data definition also cause complexity in the area of type identity.
In the following paragraphs we will explore some of the major issues connected with type identity, as related to the various data definition facility
categories discussed earlier.

4.2.1 Data structuring

4.2.1.1 Arrays

The specification of an array consists of several parts: an underlying
(or component) type, and a number of bounds specifications. In order for
two array objects to have the same type, the underlying types must be
identical, and the number of dimensions must be the same. Whether type
identity for arrays implies that the corresponding pairs of bounds must be
the same depends on the HOL's policy on bounds determination and whether
type checking is carried out at compile-time or run-time.

Bounds determination generally comes in three varieties: static (fixed
at compile-time), dynamic (fixed at scope-entry time), or flexible (allowed
to change at run-time). The simplest approach is static bounds, illustrated
by languages such as FORTRAN and PASCAL. With this scheme, total compile-
time checking of array sizes is possible, provided that bounds specifications
are required for formal array parameters.

One of the innovations in ALGOL 60 was a facility for handling dynamic
arrays; we here summarize some of the issues which such a feature raises
with respect to type identity.

1) If type-checking is to be carried out at compile-time, then
obviously the bounds sizes cannot be considered to be part of an array
object's type. Thus an array of N+6 reals has the same type as an array of
10 reals; also, an array of 10 reals has the same type as an array of 100
reals.

2)   In the absence of some sophisticated work by the compiler, a run-time expense may be incurred for dynamic arrays even when this facility is not used.   The issue here is the representation of static vs. dynamic arrays. In principle, a static array does not require any size information (i.e., a dope vector) stored with the object at run-time.   However, such an array may be passed by reference as an argument to a routine whose formal parameter is a dynamic array.   Since such a routine will perform subscripting and bounds checking via a dope vector, it will be necessary for the array argument to include this information.

It is worth pointing out the approaches to these issues which are taken in existing languages.   In ALGOL 60, it is not permitted to specify bounds (or the number of dimensions, for that matter) for formal array parameters [Na 63, Section 5.4.1]; thus the "type" of an array is basically determined by the component type.   Leaving the number of dimensions unspecified has been cited by Wichmann as a trouble spot with respect to compilation, since the checking which is necessary to ensure a match between the number of dimensions in argument and formal parameter "could involve an arbitrarily long chain of array parameter passing, and in any case is not possible if independent compilation is allowed with only the usual specification of module parameters" [Wi 73, p. 162].

The ECL language provides a clean solution to the issues raised by dynamic arrays, but does so via run-time type checking.   When the specification of the type "array of N+6 reals" is encountered, the (run-time) value of N is used to evaluate the size, which becomes part of the type.   Thus an array of N+6 reals has the same type as an array of 10 reals only if $N = 4$. Since the size information is stored with the type, there is no need to also keep this information with the array object.   In order to permit the writing of routines which in different invocations take array arguments of differ-ent sizes, ECL provides the ability to define "size-unresolved" data types -- e.g., simply array of reals.   Objects of such a type must include dope vector information; moreover, an array of reals is a different data type than, say, an array of 10 reals.

One aspect of the array facilities so far considered is that once the bounds of an array have been determined, there is no way to alter them. Sometimes, however, it is desirable to have an array grow or shrink at run-time, e.g. with strings, which may be considered as arrays of characters. This kind of facility, called "flexible arrays", is found in a small number of languages, such as ALGOL 68 and SNOBOL.   The type checking issues which arise in connection with flexible arrays are not fundamentally different from those concerned with dynamic arrays, though the language must decide whether the flexibility attribute is part of the data type. The main impact of flexible arrays is upon the storage allocation philosophy of the language, since some kind of run-time free-storage management is necessary.

4.2.1.2 Records

A record specification consists of a sequence of components each of which comprises a field name and a type specification. Although most of the problems with type identity for records are inherited from the constituents of the records, there are several issues specific to this data structuring mechanism. For example, what are the roles of the field names, the constituent type specifications, and the order of the components, in defining the type which is denoted by a record specification? Are record(A: integer; B:boolean), record(B: boolean; A: integer), and record(C: integer, D: boolean) the same type? How about record(A: integer; B: boolean) and record(A: real; B: char)? Though these may not appear to be the burning issues of the day, they illustrate that even seemingly straightforward features will raise more questions regarding data types than might have been expected.

Some languages, such as JOVIAL and TACPOL, provide "tables" as a substitute for a general array and record facility. A table can be viewed as a one-dimensional array of records, and subscripting a field-name yields the component of the selected table entry. A conceptual problem with such a scheme is that although a field name thus behaves in some contexts as a legitimate data object (actually, an array) in terms of subscripting, in fact the defined object will generally be noncontiguous and not usable as a normal array.

4.2.1.3 Enumeration types

An enumeration type allows the programmer to refer to symbolically named data instead of using explicitly their representation as small integer values. The basic idea here is not new; it has appeared in languages such as JOVIAL and CMS-2, as well as more recently in PASCAL and CS-4.

Despite the apparent simplicity behind the notion of an enumeration type, there are a number of subtle issues which arise. An immediate question concerns uniqueness of the symbolic names. Is it legitimate to have the declarations[1]

      var S1: (red, orange, yellow);

        S2: (cherry, lemon, orange)

or must the two "orange"s be distinguished? The tradeoff is between user convenience and language/implementation complexity. If overlapping enumeration type-specifications are allowed, several implementations are possible:

1) The type of an enumeration literal, such as orange in the above example, is dependent on the context. For example, in S1:=orange the type would be that of S1.

2) The type of an enumeration literal is an enumeration type consisting of a single value, viz. that literal. The language could handle assignments between enumeration types (say from E1 to E2) as follows. If E1 and E2 are disjoint (i.e., have no literals in common), then the assignment is in error at compile-time. If E1's values are totally contained within E2's values, then the assignment is legal, but a run-time conversion will probably be necessary (on account of representational differences between the types). In all other cases, a run-time check is necessary to ensure that the source value is within the destination type's value, and a run-time conversion will likely be needed.

The question of whether enumeration type specifications may overlap is related to the issue of what exactly "type" means in connection with enumerations. If no overlap is permitted, then it is reasonable to adopt the convention that different enumeration type-specifications denote distinct types. If overlap is allowed, then such a convention becomes less palatable, especially if the language follows the advice of C. A. R. Hoare[2] and does not permit the same value to belong to different types. An alternative is to assume the existence of a hypothetical universal enumeration type, analogous to integer; different enumeration type-specifications then denote subsets or subranges of this universal type, in the same way that subranges of the integer type are specified.

---

[1] The notation used in the examples in this paper is based on the PASCAL language [JW 75].

[2] In his review of an earlier version of [DD 76], Hoare offers the following comments [Hr 75, p. 6]: "One of the important simplifying principles in thinking about types is: EVERY VALUE, VARIABLE AND EXPRESSION BELONGS TO ONE AND TO EXACTLY ONE TYPE. Of course I can't prove this principle. It's just that everything gets very messy if you don'd hold firmly to it."

Another issue related to enumeration types is whether they should be ordered or not. Most languages define an ordering based on the sequence in which the literals appear in the type-specification. For example, in PASCAL the PRED and SUCC functions and the relational operators are defined for enumeration values. However, in applications where a natural ordering is not present, it is not possible to prevent these routines from being (mis)used.

4.2.1.4 Subranges

A subrange type-specification can be regarded as denoting some type with ordered values (most typically <u>integer</u> but possibly an enumeration type or <u>real</u>) together with a predicate which asserts that the data object's value falls within the specified limits of the subrange. Languages which allow the specification of subranges include PASCAL and CS-4.

One issue arising with subranges is whether different subrange type-specifications denote the same type. The simplest solution, especially considering the comments of Hoare cited in the previous section, is for each subrange type-specification to result in the same type (<u>integer</u>, <u>real</u>, or an enumeration type). Otherwise, a given value would belong to an unbounded number of types: e.g., 5 belongs to 1..10, 1..20, 4..30, etc. Also, in order for the arithmetic operators to work on subrange values, we would have to view the situation as though an implicit conversion were being performed.

Having decided that subrange does not distinguish type, we are now confronted with the major question of when to perform the checking which is associated with the subrange predicate. Sometimes the check can be made entirely at compile-time; e.g.

   <u>var</u> I: 1..100; J: 10..20; ...I:=J; ...

In general, however, run-time code is necessary; moreover, there can be non-trivial degradations of efficiency if care is not taken by the compiler. One example is the statement I:=I+1, in which no check should be made vs. the lower bound of I's subrange. Another example is more subtle:

   <u>var</u> I: 1..10;
     ⋮

   <u>procedure</u> P(<u>var</u> I1: 5..15);
     <u>begin</u> ...I1:=12; <u>goto</u> L{non-local goto} ...<u>end</u>;
     ⋮

   <u>begin</u>...I:=5; P(I);...L:<u>write</u>(I)...<u>end</u>

The assignment I:=5 is valid. When P is called, the argument value should

be compared against the subrange for I1; this will check. But what happens
now on the assignment I1:=12? This is in-bounds for I1 and will thus not be
detected as an erroneous assignment to I. Perhaps the postlude code for
P(I) will check that I is in the correct subrange, but in the example the
non-local exit will lead past the checking code. Thus, at label L, I does
not have a legal value.

The solutions to this problem are not very attractive. One possibility
is to make it a compile-time error to pass a variable by reference to a
procedure with a subrange formal parameter, unless the variable's range
includes the formal parameter's subrange. However, this places a restriction
on when two objects of the same type may be used interchangeably.

4.2.1.5 Unions

The union type-specification has its origins in the desire to reuse the
same storage area for objects of different types. In early languages, this
facility was not regarded as a type-specification. For example, FORTRAN
realizes unions via its EQUIVALENCE statement, COBOL via the REDEFINES and
RENAMES clauses, and PL/I via the DEFINED attribute. The emergence of
unions as a type specification is illustrated in the CELL structure of
TACPOL [Lt 71, Section 10.4.6]. In each of these, however, the concept
realized is that of "free union", and there is no protection against defining a data object to be of one data type, then using it (via the name of the
overlaid object) as though it were of another type.

Several languages attempt to provide a "safe" form of union (called
"discriminated" union in [Hr 72, pp. 109ff]) which obtains storage overlay-
ing but also includes restrictions on the usage of union objects. In PASCAL,
this feature is the "variant record"; CS-4 offers the union facility. In CS-4
a union type-specification consists of a sequence of components each of which
comprises a field name and a type specification. An object having union type
contains at any time exactly one of these components; a field in the object,
commonly called the "tag" and not directly accessible to the programmer, indicates which alternative holds.

Some of the issues surrounding type identity for union objects are
inherited from the component type-specifications. Others are related to
issues arising in records: what are the roles of the field-names, the
constituent type-specifications, and the order of the components, in
defining the type which is denoted by a union specification? However, the

most critical questions pertain not to the relationships between (whole) union objects, but to the behavior of the components. One major problem is the tradeoff between run-time efficiency and program security. Consider the declaration:

var U: union(A: integer; B: ↑integer);

To use U as an integer, the programmer specifies U.A; to use U as a pointer to an integer, the programmer specifies U.B. For strict security, the compiler should generate a run-time check for each such qualification; e.g. U.A would expand into: if TAG(U)=A then U.A else error. However, such a check is prohibitively expensive, especially in contexts where the value of the tag is "known" to be A. Such a context is provided frequently in the form of a case dispatch on the tag field. On the other hand, if the compiler does not provide the checking code, then a programmer can take advantage of this and deal with U as a free union.

A somewhat more subtle problem can arise even if the compiler does produce run-time checking code. Consider a procedure P which has an integer I as a formal parameter by reference and which uses the data name U as a free variable. Suppose that TAG(U)=A, and that P is called with U.A as argument. Now imagine that, in the body of P, U is assigned a new object with tag field B (such an assignment is presumably legal). But now there are two names (I and U.B) referring to the same storage area under different type assumptions. This situation illustrates some of the dangerous interactions between union types and such language features as free variables and by-reference parameter passing.

4.2.1.6 Pointers

The merits and drawbacks to pointers in a high-order language have been dealt with elsewhere -- e.g. [Hr 73, BEL 76, Ki 76] -- and we will not reiterate these arguments here. Instead, we consider the implications with respect to type safety when a pointer facility is present.

An immediate problem which arises, when a HOL provides data structuring but not type definition, is that there is no convenient way to indicate the type of object being referenced by a pointer. This situation is illustrated in PL/I; a variable declared with POINTER attribute can reference any BASED data object (and can also contain the ADDRess of any variable). There is nothing which prevents the programmer from setting a pointer to reference an object of one type and then interpreting the pointed-to data as though it had some other type.

It should be noted that, notwithstanding the fact that untyped pointers defeat type checking, there is one benefit which results from such a facility: viz. the type equality issue is simplified. In our consideration of type definition features below, we will see the other side of this coin: when programmer-named types are allowed and the language supports typed pointers, strong type checking is facilitated but the type identity issue becomes complex.

4.2.1.7 Packing

Some languages permit the programmer to specify data-space-optimizing directives to the compiler in the form of "packing" attributes with a type-specification. The issue then arises as to whether the packing should be considered part of the data type. This is a case where objects which differ only in packing have the same behavioral properties but different representations; the types should be considered the same with respect to assignment (an implicit conversion routine can perform the mapping between representations) but not with respect to by-reference parameter passing.

A subtlety which arises with packing is that the way in which it filters through a type-specification is likely to be machine -- or even implementation -- dependent. For example, assume that X is declared to be a packed record(A: char; B: integer; C: array [1..10] of boolean). Then presumably X.C is a packed array, but is it also the case that X.A is a packed char, X.B is a packed integer, and X.C[i] is a packed boolean?

4.2.2 Type definition

In a language which allows user definition of data types, an immediate question concerns the relationship between the type denoted by a name and that denoted by the type specification used as the definition for the name. As an example, consider the following PASCAL declarations:

```
      type T1 = array [1..100] of real;
           T2 = array [1..100] of real;
      var  v1: T1;
           v2: T2;
           v3: array [1..100] of real;
```

Does v1 have the same type as v2? How about v1 and v3? Unfortunately, neither the PASCAL Revised Report [JW 75] nor the axiomatic definition [HW73] offers any explicit information on the subject. In fact, it is not

obvious what the interpretation should be, and different solutions are
presented in different languages. In ALGOL 68, T1 and T2 would be identical,
since the name is taken simply as a shorthand for its definition [Ko 75].
An alternative approach was taken in an early version of CS-4 [Mi 73];
according to these rules, the type denoted by T1 would be distinct from
array [1..100] of real. The ECL language supports both approaches. The
normal behavior is for the types to be identical; a user desiring to distinguish T1 from array [1..100] of real would do so by specially marking the
array type specification.

The above situation illustrates one of the many tradeoffs which must
be faced by a language designer. The simplest solution, in terms of implementation and description, is probably the ALGOL 68 approach. Most uses of
type definition are likely to be for purposes of notational shorthand, so
that this approach is consistent with programming practice. On the other
hand, there are also many cases where the programmer desires the protection
that would result from treating a type name as a distinct type instead of
as a notational abbreviation. (Consider if instead of the names T1 and T2
we had used Column_Vector and Row_Vector.) The price for such protection
is complexity; e.g. in the description of conversions.

An alternative approach to the treatment of named types is provided in
the language SPL/I [Ks 76]. Here the user must name each specification of
a composite type (a declaration like that for v3 above would be illegal),
and distinct names imply different types. This provides the protection of
strong type checking and simplifies the compiler's task of checking for type
identity, at the expense of possibly requiring a large number of type names.

One of the stickiest issues which arises in a language with a type
definition facility has to do with type identity when the language allows
pointers or recursive data types. One problem is that, in non-trivial
cases, there are likely to be differences of opinion as to when two types
are identical. Consider:

        type LIST1 = record(A: integer; B: ↑LIST1);
             LIST2 = record(A: integer; B: ↑LIST2);
             LIST3 = record(A: integer; B: ↑LIST1);

Should types LIST1 and LIST2 be considered identical? How about LIST1 and
LIST3? The answers are not obvious; in general, the solution must be
implemented as an algorithm which compares two directed graphs (possibly
cyclic) for some sort of equivalence. One approach is given in [Mi 73,
Section 2.5]; another technique is to apply finite-state-machine equivalence

methods (an example appears in [Me 75, Section 2]).

An important aspect of a language supporting type definition facilities which include pointers is that the safety which goes with typed pointers can now be realized. Assuming that the language requires that pointer type-specifications always include a specification of the type of the pointed-to data, we cannot have the PL/I-like situation where a pointer is created to reference data of one type and is then used as though the data were of another type. (Some languages, such as ECL, allow "united pointers" which can reference objects from one of several programmer-specified types; such a facility can be viewed as realizing a union of several (single) pointers.)

In a HOL which allows user type-definitions, there may be subtle inter-actions with other language features. One example is the issue of determin-ing the data type of a subscripted array object, especially if array "slicing" is permitted. To illustrate this, assume the declarations
    type T = array [1..10] of integer; var X:T;
What is the type of X[*] (where the * subscript is intended in the PL/I sense) -- is it T, or array [1..10] of integer? The answer may depend on whether the language supports "partial slicing." One might expect that the type of X[*] should be that of X (viz. T); however, if it is permissible to have the form X[1 THROUGH 5] (which clearly cannot have type T), and the * subscript is defined as "lower-bound THROUGH upper-bound," then X[*] will have the type array [1..10] of integer. As another example, suppose that it is desired, when selecting either a row or a column of a matrix, to obtain an object of type vector. Neither of the possible sets of declarations below will work:
    1) type vector = array [*] of real;
            matrix = array [*] of vector;
    2) type matrix = array [*,*] of real;
In the first case, the selection X[i] yields a vector (assuming X to be a matrix), but the column selection X[*,i] produces an array [*] of real. In the second case, neither selection form yields an object of type vector.

4.2.3 Data abstraction

A great deal of attention has been focussed recently on the subject of data abstraction in programming languages. In this section we attempt to identify some of the issues which arise, primarily in connection with type safety, when data abstraction is present in a language.

4.2.3.1 What is a "data type"?

An example which is frequently used to illustrate data abstraction is
that of a STACK of elements; the same abstraction can be invoked regardless
of the type of the element. Given an object defined to be, say, a STACK of
integers, what is then the type of this object? Is it simply STACK, or is
it STACK of integers? That is, should we regard a data abstraction as a
type or as a type generator? It is probably not possible to give a general
answer to this question, since the kinds of compile-time facilities available will be relevant. However, the answer provided by a language has a
direct impact on the type checking which is performed. Suppose that D is a
parameterized data abstraction, and that a routine P expects an argument
whose type (or type generator) is D. In the specification of P's formal
parameter, what are the rules governing the instantiation of D? Presumably
it is possible to omit the instantiation altogether (e.g., in the PUSH
routine, the parameter is declared as a STACK, and not as STACK (type-
specification)). If the instantiation is included, must an actual parameter which is a D have identical attributes to those specified in the
formal parameter? Are the rules different depending on whether the parameter binding (for the procedure) is by-value or by-reference? May parameters to a data abstraction be run-time computable?

To illustrate the above issues, consider the following definition (in
a suitably extended PASCAL):

           type D = abstraction(I: integer; T: type);
                      ⋮
                   procedure P(var X: D);
                      ⋮
                   procedure Q(var X: D(20, real));
                      ⋮
                   end; {of abstraction definition}
           var V: D(10, integer);
              ⋮
            P(V);
              ⋮
            Q(V);
              ⋮

Presumably the call P(V) is permissible. What about Q(V)? If the formal
parameter X in Q had been a value parameter, would the call be legal?
Should the rules pertaining to parameter passage (and thus type checking)
for objects having abstract data types be specified by the language, or

should the programmer have control over the behavior? If the latter, then how?

4.2.3.2 Conversions

A data abstraction issue which is not directly related to type checking but is worth mentioning here, is how to capture user-defined (explicit) conversions. The problem is that a conversion routine typically must know the representations associated with both the source and the destination type, but the rules for data abstraction generally require the routine to be explicitly part of only one of the types and thus unable to use the representation of the other.

4.2.3.3 Efficiency

The generality which is obtained in an example like the STACK abstraction illustrates a tradeoff between compiler complexity and efficiency of code space. The problem is that an abstraction routine with a parameter whose data type is an uninstantiated abstraction cannot in general be compiled separately from an invocation of the routine. For example, it is not possible to compile a single copy of the PUSH routine which will work for both a STACK of integers and a STACK of booleans. The most direct solution is to compile each call on an abstraction routine as though it were a macro invocation (i.e., as open code at the point of call). Though this has the advantage of faster execution time, the expansion of the code space may be prohibitively expensive. Unfortunately, an alternative approach -- to compile a separate copy of a routine for each different instantiation of the routine's argument -- may cause non-trivial bookkeeping problems for the compiler.

4.3 INTERFACES

In our discussion of type safety issues thus far, we have been assuming the existence of a single unit of compilation. The situation is somewhat more complicated when data type information is used across program interfaces. The two most common instances of this are separate compilations and file I/O.

4.3.1 Separate compilations

The problem in separate compilations is that a procedure may be compiled expecting a formal parameter of one type, and a separate program may
call the procedure with an argument of another type. This is an especially
serious situation in large programming projects, where a number of programmers are producing separately compiled modules. A variety of solutions
has been developed in response to this situation. In PASCAL, the original
approach was to avoid the problem by not allowing separate compilation; as
stated in [Wr 71, p. 317] (emphasis in the original): "The compiler
generates absolute code. The gain in compilation speed and particularly in
avoiding the use of standard relocation loaders more than outweighs the
doubtful advantage of being able to merge 'binary' programs after compilation. If a compiler is available with a speed practically equal to that of
a relocation loader or linkage editor, there is no point in keeping
relocatable binary versions of a program; merging of programs should occur
at the source language level." However, in a recent implementation of
PASCAL (the PASREL compiler for the PDP-10), separate compilation is supported, but without type checking across program interfaces. Several
languages include provisions for supporting such checking. In ALGOL 68-R
[CBM71, pp 23-24], a "KEEP-list" is used to ensure that along with the
relocatable binary code comprising a segment, specifications of the kept
names are preserved. Thus, KEEPing a routine name should result in the
preservation of the specifications for the types of the formal parameters.
The CS-4 language [BDFLP75, Section 7.3.1] extends the notion of the KEEP-
list to include provisions for filtering and/or renaming the information
which is used from a separately compiled program. This is realized in the
ACCESS directive, which not only ensures that type checking is performed
along the interface between separately compiled programs, but also protects
the ACCESSing program against possible name conflicts. In the SUE System
Language [CH 74], one of the design objectives was "to facilitate separate
compilation of hierarchically related programs." The unit of recompilation
is the internal procedure. All the information needed to recompile a given
procedure will have been declared in data and context blocks of containing
procedures. This facilitates type checking across separate compilations.

The expense of maintaining type checking across separate compilations
is that symbol table information must be preserved along with the relocatable code. Since such information will likely include intricately linked
data structures (e.g. to represent the data types themselves), it is a non-
trivial issue to deal with the information in an efficient manner. This is

especially true considering that the compiled program and its symbol table
are generally placed on backing store.

4.3.2 File I/O

Files present unique problems regarding type safety, since a file will
typically outlive the process which creates it. In most languages, one can
write a file containing data of one type, then read the same file as though
its contents were of a different type. Generally the only checking performed
is with respect to the organization of the file (e.g. random vs. sequential
access) and not with respect to the contained data.

One approach to this situation is presented in CS-4's Operating System
Interface [GL 75, Section 2.1.2]. Here the programmer specifies the type of
file in terms of its organization and the data type(s) of the contained
information. In order to use a file defined externally, the programmer must
ACCESS the definition, thus ensuring that file creation and file use share
the same assumptions about the composition of the file.

4.4 UNTYPED DATA

In the majority of applications, strong type checking is necessary for
facilitating the production of reliable software. However, there are a number of areas in which the major concern is the machine-dependent representation of data. Just as the routines inside a data abstraction must have
access to the (high level) description of the representation of instances
of the abstraction, so too some routines dealing with certain data objects
must have access to the low level (machine dependent) representation of the
data. Such a situation is frequent in real-time applications (e.g. interpreting the contents of sensor data buffers in a tactical system), where
efficiency constraints or processing requirements demand taking advantage of
the hardware representation.

There is at present a certain amount of controversy surrounding the way
in which this situation should be handled in a HOL. Dijkstra offers the
following suggestions [Di 75, pp. 2,3]:
     ... in the past, when we used "low level languages" it was considered
     to be the purpose of our programs to instruct our machines; now, when
     using "high order languages", we would like to regard it as the purpose

of our machines to execute our programs. Run time inefficiency can be viewed as a mismatch between the program as stated and the machinery executing it. The difference between past and present is that in the past the programmer was always blamed for such a mismatch: he should have written a more efficient, more "cunning" program! With the programming discipline acquiring some maturity, with a better understanding of what it means to write a program so that the belief in its correctness can be justified, we tend to accept such a program as "a good program" if matching hardware is thinkable, and if with respect to a given machine [the] aforementioned mismatch then occurs, we now tend to blame that computer as ill-designed, inadequate and unsuitable for proper usage. In such a situation there are only a few true ways out of the dilemma

1) accept the mismatch
2) continue bit pushing in the old way, with all the known ill effects
3) reject the hardware, because it has been identified as inadequate...

  I cannot suggest strongly enough each time to select one of the three ways out of the dilemma, and not to mix them. When the second alternative "continue bit pushing in the old way, with all the known ill effects" is chosen, let that be an activity with which the HOL project does not concern itself: if it does, the "ill effects" will propagate through the whole system.

An alternative approach is implicit in the notion of "rep type" in [PSW76], which is a set of modes with identical representations. As stated by these authors:

> The desire for compile-time checking interferes with abbreviation and code sharing because strong type checking tends to prevent code developed to work with data of one type from use on data of another type, even when its application is meaningful [p. 150]... One of the most frequent complaints about languages with strong type checking is that one is prevented from utilizing the common properties of two modes [p. 151]... Our position is that representation-dependent programs will be written whenever cost considerations demand it; it is better to provice a mechanism that allows the control of such dependency than to force the programmer to use dirty tricks [p. 153].

Unfortunately, trying to strike a compromise of the sort suggested by [PSW76] is difficult in practice. When one attempts to satisfy two conflicting goals in order to gain the advantages of both, the result is frequently a system which combines the disadvantages instead. There are, however, a variety of languages which contain type checking as well as

explicit escapes from such checking.   The UNSPEC function in PL/I (which may
be used as a pseudovariable) enables the programmer to treat any data object
as a bitstring.   Somewhat more restrictive is the notion of a UNIVersal type
in Sequential PASCAL [BHH 75].   If a formal parameter to a routine has type
UNIV T2 and an argument has type T1, then a call on the routine with the
given argument is legal if both types' instances are represented in the same
number of store locations and neither type involves pointers.   "The type
checking is only suppressed in routine calls. Inside the given routine the
parameter is considered to be of non-universal type T2, and outside the
routine call the argument is considered to be of non-universal type T1"
[BHH 75, p. 32].   CS-4 provides a set of features for dealing with machine
dependencies [BDFLP 75, Chapter 8].   An encapsulated direct code facility
allows the insertion of assembly language in certain contexts, and CS-4 also
permits the programmer to define data layouts in a machine-dependent manner
(e.g. with overlapping fields), including the allocation of data in absolute
memory locations.

5. CONCLUSIONS

The basic result which emerges from this study is that, in contemporary
High Order Languages, the subject of data types and type checking is
characterized by a relatively large number of (relatively) minor issues.
It is not the case that we can point to one or two overriding problems,
investigate their potential solutions, and mechanically decide on an
appropriate set of constructs. Instead, we have the situation where the
most fundamental facilities (e.g., arrays) cause difficulties, and where such
apparently innocent features as enumeration types and subranges conceal an
assortment of problems.

These issues may be regarded as manifestations of a larger problem --
the agony of deciding on tradeoffs among equally desirable goals. For
example, a language designer must face the dilemma of balancing the power and
efficiency needed to support the intended applications, with the security
required for program reliability, without paying too highly in language complexity. Hard choices must be made; improvements in one area are typically
accompanied by sacrifices in another. It is hoped that the survey conducted
in this paper has shed some light on the tradeoffs which affect the decisions
concerning a language's treatment of data types and type checking.

Acknowledgements

The author would like to acknowledge the influence of the members of
the CS-4 design group on the ideas expressed here. In particular,
discussions with Tim Dreisbach, Jim Miller, John Nestor, and Larry Weissman
have been helpful in exposing various subtle issues surrounding data types.

REFERENCES

[ACM 76]

Association for Computing Machinery, Proceedings of Conference on Data: Abstraction, Definition and Structure, Salt Lake City, Utah, March 22-24, 1976.

[BDFLP 75]

Brosgol, B. M., T. A. Dreisbach, J. L. Felty, J. R. Lexier, G. M. Palter, CS-4 Language Reference Manual and Operating System Interface, Part I; Intermetrics, Inc., Cambridge, Mass., October 1975.

[BEL 76]

Berry, D. M., Z. Erlich, C. J. Lucena, "Correctness of Data Representations: Pointers in High Level Languages," in [ACM 76], pp. 115-119.

[BHH 75]

Brinch Hansen, P. and A. Hartmann, Sequential PASCAL Report, California Institute of Technology, Pasadena, Calif., July 1975.

[CBM 71]

Currie, I. F., S. G. Bond, J. D. Morison, "ALGOL 68-R," in [Pe 71], pp. 21-34.

[CH 74]

Clark, B. L. and F. J. B. Ham, "The Project SUE System Language Reference Manual," Report CSRG-42, Univ. of Toronto, Canada, 1974.

[DD 76]

Department of Defense, Requirements for High Order Computer Programming Languages "Tinman", June 1976.

[DDH 72]

Dahl, O-J., E. W. Dijkstra, and C. A. R. Hoare, Structured Programming, Academic Press, London, 1972.

[Di 75]

Dijkstra, E. W., "On a language proposal for the Department of Defense," EWD514, Sept. 17, 1975.

[GL 75]

Grimes, D. E. and J. R. Lexier, CS-4 Language Reference Manual and Operating System Interface, Part II; Intermetrics, Inc., Cambridge, Mass., October 1975.

[Gu 76]

Guttag, J. "Abstract Data Types and the Development of Data Structures," in supplement to [ACM 76], pp. 37-46.

[Ha 76]

Hammer, M., "Data Abstractions for Data Bases," in [ACM 76], pp. 58-59.

[Ho 76]

Horning, J. J., "Some Desirable Properties of Data Abstraction Facilities," in [ACM 76], pp. 60-62.

[Hr 72]

Hoare, C. A. R., "Notes on Data Structuring," in [DDH 72], pp. 83-174.

[Hr 73]

Hoare, C. A. R., "Recursive Data Structures," Stanford Artificial Intelligence Laboratory Memo AIM-223, Stanford University, Stanford, Calif., October 1973.

[Hr 75]

Hoare, C. A. R., "Comments by Prof. C. A. R. Hoare on: 'Tinman" Set of Criteria and Needed Characteristics," Working Paper, December 5, 1975.

[HW 73]

Hoare, C. A. R. and N. Wirth, "An Axiomatic Definition of the Programming Language PASCAL," Acta Informatica 2, pp. 335-355, 1973.

[Hw 74]

Holloway, G., J. Townley, J. Spitzen, B. Wegbreit, ECL Programmer's Manual, Technical Report 23-74, Center for Research in Computing Technology, Harvard University, Cambridge, Mass, December 1974.

[JW 75]

Jensen, K. and N. Wirth, PASCAL User Manual and Report, Springer-Verlag, New York, 1975.

[Ki 76]
    Kieburtz, R. B., "Programming without Pointer Variables," in [ACM 76],
        pp. 95-107.

[Ko 75]
    Koster, C. H. A., "The Mode System in ALGOL 68," in [Sc 75], pp. 99-114.

[Ks 76]
    Kosinski, M. S., <u>SPL/I Language Reference Manual for Compiler Release
        4.0</u>, Intermetrics, Inc., Cambridge, Mass., July 1976.

[Li 74]
    Liskov, B., "A Note on CLU," Computation Structures Group Memo 112,
        Massachusetts Institute of Technology, Cambridge, Mass., November
        1974.

[Lt 71]
    Litton Systems, Inc., Data Systems Division, CPCEI Specification for
        Compiler/Assembler for Fire Direction System, Artillery AN/GSG-
        10()(V), Vol. 1, April 1971.

[Me 75]
    Meertens, L., "Mode and Meaning," in [Sc 75], pp. 125-138.

[Mi 73]
    Miller, J. S., C. M. Mikkelsen, J. R. Nestor, B. M. Brosgol, J. T.
        Pepe, R. Fourer, <u>CS-4 Language Reference Manual</u>, Intermetrics, Inc.,
        Cambridge, Mass, December 1973.

[Na 63]
    Naur, P. (ed.), "Revised Report on the Algorithmic Language ALGOL 60,"
        <u>Comm. ACM</u> 6, pp. 1-17, January 1963.

[No 76]
    Nordström, B., "An Outline of a Mathematical Model for the Definition
        and Manipulation of Data," in [ACM 76], pp. 1-11.

[Pe 71]
    Peck, J. E. L. (ed.), <u>ALGOL 68 Implementation</u>, North Holland Publishing
        Company, Amsterdam, 1971.

[PSW 76]

    Parnas, D. L., J. E. Shore, D. Weiss, "Abstract Types Defined as
        Classes of Variables," in [ACM 76], pp. 149-154.

[Sc 75]

    Schuman, S. A. (ed.), <u>New Directions in Algorithmic Languages 1975</u>,
        IRIA, France, 1975.

[St 71]

    Standish, T. A., "Data Structures: an Axiomatic Approach," Harvard
        University, Cambridge, Mass., January 1971.

[Wi 73]

    Wichmann, B. A., <u>ALGOL 60 Compilation and Assessment</u>, Academic Press,
        London, 1973.

[Wr 71]

    Wirth, N., "The Design of a PASCAL Compiler," <u>Software-Practice and
        Experience</u>, Vol. 1, pp. 309-333, 1971.

MODELS OF DATA OBJECTS AND DATA TYPES

John R. Nestor

Intermetrics, Inc.
701 Concord Avenue
Cambridge, Massachusetts   02138
617-661-1840

Abstract

Several models for data objects and for data type relationships are
discussed and compared.
The models for objects discussed are
1. Representational model in which representations are visible.
2. Behavioral model in which representations are hidden.
3. Operational model in which multiple hidden representations
   are permitted.
For each model the handling of shared information and aggregates is discussed.
Several kinds of type relationships are considered: mixed type
operations, generic operations, polymorphic operations, representational
relationships, and component relationships. Two programming language
models that permit objects having any of several types to be used in a
single context are discussed.
1. Conversion model in which conversion functions are used.
2. Lattice model in which bidirectional mappings are used.
Finally some possible research directions for developing improved
models are suggested.

This work was supported by Contract N00123-76-C-1688, Naval
Electronics Laboratory Center, San Diego, California.

1.0 INTRODUCTION

Recently, interest in the treatment of data in programming languages has increased. This is due partially to a greater appreciation of the role of data in creating reliable programs [Hoare 75] and partially to new program language features [Wulf 74, Liskov 75, Brosgol 75] that provide users with more flexibility and protection for their data structures.

Although methods for defining data types have been extensively studied and discussed [Fisher 73, Morris 73, Reynolds 74, Liskov 75a, Wulf 76, SIGPLAN 76], relatively little attention has been directed toward the study of data objects as entities distinct from their types or toward the study of how different types are related. This paper addresses these two areas by providing a survey and comparison of several models based on features in existing programming languages and on several proposals for new language features. Section 2.0 presents models for data objects and Section 3.0 discusses models for the structuring of related types.

Many of the ideas discussed here have resulted from the design effort for the CS-4 language [Brosgol 75, Nestor 75, Nestor 76].

2.0   OBJECTS

An object is an abstract model for memory used by a programming language. In this section, three object models are considered. These models
differ primarily in the way in which representations are handled. In the
representational model, representations are visible. In the behavioral
and operational models, representations are hidden but only in the operational model can multiple representations for a type exist in the same
program. Finally, some suggestions for a more advanced object model are
presented.

The naming of objects is not a primary consideration here. A name
is assumed to be bound to a single object during the lifetime of the object.

2.1 REPRESENTATIONAL MODEL

In the representational model, each object (Figure 1) consists of a changeable value association which is uniquely labeled by a value, called the Lvalue of the object. The value association associates with the object another value, called the Rvalue of the object. A value is a primitive, indivisible member of some value set. For simplicity, the value set for both Lvalues and Rvalues is assumed to be the set of all bit patterns of a specific fixed length. The Lvalue of an object is fixed; however, the value association of an object can be changed to associate the object with a new Rvalue. An object can optionally be named by associating a name with its Lvalue.

Objects are updated by an assignment having the form

        E1 := E2

where E1 and E2 are each expressions. When an assignment is performed, E1 is evaluated to produce a value which must be the Lvalue of some object. E2 is evaluated to produce a value. The value association of the object whose Lvalue was produced from E1 is changed so that the Rvalue of that object is the value produced from E2.

To make assignment operate in a conventional fashion, E1 and E2 are evaluated differently. The two kinds of evaluation are called L-evaluation (for E1) and R-evaluation (for E2). Consider an assignment involving two objects named A and B (Figure 2).

        A := B

The left hand side, A, is L-evaluated to produce the Lvalue associated with A. The right hand side is R-evaluated to produce the Rvalue of the object whose Lvalue is associated with B. The value association of A is then changed to associate the Rvalue from B.

This model provides only one type of value (a bit pattern); however, most programs are best expressed in terms of several additional types of values (e.g., integers, reals, Booleans, characters, etc.). Each additional value type is achieved by representing each of its values by some bit pattern (e.g., integer values might be represented in two's complement binary).

135

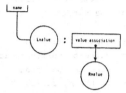

Figure 1   An object using the Representational Model

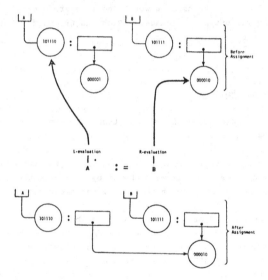

Figure 2   Assignment using the Representational Model
(values are assumed to be 6 bits long)

Operations are normally designed for use with the representation for
only one type of value (e.g., an integer + operator might add two bit
patterns using two's complement addition). When a sufficient set of operations, together with some way for expressing literal values, is provided
for some type, there is no need for the user to know the representation
that is used for values of that type (e.g., the user need not be aware of
whether integer values are represented in one's complement or two's complement). This leaves each implementation free to choose a representation
that is most appropriate for the particular target computer.

It is the programmer's responsibility to use only those operations
which are meaningful for the current representation used for the objects
to which they are applied. Using an operation on an object whose representation is not that for which the operation was intended can result in
errors that are not detected during compilation (if the use was accidental)
or a severe transportability problem (if the use was intentional).

The representational model corresponds closely with the memory of most
computers (each value association is a word, an Lvalue is an address,
and an Rvalue is the contents of a word) and is therefore quite easy to
implement. Several untyped languages [Richards 69, Wulf 71] handle objects
in a way that is similar to this model.

2.1.1 Sharing and Pointers

An object is said to be shared when there are two or more paths for
referencing that object.

A simple kind of sharing occurs when an object has two names. A
useful example of this is a parameter bound by reference where the formal
parameter name is associated with the actual parameter object.

A more general kind of sharing is achieved by permitting the Rvalue
of one object to be the Lvalue of some other object. The first object is
called a pointer to the second object. To produce Lvalues during
R-evaluation, a special ADDR operator is used. R-evaluation of the ADDR
operator is equivalent to L-evaluation of its operand (L-evaluation of
the ADDR operator is illegal). For example the assignment

A := ADDR B

results in the Rvalue of A being the Lvalue of B (Figure 3). To use the

value of a pointer object, an @ (dereference) operator is used. During
R-evaluation the result of the @ operator is the Rvalue of the object
whose Lvalue is the result of R-evaluating the operand. L-evaluation of
the @ operator is equivalent to R-evaluation of its operand. For example
the expressions

@ A

B

both refer to the same object (Figure 3).

2.1.2 Aggregates

An aggregate is a collection of closely related objects, called components, each with its own Lvalue and Rvalue. Commonly used aggregates
include arrays and structures (records).

By arranging the Lvalues of the components of an aggregate in a
standard pattern (frequently the Lvalues of array components are arranged
in an arithmetic sequence) it is possible to use a single Lvalue to refer
to the entire aggregate. If the Lvalue of an aggregate is set equal to the
Lvalue of its first component, then the Lvalues of each of the components
can be obtained by applying simple operations to the Lvalue of the
aggregate (normally adding a constant offset). It is convenient to place
the Lvalue of an aggregate in the Rvalue of another object through which
the aggregate is referenced. For example consider an array with five
components referenced via the object A (Figure 4). Then the I-th component
is referenced by

@ (A+I)

Note that if I is not in the range 0 through 4, then the reference is
erroneous. It is the user's responsibility to perform any necessary
checking on I before evaluating this reference.

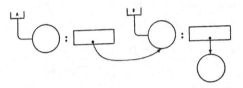

Figure 3 A pointer using the Representational Model

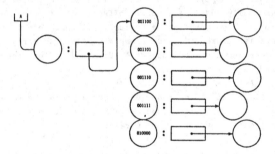

Figure 4 An array using the Representational Model

2.2 BEHAVIORAL MODEL

In the representational model, two kinds of information were required
to completely characterize the behavior of each type of values:
1. Behavioral Information -- This information specifies how each value
    behaves when appropriate operations are applied.
2. Representational Information -- This information specifies the bit
    pattern that is used to represent each value.
In the behavioral model, each type is characterized by only the behavioral
information. The representational information is supplied when a type is
implemented. Representational information is not available to the user of
the type.

Objects in the behavioral model contain a type in addition to a value
association (Figure 5). The type defines two properties for objects
having the type: a value set and a set of basic operations. The only
values that can be associated with an object are those in the value set of
the type of the object. The set of basic operations define the ways in
which an object having the type can be used. Any other operations which
use an object having the type must be implemented in terms of the basic operations of the type. Note that behavioral objects have no Lvalue. An
object is named by associating the name directly with the object.

The behavioral model offers several advantages over the representational model.
1. Understandability -- The user need not be aware of the representational
    information to use languages that employ the behavioral model.
2. Reliability -- It is possible to check (usually during compilation)
    that each operation is applied only to objects having the correct
    types for that operation.
3. Modularity -- It is possible to have several versions of a type, all with
    the same abstract behavior but each implemented with a different repre-
    sentation. Only one version of the type can be used in a single com-
    pilation of a program. Since the representation of a type is not
    known to the user of the type, later compilations of the same program
    can use other versions of the type without making any changes to
    places in the program that use the type.

Assignment, which is usually one of the basic operations, again has
the form

        El := E2

where El and E2 are expressions. Expression evaluation in this model can
result in either an object or a value depending on the particular expression
(function and operator applications usually produce values). The assignment
changes the value association of the object produced by evaluating El
(it is an error if a value is produced) to associate the value produced or
the value of the object produced by evaluating E2. If the value from the
right hand side is not in the value set of the type of the object on the
left hand side, then the assignment is in error.

    Strongly typed languages [Jensen 75, Liskov 75] handle objects in a
way that is similar to this model.

2.2.1 Sharing and Pointers

    Sharing can be achieved by allowing objects to be values. A type
whose value set contains objects is called a pointer type. To simplify
type checking, each pointer type is restricted so that its value set
includes objects having only a single type. Figure 6 shows an example of
a pointer object.

    Some languages [Dahl 70, Liskov 75, Wulf 74] achieve sharing by
including a single hidden pointer as part of each object (see Figure 7).
Each object now has two independently modifiable associations: a reference
association and a value association.

    There are two kinds of assignment that update the two kinds of
association. The first kind of assignment is a reference (sharing) assignment. When a reference assignment

        L ← M

is performed upon the objects shown in Figure 8a, the result is shown in
Figure 8b. Note that the value association that was originally used for L
is no longer needed. An implementation using this kind of object requires
some kind of garbage collection for these lost value associations. The
second kind of assignment is a value (copy) assignment. When a value
assignment

        M := N

is performed upon the objects in Figure 8b, the result is shown in Figure 8c.

141

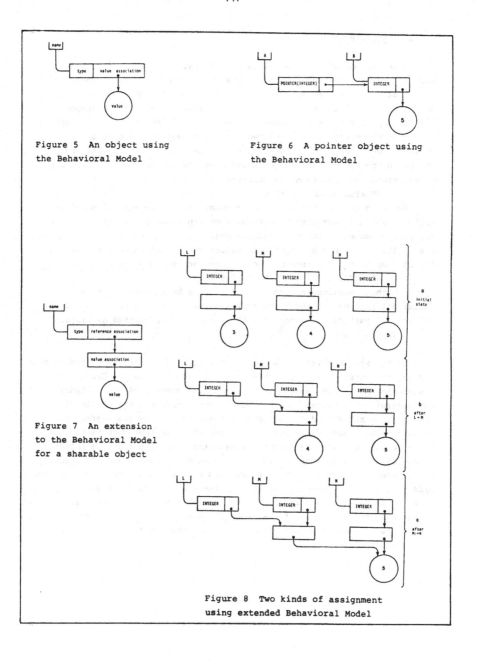

Figure 5 An object using
the Behavioral Model

Figure 6 A pointer object using
the Behavioral Model

Figure 7 An extension
to the Behavioral Model
for a sharable object

Figure 8 Two kinds of assignment
using extended Behavioral Model

2.2.2 Aggregates

Since values are considered to be indivisible, component selection cannot be done by a single selector operation which produces a component object as a result. As an example consider a complex object consisting of RE (real) and IM (imaginary) components as shown in Figure 9. Suppose that the RE component is to be incremented by 1.0. Since no object corresponding to the RE component can be produced, a pair of selector operations is required, one operation for getting the value of the RE component and another operation for updating the value of the RE component. Using a pair of selectors, the increment is performed by

    UPDATERE(C,GETR(C)+1.0)

To avoid this rather complicated notation, the behavioral model can be modified so that aggregate objects have multiple value associations, one for each component. The same complex object is shown using this scheme in Figure 10. It is now quite easy to select out an object corresponding to the RE component. The increment operation can now be written as

    SELECTRE(C) := SELECTRE(C)+1.0

Although this notation is more natural, it has been necessary to include additional information about the representation that was not required before. In particular, a complex number must be represented as disjoint RE and IM components.

To see why information about the partitioning of components should be hidden, the complex example is extended. In addition to the Cartesian components, RE and IM, access to two polar components, MAG (magnitude) and ANG (angle), is considered. The MAG and ANG components are completely dependent on the RE and IM components; therefore, a complex object need contain value associations for only two of these four components. If a complex object has RE and IM value associations, then a single selector operation is possible for the RE and IM components but a pair of selector operations is required for the MAG and ANG components. A similar situation arises if a complex object instead contains MAG and ANG value associations. If a single selector operation is made available for a component using either of these value association forms, then it is impossible to change to the other value association form without changing the set of selector operations in an incompatible fashion.

As another example, consider a sparse matrix, a two-dimensional array of real components, most of which have the value zero. To conserve on storage, this kind of matrix is represented by a one-dimension varying size array. Each element of this array corresponds to some non-zero element of the matrix and includes a position in the matrix (two integers) and an element value (a non-zero real). When a component which currently has a zero value is selected, there is no way to produce an object since there is no value association in the representation for that component. If a component with a non-zero value is selected, an object can be produced; however, if the value of that selected component is then set to zero, its value association should vanish! For a sparse matrix, it is clear that a single selector operation is impossible. Component selection must be done by a pair of selector operations.

2.2.3 Implementation of User-Defined Types and Built-In Types

Many languages [Liskov 75, Wulf 75, Palme 76, Wirth 76, Brosgol 75] provide abstraction mechanisms for implementing user-defined types. A type definition defines an abstract type by specifying a representational type and a set of basic operations. An abstract object is implemented by a representational object having the representational type (Figure 11). Inside the type definition, it is possible to change an object to its representational object and vice versa. The basic operations supply the abstract behavior for objects with the abstract type. These operations are implemented in terms of the operations for objects having the representational type. The value set of the abstract type is an equivalence class over the value set of the representational type. Two representational values are equivalent abstract values if there is no way to detect a difference in the abstract behavior of an abstract object whose representational object has those values.

Built-in types can be considered in a similar manner to user-defined types. For a built-in abstract type, the representational type is similar to the bit pattern "type" of the representational model. Basic operations are implemented by target computer instructions that manipulate these bit patterns.

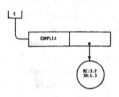

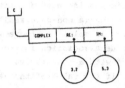

Figure 9 A complex object
using the Behavioral Model

Figure 10 A complex object
using the Behavioral Model
with multiple value associations

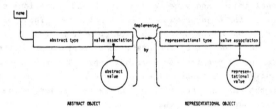

Figure 11 An object in the Behavioral Model
together with its representational object

2.3 OPERATIONAL MODEL

A major advantage of the behavioral model was that the representational type for an abstract type can be changed while leaving the abstract behavior the same. Although this permits different representations for an abstract type, only a single representation can be used in a single program. The operational model provides additional flexibility by permitting multiple representations for an abstract type to be used in the same program.

In the operational model, an object, in addition to its type, has either one or both of two procedural capabilities: an R (read) capability and a W (write) capability (Figure 12). A variable object has both capabilities. A constant object has only an R capability. A write-only object has only a W capability (this is useful for output parameters). Each capability, if present, grants the right to invoke an associated procedure. The R capability is for an R procedure which has no parameters and when invoked returns the value of the object. The W capability is for a W procedure which when invoked takes a value as an input parameter which replaces the current value of the object.

Assignment has the form
        E1 := E2
where E1 and E2 are expressions. In this model, the result of evaluating an expression is usually an object (function and operator applications usually produce constant objects). When the assignment is performed, the expressions are first evaluated to produce objects O1 and O2. Object O1 must have a W capability and object O2 must have an R capability. The value of O1 is then updated to be the value of O2 by
        W_PROCEDURE[O1](R_PROCEDURE[O2]())
where object procedure selection is shown by brackets and procedure invocation is shown by parentheses.

The full CS-4 language [Nestor 75, Nestor 76] handles objects in a way quite similar to the operational model presented here.

2.3.1 Implementation of User-Defined Types and Built-In Types

As in the behavioral model, the implementation of an abstract type
specifies a representational type. This representational type serves in
the operational model as the primary representation. The primary representation is the representation used for values returned by the R procedure and passed to the W procedure of objects having the abstract type.

Figure 13 shows an object with a standard representation. In this
case, the only effect of the R (or W) procedure of the abstract object is
to call the R (or W) procedure of the representational object.

In addition to the primary representation, arbitrary alternate
representations are possible. To create an abstract object with an alternate representation, a mapping is applied to an object (or set of objects)
having the desired alternate representation (Figure 14). The mapping contains two functions: an R map function which converts values from the
alternate representation to the primary representation and a W map
function which converts values from the primary representation to the
alternate representation. The resulting abstract object has an R
procedure formed by the composition of the R map function and the R procedure of the representational object and a W procedure formed by the
composition of the W procedure and the W map function of the representational object. The procedure for a standard representation can also
be considered to be composition in which the R and W map procedures
are each an identify function.

Objects of a given type having either the primary or an alternate
representation can exist simultaneously and be used interchangeably in
a single program.

Note that so far no value associations have appeared for the operational model. Each object shown has obtained its value from the value
of its representational object. Objects with built-in types have no
representational object but must, instead, have R and W procedures
which reference a value association (Figure 15). This value association
resembles an object in the representational model.

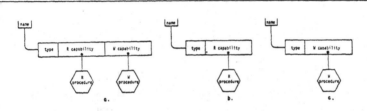

Figure 12 Objects using the operational model

a.   a variable object

b.   a constant object

c.   a write-only object

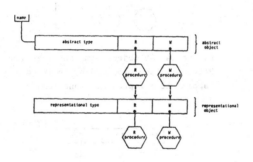

Figure 13 An object with a
Standard Representation

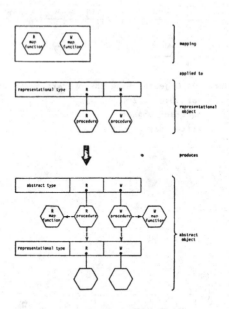

Figure 14 An object with an Alternate
Representation produced by applying a
mapping to a representational object

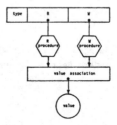

Figure 15 An object with a built-in
type together with its representation

2.3.2 Some Simple Uses for Alternate Representations

2.3.2.1 Packing

Packed representations can be used in places where unpacked representations are required (and vice versa) if a mapping is first applied. The R map function performs the unpack operation and the W map function performs the pack operation.

2.3.2.2 Range Checking

It is often desirable to have classes of types which differ only in the range restrictions that are placed upon their value sets. When an object, whose type has value set V1, is to be used in a place that requires an object whose type is in the same class but whose value set is V2 (e.g., assignment, parameter passing), a mapping is applied. The R map function raises an error when an access is attempted and the object has a value (in V1) which is not in V2. The W map function raises an error when an attempt is made to store a value (in V2) which is not in V1.

2.3.2.3 By Name and By Reference Parameters

In the previous models, by name parameters could not be considered to be objects. The operational model makes it possible to treat by name parameters as objects. The R (or W) procedure of a name parameter object, when invoked, evaluates the actual parameter expression and then invokes the R (or W) procedure of the resulting object.

By reference parameters are handled similarly, the only difference being that the actual parameter expression is evaluated only once at the point where the call is made.

2.3.3 Sharing and Pointers

A pointer object is shown in Figure 16. Note that a pointer requires its own value association.

If there is a mapping that takes an object with type T1 and produces an object with type T2, it seems reasonable to use this mapping to permit assignment of an object with type POINTER(T1) to an object with type POINTER(T2). When the assignment is performed, the mapping is applied to the value to be assigned (the pointed-to object).

Suppose that there is also a mapping from T2 to T1. Now consider the program

```
        VARIABLE X IS POINTER(T1),
                 Y IS POINTER(T2);

        ...
        WHILE condition REPEAT
           ...
           X := Y;
           ...
           Y := X;
           ...
        END
        ...
```

Each of the assignments applies another layer of mapping to the value assigned. Since each layer will require some amount of memory, the amount of memory needed here can grow without bound. When the value is finally discarded, the memory must be freed. This requires either a substantial bookkeeping overhead or a garbage collector.

In the full CS-4 language [Nestor 76] a restriction is placed on pointers to avoid this overhead. The pointed-to object is restricted so that only the primary representation is permitted. This allows an efficient implementation in which the value association of a pointer is implemented by a memory location containing the address of the pointed-to object.

The kind of overhead that occurs in the operational model for un-restricted pointers does not occur for some other data structures that have been suggested as replacements for pointers (e.g., arrays, recursive data structures).

2.3.4 Aggregates

In the operational model, all components of an aggregate can always be accessed by a single selector operation and this is possible without placing any restrictions on the partitioning of the representation. Any component object can be produced by applying an appropriate mapping to the aggregate object.

As an example, a complex object is again considered with selectors available for the RE, IM, MAG and ANG components (Figure 17).

Consider the mapping for selecting the RE component. The R map function extracts and returns the RE part of the value. The W map function first extracts the old IM part of the value, then combines this with the new value for the RE component and returns this result. It is interesting to note that there is no way to apply a component selection mapping to a write-only aggregate object to produce a usable component object since the component object W procedure requires the R procedure of the aggregate object.

Next consider a mapping for selecting the MAG component. The R map function extracts the current RE and IM parts of the value and returns the square root of their squares. The W map function first computes the current value of the ANG component from the RE and IM parts. This old ANG value, together with a new MAG value, forms a complete polar value. This polar value is converted to a Cartesian value which is then returned.

As a second example, a sparse matrix is reconsidered. Component selection is again achieved by applying a mapping. The R map function obtains the complete matrix value, replaces the value of the selected component and returns this new matrix value.

In the operational model, every time a component of an aggregate is accessed or updated, it is necessary to access the entire aggregate value. For a sparse matrix, it is necessary to create the full two dimensional representation every time a component is referenced.

To avoid accessing the entire aggregate value, objects are extended to include, in addition to R and W capabilities, a SELECT capability (Figure 18) for a SELECT procedure. The SELECT procedure can work directly with the representation to produce selected component objects.

Using this scheme, a complex object represented by RE and IM components is shown in Figure 19. When the RE or IM component is selected,
by invoking the SELECT procedure with the actual parameter RE or IM, the
resulting component object references only one of the two representational
objects. The selection of the MAG or ANG component, however, would require
the application of a mapping to the complete complex object.

Component selection for a sparse matrix would result in a component
object with the following procedures. The R procedure first searches for
the specific component in the representation. If the component is found,
the associated value is returned; otherwise, zero is returned. The W
procedure searches the representation for the specific component. There
are then four cases:

1.   (component found, zero stored) - the component is removed
      from the representation
2.   (component found, non-zero stored) - component is updated
3.   (component not found, zero stored) - no action
4.   (component not found, non-zero stored) - component added
      to the representation with the new value

2.3.5 Implementation Considerations

In cases where the representation of a referenced object can be
determined during compilation, the operational model can be implemented
as efficiently as the behavioral model.

In cases where the representation of a referenced object is not known,
specifically the case for parameters passed by reference, the operational
model is substantially less efficient. For parameters passed by reference,
it is necessary to pass the R and W procedures rather than an address. An
optimizing compiler, however, should be able to implement parameters passed
by reference by addresses in those cases where the actual parameters in
all calls have the same representation.

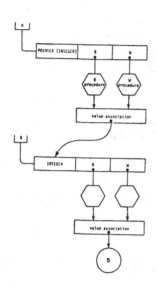

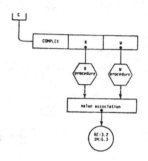

Figure 16 A pointer object
using the Operational Model

Figure 17 A complex object
using the Operational Model

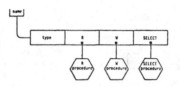

Figure 18 An aggregate object
using the Operational Model
extended with a SELECT capability

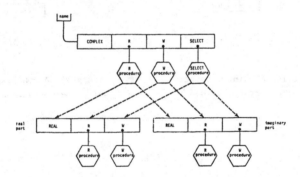

Figure 19 A complex object using
the Operational Model with SELECT
capability. The representation is
by two real objects corresponding
to the RE and IM components.

155

2.4 FUTURE DIRECTIONS

The major limitation of the operational model is that there is a single primary representation to which all other representations must be mapped before being used. The disadvantages of this can be seen in an assignment involving two sparse matrices. In this case, a non-sparse copy of the value being assigned must be created when the primary representation is non-sparse.

An advance over the operational model would be a model which permits multiple representations of a type to be used simultaneously yet does not identify any of these representations as primary. All representations exist on an equal basis.

In this model, an object contains capabilities for each of the basic operations of the type of the object. These basic operations can then be designed to operate efficiently for the particular representation.

When an object is passed as a parameter to a procedure, only the capabilities that are needed by the procedure need be passed. Jones and Liskov have suggested a notation for specifying parameter capabilities using a behavioral model for objects and have indicated its utility [Jones 76].

The major difficulty of this model occurs for operations which involve several objects. If these objects can have different representations, then the number of required implementations of the operations can become overwhelming. In the case on an n-nary operation which can operate on any combination of m representations, a total of m^n implementations of this operation are potentially required.

A possible answer may be providing those implementations of an operation which are most critical. When a combination of representations occur for which no implementation exists, mappings could be applied so that one of the existing implementations could be used.

3.0   RELATIONSHIPS OF TYPES

In programming languages that have typed data, there are many kinds of relationships between the various types. In Section 3.1 several kinds of type relationships are considered and briefly discussed. In Section 3.2 programming language models that express type relationships are considered.

3.1   KINDS OF TYPE RELATIONSHIPS
3.1.1   Mixed Type Operations

An operation, which has parameters and/or a result which are of several different types, is called a mixed type operation. An example of a mixed type operation is a comparison operation which compares two integer objects and produces a Boolean result.

A particularly important kind of mixed type operation is a conversion operation. A conversion operation takes a single object having a source type and produces a result having a target type. The conversion operation maps each valid value in the value set of the source type to some corresponding value in the value set of the target type. Applying a conversion operation to an invalid value results in an error.

An important property of a conversion operation is whether it loses information. A conversion operation is said to lose information if and only if either (1) any values in the value set of the source type are invalid or (2) two values in the source value set map to the same value in the target value set. An example of a conversion that has no information loss is a conversion that maps each integer to a character string containing a sequence of decimal digits that represent the source integer. A conversion that loses information is the conversion from real to integer where fractional parts are truncated. A somewhat less obvious case of information loss occurs when integers are converted to reals. Information loss occurs here when the number of digits in the integer exceeds the precision of the real.

Data abstraction mechanisms in current programming languages [Liskov 75, Wulf 74] require that each type definition include the basic operations for that type. These basic operations are the only operations that have access to the representation. When an operation involves two (or more) types, it is not always clear that it is desirable (or in some cases

even possible) to place that operation in one of the two type definitions.
If placed in one type definition, the representation of that type is
accessible but the representation of the other type is not. One solution
to this problem (used by CS-4 [Nestor 75]) is to permit a data abstraction
to make different sets of information accessible to different external parts
of the program. In Figure 20, two type definition modules for types T1
and T2 are shown. Each definition includes a specification of the representational type and the set of basic operations. In addition to the two
type definitions, there is another module, X12, containing those mixed
type operations which involve both types. Each of the modules T1, T2,
and X12 is considered to be surrounded by a protection wall which makes
accessible selected information to selected external program parts. Using
this mechanism, the representation of T1 and T2 is made accessible to X12
but not the main program.

3.1.2 Representational Relationships

Each abstract data type is related to its representational type.
Within the implementation of a data type it is possible to change an
abstract object having the abstract type to a representational object
having the representational type and vice versa.

It is important, however, that the relationship between an abstract
type and its representational type not be known to the user of the abstract
type. If this relationship is known, then the representation of the abstract
type can not be changed without changes to those places where the relationship is used.

When two abstract types have the same representational type, sometimes
the abstract types can share a common implementation for some abstract operation. In this case it is desirable to have only a single implementation of
the operation that can be used by both types. This can be done by writing
a single copy of the operation which operates upon the common representation
and placing a short abstract operation in each of the abstract types whose
purpose is to call the operation on the representation. There are two
problems with this approach: first, two calls (together with their overhead) are executed each time the abstract operation is called, and, second,
having to code the short abstract operations is notationally inconvenient.
Both problems can be eliminated by providing a way of "promoting" operations upon the representation when an abstract type is defined (Figure 21).

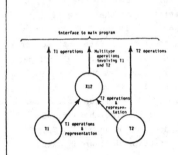

Figure 20 Modules with
protection walls used to
define mixed type operations.

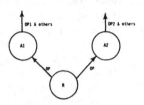

Figure 21 Two abstract
types A1 and A2 sharing a
common representational
type R. A common operation
OP is promoted through A1
to form OP1 and through A2
to form OP2.

3.1.3 Operations That Apply to Multiple Types

Sometimes a single operation can be applied at different calls to
parameters of different types. There are two basic kinds of operations
with this property: generic operations and polymorphic operations.

A generic operation [Schuman 75] has several different associated
bodies, each of which operates on a single set of parameter types. The
particular body used for each call is selected based on the types of the
actual parameters. An example of a generic operation is a + operator
which has one body for two integer operands and another body for two real
operands.

A polymorphic operation has only a single body that is used for all
parameter types. An example of a polymorphic operation is a sort procedure which will sort a one-dimensional array of components when an
assign (:=) and a compare (>) operation are defined for the component type.
Note that polymorphic operations are possible only when there are generic
operations on which to base their implementations.

3.1.4 Component Relationships

Each aggregate type is related to the types of its components. This relationship is present in the selector operation for the aggregate type. The selector operation is a mixed type operation.

3.2 PROGRAMMING LANGUAGE MODELS

In this section, two programming language models for type relationships are discussed. Each model permits the use, in certain contexts, of objects having any of several types. For each context, there is some rule establishing the set of permitted types.

The only kind of context for an object considered here, is use of the object as an actual parameter for some procedure. Other contexts in which an object can be used, such as in language commands, can be treated in the same way by considering a command to be a call, with an unusual syntax, to some built-in procedure that implements the command.

The models presented here differ in the way in which an object, in some context, is manipulated into a form which can be transmitted to the procedure. In both the conversion model and lattice model, there is a single distinguished target type for a context. Objects having other types are operated upon to form objects having the target type. In the conversion model, values can be transmitted only from the object to the procedure. The lattice model, in addition, permits values to be transmitted from the procedure to the object. In the lattice model, there is no distinguished target type for polymorphic procedures. In this case, objects are transmitted directly.

The models discussed here are restricted to those that can be used conveniently in a language that supports user-defined types. Only those models which can be extended to include a new user-defined type are considered.

3.2.1 Conversion Model

In this model, for each context there is a distinguished type. The
only objects that can be transmitted are those having the distinguished
type. To make it possible to use, in some context, an object having a
type other than the distinguished type for that context, a set of conversion functions is defined. A conversion function takes as input an object
of a source type and produces as a result a (read-only) object having a
target type.

Conversions are frequently used to define mixed type arithmetic.
Suppose, the arithmetic operators +, -, * and / are generic and have
two bodies: one body takes two integer operands and produces an integer
result and the other body takes two real operands and produces a real
result. If there is a conversion function from integer to real, then each
of the arithmetic operators should also operate on one real operand and
one integer operand to produce a real result. The integer operand would be
converted to a real before being transmitted to the conversion function.

There are many ways in which conversions can be defined. Some
languages [Van Wijngaarden 69] have complicated, built-in rules for
determining which conversions can be applied in each of several kinds of
contexts. This kind of approach is not easily extended to include rules
for new user defined types. Three ways of defining conversions that can
be easily extended are considered here.

I. Simple Conversion Model

Here there is a single set of conversions, CV, in each scope. Each
element of the set has the form

    (Ts,Tt,F)

where Ts is a source type, Tt is a target type and F is a function that
takes a parameter having type Ts and produces a result having type Tt.
The types Ts and Tt are required to be different types. The set of
conversions for a scope is the union of the set of conversions defined
in that scope and the set of conversions for the immediately enclosing
scope.

For each context, a distinguished type, DT, is specified in the
formal parameter declaration for that context. An object having type
DT can be transmitted directly. An object having type T can be used if
there exists an f such that (T,DT,f) is in CV. The function f is applied
to the object before transmission.

This approach is ambiguous if there are two or more elements in CV
that have the same source and target types. This ambiguity can be
avoided if no two elements are permitted to have the same source and
target types. Another approach is to add an additional rule that always
selects a unique element from CV. One possible rule is to use the most
recently defined conversion.

II. Cast Context Conversion Model

In the simple conversion model, the same conversion rule is used
for all contexts having the same distinguished type. In the cast
context conversion model, a different rule can be associated with each
context.

A cast rule for a distinguished type, DT, is a set of conversions to
type DT. Each element has the form
$$(Ts,F)$$
where Ts is a source type different from DT and F is a function that takes
a parameter having type Ts and produces a result having type DT.

A cast rule C is said to be valid for type T if
$$\exists (t,f) \in C \mid t=T$$
Application of cast rule C, which is valid for type T to object O having
type T, is equivalent to
$$f(O) \text{ where } (T,f) \in C$$

For each context, a distinguished type, DT, and a cast rule for
that distinguished type, CDT, is specified in the formal parameter
definition for that context. An object having type DT can be transmitted
directly. An object having type T can be used if CDT is valid for T. The
cast rule CDT is applied to the object before transmission.

One design decision to be made for this model is whether all elements
of a cast rule must be defined before the cast rule is referenced in a
formal parameter definition. It seems reasonable to permit a cast rule
to be extended even after it has been referenced to account for new
user-defined types.

The comments on resolving ambiguitites in the simple conversion
model also apply to cast rules.

III. Cascaded Conversion Model

Frequently, it is desirable to use a composition of several conversion
functions. For example, when an integer object is used in a context
whose distinguished type is complex, two conversion functions might be
used: one from integer to real and another from real to complex.

A cast rule for a distinguished type, DT, is a set of conversions
to type DT. Each element has the form
    (Ts,Cs,F)
where Ts is a source type different from DT, Cs is a cast rule for Ts,
and F is a function that takes a parameter having type Ts and produces
a result having type DT.

A cast rule C is said to be valid for type T if
    $\exists (t,c,f) \in C \mid (t=T) \vee (c$ is valid for $T)$
Application of a cast rule C which is valid for type T to an object O
having type T is equivalent to either
    $f(O)$ where $\exists c \mid (T,c,f) \in C$
or $f($application of c to O$)$ where $((T,c,f) \in C) \wedge (c$ is valid for type $T)$.

For each context, a distinguished type, DT, and a cast rule for
that distinguished type, CDT, is specified in the formal parameter
definition for that context. An object of type DT can be transmitted
directly. An object having type T can be used if CDT is valid for T.
The cast rule CDT is applied to the object before transmission.

Ambiguities tend to occur more frequently in this model due to the
cascading of cast rules. A selection rule here might attempt to
minimize the number of conversion functions needed.

When a new user-defined type is declared, it is desirable to specify any additional conversion functions and rules that involve that type as a part of the declaration. Suppose a new type NT is being declared and it is to be related, by means of conversions, to an existing type ET. Then two conversion functions can be defined with NT: one from ET to NT and another from NT to ET. The first would be used to build a new cast rule(s) for NT and the second would be added to an existing cast rule(s) for ET.

There are several disadvantages to the inclusion of a conversion model in a programming language.

1. Reliability - When many conversions are defined, the extent to which a program can be checked during compilation is severely restricted because a larger set of object types are permitted in each context.

2. Complexity - The introduction of conversion rules greatly increases the complexity of a language. In addition to the complexity of the conversion rules, generic functions are complicated when body selection can be based on the validity of a cast rule.

3. Generality - A conversion is a one way operation. It can be used when the value of an object is to be transmitted to a procedure (an input context) but not in cases where a value is transmitted from the procedure to the object (an output context).

4. Efficiency - Conversion functions are invoked automatically when needed and require no special attention on the part of the user. A user who is not aware of this hidden overhead may produce less efficient results.

5. Understandability - The ability of a user to define conversion functions and rules can result in programs that are difficult to understand. Particularly confusing effects occur when the conversion functions lose information.

3.2.2 Lattice Model

The lattice model corrects some of the problems found in the conversion model. The conversion model uses a mapping (see section 2.3.1) rather than a function to change an object in some context to a new object having the distinguished type for that context. This permits the same type relationships to apply to both input and output contexts. The lattice model also restricts the kinds of permitted type relationships in order to produce less complexity and more reliability. The lattice model is used in the full CS-4 language [Nestor 76].

In the lattice model, related types are grouped into a type class, and related type classes are grouped into a mode. Each type belongs to a single type class and each type class belongs to a single mode. It is convenient to say that a type belongs to a mode when the type belongs to a type class that belongs to the mode. A mode is specified by a mode declaration which serves as the primary language facility for creating new types. Each mode declaration contains representational information and basic operations for objects having any of the types belonging to the mode.

Each type consists of a mode part and a set of traits. The mode part is the mode to which the type belongs. Each trait is named and has a fixed value. All types that belong to the same mode have exactly the same trait names. Different types having the same mode part are distinguished by having different trait values.

Each trait is either a class trait or a type trait. Two types belong to the same type class if and only if they have the same mode part and class trait values. Therefore, class trait values distinguish type classes belonging to the same mode and type trait values distinguish types belonging to the same type class.

An object, O, whose type, T, belongs to a type class, TC, can be used in any context whose distinguished type, DT, belongs to TC. If T is the same as DT, then the object can be transmitted directly. Otherwise, a mapping from T to DT is applied to O and the resulting object is transmitted. Since DT and T belong to the same mode, the mapping is specified as one of the basic operations of that mode.

To enhance reliability and to yield an easily understood language, type traits are restricted. Only two kinds of properties are considered to be type traits.

1. Representational Properties - If two types have exactly the same abstract behavior but different representations, they are distinguished by a type trait. An example of this would be a packing trait which specifies either loose or dense packing. Another example is a trait that specifies whether a matrix has a sparse or non-sparse representation.

2. Range Properties - Many programming language types are based on mathematical models involving sets having an infinite cardinality. To permit these models to be represented on a finite machine, range restrictions must be made. Types which are based on the same mathematical model, but have different range restrictions, are distinguished by a type trait. Examples of a range trait are upper and lower value bounds for integer and real types and precision for real types.

Any other properties that distinguish types belonging to the same mode are considered to be class traits.

All types belonging to the same type class form a lattice. For two types, T1 and T2, belonging to the same type class and differing only in their range traits, T1<T2 if the value set of T1 is a proper subset of the value set of T2. To permit a greatest lower bound to always be defined, a special type VOID, with an empty value set, is introduced with the property that for any type T belonging to the type class other than VOID, VOID<T. Types which differ in some representational property are also ordered so that if the representation of T1 is preferrred to the representation of T2, then T2<T1.

Two important type relationships are displayed in this lattice. When an object having type T1 is used in a context with distinguished type T2, the set of values that can be transmitted is the value set of the meet (greatest lower bound) of T1 and T2. In conditional expressions, such as
IF b THEN E1 ELSE E2 FI
where E1 is an expression having type T1 and E2 is an expression having type T2, then the type of the conditional expression is the join (least upper bound) of E1 and E2.

It is also convenient to form a type specification lattice that contains all type classes and modes. A type class consists of a mode part and a set of class traits. All type classes are also type specifications. Each class trait of a type class must have a value; however, each class trait of a type specification can either have a value or be unresolved. If S1 and S2 are two type specifications having the same mode part and class traits except a single class trait which has a value in S1 and is unresolved in S2, then S1<S2. Note that a type specification in which all traits are unresolved is considered to be a designation for the mode which is the mode part of that type specification.

Type specifications that have different mode parts are joined by a special type specification
ANY(S1,S2,...,Sn)
where each Si is a type specification and no two type specifications belong to the same mode. The lattice relation for this type specification is
ANY(S1,S2,...,Sn)>Si for all i where $1 \leq i \leq n$

To complete the lattice, two special type specifications, ANY and VOID, are defined with the properties
S<ANY where S is any type specification $\neq$ ANY
VOID<S where S is any type specification $\neq$ VOID

A type specification can be used instead of a type in a formal parameter definition of a polymorphic procedure. An actual parameter to a polymorphic procedure is said to be in a polymorphic context. An object O, whose type T belongs to type class C, is acceptable in a polymorphic context that has a type specification S if $C \leq S$.

Objects in polymorphic contexts are transmitted directly. In the CS-4 language, polymorphic procedures are restricted to have only open (inline) expansions. Since only a single type for each parameter need be handled in each expansion, the implementation is straightforward.

3.2.3 FUTURE DIRECTIONS

Further study of techniques for implementing closed polymorphic procedures is needed. The implementation problems encountered here are quite similar to those discussed for the advanced object model (section 2.4).

In the lattice model, all types that belong to a single type class must be implemented in a single abstract declaration (mode). It is desirable in languages with user-defined types to permit a type class to be specified in multiple declarations. This reintroduces some of the complexity found in the conversion model.

An alternate view of type relationships, that considers types to be equivalence classes of objects, has been proposed by Parnas, Shore and Weiss [Parnas 76]. Further development of this model and techniques for implementing it are worth pursuing.

ACKNOWLEDGEMENTS

I would like to thank Dr. James S. Miller, Mr. Timothy A. Dreisbach, Dr. Benjamin M. Brosgol and Ms. Mary S. Kosinski of Intermetrics, Inc., Dr. John Shore, Dr. David Parnas and Mr. David Weiss of Naval Research Laboratory and Mr. Paul R. Kosinski of IBM Research for many helpful discussions of the ideas in this paper. John Bates prepared the diagrams included here. I am especially grateful to Miss Judy Haigh for preparing the final version of this manuscript.

168

REFERENCES

[Brosgol 75]
   Brosgol, B.M., Dreisbach, T.A., Felty, J.L., Lexier, J.R., Palter, G.M.,
   CS-4 Language Reference Manual and Operating System Interface,
   Part I, Intermetrics, Inc., 701 Concord Avenue, Cambridge,
   Massachusetts 02138, IR# 130-2, October 1975.

[Dahl 70]
   Dahl, O.J., Myhrhaug, B. and Nygaard, K., SIMULA Common Base Language,
   Norwegian Computing Center, Norway, 1970.

[Fischer 73]
   Fischer, A. and Fischer, M., "Mode Modules as Representations of Domains",
   ACM Symposium on Principles of Programming Languages, Boston, 1973.

[Hoare 75]
   Hoare, C.A.R., "Data Reliability", in [SIGPLAN 75].

[IFIP 75]
   IFIP Working Group 2.1 on ALGOL, New Directions in Algorithmic Languages,
   Institut de Recherche D'Informatique et D'Automatique, France, 1975.

[Jensen 75]
   Jensen, K. and Wirth, N., PASCAL User Manual and Report, Springer-Verlag,
   New York, 1975.

[Jones 76]
   Jones, A.K. and Liskov, B.H., "An Access Control Facility for Programming
   Languages", MIT Computation Structures Group #137, Cambridge, 1976.

[Liskov 75]
   Liskov, B.H., "An Introduction to CLU", in [IFIP 75].

[Liskov 75a]
   Liskov, B.H. and Zilles, S., "Specification Techniques for Data
   Abstractions", in [SIGPLAN 75].

[Morris 73]
    Morris, J.H., "Types Are Not Sets", ACM Symposium on Principles of
        Programming Languages, Boston, 1973.

[Nestor 75]
    Nestor, J.R., <u>CS-4 Language Reference Manual and Operating System
        Interface, Part III</u>, Intermetrics, Inc., 701 Concord Avenue,
        Cambridge, Massachusetts 02138, IR# 130-2, October 1975.

[Nestor 76]
    Nestor, J.R., <u>Full CS-4 Language Definition</u>, Intermetrics, Inc.,
        701 Concord Avenue, Cambridge, Massachusetts 02138, IR# 193-1,
        (to be released late 1976).

[Palme 76]
    Palme, J., "New Feature for Module Protection in Simula", SIGPLAN
        Notices, Volume 11, Number 5, May 1976.

[Parnas 76]
    Parnas, D.L., Shore, J.E., and Weiss, D., "Abstract Types Defined as
        Classes of Variables", in [SIGPLAN 75].

[Reynolds 74]
    Reynolds, J.C., "Towards a Theory of Type Structure", Colloquium on
        Programming, Paris, April 1974.

[Richards 69]
    Richards, M., "BCPL: A Tool for Compiler Writing and System Programming",
        Spring Joint Computer Conference, 1969.

[Schuman 75]
    Schuman, S.A., "On Generic Functions", in [IFIPS 75].

[SIGPLAN 75]
    <u>International Conference on Reliable Software</u>, SIGPLAN Notices,
        Volume 10, Number 6, June 1975.

[SIGPLAN 76]

Conference on Data: Abstraction, Definition and Structure, SIGPLAN
Notices, Volume 8, Number 2, 1976.

[Van Wijngaarden 69]

Van Wijngaarden, A. (ed.), Report on the Algorithmic Language ALGOL 68,
Numerische Mathematik, 14, Springer-Verlag, Berlin, 1969.

[Wirth 76]

Wirth, N., "MODULA: A Language for Modular Multiprogramming", Institut
fur Informatik, Eidgenossische Technische Hochschule, #18,
Zurich, March 1976.

[Wulf 71]

Wulf, W.A., "BLISS: A Language for Systems Programming", CACM, Volume 14,
Number 12, December 1971.

[Wulf 74]

Wulf, W.A., "ALPHARD: Toward A Language to Support Structured Programs",
Carnegie-Mellon Research Report, Carnegie-Mellon University,
Pittsburgh, April 1974.

[Wulf 75]

Wulf, W.A., "Abstraction and Verification in Alphard", in [IFIP 75].

ENCAPSULATED DATA TYPES

and

GENERIC PROCEDURES

Alan J. Demers
James E. Donahue
Ray T. Teitelbaum
John H. Williams

Computer Science Department
Cornell University

This work was supported in part by NSF grants MCS76 - 14293 and
GJ - 42512 and by RADC grant # F30602 - 75 - C - 0121

1. Introduction

In this paper we consider two programming language capabilities, encapsulated data types and polymorphic procedures, and their mutual dependence and effect on each other. The paper is organized as follows. In this section we give our motivation for studying these capabilities and introduce some general questions addressed by our research. In section 2 we consider carefully what is meant by such notions as data types, type checking and parameterized types. In section 3 we present an overview of various encapsulation mechanisms and compare and contrast their relative advantages and limitations. Finally, in section 4 we explore polymorphic constructs in general and generic procedures in particular.

Our reasons for studying encapsulated types and generic procedures are threefold. First, the IDA report [Fisher 1976] popularly known as the "Tinman," includes capabilities requiring the presence of an encapsulation mechanism and generic procedures as "needed characteristics" of the language. The requirements pertaining to the inclusion of an encapsulated data type facility are the following. Requirements E1 and E2 say that "the user of the language will be able to define new data types and operations within programs," and "the use of defined types will be indistinguishable from built in types." Requirement E5 states that "type definitions will permit definition of both the class of data objects comprising the type and the set of operations applicable to that class," and E8 states that "the user will be able to specify the initialization and finalization procedures for the type." The need for a "generic procedure" capability arises specifically from requirement C8. Although the very first requirement specifies that the language be "strongly typed," C8 indicates that "specifications of the type...of parameters will be optional on the formal side". We interpret this requirement to mean that procedures may be "generic," i.e., procedures may operate on data of more than one type. As specified in C8, the types of the parameters are to depend on the types of the arguments supplied with each call.

Second, the different approaches described in the literature [Liskov 1976,Dahl 1968] for providing an encapsulation capability, while starting with basically the same philosophy and goals, have resulted in distinctly different mechanisms. We feel that a comparative study of these various approaches will provide a clearer understanding of the essence of data encapsulation and its realization in programming languages.

Third, the two notions, encapsulated types and generic procedures, are very closely related. Underlying both are the notions of "data type" and "type-checking." A clear understanding of each of these ideas should have beneficial effects on any design of both facilities.

In the course of our research we have concentrated on these fundamental, underlying issues and their impact on the notions of encapsulated types and generic procedures. In order to indicate the nature and direction of our approach, we briefly introduce some of these questions and issues in this section; each of these notions will be considered in more depth in the remaining sections.

i) We wish to be able to distinguish between the capabilities provided by the fundamental notion of data encapsulation and the specific capabilities resulting from a particular method of encapsulation. For example, is the difference between associating operations with a type as in CLU [Liskov 1976] and associating operations with individual data objects as in SIMULA [Dahl 1968] an important and fundamental distinction? Or, are these two approaches just different mechanisms for achieving the same capability? All approaches to data encapsulation purport to provide greater "data security" and to permit a more abstract treatment of data structures during the programming process. This should allow greater program modularity. But are there other "features" and restrictions resulting from the particular choice of encapsulation mechanism which do not follow from the desired properties of data encapsulation, but are merely curious by-products of a particular approach? We will pursue this question in more depth in section 3.

ii) We attempt to give a rigorous definition of the notions of "type checking" and "strongly typed" and to consider carefully when two types should be considered equivalent. In the next section, we present semantically motivated definitions of type, type equivalence, and strong typing which are consistent with more informal notions and provide the basic principles used in allowing type definitions.

iii) Whatever mechanism is chosen for providing user-defined (encapsulated) types, should the language permit abstraction as part of the mechanism, i.e., should the language include parametrized types? In particular, what effect does parameterization have on our definitions of "type," "type equivalence," and "strong typing?" We will consider this in more depth in section 2 and also in section 4 where we consider abstraction of objects with respect to type, resulting in the possibility of polymorphic procedures and types.

iv) One of the important considerations in adding any feature to a language is its impact on other features and on the resulting implementability of the language. All implementations of languages with an encapsulation facility have assumed the existence of a run-time heap and the need for pointers. It is important, particularly for an effort like the forthcoming DoD design, to know whether a heap is an inherent necessity of encapsulated types or just a by-product of a particular approach. In section 3 we consider an encapsulation mechanism which implies neither pointers nor a heap.

v) Another important consideration in adding a feature to a language is its impact on the language definition. That the syntax of the extension should be compatible with the rest of the language is fairly evident, but it is even more important that the meaning of the new construct admit of a clean and simple semantic description. This consideration is one which permeates the entire paper but will be particularly stressed in section 2.

We now proceed to consider these topics in greater detail
in the remaining three sections.

2. Basic issues in providing type definition facilities

2.1 What is a "type?"

To be successful in providing a type definition facility, we
must first understand what we mean by a "type." In this section,
we discuss some currently used meanings of type and suggest an improved interpretation, more suited to our goal of defining a type
encapsulation mechanism.

Perhaps the most basic notion of type in current use is that
a type is defined by a set of values. Thus, the meaning of a type
definition should be to define a new set of values in the value space
allowed in the language. In languages like PASCAL where variables
have immutable type, this notion of type fits well with our natural
view of stack-oriented storage allocation for variables. Thus,
"a data type defines the set of values a variable may assume."
[Jensen and Wirth 1975, pg. 12]

The basic problem with this approach is its lack of precision.
A good example of the confusion involved is seen in the continuing
debate over the extension of PASCAL to allow procedures which accept
differing size arrays as arguments. The controversy can be simply
stated as follows. Clearly, one should be able to partition

array [integer] of integer

from

array [integer] of boolean

using the type mechanism in the language. A more subtle question is whether

array[1..10] of integer

should be viewed as distinct from

array[1..11] of integer.

PASCAL says yes; one can form subsets of the value space based on differing subscript bounds. PL/I says no; one need not (indeed, cannot) partition the value space that finely. And, by viewing types as simply subsets of values, we have no criterion for favoring a particular interpretation. Any mechanism that allows some partitioning of the value space, however fine or coarse that partition may be, is a type definition facility.

Recent work on data type definitions has moved away from viewing types as sets of values and has focused more on the behavior of objects under certain operations, e.g. [Morris 1973, Liskov and Zilles 1974, Guttag 1975]. This approach merely disguises the question of what is a type and certainly does not solve it. Just as we can ask how finely "type" should partition the value space, so we can just as readily ask how finely "abstract type" should partition the behavior space. Are two stacks different or alike, for example, if they impose different limits on the size or maximum number of elements that may be pushed onto them? Again, rather than answering this rather basic question, most papers on "abstract data types" leave this as a matter of taste.

The approach we take to the question of "what is a type" is based on the semantic role of types in an imperative language. We view a type as defining the following basic operators:

1. <u>Variable declaration</u> - given a new type, in imperative languages we can now declare and possibly initialize variables of the type.

2. <u>Value production and assignment</u> - given a variable of the type, we can produce the value currently possessed by the variable. Assignment allows this value to be changed.

3. <u>Value comparison</u> - given two values of the type, we need some mechanism to compare them. This may be as simple as allowing equality tests, but could also include less than and greater than for types with some defined ordering.

4. <u>Constant denotation</u> - a type declaration provides some interpretation of the syntactic constant symbols introduced.

5. <u>Component selection</u> - types introduce an interpretation of the component selection operators [ ] (subscription) and . (attribute selection) applied to variables and values.

Now, the distinction between different types is clear. If two types differ in terms of the meaning of the operators each definition provides, then they must be considered to be different types.

This is certainly a restrictive notion of type, in that we would not consider

<u>array</u> [1..10] <u>of</u> <u>integer</u>

and

<u>array</u> [1..11] <u>of</u> <u>integer</u>

to be the same types using this approach. However, as we will see

below, this view substantially simplifies answering the questions
of:

1. What should "type checking" mean in the presence of
    user-defined types? When is "compile-time" type checking
    not possible?

2. How should parameters to types be handled? What effect
    do they have on type-checking?

3. What do polymorphic constructs mean? Can we define types
    and procedures that are polymorphic and still guarantee
    strong typing?

We examine the first two questions below; polymorphism is
discussed in some detail in Section 4.

2.2   What do we mean by "type-checking?"

The second most confusing aspect of type, after deciding what
type should mean, is to decide what "type-checking" should mean.
Most discussions of type-checking [Ledgard 1972, Gannon and Horning
1975, Wirth 1975] view type-checking as a purely syntactic operation:
we record the type of each identifier, and if there is a conflict
between the type required in some context and the type supplied,
the program is taken to be erroneous. Thus a language like PL/I
with its automatic conversions is said to defeat the purposes of
type-checking as an error detection facility.

The difficulty with this simple approach to type-checking is
that type identifiers have a semantic, as well as a syntactic
interpretation (the inclusion of type definitions makes this

position inescapable). Thus without a clear semantic interpretation of type-checking and type equivalence, we have no assurance that whatever approach we take does not introduce errors, rather than catch them.

Our approach to type-checking and type equivalence is based on the following definitions. We will say that a language is statically typed iff the meanings associated with all occurrences of the basic operators (i.e. the operators for which meaning is given by type definitions) is statically determined. Otherwise, we will say the language is dynamically typed. There are two basic ways of providing static typing. One is the approach taken in BCPL [Richards 1969] or BLISS [Wulf et al. 1971], where each basic operator has only a single meaning (x := y means "move k bits from x to y"). The other approach is that common to Algol-like languages. If all identifiers are typed and the meaning of all types is statically determined, then it is clear that we can determine the meaning of all panmorphic operators strictly from their appearance in the program text.

The difficulty with static typing is in the semantics of parametric constructs, e.g., procedures. If a language is statically typed by requiring the typing of identifiers, then the meanings of the basic operators applied to the parameters will be determined from their type. Now, if we are to protect against the production of spurious results, we must ensure that applications of the parameterized construct to arguments produce results only when the meanings of the basic operators on the arguments are equivalent to their meanings as derived from the parameters specifications. We say that a language is <u>strongly typed</u> iff the application of a parametric construct to a set of arguments produces the semantically distinguished result "type error" if there is such a conflict in meaning; otherwise, it is said to be <u>weakly typed</u>. PL/I external procedures are an example of a language construct that is statically, but weakly typed, since there is no check that the argument and parameter types agree. A stronger notion of typing, which we will call <u>protective typing</u>, is also common to Algol-like languages (in particular, to PASCAL). We will say a language is <u>protectively typed</u> iff all programs containing an application of a parametric construct producing "type error" have meaning "type error". Thus,

```
p : procedure (integer x,y);
       x := y
  end;
  var x,y : real;
  if false then p(x,y) fi
```

has the semantic meaning "type error" in the case of protective, but not strong, typing. Note that with strong typing the production of "type error" is a property of parametric constructs, with protective typing a property of the programs which use them.

Thus, to guarantee at least strong typing, we must guarantee the type equivalence (in our semantic sense) of parameters and arguments. Clearly, since we are defining type equivalence in purely semantic terms, the equivalence of two types will in general be undecidable. However, we can be more restrictive and give simple, sufficient conditions for type equivalence that will ensure a strongly typed language.

For the moment, we will simply assume some type definition mechanism without any particular biases toward syntax. One cah read the following believing we are talking about either SIMULA or CLU without confusion. If the type definitions include no occurrences of free identifiers (as, for example, one could regard the definitions of the primitive types in Algol), then it is clear that in the absence of any redefinition of the type, all occurrences of the same type identifier are semantically equivalent. Thus, if we severely restrict the forms of type definitions we allow, type equivalence, and thus strong or protective typing, becomes no more difficult to guarantee than before.

Note that this view of types requires us to assume that distinct type definitions are never equivalent. If we allow arbitrarily complex forms of definition, then even if we go so far as to disallow free identifiers in the definition, we can not hope to be able to prove semantic equivalence of the definitions. Therefore, we are forced to say that any two distinct definitions define semantically distinguishable (and thus not equivalent) types.

If we now allow free identifiers to appear in type definitions, the use of static scope allows us to simplify the process of

guaranteeing type equivalence. If all free identifiers appearing
in a type are statically bound and all type identifiers appearing
in the definition are handled in the same way, then as before
all occurrences of the type identifier will be guaranteed to
be semantically equivalent.

Two points need to be made here. First, if we view type
definitions as being a purely syntactic device and replace each
occurrence of a type identifier by the syntactic definition of the
type, then the appearance of two occurrences of a type identifier
need not specify the same type. For example, given a definition
of the form

> type T = array [1..n] of integer,

then if we view types as "macro expansions," the two occurrences
of T in

> const n = 5;
>
> var x : T;
>
> begin
>
> > const n = 10;
> >
> > var y : T

are definitely not equivalent types. To guarantee the semantic
equivalence of two occurrences of T in this case we must check the
values associated with the free variables in each occurrence.
This approach has the disadvantage that if we allow free type
identifiers in type definitions (which seems perfectly natural),
the determination of the equivalence of two occurrences of the
same type identifier may involve an unbounded number of comparisons.

The second point is that we can nicely classify types based
on the free identifiers occurring in their definition. If we
have a language allowing:

1. constant declarations, like the const declarations of
   PASCAL, which allow us to name constants known at compile-
   time,

2. value declarations, like the const declarations of Euclid
   [Lampson et al.,1976] and the non-ref declaration of Algol68,
   which allow us to bind values (which are computed during
   execution of the program) to identifiers, and

3. variable declarations, which simply allow us to declare new
   variables,

then we can classify types into the following three categories:

1. Constant types. A constant type refers only to
   free identifiers which are constants or constant
   types.

2. Value types. A value type refers to free identifiers
   which are constants or values or constant or value types.

3. Variable types. A variable type refers to free identifiers
   which are constants, values or variables or constant,
   value, or variable types.

2.3 Parameterized Types

The final basic question to be decided in providing a
type definition facility is whether to allow types to be parameterized and, if so, how the addition of parameters should effect the
type-checking mechanism. The answer to the first part of this
question seems obvious - yes, types should allow the possibility
of being parametric. The answer to the second part is far less
clear. Indeed, the two most widely discussed type definition
facilities, those in Simula and CLU, adopt different approaches.

In Simula, type (or _class_) equivalence is independent of
the particular values assigned to class parameters by any two
instances of the _class_. For example, given the following definition
of histogram [Dahl, Dijkstra, and Hoare, pg 182]:

    class histogram (x,n); _array_ x; _integer_ n;

        begin _integer_ N; _integer_ _array_ T [0 : n];

            procedure tabulate (y);... _end_;

            real _procedure_ frequency (i);... _end_;
            .
            .
            .
        end of histogram;

any two variables of type ref(histogram) have the same type, independent of whether one is assigned a value of

histogram (A,10) or histogram (B,12).

One can argue that, even in terms of the notion of type introduced above, this is a reasonable treatment of parameters; but this is only true because of the introduction of the level of indirection given by the use of ref. Since all operations on class values involve manipulating the references to the values, rather than the values themselves, one can certainly think of a class definition as defining a single new type, ref(class), independent of any of the arguments supplied to create new instances of the class.

CLU, on the other hand, views the application of a type generator (i.e., a parametric type definition) to distinct arguments as defining distinct types. In part, however, this is because type generators allow types as arguments, in which case the choice seems clear. At this point, we are not considering the possibility of polymorphic types, so our choice of how to treat parameters is not so readily determined.

However, if we view type definitions in the semantic sense described above, we can see a clear justification for adopting the CLU approach. The semantics of a type definition, as we noted earlier, is clearly dependent on the meanings assigned to the free identifiers occurring in the definition. Therefore, if we allow type definitions to be abstracted with respect to some free

identifier appearing in the definition, then the application of
the type definition to distinct arguments will produce semantically
distinct types. Where earlier we could guarantee semantic
equivalence of types by requiring that they refer to the same
type identifier, now our requirement for type equivalence must
be extended to require that we have the same type identifier
applied to the same arguments.

Uniformity thus would suggest that if we allow constant,
value, and variable declarations and allow identifiers declared
as such to appear free in type definitions, then we should allow
constant, value and variable parameters to type definitions. As
an indication of the sort of parameterization we have in mind,
we give type definitions that correspond to the sorts of arrays
one finds in PASCAL, PL/I, and Algol68.

PASCAL arrays require constant bounds declarations, so
we could specify such arrays by

type PASCAL_Array (integer const n,m) =

static array [n..m] of integer

(for the moment, we will consider only integer arrays). By
contrast, PL/I allows bounds specifications to be computed
during execution, so we have

type PL/I_Array (integer val n,m) =

dynamic array [n..m] of integer.

Finally, Algol68 (or CLU) allows flexible arrays, where the bounds
can change during execution of a program. One way to mimic this
behavior is to assume that the array constructor can take variables

as the bounds specifiers and then uses the values of these variables
when checking subscript validity. (This example is slightly
complicated by the fact that these variables are not directly
accessible outside the type and that there are obvious differences
in best storage allocation strategies in these three cases, but
the basic point should be clear.) Thus, we can regard Algol68
flexible arrays as similar to the following type:

> type Algol68_Array(integer var n,m) =

> Flex array [n:m] of integer.

Our choice of parameterization options however, may be
tempered by our wish to have efficient mechanisms for providing
strong or protective typing. If we allow only constant parameters,
then type equivalence remains a compile-time property, thus
ensuring our ability to guarantee strong typing with no run-time
overhead. Allowing value parameters changes type equivalence to
a property that can only be determined during execution and thus
exacts some penalty (which we may be perfectly willing to accept)
to guarantee that the language remains strongly typed. The
addition of variable parameters certainly causes some additional
problems which remain for future research.

One final question about parameterized types is their use in
parameter specifications, e.g., in procedure declarations.
If we agree with the principle that types are always required,
then to specify the type of a procedure parameter, we must specify
the parameterized type identifier and the arguments applied to
the type definition. Thus, if we have (following [Wirth 1975]),

> type table (m,n) = array [m..n] of integer,

then a function Sum, summing the values of its table argument,
would be specified as

> function Sum (t:table(m,n))

for some m,n, rather than simply as

> function Sum (t:table).

But this seems to get us back to one of the basic criticisms of
PASCAL (one Wirth himself [1975] has agreed needs change) - that
we cannot write procedures and functions operating on differing
sized arrays. Two points need to be made here.

First, if we truly believe in using the type mechanism to
catch programming errors, then the full specification of the types
of parameters is clearly preferable, as the following example
illustrates.   If we look at Wirth's program for the function
Sum using the table data type, we have

```
function Sum (t:table; u,v: integer): integer;
    var i,s: integer;
    s := 0;
    for i := u to v do s := s + t[i];
    sum := s
end;
```

Now, if we declare

> var A : table (1,100);

we can call Sum (A,1,5), which does not sum the entire array, but
only a small portion of it.

On the other hand, we could just as easily write Sum as

```
function Sum (u,v:const integer; t:table(u,v)):integer;

        var i,s : integer;

        s := 0;

        for i := u to v do s := s + t[i];

        sum := s

        end;
```

making clear that u and v must give the lower and upper bounds
of the table t.   By the simple trick of allowing constant
parameters to procedures and "Currying" the parameter list, we can:

1. allow the type-checking mechanism to increase the range
   of errors that are detectable as producing "type error,"
   and

2. allow procedures (or other parametric constructs like
   type definitions) to operate on objects of types which
   differ only through their parameters.

Admittedly, in the case of several parameters of types each of
which have parameters, this simple-minded approach becomes somewhat
cumbersome and error-prone of its own accord.   But this problem
seems to yield to a little syntactic sugaring.   Belabouring our
table example just a little more, one can easily see how we could
translate

```
    function Sum (u,v:const integer, t:table(u,v)):integer;
```

into

```
    function Sum(t:table(new u, new v:const integer))
```

thus removing the necessity to pass explicitly the parameters of
the type table at each call.

3. Encapsulation Mechanisms

It is difficult to define precisely what a "data type encapsulation facility" is. We can, however, list some desirable goals which such a facility should be designed to achieve:

1. Objects of a given (user-defined) type are protected against invalid or unauthorized access. As an example of an invalid access, consider representing nonempty intervals on the real line by pairs (x,y). The assignment x := y + 1 would give the object a meaningless value, and should be forbidden.

2. Except for type definitions themselves, a program is independent of the particular representation chosen for objects of user-defined types.

Both (1) and (2) can be achieved by "hiding" the internal structure of an object from all but a few trusted procedures whose definitions are part of the "encapsulated definition" of the object.
As result of (1) and (2),

3. Program modularity is enhanced, and

4. Correctness proofs can be factored across type definition boundaries. That is, one can prove the correctness of a program using axiomatic descriptions of its user-defined types, then prove independently from the type definitions that the axioms are, in fact, satisfied.

Existing and proposed type definition facilities exhibit a number of different approaches to achieving the above goals.
One apparent distinction is the association of operators with types,

as in CLU, or with individual objects, as in Simula. A second
and, in our estimation, more fundamental distinction is made by
Reynolds [Reynolds 1975]. He identifies two basic approaches, which
he calls "user-defined types" and "procedural data structures".

In the user-defined types approach, each type defines an
internal representation, which is common to all objects of the type.
The program is divided into an "inner" region, in which the representation is known, and an "outer" region or abstract program from
which the representation is hidden. The abstract program can
manipulate data objects only by using primitive operations
which are defined as procedures in the inner region. Thus, operations
are associated with types, and a type is characterized (so far as
the abstract program is concerned) by the primitive operations
which can be performed on objects of the type.

Just as a type can be characterized by its primitive operations,
an object of the type can be characterized by the effect of these
operations applied to the object. Thus, if integers are characterized by the operators +, *, ..., then a particular integer
"a" is characterized by the unary functions $\lambda b.a+b$, $\lambda b.a*b$,
and so forth. Taking this viewpoint, each part of a program
which uses procedural data can specity its own representation,
independent of the representation used elsewhere in the program
for data of the same type. Associated with each data object is
a collection of procedures for performing primitive operations
on the object.

Evidently, an implementation of procedural data structures

must be Simula-like, in the sense that operations are associated with objects rather than with types. Similarly, user-defined types fit naturally into a CLU-like language. We feel, however, that the important component of the Reynolds distinction is not the association of operators with objects or types but rather the possibility of having several different representations for objects of the same type.

If each type has a unique representation, then Simula-like and CLU-like approaches can be made quite similar by use of a simple selective exporting mechanism. In fact, Koster [Koster 1976] argues that (more complex) selective hiding is the essential part of an encapsulation system.

On the other hand, the flexibility of having more than one representation for objects of the same type could be useful in dealing with infinite objects, for example, where a single representation may be inadequate to describe all the objects with which the program must deal. There are serious disadvantages however. Without a unique representation, the procedures internal to one object can assume no knowledge about the internal structure of other objects of the same type. To make it possible to implement the primitive operations, we are often forced to export record components which we would prefer to keep hidden from the abstract program.

We now illustrate the above concepts by a running example. We shall implement a two-dimensional vector space over the real numbers using both Simula-like and CLU-like approaches and

variations thereof. For our purposes, a vector space is characterized by:

   addition of vectors

   multiplication of a vector by a real

   unit basis vectors, $\underline{u}$ and $\underline{v}$

   assignment (:=)

   equality test (=)

Ideally, a user of our vector space implementation should have
access to the above attributes of vectors and to no other attributes.

   Our syntax is based on PASCAL. All identifiers are assumed
hidden unless explicitly exported. In particular, exporting a
record identifier does not automatically export its field
identifiers, as it does in EUCLID [Lampson et al, 1976].

   The vector space example does not require reference variables
or a heap. Instead, we assume storage objects are allocated on
a run-time stack at block entry.

   First we develop a Simula-like, procedural implementation of
vectors. The heading of our type declaration looks like:

```
type vector = record exports rprod, vsum;
   var x,y : real;
      .
      .
      .
```

The procedure to implement multiplication by a real is fairly straightforward. If A is a vector and r a real, the call A.rprod(r)
will have the effect A := r * A. The procedure body is simply

```
        procedure rprod (value r : real);
            x := x*r;   y := y*r
        end;
```

When we try to write an analogous procedure for vector addition,
however, we are faced with a problem. The obvious approach:

```
        procedure vsum (value B : vector);
            x := x+B.x;   y := y+B.y
        end
```

is not a legal program, because statements in the body of vsum
cannot access the hidden (i.e., not explicitly exported)
attributes x and y of B.

This problem, which we alluded to earlier, is inherent with
procedural data structures. The fact that a procedure can have access
to the internal structure of only one object at a time makes it
difficult to write procedures with more than one argument of a
given type.

To make it possible for us to write vsum, at least read
access to x and y must be exported from vector; e.g.:

```
type vector = record exports vsum, vprod, xval, yval;
var x,y: real;
function xval(): real;
return x
end;
        .
        .
        .
procedure vsum (value B : vector);
    x := x+B.xval();
    y := y+B.yval()
end;
```

Exporting even read-only access to x and y clearly compromises
our stated goal of representation hiding. From the abstract
description of a vector space given above, and recalling that
u is the unit vector of the vector space, there is no way to
predict whether u.xval() returns $0, \sqrt{2}/2, 1$, or even 10; there are
perfectly valid implementations producing any of these values.

As vsum is coded above, A.vsum(B) has the effect A := A+B.
We can also write

    procedure vsum2 (value B,C : vector);

      x := B.xval() + C.xval();

      y := B.yval() + C.yval()

    end;

The call A.vsum2(B,C) results in A + B+C. In fact, both vsum
and vsum2 may be needed since there are good reasons for prohibiting procedure calls such as A.vsum2(A,B) in which some
actual parameter appears more than once.

Both vsum and vsum2 are written as procedures which assign
to the components of their associated vector objects. Perhaps
a more natural form of the vector sum function would be invoked as
if it were an infix operator: A := B.vsum3(C). This raises the
general question of writing functions which return vector values
(as distinct from refs to vector objects, as in Simula). To
return a vector value, we need a function which constructs a
vector from the values of the components. We could use the
identifier "vector" for this function without causing any
confusion; e.g.,

```
function vsum3 (value B,C: vector) : vector;
    return vector (B.xval() + C.xval(), B.yval() + C.yval())
end;
```

Such a value constructor is, of course, quite different from the SIMULA operator

```
new vector
```

which returns a ref to a new storage object.

It might appear that we could have written vsum3 without the built-in value constructor by declaring a vector variable within the body of vsum3 and returning the local variable. Unfortunately, such a function requires that write access to x and y be exported from vector. This write access can be in the form of setx and sety procedures which do validity checking. In our example, however, there is no checking to be done, and we obtain:

```
type vector = record exports vsum4, rprod, xval, setx, yval, sety;
    var x,y : real;
    function vsum4 (value B,C : vector) : vector;
        var A : vector;
        A.setx (B.xval() + C.xval());
        A.sety (B.yval() + C.yval());
        return (A)
    end;
    procedure setx (value xx : real);
        x := xx
    end;
```

```
    procedure sety (value yy : real);

        y := yy

    end

end
```

Of course, the procedures setx and sety are unnecessary. We
might just as well have exported x and y directly, since they are
completely unprotected now anyway.

Now consider the unit vectors u and v. The most natural way
to supply these vectors is probably

```
    value u : vector := vector (1.0,0.0);

    value v : vector := vector (0.0,1.0);
```

but again there are a number of problems. These statements
cannot be placed outside the vector type definition unless the
value constructor is exported. From a hiding standpoint at
least, exporting the value constructor is as undesirable as
exporting setx and sety. Placing the statements inside the type
definition, on the other hand, results in unbounded recursion. The
only viable solution seems to be attaching u and v functions to
every vector; e.g.,

```
    function u() : vector;

        return vector (1.0,0.0);

    end;
```

This works, but has the unnatural property that a unit vector can
be accessed only as a component of some other vector; e.g., as
a.u().

The attempt to declare u and v as values raises
another question in connection with value parameters which we
have been ignoring up to this point. We have assumed that a function
reference like B.xval() is valid if B is a value parameter.
It seems clear, however, that in the same situation the procedure
call B.setx(2.5) should be prohibited. Otherwise, B would be a
value parameter in "name" only; e.g., using setx and sety, one
could achieve the semantics of a variable parameter. We believe
one solution to this problem is to prohibit side effects of
functions and to allow references to function but not procedure
components of vector values. This question deserves further
consideration.

Nearly all of our problems in the foregoing examples came
from the restriction that procedures internal to one object of
a type have no knowledge of the internal structure of other objects
of the same type. If we wish to provide the full generality of
Reynolds' "procedural data structures," then this restriction seems
to be inherent since, in principle, objects of the same type might
have different internal representations. For example, there
might be a second declaration of the type vector:

```
type vector = record exports rprod, vsum, xval, yval;
    var r,θ : real;
        .
        .
        .
    procedure rprod (value x : real);
        r := r*x
    end
        .
        .
        .
```

```
function xval() : real;

    return r*cos(θ)

end
        .
        .
        .
end
```

The two kinds of vector objects could coexist, and they would be indistinguishable.

To allow procedures in each kind of vector knowledge of both vector representations would require some additional mechanism, which does not seem worth pursuing. However, if only one definition is allowed for each type, so that all objects of a type are required to have the same representation, then the procedures internal to one object can be allowed access to the internal structure of other objects of the same type, while the internal structure still remains hidden from statements outside the type definition. To do this, we extend our hiding mechanism to allow three posibilities: an attribute may be hidden, exported to the entire program, or shared among all objects of the type. The resulting program is as follows:

```
type vector = record exports vsum, rprod, u,v;

                shares x,y;

var x,y: real;

function vsum (value B : vector): vector;

    var C : vector;

    C.x := x+B.x; C.y := y+B.y;

    return C

end;
```

```
function rprod (value r : real) : vector;

    var C : vector;

    C.x := r*x; C.y := r*y;

    return C

end;

function u() : vector;

    var uu : vector;

    uu.x:= 1; uu.y:= 0;

    return uu

end;
         .
         .
         .
end;
```

Though still SIMULA-like, this approach is really closer in spirit
to Reynolds' "user-defined types" than to "procedural data structures."
Operations are associated with objects rather than types;
however, all objects of a given type have the same representation
and each type divides the program into an inner region (the
procedures internal to the type definition) in which the
representation is known, and an outer region from which the representation is hidden.

In order to contrast the two approaches, we now redevelop the
vectorspace example in a CLU-like language. The type declaration
for vectors and the procedures which operate on vectors are enclosed
in a capsule, which defines a scope within which the attributes
of vector are known. One can declare a vector outside the
capsule, but the vector can be manipulated only by procedures
defined within the capsule. For example:

```
capsule vectorspace exports vector, u,v, vsum,rprod;
type vector = record
    var x,y : real
end;

value u : vector := vecval(1.0,0.0);
value v : vector := vecval(0.0,1.0);
function vsum (value B,C : vector) : vector;
    var A : vector;
    A.x := B.x+C.x; A.y := B.y+C.y;
    return A
end
function rprod (value r : real, value B : vector) : vector;
    var A : vector;
    A.x := r*B.x; A.y := r*B.y;
    return A
end;
function vecval (value xx,yy : real) : vector;
    var A : vector;
    A.x := xx; A.y := yy;
    return A
end
end
```

Several points deserve to be made about this example. First,
the program given here is quite similar to the analogous program
written in CLU. The rep and cvt features of CLU are missing;
however, their function is performed by a type declaration for
vector which is internal to the capsule. Thus, there is no

"representation type" equivalent to vector within the capsule
as there is in CLU. Moreover, obvious language extensions would
allow the capsule vectorspace to contain several internal type
declarations or to contain variables through which the vectorspace procedures could communicate.

Second, creation of the read-only basis vectors u and v, an
awkward problem in the SIMULA-like example, has become straightforward.

Third, a capsule is a purely syntactic device used to
define a scope. Alternatively, we could view a capsule as a
type declaration. Under this interpretation, an object of the capsule type is a record, some of whose fields are themselves types
or procedures. This is essentially the viewpoint taken by the
designers of Euclid, and it has the advantage of treating
capsules and records in a uniform way. The resulting program is
as follows:

```
type vectorspace = record exports vector,u,v, vsum, rprod;
    type vector = record exports x,y;
        var x,y : real;
    end;
    value u : vector := vecval(1.,0.);
    value v : vector := vecval(0.,1.);
    function vsum (value B,C : vector) : vector;
        var A : vector;
        A.x := B.x+C.x;
        A.y := B.y+C.y;
        return(A)
    end;
```

```
function rprod (value r : real, value B : vector) : vector;
    var A : vector;
    A.x := r*B.x; A.y := r*B.y;
    return (A)
end;
function vecval (value xx,yy : real) : vector;
    var A : vector;
    A.x := xx; A.y := yy;
    return (A)
  end
end
```

We have not included any default exporting conventions in
our example language; i.e., the components of a record are not
exported automatically with the record name, as they are in
Euclid. Thus, x and y are not accessible from outside vectorspace, even though the type name "vector" has been exported.

Although this new program differs very little from the previous
one, it represents a considerable shift in philosophy back
toward SIMULA, since operators are again associated with objects
rather then with types. The difference between this example and
the first one is that now the procedures which operate on vectors
are associated with a vectorspace object rather than with a
vector. To use vectors, we must first instantiate a vectorspace, then instantiate vectors within it. In fact, we can
instantiate several different vectorspace objects at once:

<u>var</u> VS_1, VS_2: vectorspace;

<u>var</u> A_1,B_1: VS_1.vector;

<u>var</u> A_2,B_2: VS_2.vector;

We feel that there are compelling reasons for treating VS_1.vector and VS_2.vector as distinct variable types. By the semantic characterizations of variable types and of type equivalence given in Section 2, one cannot decide these properties without knowledge of the bindings of free identifiers referred to in the type definitions. The definition of vector is internal to vectorspace and hidden from the abstract program; hence the abstract program should make no assumptions concerning equivalence of vector types.

Thus, the above program segment creates two indistinguishable but separate vectorspaces, VS_1 and VS_2, and two vector variables belonging to each vectorspace. Statements such as $A_1 := A_2$, $A_1 := VS_2.vsum(A_2,B_2)$, or $A_1 := VS_1.vsum(B_1,B_2)$ are considered to have type errors.

One final remark about the vectorspace example: there is nothing to prevent our moving the definitions of vsum and rprod inside the defintion of vector, yielding a program which is virtually identical to our final SIMULA-like example. The use of internal type definitions appears to combine the virtues of the SIMULA-like and CLU-like approaches, provided all objects of a particular type are required to have the same representation.

4. Polymorphic constructs and generic procedures

Perhaps one of the most overworked, but least understood, words in language design and description (after "type") is "generic," as in "generic procedures." The dictionary meaning of generic is "applied to a large group or class." When applied to programming languages, this usually means that a generic procedure or operator is one that can be applied to different classes of arguments. There are two basic ways such a facility can be provided; an example will serve to show the difference between the two approaches.

Consider the program fragment

<pre>
        <u>var</u> u,v: integer;
        <u>var</u> x,y: real;
          u: = v;
          x: = y
</pre>

In both assignments, the same syntactic form (:=) is used, and the selection of the appropriate semantic interpretation of the symbol for assignment is determined from context. Note, however, that the meanings of <u>both</u> integer and real assignment are known; the only question is which of the set of possible interpretations to choose. This sort of mechanism (similar to the PL/I "generic" facility), we will call <u>syntactic overloading</u>.

Now, the reason we know the meaning of integer and real assignment is that the surrounding environment provides a meaning for these type identifiers. Just as we previously described the possibility of abstracting constructs (particularly types) with

respect to values, so we can similarly entertain the possibility
of abstracting a construct with respect to a type identifier.
For example, we can define a type abstracted (or "polymorphic")
swap procedure as follows:

```
procedure Swap(T: type, var p,q: T);
    var x: T;
    begin
        x: = p;
        p: = q;
        q: = x
    end;
```

Unlike our earlier example, inside the body of Swap the meanings
of the assignments are not known since the type T is
not bound in the enclosing environment. This sort of mechanism,
which is basically a restrictive form of dynamic typing (as we
defined this term in Section 2), we will call type abstraction.

The addition of some kind of mechanism to allow syntactic
overloading seems to be a rather minor bit of syntactic sugaring,
because we are simply providing a mechanism for referring to
several operators using the same symbol. Indeed, throughout this
paper we have consistently overloaded the assignment operator
without any particular concern. Thus, we will focus our attention
instead on the inclusion of type abstraction, which seems to raise
some more basic semantic issues.

If we wish to leave some basic operations inside a procedure
(or type) definition unspecified at the time of declaration of the
procedure, then we can either:

1. leave certain types unspecified (or perhaps partially
   specified), thus making it impossible to determine the
   meanings of operators provided by a type. Then, for each
   call, we infer the missing type information from the forms
   of the arguments and supply the missing interpretations.

2. explicitly abstract the construct with respect to a type
   and then supply a type argument as part of each call. For
   example, our Swap procedure described above was written
   in this form, and would be called as

   Swap(integer, x,y)

   (assuming x and y are integer variables).

Our example of Swap provides a compelling reason for the
selection of the second alternative. In the body of Swap, the declaration of the variable x cannot be independent of the type associated
with the parameters. Thus, if we leave the type of the parameters
p and q unspecified, we must also leave the type of x unspecified
and deduce the types of all three from each call of Swap. But
then, why can't we leave all declarations untyped and leave all the
deductions about the necessary types of all variables to the
compiler? Obviously, if we believe in the error detection advantages of types, this approach must be discarded.

An intermediate approach to our two proposed alternatives
is found in [Gries and Gehani 1976]. There they suggest that
types should be allowed as parameters, but not as arguments. Thus,
we would write Swap as above, but instead of calling Swap by

$$\text{Swap}(\underline{\text{integer}}, x, y)$$

we could simply use

$$\text{Swap}(x, y).$$

The compiler would then have the responsibility to decide the types required for the call to be correct.

The approach we are currently favoring simply allows type abstraction and application. Thus, we would expect to call Swap using

$$\text{Swap}(\underline{\text{integer}}, x, y)$$

or

$$\text{Swap}(\text{table}(10, 20), t_1, t_2)$$

(using our earlier definition of the table data type). Note that our desire to state in exact semantic terms what we mean by a type pays ample dividends. First, we know what a type "means," so its use as an argument to a procedure call is not as strange as it first seems. A type supplied as an argument simply makes available the operators (e.g., declaration and assignment) defined by the type.

Moreover, we even have the first glimmer of hope for knowing how to compile a polymorphic procedure. If types make available a set of basic operators, then inside a procedure abstracted with respect to a type T, we simply cannot access the T operators directly; instead, we must access them indirectly for each type argument supplied. But this can be implemented by viewing a type parameter as being a transfer vector with one element for each basic operation. Then type application is simply initializing

the vector with the appropriate values to access the operations
of the type argument. And the question of whether the compiler
should generate a new version of the procedure for each different
argument list supplied becomes a question of code optimization, as
it naturally should be.

Although we have not fully developed all the details of this
approach to polymorphic procedures, we have reason to believe that
the problems involved, including the question of type-checking,
are manageable. Certainly the most thought provoking aspect is
what effect polymorphic constructs have on type-checking. Using
our definitions from Section 2, we can at least make the following
basic observations.

If we assume that the operations provided by types are strongly
typed (i.e., they check the types of their arguments), then we
should be able to guarantee strong typing in the language by a
simple inductive argument on the complexity of the structure
of a program. The most interesting case, however, is to
guarantee protective typing when only constant types are allowed
as arguments. Since protective typing makes the production of
"type error" a property of programs rather than operations, it
is clear that the body of the polymorphic procedure (or type)
definition will need to be checked with each set of arguments
supplied in calls. But this does not seem to be unfamiliar
ground; there are just a number of details to be worked out.

5. Conclusion

We began this research with the goal of defining an "encapsulated data type mechanism." However, our interest in also
providing generic procedures and the complexity of existing encapsulated type facilities soon led us to separate the problem into
two orthogonal subproblems:

1. What does it mean to define a new type? Even more simply
   put, what does type mean? How do type definitions and
   programs using them interact and how should type abstraction
   be handled?

2. Is encapsulation simply a matter of using the naturally
   occurring scope boundaries of a language to "hide
   information?" If so, how can one best use the new scope
   provided by a type definition to the best advantage? What
   do we mean by hiding?

This paper describes our preliminary views on both of these
questions. While we have not fully worked out all of the details,
we are encouraged by our initial progress for the following
reasons:

1. We seem to have developed a sufficient understanding of
   what type means to be able to make precise statements
   about the type-checking in any language we eventually
   design. Our goal is <u>to prove rigorously</u> that we have
   defined a strongly (or protectively) typed language
   when we finish.

2. Our careful examination of type has greatly affected our view of generic and polymorphic procedures. We are now convinced that the success of our language design can be measured in part by the degree to which polymorphic constructs become a natural extension of our basic principles. In particular, our proof of correctness of our type-checking mechanism should include the possibility of type abstraction.

3. Our approach to encapsulation has been to explore how we could naturally use the scope boundaries provided by type definitions to hide information. By restricting ourselves to mechanisms which only allow or disallow names to be known across scope boundaries, we may not be able to do everything one could imagine of an encapsulated type facility. However, we do expect to produce a mechanism with a simple implementation, simple semantics, and general ease of use for most problems.

We are beginning to put the pieces together to produce a complete design and implementation of a language incorporating the ideas described above.

213

REFERENCES

[Dahl et al. 1968]

Dahl, O.-J., K. Nygaard and B. Myhrhaug, The Simula 67 Common Base Language, Norwegian Computing Center, Oslo, Technical Report.

[Dahl, Dijkstra and Hoare 1972]

Dahl, O.-J., E.W. Dijkstra and C.A.R. Hoare, Structured Programming, Academic Press, 1972.

[Fisher 1976]

Fisher, David, Department of Defense Requirements for High Order Computer Programming Languages ("TINMAN"), June 1976.

[Gannon and Horning 1975]

Gannon, J.D. and J.J. Horning, "The Impact of Language Design on the Production of Reliable Software", Proc. International Conference on Reliable Software, Los Angeles, April 1975, pp. 10-22.

[Gries and Gehani 1975]

Gries, David and Narain Gehani, "Some Ideas on Data Types in High Level Languages", Department of Computer Science, Cornell University, TR 75-244.

[Guttag 1975]

Guttag, J.V., The Specification and Application to Programming of Abstract Data Types, Technical Report CSRG-59, Computer Systems Research Group, Toronto, 1975.

[Jensen and Wirth 1975]

Jensen, Kathleen and Niklaus Wirth, PASCAL User Manual and Report, Springer-Verlag, 1975.

[Koster 1976]

Koster, Cornelis H.A., "Visibility and Types" Proc. of Conference on Data: Abstraction, Definition and Structure, SIGPLAN Notices, Volume 8, Number 2 (Special Issue), 1976, pp. 179-190.

[Lampson et al. 1976]

>   Lampson, B.W., J.J. Horning, R.L. London, J.G. Mitchell, and G.S. Popek, Euclid Report (draft), private communication, 1976.

[Ledgard 1972]

>   Ledgard, Henry F., "A Model for Type Checking — with an Application to Algol 60", Comm. ACM, Volume 15, Number 11 (November 1972), pp. 956-966.

[Liskov and Zilles 1974]

>   Liskov, Barbara and Steven Zilles, "Programming with Abstract Data Types", Computation Structures Memo 99, Project MAC, M.I.T., March 1974.

[Liskov 1976]

>   Liskov, Barbara H., "An Introduction to CLU", Computation Structures Group Memo 136, Laboratory for Computer Science, M.I.T., February 1976.

[Morris 1973]

>   Morris, James H., Jr., "Protection in Programming Languages", Comm. ACM, Volume 16, Number 1 (January 1973), pp. 15-21.

[Richards 1969]

>   Richards, M., "BCPL: A Tool for Compiler and System Writing", Proceedings of the SJCC, Volume 34, 1969, pp. 557-566.

[Reynolds 1975]

>   Reynolds, John C., "User Defined Types and Procedural Data Structures as Complementary Approaches to Data Abstraction", Conference on New Directions in Algorithmic Languages, IFIP Working Group 2.1, Munich, August 1975.

[Wirth 1975]

>   Wirth, Niklaus, "An Assessment of the Programming Language PASCAL", Proc. International Conference on Reliable Software, Los Angeles, April 1975, pp. 23-30.

[Wulf et al. 1971]

>   Wulf, W.A., D.B. Russell and A.N. Habermann, "BLISS: A Language for Systems Programming", Comm. ACM, Volume 14, Number 12 (December 1971), pp. 780-790.

Run-time Checking of Data Access in Pascal-like Languages

Charles N. Fischer and Richard J. LeBlanc
Computer Sciences Department
University of Wisconsin
Madison, Wisconsin

I. Introduction

The techniques for run-time checking discussed in this paper
were developed in the course of designing a PASCAL compiler for
the UNIVAC 1110. The design of these techniques follows three
basic principles:

(1) Any existing language restriction should be checkable,
    either during compilation or at run-time.

(2) Run-time checks should be efficient, limited to a few
    in-line instructions, if possible.

(3) If a particular language feature requires run-time
    checking, only usage of this feature should bear the extra
    overhead.

Two features of PASCAL that require run-time checking will be
considered: discriminated union (DU) types (records with
variants) and pointer types. Reference to a field in an object
of a discriminated union type requires a check of the tag field
to verify that the referenced field is part of the currently
active variant. Use of a pointer requires a check that the
pointer references a correctly allocated object from the dynamic

storage pool (heap) and that the object has not been freed since the pointer was set (PASCAL allows explicit heap deallocation).

The existence of complete checking of all language requirements is crucial to the development of reliable software as economically as possible. Advanced language features that aid in program construction tend to do so by restricting generality. Their usefulness is clearly impared if such restrictions are not enforced at compile-time or run-time. The enforcement of language restrictions is a valuable debugging aid, allowing the system to explicitly point out errors that otherwise might only be detected as hardware interrupts or incorrect results. Indeed, it might well be suggested that such run-time checking ought to be considered an integral part of a language, disabled only in special cases (or by compiler optimization).

The features of PASCAL requiring the run-time checks discussed in this paper would be part of a language conforming to the specifications found in the Tinman document. The language ultimately designed must either require such run-time checks as part of its implementation or include sufficient restrictions to eliminate their necessity.

Basic Checking

The discriminated union types of PASCAL bear some resemblance
to features found in ALGOL 68 (type unions) and SIMULA 67
(classes), but have important differences worth noting here.
The discriminated union type is a single type that includes a
tag field which may be dynamically changed, thus altering the
run-time accessibility of some (or all) of the record's other
fields. The type union concept in ALGOL 68 allows a given
variable to take on values of disjoint types at different times
during its existence. The use of prefixed classes in SIMULA 67
allows the creation of objects that look much like PASCAL's
variant records, but their interpretation is fixed when they are
allocated and may not be changed dynamically.

The variants of a discriminated union are typically allocated
such that they overlay one another (to do otherwise would
eliminate much of the utility of this feature). The language
specifications require that only fields of the variant indicated
as currently active by the value of the tag field may be
referenced. If each variant of the union has a single label (as
is usually the case) a simple run-time check is possible - the
tag value is compared with the variant label of the field
referenced before access is allowed. Note that this check is of
no greater complexity than a subscript check and thus satisifies
principle (2).

PASCAL allows variants to have multiple labels, a feature which requires a more complex check. A sequence number field can be stored along with the tag field in this case. Whenever the tag field is set, the index of the newly active variant (if any) to which the tag corresponds is computed and stored. Reference checks then use this sequence number field just as the tag field is used in the single label case. This solution satisfies principle (3) - only users of this feature bear its extra cost.

As previously discussed, determination of the legitimacy of a pointer requires verification that it references a correctly allocated object and that this object has not been freed since the pointer was set. In PASCAL, pointers may only refer to dynamically allocated objects created explicitly by the procedure NEW. Thus dangling pointers due to scope problems do not exist. However, storage is reclaimed in the dynamic allocation pool by way of deallocation explicitly specified by the user. Such a process can obviously lead to dangling pointers. Note that the existence of discriminated union types prevents an implementation of implicit garbage collection (such as the mechanism in SIMULA 67). A pointer set while one variant is active is still a legitimate pointer when the tag is changed, though it may not be referenced as such. In combination with the fact that variants are overlayed, discriminated unions are another source of illegitimate pointers, allowing a field to be initialized as an integer, for instance, under one variant and interpreted as a pointer under another. There is also the general problem of using uninitialized pointers, regardless of whether they are fields of variants.

The most desirable checking mechanism is one that does not require the subdivision of the heap into subspaces for individual types (termed classes in the first definition of PASCAL [5], but since eliminated). Such a restrictive arrangement would include the possibility of program termination due to only one subspace being exhausted when other storage is still available. The solution chosen was to represent a pointer as a pair (key, address) and heading each allocation from the heap with a lock field. When a pointer is used, the key value must agree with the lock field of the object referenced. This is again a very efficient run-time test. It does not provide absolute security since the key field is simply a bit pattern that could be fabricated by a malicious user. This relative security is considered acceptable due to the very low probability of the fabrication being accidental.

III. Generation of Run-Time Checks

There is a significant difference between the kind of checking discussed thus far and the more familiar process of subscript checking. Consider the PASCAL statement

    P->.A[F(I)] := G(J)

where A is a field of a discriminated union. A pointer check and a tag check as well as a subscript check are required. A simple-minded generation scheme (especially in a one-pass compiler) would generate these checks to be performed before the evaluation of F(I) and G(J) (i.e., a simple left-to-right generation order). However, either function, as a side effect, could invalidate one of the checks by either deallocating the object referenced by P or changing the tag to make A inaccessible. Subscript checks merely require that a value be in a range, a check unaffected by potential side effects of expression evaluation. Pointer and tag checks test the validity of a reference, something that can change quite abruptly in PASCAL.

In the previous example, the generated checks must be executed just before the object referenced is to be used. This is done by buffering (at the semantic routine level) the qualification of a variable. These semantic routines are not executed until an actual reference to the variable is required, ensuring that side effects occur before the checks are executed.

The buffering scheme is such that F(I) would be evaluated as the subscript to A and its value saved until after evaluation of G(J), for use in generating a subscript test when the qualification is computed. Had the subscript expression been a simple variable, for instance I, its value would not have been automatically protected during evaluation of G(J). Under a requirement of strict left-to-right evaluation, the value of I would have to be copied into a temporary until its use in the qualification of the left hand side of the assignment.

The buffering scheme is a useful solution to more general problems when objects can vary in structure as side effects of function evaluation. For instance, if PASCAL included flex arrays (whose bounds can change dynamically) the generation of a subscript test would move into the same class as pointer and tag checks, since the range against which the value was to be tested could vary with time. The buffering mechanism handles this with no modification since in the given example, the subscript test is generated immediately before the indexing and assignment operations are performed.

IV. Checking "By-reference" Procedure Parameters

When a heap object or a field of a DU is used as an actual parameter, verification that it is accessible may be accomplished by the same run-time checking mechanisms discussed above. If the object is to be a "by-reference" parameter (a VAR parameter in PASCAL terminology), there exists the additional problem of verifying that the object remains accessible during execution of the procedure. This is essential if correctness of access is to be guaranteed. A number of ways of dealing with this problem present themselves.

The simplest solution is simply to disallow the use of heap objects or fields of DU's as "by-reference" actual parameters. Such a solution is obviously quite unsatisfactory, if only because these data objects are often an integral part of an algorithm (as is the case in our Pascal compiler). Further, if these objects represent arrays or records, no viable alternative to allowing their use as "by-reference" parameters exists - "by value" parameters require a (potentially expensive) copy operation and functions may only return scalar objects.

A second potential solution is to require the use of "thunks" to perform the required checks whenever an actual parameter (passed by reference) is accessed. This, however, violates principle (3) and must be rejected.

A third possibility (unfortunately, the one usually adopted by Pascal compilers) is simply to ignore the problem at run-time and issue a suitable language restriction. This, of course, violates principle (1).

The solution presented below is an attractive one in that it satisfies the basic principles as well as allowing (as will be shown later) significant optimizations in run-time checking and heap allocation.

A heap object, passed by reference, can be made inaccessible only if a DISPOSE operation is done. It is then natural to require that the DISPOSE routine bear the overhead of checking whether an object being freed is in use as a by-reference parameter. This can easily be done as follows. When a heap object is to be passed as a by-reference parameter, its address is pushed onto a stack accessible to the DISPOSE routine. Upon return from the procedure, the address is popped. All dispose operations check the addresses on this stack before proceeding. This method is clearly efficient and entails no overhead for non-heap (i.e., stack) objects. Further, it allows us to access by-reference heap objects directly (via their run-time address).

A field of a DU can be made inaccessible by assigning a new value to its tag. Thus an efficient method of preventing assignment to a tag while a field in one of its variants is in use as a by-reference parameter is necessary. This can be done by associating with every data object an access structure. This access structure is disjoint from the data object (to allow assignment of data values without transmitting access information). Each tag field of an object maps to a single bit in the access structure. This bit indicates whether or not the corresponding tag may be assigned to. All other components of an object map to null; an object containing no DU's (and thus no tags) would have a null access structure. The following DU, for example, would require an access structure of two bits:

```
R:RECORD CASE I:0..1 OF
      0: (J: RECORD CASE K: BOOLEAN OF
              TRUE: (L:REAL);
              FALSE: (M:CHAR) END);
      1: (P: REAL)
   END;
```

One bit would correspond to tag I and the other to tag K (when tag I=0). When a field of a DU is to be passed as a by-reference parameter, the usual check that the tag values are correctly set is executed first. The access structure bits corresponding to the tags are then set to "on", indicating that the tag values cannot be changed. The previous values of the bits are saved on a stack and restored upon return from the procedure call. When an assignment to a tag occurs, it is preceded by a check that the corresponding access structure bit is "off" (this check is very fast and compact). If it is "on", the assignment is unsafe as it could make a by-reference parameter inaccessable. Since assignments to tags must be checked (but of course not ordinary assignments), it is not possible to allow tags to be passed as by reference parameters. This, however, is a minor restriction as tags are always scalars and can, if necessary, be updated via function calls. When an entire DU is assigned to, a check must verify that none of the access structure bits corresponding to its tags are "on" (again this is a simple check since the number of such bits is constant and they are adjacent in the access structure). Note that no such check is needed for ordinary records. Further, observe that a DU can be passed as a by-reference parameter, even if some of its tag fields are considered "locked" (i.e., have access structure bits on). Two run time addresses are passed in such a case; one representing the DU itself, the other representing the access structure corresponding to the DU. In the procedure, this second address is used to check assignments to tag fields, exactly as outlined above.

On balance, we consider the scheme presented above to be a very attractive one. All by-reference parameters are passed in the simplest possible way (via a run-time address). Only heap objects and fields of DU's require any extra checking and such checking is quite efficient. Indeed, as shall be shown in the next section, the above techniques can be employed to significantly reduce the amount of run-time checking required by pointers and DU's.

V. Optimization of Run-time Checks

Any compiler which does thorough run-time checking must be prepared to optimize such checking wherever possible. Some checks, such as subscript and subrange tests are amenable to standard optimization techniques [3], although use of DU's can complicate matters. (A subrange variable occurring in a DU, for example, usually cannot be guaranteed, on a global basis, to contain a value within the specified range.) Careful use of subrange variables can allow many subscript checks to be folded, often at a significant gain. Further savings can be realized by using the WITH statement to optimize both pointer and DU tag checks.

The original purpose of the WITH statement was to serve as a syntatic convenience. The statement has the general form "WITH <rec> DO <statement>" where <rec> represents any record (including, of course, DU's). The WITH opens the scope of the WITH record (<rec>) to all identifiers occurring in <statement>. That is, if possible, an identifier is interpreted as a field of the WITH record, rather than as a variable name. Obviously this relieves the user of the necessity of inserting explicit qualification of fields within the scope of the WITH. Since the address of the WITH record is calculated only once (when the WITH is opened), some optimization is possible. However, even greater savings are possible if run-time checks associated with the WITH record can be optimized. If the WITH record is contained in a heap object (i.e., referenced through a pointer) or is a field of a DU then the usual run-time checks are needed when the WITH statement is entered. Just as in the case of by-reference parameters, it must be guaranteed that the WITH record remains accessible during execution of the WITH statement. The obvious solution is to use the same techniques as in the "by-reference" case. Heap addresses are saved and DU tags are "locked" when the WITH is entered; the addresses are freed and tags "unlocked" when the WITH is exited. Thus necessary tests are performed only once, when the WITH is entered, and not every time a field within the WITH is referenced. In practice such savings can be quite substantial.

It may be observed that even more optimization might be possible if one could specify not only records but also particular variants of a DU in a WITH. Fortunately, this "extension" can be simulated by enclosing all fields of a given variant in a dummy record (which is then used as a With record).

VI. Optimization of Heap Allocation

In PASCAL, any data type can be allocated from the heap. The most commonly allocated data types are usually records and DU's. In the case of DU's, it is often known at the time of allocation that only one particular variant will be used. It is then possible to effect substantial savings in space by only allocating enough space to accommodate the variant in question. If such a strategy is used, however, it is essential that the tag field never be changed (otherwise access outside of the allocation is possible). The access structure mechanism of section IV provides an excellent means of limiting access in such cases. When an allocation of a heap object with a fixed tag is requested, the tag field is set and the corresponding access structure bit is turned permanently on. Thereafter, the normal run-time checking mechanisms guarantee the integrity and safety of all references to the object.

VII. Conclusions

Until it becomes possible to rigorously prove the correctness of programs of substantial size, careful and thorough run-time checking will play an essential role in the development and maintenance of reliable software. We believe that typed pointers and discriminated unions are fundamental data abstractions which are of great use in a wide variety of programming languages and programming endeavors. It then follows that efficient, thorough and optimizable checks which monitor them at run-time are an essential adjunct to their use. Certainly our experience with PASCAL has convinced us of their utility. Although run-time checks are often held in disrepute, we should not ask ourselves, "Can I afford them?" but rather "Can I afford to be without them?".

[1] Dahl, Ole-Johan, Bjorn Myhrhhang amd Kristen Nygaard, "SIMULA 67 Common Base Language", Norwegian Computing Center, Oslo, Norway (1970).

[2] Jensen, Kathleen and Niklaus Wirth, PASCAL User Manual and Report, 2nd Ed. Springer-Verlag, Berlin (1976).

[3] Kildall, G.A., "A Unified Approach to Global Program Optimization", Conf. Record, ACM Symp. on Principles of Programming Languages. Boston, Mass, 1973. pp. 194-206.

[4] Van Wijngaarden, A. (ed), "Revised Report on the Algorithmic Language ALGOL 68", Acta Informatica, 5 (1975).

[5] Wirth, Niklaus, "The Programming Language PASCAL", Acta Informatica, 1, p. 35-63 (1971).

[6] Wirth, Niklaus, "An Assesment of the Programming Language PASCAL", Proceedings of the International Conference on Reliable Software, 21-23 April 1975, p. 23-30.

A Language Design for Structured Concurrency[*]

Jack B. Dennis
Laboratory for Computer Science
Massachusetts Institute of Technology
Cambridge, Massachusetts 02139

Introduction

Concurrency is an important aspect of all large scale computer applications -- either for the sake of making efficient use of the physical resources of a computer system, or as an inherent property of the application. A programming language, if it is to provide a basis for the construction of reliable software to meet a precise specification of function, must have un-ambiguous semantics and must support all aspects of the computations to be represented -- including concurrency.

At present, there is no generally accepted proposal for incorporating support for concurrency in high-level programming languages. Indeed, the dif-ficulties of adding such support to existing practical languages are formidable. In this note we consider a limited context for the design of a programming lan-guage that includes support for representing concurrency of computation. The context is one that appears to be of great significance in forthcoming years: interconnected microcomputers. The language LSC (Language for Structured Con-currency) is formulated to include a kind of program unit called a __system__ which is an interconnection of simpler units by links over which data values are passed. Thus, the units comprising a system may be readily assigned to different microcomputers to distribute processing activities over system com-ponents in a balanced way.

The form of multi-microcomputer system we envision as supporting execution of programs written in LSC is shown in Fig. 1. The microcomputers are inter-connected by a message routing network, and each microcomputer is equipped with

[*] This research was supported by the National Science Foundation under grant DCR75-04060.

Microcomputers

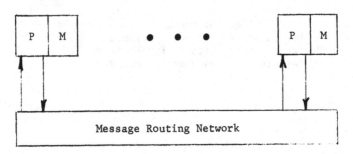

Figure 1. Suggested structure for multi-microcomputer systems.

the capability of sending and receiving messages (packets) to/from any other microcomputer over the network. We suppose that the protocol of packet transmission is designed to match the requirements of passing values over the links between units of a system expressed in LSC.

The Language

In LSC, each unit of program text has at least one input port and at least one output port. Program units may be combined to form a larger unit by connecting output ports to input ports.

The language is strictly value-oriented; that is:

1. The members of a data type are mathematical values and not subject to change.

2. Inputs and outputs of program units are strictly distinguished.

The meaning of a program in LSC can be understood in terms of just three basic mechanisms (in addition to primitive operations on the data types of the language):

1. Transmission of data values from one unit to another.

2. Definition of bindings of identifiers to values.

3. Functional application.

We discuss the general structure of the three kinds of program units in LSC, and give some examples of LSC programs.

Each program unit written in LSC has the same form of interface specification:

⟨unit name⟩: ⟨keyword⟩(⟨arg-list⟩⟨separator⟩⟨res-list⟩)

There are three types of program units:

1. system: ⟨keyword⟩ ::= <u>system</u>
              ⟨separator⟩ ::= <u>sends</u>

2. procedure: ⟨keyword⟩ ::= <u>procedure</u>|<u>recproc</u>
              ⟨separator⟩ ::= <u>returns</u>

3. module: ⟨keyword⟩ ::= <u>module</u>|<u>recmod</u>
              ⟨separator⟩ ::= <u>yields</u>

A unit that is a procedure or module may be indicated as recursive, in which case use of the ⟨unit-name⟩ inside the unit refers to the unit itself.

Systems

A program unit that is a system is simply an interconnection of simpler units which may be systems or procedures or modules. Each connection link is labelled by an identifier and the connection pattern is described by statements such as

A(x1, x2) <u>defines</u> (y1, y2)

which means that program unit A has two input and two output ports; that it receives input values from links x1 and x2; and that it sends values to links y1 and y2. Each link may be mentioned many times as the source of data values, but must be mentioned exactly once as a destination for data values. A statement

x := 0

means that in the initial condition of the program, link x presents the value 0 to the associated input port.

Example: Let us write in LSC a system that implements a second order digital filter; given the sequence of input values x_0, x_1, ..., the sequence of output values y_0, y_1, ..., is to be computed according to the recursive formula

$$y_t = x_t + k_0(y_{t-1} + k_1 y_{t-2}), \quad t = 0, 1, \ldots$$

where

$$y_{-1} = y_{-2} = 0$$

Figure 2 shows a suitable LSC system drawn as an interconnection of simpler program units. The textual form of this system is:

```
Filter: system(x: real sends y: real);

    p0: real := 0;
    p1: real := 0;
    s: real;

    Add(x, p1) defines s;
    Add(s, p0) defines y;
    Mult(y, k0) defines p0;
    Mult(p0, k1) defines p1;

end Filter;
```

The above program Filter will not deadlock. However, there is no guarantee that program units that are or contain LSC systems are free of dead-

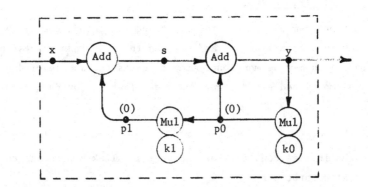

Figure 2. The second order filter as an LSC system.

lock. The translator must check that constraints are met that ensure "liveness." This check is easy if the nesting of systems is only one or two levels, but requires inspecting the internal structure of any component units that are LSC systems. In contrast, LSC procedures and modules are inherently free of any possibility of deadlock (except, of course, waiting for input).

Procedures

Procedures in LSC are conventional, but are restricted to eliminate side effects. They have the property that (unless they loop indefinitely or reach an error condition) they produce one value at each output port each time they have received one value at each input port. We prefer to use recursion rather than iteration to express repeated evaluation of program fragments for ease of understanding. The translator can determine when a stack of activation records is not required for correct execution.

A procedure may contain invocations of procedures (including itself), but may not contain invocations of program units that are systems or modules.

Example: In LSC the factorial function would be written as follows:

fact: recproc (n: integer returns f: integer);

f = if n = 0 then 1
                else n x fact(n - 1);

end fact;

Modules

In an LSC program unit that is a module, an input or output port is viewed from inside the module as passing a single value of the data type stream of t, where t is the data type associated with the port when viewed from outside the module. The body of a module is written in terms of four basic operations on streams (of type stream of t):

1. empty: stream of t ──→ boolean
        empty(s) tests if s is the empty stream [ ].

2. first: stream of t ──→ t

3. rest: <u>stream</u> <u>of</u> t ⟶ <u>stream</u> <u>of</u> t

>   <u>first</u>(s) yields the first element of s
>
>   rest(s) yields the stream containing all but the
>   first element of s.

4. <u>cons</u>: t × <u>stream</u> <u>of</u> t ⟶ <u>stream</u> <u>of</u> t

>   <u>cons</u>(x, s) forms a stream by adding a new first element x
>   to the stream s.

We have that if <u>empty</u>(s) = <u>false</u> then

>   s = <u>cons</u>(<u>first</u>(s), <u>rest</u>(s))

Using the above stream operations, modules may be written which produce fewer or more values at their output ports than they have received at their input ports. Thus modules are more expressive than procedures. Yet such modules are guaranteed to be determinate in their operation; they define functional dependencies of their sequences of output values upon the sequences of input values. By the theory of interconnected systems [Patil, Kahn], any system built by connecting procedures, modules, and similarly constructed subsystems will be determinate in the same sense.

> Example: The following LSC module illustrates the use of stream operations to describe determinate processing of a sequence of integer values. The sequence of output values contains all members of the sequence of input values that are not evenly divisible by three.

```
select: recmod (x: integer yields y: integer);

          if empty(x) then y = [   ]
                      else

      begin
          f, r = first(x), rest(x);
          y = if f ÷ 3 = 0
                   then select(r)
                   else cons(f, select(r));
      end

end select;
```

Note that an LSC module should be regarded more as a specification of what task is to be performed rather than a prescription of how the task should be implemented. Note also that an implementation must be capable of transmitting output values without waiting until all input values have been received; thus an LSC module implementation has a behavior related to the behavior of a system of coroutines.

Nondeterminate Programs

It appears that the operation of merging two streams by nondeterminately interleaving their values should be seriously considered as a high level construct for expressing nondeterminate computations. Hence, we include in LSC the operation

$$\text{merge}: \underline{\text{stream}} \ \underline{\text{of}} \ t \ \times \ \underline{\text{stream}} \ \underline{\text{of}} \ t \longrightarrow \mathcal{P}(\underline{\text{stream}} \ \underline{\text{of}} \ t)$$

The value of merge(s1, s2) is any stream s formed by choosing successive elements of s1 and s2. Our final example illustrates the use of the merge operation in the implementation of a basic problem of nondeterminate computation: an abstraction of the airline seat reservation problem.

> Example: The system shown in Fig. 3 handles the booking of seats on one flight of an airline. Requests arrive at ports 1 and 2 from two agents and responses are sent to the two agents at ports 3 and 4, respectively. A request may be an inquiry about the status of booking (INFO), or a request that so many seats be reserved (RES), or cancelled (CAN). The response is the number of booked and available seats (INFO), or a boolean value indicating success or failure (RES, CAN). The flight is assumed to have 100 seats.
>
> The function of the Input subsystem is to tag each request with its origin and to merge requests from both sources into one stream for processing by Main. The tagged responses generated by Main are separated by Output according to agent, and directed to the appropriate output port.
>
> The program unit Main is another example of an LSC module whose function is expressed by means of the recursive definition of a function on streams. The Process module has two arguments: the stream of

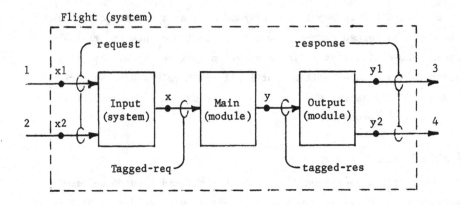

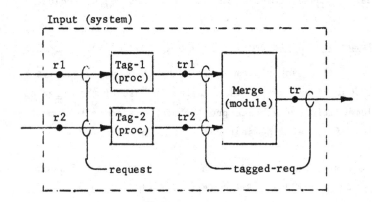

Figure 3. The Flight program as an LSC system.

requests to be processed, and the state of booking for the flight. It specifies that the job to be done is to act on the first request to de-determine the response and the new state of booking, and append this response to the response stream that results from processing the re-mainder of the input in the new state. The texts in LSC of the sys-tems, modules and procedures making up the Flight system are presented below:

```
Flight:  system(x1, x2: request sends y1, y2: response);

    request = oneof[INFO: null,
                    RES, CAN: integer];
    response = oneof[INFO: [booked, available: integer],
                    RES, CAN: boolean];
    tagged-req = [req: request, tag: integer];
    tagged-res = [res: response, tag: integer];
    x: tagged-req; y: tagged-res;
    input(x1, x2) defines x;
    Main(x) defines y;
    Output(y) defines (y1, y2);
end Flight;


Input: system(r1, r2: request sends tr: tagged-req);

    tr1, tr2: tagged-request;
    Tag-1(r1) defines tr1;
    Tag-2(r2) defines tr2;
    Merge(tr1, tr2) defines tr;
end Input;


Tag-1: procedure(r: request returns tr: tagged-req);

    tr = [req: r, tag: 1];
end Tag-1;


Tag-2: procedure(r: request returns tr: tagged-req);

    tr = [req: r, tag: 2];
end Tag-2;


Merge: module(in1, in2: stream of tagged-req
        yields out: stream of tagged-req);

    out = merge(in1, in2);
end Merge;
```

```
Main: module (in: stream of tagged-req
      yields out: stream of tagged-res);

    Process: recmod(in: stream of tagged req, booked: integer
            yields out: stream of tagged-res);
        if empty (in) then out = [   ]
                        else
        begin
            x,y = first(in), rest(in);
            rq = x.req; tg = x.tag;
            rs, new = tagcase rq of
                INFO: ([booked: booked, available: 100 - booked], booked);
                RES: if booked + rq ≤ 100
                        then (true, booked + rq)
                        else (false, booked);
                CAN: if booked - rq ≥ 0
                        then (true, booked - rq)
                        else (false, booked);
                endcase;
            out = cons([res: rs, tag: tg], Process(y, new));
        end;
    end Process;
out = Process(in, 0);
end Main;
```

```
Output: recmod(in: stream of tagged-res
         yields out1, out2: stream of response);

    if empty(in) then out1 = out2 = [  ]
                      else
    begin
        x,y = first(in), rest(in);
        y1, y2 = Output(y);
        out1, out2 = case x.tag of
            1: (cons(x.res, y1), y2);
            2: (y1, cons(x.res, y2));
            endcase;
    end
end Output;
```

References

Brinch-Hansen, P. The programming language concurrent Pascal.
IEEE Trans. on Software Engineering 1, 2 (1975).

Kahn, G. The semantics of a simple language for parallel programming.
Proceedings of the IFIP Congress, 1974.

Patil, S. S. Closure properties of interconnections of determinate systems.
Record of the Project MAC Conference on Concurrent Systems and Parallel Computation, ACM, New York 1970, 107-116.

Weng, K-S. Stream-Oriented Computation in Recursive Data Flow Schemas.
Technical Memo 68, Laboratory for Computer Science, Massachusetts Institute of Technology, Cambridge, Mass., October 1975.

LANGUAGE FEATURES for

PARALLEL PROCESSING and RESOURCE CONTROL

Gregory R. Andrews
James R. McGraw

Cornell University
September, 1976

Languages for parallel programming should meet four goals:
expressiveness, reliability, security, and verifiability. This paper
presents a set of language features for describing processes and
process interaction, gives examples of their use, and briefly discusses
their relation to the goals. Two constructs, resources and protected
variables, are introduced as the mechanisms for describing interaction.
Resources are extensions of the monitor concept of Hoare; protected
variables are global variables which can only be accessed by one
process at a time. Two types of access control are introduced:
restrictions on scope rules for static access, and capabilities for
dynamic access. Examples include the interface to machine devices,
files and virtual devices, device scheduling, device reservation,
and buffer allocation.

This work was supported in part by the National Science Foundation
under grants GJ41115 and GJ42512.

1.0 INTRODUCTION

In order to increase the reliability of parallel programs,
a number of high-level language features have been proposed in
recent years. The work of Brinch Hansen [1,2], Hoare [5] and
Wirth [13,14] is especially noteworthy and has led to numerous
refinements and extensions [for example, 7 and 11]. In this
paper, we present a unified set of language features to specify
and control processes and their interaction. In particular, we
describe language mechanisms for processes, resources, shared
variables and protection. We then demonstrate the use of our
tools by specifying an interface between machine hardware and
high level programs.

The next section of the paper describes a syntax for
processes and presents four process control operations. Then
we discuss mechanisms for process interaction and describe two
new features: resources (an extension of monitors [5]) and protected variables. The fourth and fifth sections describe
mechanisms for static and dynamic allocation and access, respectively. A scope restriction mechanism is introduced to limit
static access; dynamic access is controlled by resource
capabilities and pointers to protected variables. One major
difficulty in any high-level language is designing a machine
independent interface. This problem is accentuated in systems
languages because of the need of systems programs to control
machine resources. In the sixth section of the paper, we show
how our language-defined resource construct can be used to re-

present machine resources, such as devices and clocks, as well as logical resources such as files and message buffers. The use of protected variables and pointers to efficiently manage IO buffers is also illustrated. Consequently, our language allows the definition of all process interaction, whether for programmed or machine resources.

Four specific goals have guided the work presented here: expressiveness, reliability, security, and verifiability. They are, we feel, the yardstick against which any systems language should be measured. First, the language must be sufficiently rich to enable a wide variety of policies to be naturally expressed. To use the distinction so aptly drawn by the Hydra group at Carnegie-Mellon [15], language features are the mechanisms by which system policies are described. As such, the features must be devoid of policy decisions which might preclude the efficient implementation of reasonable systems algorithms. Our focus is upon describing systems of interacting processes. Therefore, we are concerned, when implementing a system, with scheduling the activity of processes, defining the means by which they interact, controlling access to shared resources, and allocating resources. To be useful, our language features must make it possible and easy for us to perform these tasks. Related to the richness of expression, is the goal of uniformity of expression. Similar concepts should have a compatible representation and similar operations should have the same interpretation.

The second design goal is to insure that programs are reliable. Reliability means that all time-dependent errors which could result from the activity of parallel processes are detected at compile time. This requires that no two processes ever have access to the same variable(s) at the same time. The most insidious errors in systems programming are those which occur asynchronously. In our opinion, the main argument in favor of using high-level languages for systems programming, as long as they are "good" languages, is to increase the reliability and security of systems. A good language at a minimum is sufficiently structured that all access paths and access overlap can be enumerated at compile time. Our language features meet this requirement.

Our third design goal, security, has two aspects: access restriction and guaranteed service. First, every module (process, procedure, block) in a program should only have access to what it requires to carry out its function. In addition, data should only be accessed by valid operations (data encapsulation). Global variables are therefore bad because they violate this notion. There are also many situations where access should be further restricted to a subset of the valid operations; for example one process can only send messages of a certain type while another can only receive. For efficiency, all static access restrictions should be enforced at compile time. As we argue in section five, some dynamic access control is required to efficiently manage dynamic resource allocation. We introduce capabilities for this purpose. The cost of their use must be and is minimal, however.

The other aspect of security is guaranteeing service. Whereas access control is concerned with preventing invalid operations, guaranteed service is concerned with allowing valid operations, if they are attempted. This requires that no process can become deadlocked [6] and that all scheduling mechanisms are fair. Although absence of deadlock is a property of a program that cannot be guaranteed a priori just by programming in a particular language, the language can provide enough structure to make it possible to decide if a given program contains a deadlock possibility. We comment on the relation between languages and deadlock at the end of the paper.

The fourth and final goal motivating our work is the ability to prove the correctness of programs. Work in program verification affects language design by indicating which language constructs are hard to handle (e.g. procedures as parameters) and which lead to more readily verified programs (e.g. encapsulated data types). The semantics of our language proposals have not yet been formalized, so we are not completely sure of their impact. We have not, however, knowingly made any choices which lead to difficulty. And we have retained the axiomatic structure proposed by Hoare [5] in our resource facility.

The following sections describe our process specification and process interaction proposals. At the end of the paper we comment further upon their relationship to the four goals described above. The language notation is based upon Pascal syntax [12]. As a base, we assume a sequential language like Pascal; our proposals are extensions to the base.

2.0 PROCESSES

Any language for parallel programming must provide a means for describing processes. In order to enhance reliability, parallel activity should be clearly separated from sequential activity. And if the language is to be useful for writing systems programs, it must be possible to control the scheduling and execution status of processes. As stated in the introduction, a parallel language should merely provide the mechanisms for creating and controlling processes; control policies themselves are expressed by algorithms in the program of a system. In this section, we present a process data type and describe the operations on process objects.

Because processes are like procedures in that they contain declarations and code, we choose to represent them syntactically by the following notation:

```
pname: process;
       local declarations;
       body;
       end pname;
```

Processes in Concurrent Pascal [1] and Modula [13,14] are declared similarly.

Processes are manipulated by four operations: setstate,

changestate, activate, and suspend. When created, a process
cannot yet execute. First it requires a scheduling state and
then it must be activated. A process state consists of a priority,
time limit, and time quantum. Process scheduling is based on
priorities and uses time quantums for splitting time among equally
high priority processes. At all times, one of the highest
priority, active processes is executing. It executes until it
blocks waiting for an event (see next section), is suspended,
or exceeds its time quantum. A blocked process waits until
awakened by another process, a suspended processes waits for
activation, and a process which exceeds its quantum waits its
turn for another quantum. If a process executes for a total
amount of actual time in excess of its time limit, it is automatically suspended.

In addition to a scheduling state, each process has a
status: running, ready-active, ready-suspended, blocked-active,
or blocked-suspended. The running process is executing on a
processor; ready and blocked indicate whether or not a process
is waiting for an event; active and suspended indicate whether
or not a process has been allowed by its controller (e.g. its
creator) to continue execution. A more detailed discussion of
these five execution states can be found in [10].

To manipulate the scheduling state and status of a process, four operations can be used. First, if a process pn has been
created, its scheduling state can be set or changed by invoking:

```
        pn.setstate(priority,quantum,limit);
```

The process can then be activated by:

```
            pn.activate;
```

These operations are always executed in order to start a newly
created process. Should it be necessary to ever suspend the process, it can be done by:

```
            pn.suspend;
```

Finally, it may be necessary or desirable to examine
a process state, perhaps before changing it. This can be done
by calling:

```
        pn.readstate(priority,quantum,limit,used);
```

which returns four values. The "used" parameter is set to
indicate how much time the process pn has currently used. We
now describe the mechanisms for process interaction.

3.0 PROCESS INTERACTION

    In any system with multiple processes, interaction will
occur. Processes compete for access to limited, reusable resources and cooperate by exchanging information and synchronization
signals. A programming language can permit processes to interact
in at least four different ways:

    (1) through a language defined message passing
        facility;

    (2) through encapsulated, synchronized data
        types such as monitors;

(3) through access to shared reentrant procedures; and

(4) through access to global variables and types, such as buffers.

We propose three facilities for interaction: <u>resources</u> to implement shared data types requiring exclusive access, reentrant shared procedures, and <u>protected</u> variables to allow processes to access global data one at a time. A system wide message passing facility can be designed using our resource type. We do not feel that the language should define the message passing facility, however, because policy decisions would then have to be made. For example, how much information can be passed, what is its type, and is it passed by value or reference?

3.1 Resources

A <u>resource</u> is an extension of a <u>monitor</u> and is used for much the same purposes. The two main differences are that we allow resource operations to execute in parallel when possible and we distinguish between static resources controlled by scope rules and dynamic resources controlled by capabilities. We use the term resource to emphasize that the resource construct is the way in which any machine <u>or</u> logical system resource is represented. They are used in encapsulate each machine device and describe its operational interface to the software system. This is illustrated in section 6.

A resource has the following form:

rname: <attribute> <u>resource</u>;

        <u>entry</u> $operation_1, \ldots, operation_m$;

        <u>parallel</u>* $procedure_1, \ldots, procedure_p$;

        data declarations

        <u>procedure</u> $operation_1$ (parameters);

                <u>end</u> $operation_1$;

            .

            .

            .

        <u>procedure</u> $operation_m$ (parameters);

                <u>end</u> $operation_m$;

        local procedures

        initialization code

        <u>end</u> rname;

The *'d component (<u>parallel</u> phrase) is optional. The attribute is either <u>static</u> or <u>dynamic</u>; it governs storage allocation and access control. A static resource is allocated storage when its declaration occurs whereas a dynamic resource is allocated storage via a create operation. These two topics are discussed in detail in the next two sections.

When a resource instance is created, the initialization code is executed. It initializes the local data of the resource. Subsequent access to the local data is provided by calls on the <u>entry</u> operations. A call has the form:

        rname.operation(actual parameters);

where rname is a resource name. Within resources, synchronization of operations is provided by <u>wait</u> and <u>signal</u> operations on <u>condition</u> variables just as within monitors.

The normal mode of execution within resources is exclusive access to the local data. When an entry operation calls a local utility procedure or calls outside to another resource or global procedure, it retains exclusive control of the resource. Control in the normal (monitor-like) situation is relinquished when the resource operation returns, a <u>wait</u> is executed on a condition variable, or a <u>signal</u> is executed which awakens another process.

Two situations arise where exclusive access is unnecessary and leads to inefficient or clumsy problem solutions. One occurs when one or more resource operations only examine the local data; the other when one resource is used to schedule access to another, for example a disk or drum scheduler. Whenever it is possible for resource operations to overlap without disrupting integrity, the <u>parallel</u> phrase can be used. It has the form:

$$\underline{\text{parallel}} \ \text{procedure}_1, \ldots, \text{procedure}_p;$$

and names all those procedures defined by <u>or</u> called by the resource which can be executed in parallel. The effect of calling a <u>parallel</u> procedure is to give up exclusive resource access; on return it must be regained, however.

To insure data integrity, only one process at a time must be able to modify the resource data, namely the process which has exclusive resource access. Therefore, parallel procedures must not be able to modify the resource data in any way. To insure this, two constraints are placed on resources: first, parallel procedures inside a resource cannot assign values to resource data; second, no resource data can be passed as a parameter. The reason for the second constraint is that parameters are passed by reference, which could cause implicit assignments. Both of these constraints can easily be checked by a compiler.

An example of a simple resource employing the parallel phrase is shown in Figure 1. It solves the famous reader/writers problem [3] assuming readers have priority over writers. Another example, device scheduling, is shown in Section 6. The reader writer resource, named rw, implements local data, store, of type T. The data is examined by calls to rw.read(d) and updated by calls to rw.write(d) where d is of type T. Within the resource two extra variables, oktowrite and readers, are used for synchronization of read and write. Variable oktowrite is a condition which writers wait for if other processes are reading; readers indicates the number of processes actively reading. Because more than one process can safely read at once, actual reading takes place in a local, parallel procedure doread.

In the solution, read and write are executed as critical sections since they are not in the parallel phrase. Therefore, no two writes can occur at the same time. Simultaneous reading and writing is prevented because writing proceeds only when the value of readers is zero and readers is only set to zero if no process is inside either read or doread. Concurrent reading is permitted by having a separate, parallel doread procedure which is invoked by read. Other variants of the readers/writers

Figure 1

Readers/Writers

```
type T = record  · · ·  end;

rw: static resource;
    entry read, write;
    parallel doread;

    var store: T;
        oktowrite : condition;
        readers : integer;

    procedure read(var d:T);
        readers := readers + 1;
        doread(d);
        readers := readers - 1;
        if readers = 0 then oktowrite.signal;
        end read;
    procedure write(var d:T);
        if readers > 0 then oktowrite.wait;
        /* write */
        store := d;
        if readers = 0 then oktowrite.signal;
        end write;
    procedure doread(var d:T);
        /* read */
        d := store;
        end doread;
    /* initialize readers */
      readers := 0;
end rw;
```

problem have similar _resource_ solutions.

We feel that our algorithm is superior to that in [5] because we completely capture the solution in one place. Hoare's solution requires that each process call a monitor to request and release permission and then access the store directly. The drawbacks are that (1) processes must be trusted to get permission before attempting access and (2) they require direct access to the global store. Insuring that the store is not erroneously accessed by concurrent processes would be very difficult, if not impossible to insure. The whole advantage of monitors is encapsulating data and enforcing exclusive access constraints. Yet the monitor solution to readers/writers throws both advantages away. We were lead to our _parallel_ construct for these very reasons.

3.2 Shared Procedures

In addition to sharing resources, for efficiency we allow processes to share the code of global procedures. We therefore require that procedures be pure (reentrant). This implies that compilers for a language containing our extensions must allocate separate local storage for each activation of a shared procedure and that compiled code must not modify itself. Both requirements are easily met with known techniques. If a procedure needs local storage (own variables) which is retained from call to call, then the procedure must and should be implemented as an operation in an encapsulated _resource_.

3.3 Protected Variables

Whenever data is shared, we must insure that it can only be accessed by one process at a time. If multiple access paths exist, then the data must be contained within a <u>resource</u>. There are situations, however, where data is shared but only one process at a time has access to it. For example, buffers used in IO processing are often stored in a global pool used by several input, output and/or user processes. Each individual buffer is used by only one process at a time, however, and is accessed by simple read and write (assignment) operations. If shared variables, such as buffers, are implemented in resources, there is significant execution overhead caused by procedure calls to do reads and writes and by unneeded mutual exclusion. For those situations where simple data types, such as records or arrays, are shared but only one access path at a time ever exists, we propose using <u>protected</u> variables.

A protected variable is any variable declared with a <u>protected</u> attribute. Operations on the variable are exactly those for its type, but a protected variable can only be accessed by using a variable of type <u>pointer</u>. To illustrate the declaration and use of protected variables and pointers, we declare a <u>protected</u> type and two pointers as follows:

$$\underline{\text{type}}\ T = \underline{\text{protected}}\ \texttt{<basic type>};$$
$$P_1, P_2: \underline{\text{pointer}}\ \underline{\text{to}}\ T;$$

Once p_1 is bound to an instance of T (see Section 5), the contents of the instance are referenced by:

$$*p_1.\text{field}$$

where the .field, if present, names a subfield of T. Pointers themselves can be assigned and passed as parameters. To insure that only one pointer is ever bound to the same instance, however, assignment and parameter passing both destroy one pointer when transferring its value to another.

The use of protected variables and pointers to implement a buffer pool manager is shown in Section 6. Their allocation and access control are discussed further in Section 5.

4.0 STATIC ALLOCATION AND ACCESS

The two previous sections defined language facilities for process definition and interaction. In this section and the next, we show how these facilities are created and controlled, and also show how they interact with common sequential language constructs. Each object defined in a program (variables, structures, procedures, resources, and processes) is either statically or dynamically controlled. This section defines the allocation, access, and implementation of static objects.

4.1 Allocation

Every static object obeys the standard ALGOL rules for allocation. When a declaration is encountered (at the beginning of a block) space is immediately allocated and the object comes into existence. The object remains until the block in which

its declaration appears is exited. At that time, the space

for the object is deallocated.

The syntax for declaring static objects is fairly stand-

ard. All of the normal sequential language objects (variables,

arrays, records, procedures) are declared with conventional

Pascal syntax; the syntax for processes, static resources, and

pointers has been illustrated in previous sections. The only

other static object type is capability. Although both capabilities

and pointers are used to represent dynamic objects, they them-

selves have static control. The syntax for a capability declar-

ation is:

name: capability for <dynamic resource def>;

As in PASCAL, new types can be defined. The type de-

finition itself falls under static control even if it defines a

dynamic type of object. An example of the declaration and use of

a type is:

```
type terminal = process (parameters);
               declarations
               code
               end terminal;
console: terminal (actual parameters);
```

As shown, a type declaration can be parameterized. Type declarations

for other objects all have the same form.

4.2 Scope of Access

The maximum scope of access for any static object is the range of the block in which the instance is defined. Algol-like scope rules allow inner blocks to access global objects, unless the inner block re-defines a global name. With the introduction of process and resource blocks, this rule is too strong. Two of our design goals can be achieved by modifying Algol's default scope rules. First, simultaneous access to data objects by two processes can be prevented by only permitting a data object to be accessible in a single process environment. Second, the transmission of rights for a dynamic object from one process environment to another can be limited to parameter passing. These two goals have lead to the default scope rules shown in Figure 2 which indicates the types of objects which are accessible to a block if they are declared global to it.

The only entry which might cause confusion is the starred one. Normally, internal procedures are permitted to access global variables. If the procedure can be called from different processes, however, simultaneous data access is possible. Therefore, the rule (enforceable at compile time) is that a procedure may access global variables only if it will be called solely from the process environment that defined it.

The default scope rules define the maximum allowable access policy of any program. However, many circumstances arise where it would be useful to be more restrictive. This type of con-

Figure 2

Default Scope Rules

Global Object Type	Block Types to which object is accessible[+] (if within scope of object)
1. Data declatation (integer, record, etc.)	procedure*
2. Procedure declaration	procedure, process, resource
3. Process	procedure, process, resource
4. Static resource	procedure, process, resource
5. Pointers and capabilities	procedure
6. Type declarations	procedure, process, resource

[+] not including the block declaring the object.

* allowed if all calls to the procedure are from the reach of the process in which the procedure is declared.

straint can be enforced through the use of a _scope_ clause which can be attached to the declaration of any type or instance. The general form is demonstrated with a variable declaration:

alpha: integer _scope_ $block_1, \ldots, block_N$;

Only blocks declared at the level where the _scope_ appears can be included in the block list. The effect of the clause is to permit only those blocks listed to access the object being declared. The _scope_ clause cannot be used to relax the default rules, only to further restrict them on an individual object basis.

In addition to direct access allowed by the scope rules, some objects can be passed as parameters. Simple variables and structures (records and arrays) are passed to procedures by reference. They can be passed to _type_ definitions by value only, however, because of the possibility of simultaneous access. Pointer variable and resource capability passing is described in the next section. We do not allow, or see a need which requires procedures, processes or resources to be passed as parameters.

4.3 Implementation

One of the major concerns with any proposed language feature is the efficiency of its implementation. Our constructs are good in this respect. All of the access rules can be enforced at compile time, particularly the _scope_ clause which only involves changes to the symbol table control procedures. Memory management

is only complicated slightly. For a particular process the
standard stack allocation is possible since object existence is
tied to the block structure. The possibility of nested processes
creates the only memory difficulty because it involves finding
space for a new stack. In general though, the static objects
do not cause any problems.

5.0 DYNAMIC ALLOCATION AND ACCESS

The second method of object control is dynamic allocation
and access. Only two types of objects can be controlled in this
way: protected data structures (variables and records) and
dynamic resources. The major difference between static and
dynamic control is that the access rights possessed by a process
environment for a dynamic object may vary during execution. All
dynamic objects are referenced through a form of pointer mechanism:
resources via capabilities, and protected objects via pointers.
In this section we describe dynamic allocation, the use of capabilities and pointers, and the implementation of dynamic control.

5.1 Allocation

The lifetime of a dynamic object is different from its
static counterpart. A dynamic object may be created at any time
during execution, not just on block entry. Deallocation occurs
only when no references (pointers) to the object remain instead
of on block exit. Creating a dynamic object involves three
steps: (1) defining the type of object, (2) defining a capability

(or pointer) to reference the object, and (3) executing the
create operation to generate an instance. The creation of a
dynamic resource begins with a type definition.
For example:

> type buffer = dynamic resource (parameters);
>   {body}
>   end buffer;

Step two is a simple capability declaration, in this case:

> IO_buf: capability for buffer;

Then an actual instance of the dynamic object is created by
executing:

> IO_buf := buffer.create (parameters);

Notice that both the capability name and the resource type name
must be accessed in order to accomplish the creation. This requirement will be useful later. The steps for the creation of a protected data object are almost identical. An example follows.

> type count = protected integer;
>   size : pointer to count;
>
> size := count.create;

In general, integer could be replaced by any data structure
definition.

Dynamic objects could be created without using a type
definition, but then only one instance exists and, more importantly,
only one reference pointer exists. No other block could then

refer to the object because they could not declare a name for referencing it. Although legal syntactically, untyped dynamic objects merely act like static objects.

5.2 Access Control

Every dynamic resource is accessed through capabilities [8,15]. A resource capability has two components: (1) a reference to a particular instance, and (2) a set of access rights for the instance. The maximum rights for a resource are call rights for every resource entry plus the language-defined copy right. A capability is used to call an entry by executing a statement of the form:

capability_name.entry (parameters);

The call is permitted only if the capability contains a right for that entry. This check must be made at run-time.

Capabilities are manipulated by assignment statements and parameter passing. The copy right allows the contents of one capability to be copied into another capability of the same type. The form of the copy is:

cap_name_1 := cap_name_2 {rights list};

The bracketed rights list identifies the rights to be given to cap_name_1; obviously all these rights must be possessed by cap_name_2. Rights which may appear in the list are the entry point rights and copy. The rights list may be omitted if all rights are to be copied. The copy operation does not affect the contents of cap_name_2.

Since the default scope rules (Figure 2) do not allow a capability to be shared by two processes, sharing can only occur through parameter passing. When a capability is passed, its contents are transferred to the formal parameter capability <u>and</u> the actual parameter loses all rights. On return from the call, the reverse transfer is performed. The purpose of this approach is to be able to control all capability copying by the <u>copy</u> right yet still permit the acquisition of a resource by passing an empty capability and returning with a full one, or the release of a resource by the reverse action.

A last operation that can be performed on a capability is to empty it. This action requires no right in order to execute: The form is:

$$\text{cap\_name} := \underline{\text{null}};$$

One use of this tool would be in a resource responsible for trans-ferring capabilities among processes. The resource could receive the capability in a parameter, copy it into its global information, then empty the parameter. When the resource returns, the calling process has lost its access. This is illustrated by an example in Section 6.

The control and use of <u>protected</u> data structures (via pointers) is much the same as with capabilities, but with some important differences. The purpose of the <u>protected</u> attribute is to permit a structure to move among processes. A key difference is that data structures do not have built-in exclusion to avoid simultaneous access by different processes. To solve this problem, each protected object will only be permitted to have one pointer to it at any time (implying only one process can access it at any time); the value of a pointer is simply the "name" of a protected object. This restriction simplifies the access and manipulation mechanisms for pointers. There is no copy concept because copying is forbidden. The object referenced by a pointer can be transferred to another pointer by the assignment statement:

```
name_1 := name_2;
```

This assignment both copies the pointer and empties name_2. A null value can also be assigned in order to empty a pointer.

Access to a protected object is accomplished by explicit dereferencing of the pointer. The form is:

```
*pointer_name
```

For example, if pointer_1 and pointer_2 are both pointers to protected integers, the value of the second integer can be copied by the assignment:

```
*pointer_1 := *pointer_2;
```

The result is that the pointers reference different objects which now have the same value. If the data structure is a record, the sub-fields of the record can be specified using the standard dot notation following the dereferenced pointer. Subscripts are used with pointers to arrays.

As with capabilities, parameter passing is what makes
pointers useful; it is the only way for a <u>protected</u> object to
be moved through various process environments. When a pointer
is passed, the effect is exactly the same as assigning the actual
pointer to the formal one; the calling environment loses access.
On return, the reverse assignment is made.

5.3 Implementation

There are several points that should be made concerning
the implementation of dynamic objects. The first, and probably
most troublesome, is that dynamic objects involve dynamic
allocation which implies that some form of dynamic memory management must be provided by the compiler or computer system. We
no longer have a simple stack allocation system; each object's
existence is independent of all others so some form of memory
recovery is needed. Another implementation point concerns capabilities. A run-time check of each access is needed. The overhead can be minimized, however, by implementing a capability's
rights in a bit vector. An access check then involves examining
a bit and allowing access if the bit is set. Since capabilities
are only used to reference resources, most capability accesses
will already involve the overhead of a procedure call to a
resource entry. The extra overhead of capability checking should
therefore be small. The last implementation point concerns
pointer variables. These objects can be implemented with almost
no run-time checking because no rights need to be examined. By

having only one pointer to each data object, simultaneous
multiple access is avoided without incurring the overhead of
some synchronization mechanism. The only question at run-time
is whether or not a pointer is empty. By placing an illegal
address in any empty pointer, the run-time check is made automatically by existing hardware.

6.0   IO PROCESSING - USING RESOURCES AND PROTECTED VARIABLES

As Hoare has observed [5], the utility of proposed language
features cannot be assessed without presenting a convincing
set of examples. In this section, we describe five IO
processing problems and outline solutions using our language
features. Numerous other examples can be found in [9]. First,
we use resources to define the interface between program modules
and hardware devices. Then we add another resource layer for
files to give users a higher level interface to devices and to
illustrate general system structure. Two device management
problems are then discussed: scheduling of "shared" devices
such as disks, and allocation of serial devices such as consoles.
Finally we show how protected variables can be used to solve a
typical buffer allocation problem.

6.1   Device Interface

One of our main goals has been to develop a single, uniform
way to describe all process interaction. Competition for and
sharing of physical devices is one of the most basic kinds of

interaction. A device has much in common with any abstract
data type; it has local storage and it defines operations for
accessing the storage. And like shared data types, devices
require exclusive access and synchronization. Therefore, we
propose that every addressable device (or group of identical
devices such as consoles) be represented by a resource. Wirth
has recently made a similar proposal [13, 14].

A major complaint about using high level languages for
controlling devices is that they can be inefficient compared
to machine (assembly) programs. As a result, when high level
languages have been used, machine language inserts are often
employed to code critical portions. In most cases, machine
code is used to interface to machine hardware. We do not reject
this approach but feel that it must be used with care. Therefore,
we propose that the only place where machine language is used is
within resources which interface to devices. In this way, device
peculiarities can be handled efficiently but, equally if not
more important, the device's interface to the rest of the system
is defined by a high level interface.

The general form of a device resource is:

```
device name:   static resource;
               entry operation_1,...,operation_n;

               local data - channel program storage, etc.
               ⋮

               procedure operation_i (parameters);
                   build channel programs        ⎫  machine
                   initiate task                  ⎬  language
                   interrogate completion codes  ⎭
                   end operation_i;
               ⋮

          /* initialization */

          end device name;
```

One final point should be made about the role of device
resources. We believe that machine dependency occurs in only
two places in our language: within the run-time package
implementing language features (e.g. processes) and within device
resources. It seems appropriate, therefore, for each language
implementation to contain a library of pre-defined device resources
appropriate for the target machine. Any systems written in our
language can then reference, via procedure calls to resources,
the machine devices. The same system, if implemented on another
machine with the same types of devices, would still function
correctly even if the hardware had different characteristics.
As long as the name and operations were the same, the resource
interface would be the same.

6.2 Files and Virtual Devices

Although a system process may communicate directly with
peripheral devices, it is common to provide user (application)
processes with a higher level interface implemented by a file
system. In order to illustrate general system structure using
processes and resources, we consider a simple example of a
portion of an input spooler. The system has two processes and
three resources as shown in Figure 3. The INPUT process reads
cards and writes them into a cardfile resource which in turn
stores them on disk. At some later time a USER process reads
its input from the cardfile which causes the input to be fetched
from disk.

Figure 3

A Simple Input Spooler

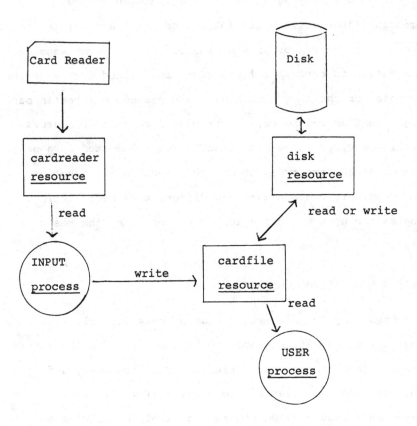

Ignoring all details of synchronization and IO buffering, the structure of this system is shown in Figure 4. Cardreader and disk are device resources as discussed in the last section. Each defines procedures to access its associated device. By using the scope phrase, access to cardreader is restricted to the INPUT process and access to the disk is restricted (in this example) to the cardfile resource. Cardfile contains two entries, read and write, used by USER and INPUT. The functions of cardfile are to implement a sequential file organization and to perform IO buffering and synchronization (synchronization is required to prevent a "card" from being read before it has been written).

The INPUT process executes a loop to read physical cards and write card images into the cardfile. The USER process gets its input by reading the cardfile. The remaining code initializes and activates the two processes.

This example is greatly simplified and not representative of a real system. Its intent is merely to illustrate the general structure of a language defined system and give an example of the use of scope restriction. One step toward realism would be to add multiple cardfiles. The INPUT process would then create a new cardfile, fill it, and then pass it on to another process (or resource) such as a job manager. Once a USER process is scheduled, it is given access to the appropriate cardfile instance. This can be achieved in our language in the following manner. First cardfile is declared as a dynamic resource type. INPUT

Figure 4

Outline of Input Spooler Code

```
System: begin

      cardreader: static resource;
                  entry read;
                     .
                     .
                  end cardreader
                  scope INPUT;

          disk: static resource;
                  entry read,write;
                     .
                     .
                  end disk
                  scope cardfile;

      cardfile: static resource;
                  entry read,write;
                     .
                     .
                  end cardfile
                  scope INPUT,USER;

        INPUT: process;
                  repeat
                     cardreader.read (b);
                     cardfile.write (b);
                  until  end of file;
               end INPUT;

         USER: process;
                  /* fetch next card by calling: */
                     cardfile.read (b);

               end USER;

      /* start processes */

      INPUT.setstate (   );
      USER.setstate (   );
      INPUT.activate;
      USER.activate;

   end system;
```

creates new instances of the type for each new card stream and passes them (via capability passing) to the job scheduler. USER then references a card file by declaring a <u>capability</u> and acquiring the actual file instance from the scheduler. The changes to cardfile and INPUT are:

```
type cardfile = dynamic resource
                entry read, write;



                end cardfile
                scope INPUT, system;
type cardfile_reference = capability for cardfile
                scope USER;

INPUT:  process;
        c :  capability for cardfile;
        c := cardfile.create;
        repeat

            cardreader.read(b);
            c.write(b);
        until end of file;
        send c to job scheduler
        end INPUT;
```

The USER process references a card file by declaring a variable cf of <u>type</u> cardfile_reference. Note how the <u>scope</u> phrase has been used to let INPUT have access to the definition of cardfile (and hence to the create operation) but only let the USER have access to cardfile_reference. In this way, USER can acquire capabilities for cardfiles but cannot create them himself. This type of access control is common in operating systems.

6.3 Device Scheduling

We now turn to a concrete example of device scheduling, in particular scheduling operations on a moving head disk. The problem involves reordering disk operations in order

to improve device utilization. The algorithm we will use, for
demonstration purposes, is the "elevator algorithm" in Hoare [5].
The basic idea is to move the disk head in complete sweeps of the
cyclinders servicing all requests for the same cylinder at the
same time.

Our solution to this problem employs two resources: disk and
userdisk. Disk is a machine interface resource as described in
Section 6.1. Userdisk is the resource available to users. It
sequences the requests, and then calls disk to carry out the request.
The code for both resources is outlined in figure 5.

The key to our solution is that disk scheduling and access can
execute concurrently. Since the disk resource procedures are
listed as parallel procedures, a process which calls disk loses
exclusive control of userdisk. This permits other processes to
enter userdisk and queue up for eventual access. When the disk
operation completes (i.e. returns to userdisk) the next process is
selected for continuation. Notice that without the parallel
feature, this organization would imply FIFO scheduling.

Hoare's solution to this problem is weaker than ours because
monitors cannot do the scheduling and access in parallel. As a
result, his users had to take three steps: (1) request device
access, (2) make the access, and (3) release the device. There
is no mechanism for enforcing this sequence and problems arise if
any user forgets or reorders some steps.

Figure 5

Disk Scheduler

```
disk: static resource;
      entry read, write;

      /* machine interface resource */
      /* read and write called only from userdisk */
      end disk
      scope userdisk;

userdisk: static resource;
          entry read, write;
          parallel disk.read, disk.write; /* to exit
                  userdisk when IO is begun */

          request queue /* tasks waiting for disk */
          condition variables /* for waiting processes */
          executing: boolean; /* true if disk in use */

          procedure read (IO parameters);
              if  executing then begin
                              c := next free condition variable
                              save task info in request queue
                              c.wait;
                              remove task info from request queue
                              end;
                  executing := true;
                  disk.read (IO parameters);
                   /* control of userdisk surrendered during call */
                  if request queue is empty
                      then executing := false;
                      else begin
                          find next task on request queue
                          c := condition task is waiting on;
                          c.signal;
                          end;

          end read;
```

```
procedure write (IO parameters);
        /* similar to read -
             calls disk.write      */
        end write;


/* initialize data */
 executing := false;
 request queue empty


end userdisk;
```

6.4 Device Reservation

With random access devices such as disks, many processes can
share the device and interleave their read and write requests. For
serial devices however, the device must be reserved if more than one
record (line) is to be read or written at one time. To allow processes
to reserve a device we need a device allocator with two operations:
request and release. Implementing the allocator is straightforward.
What is not so easy, however, is enforcing the policy that a serial
device must be requested by and allocated to a process before the
process can use it. One possible approach is to nest two resources;
the first does allocation and then calls the other to do access.
Once a device has been allocated, the allocator blocks requests from
other processes. The trouble with this approach is that every access
operation incurs the overhead of going through the allocator. A
second approach is to separate the allocator from the device, give
all processes access to both and trust that they will request the
device before using it. Unfortunately, not all processes (or even
most) are trustworthy.

With our language, we can use dynamic resources and capabilities
to insure that a device is requested before it is used. Our solution is
outlined in Figure 6. The device resource is now declared as a type
of dynamic resource. This allows a capability to be used to provide
secure access, even if only one instance of the device is generated.
The typed device declaration is only accessible to the allocator; this
insures that only the allocator can create instances of the device.

Figure 6

Device Allocation

```
type device = dynamic resource;
         entry read, write;
              :
              :
         end device
         scope allocator;

type device_capability = capability for device;
                       /* scope is global */

allocator: static resource;
         entry request, release;
         available : boolean;
         waiting : condition;
         dc : device_capability;

         procedure request (d: device_capability);
             if ¬ available then waiting.wait;
             available := false;
             d := dc { read,write} ;
                 /* give access to device but not
                    ability to copy  */
             end request;

         procedure release (d: device_capability);
             /* d is returned by calling process */
             d := null;
             available := true;
             waiting.signal; /* awaken someone
                                 if possible  */
             end release;

         /* initialize */
         available := true;
         dc := device.create; /* actually generate
                                 device resource */
         end allocator;
```

Access to the device is through device capabilities which can be
declared in any block. The allocator resource is the key part of our
solution. It implements two operations, request and release, which
enable a process to acquire access to the device and give it up,
respectively. When a process calls request it first waits for the
device to be available. Once it is, parameter d is assigned the device
capability dc, but only with read and write access. This gives
the user the ability to access the device but prevents him from copying
his one capability. Once the user is through accessing the device,
he calls allocator.release(d) where d is the device capability
previously granted. The assignment of null to d prevents the capability
from returning to the user at the end of the call. The device can then
be allocated to another process. The only weakness is the inability
to force a user to return his rights.

6.5 Buffer Allocation and Access

As our final example, we consider one further portion of a
typical IO system: buffer allocation. IO buffers are often stored in
a pool used by multiple processes. When a process requires storage
for another data record, it gets an empty buffer from the pool and
fills it with information. Once a full buffer is no longer needed, it
is returned to the empty pool. Buffers are also used to, for example,
implement a message passing system.

Our problem here is to implement a buffer allocator analagous
to the device allocator in the previous example. The buffer allocator

has two entries, request and release, which are called to fetch and return an empty buffer, respectively. As with device allocation, we want to insure that a buffer can only be accessed after it is allocated. But buffers are not like devices; they are data records instead of resources and they are only accessed by one process at a time. Therefore, we implement buffers by protected variables and access them via pointers. The request procedure of the allocator consequently returns a pointer to the allocated buffer. A call to allocator.release gives back a buffer pointer. The creation and control of buffers is very similar to that used for devices. The complete code for the allocator is shown in Figure 7. The main advantage of using protected variables and pointers instead of resources is that each buffer can be directly and therefore efficiently accessed. No access control or data integrity is sacrificed, however, because the manipulation of pointers is carefully controlled.

7.0 CONCLUSION

In the introduction we enumerated four goals guiding the work presented here: expressiveness, data integrity, security, and program verification. Our focus in this paper has been the first, namely expressing the structure and control of systems of interacting processes. In order to describe processes, we introduced a process type. To specify process interaction, we introduced resources and protected variables. As the examples have attempted to show, our language features lead to simpler problem solutions than is possible

283

Figure 7

Buffer Allocation and Access

```
type buffer = protected array 1..size of bits
              scope allocator;

type bufptr = pointer to buffer;

allocator: static resource
           entry request, release;

           bufs: array 1..N of bufptr;
                 /* stack of empty buffers */
           waiting: condition;
           top: integer;

           procedure request (p: bufptr);
               if top = 0 then waiting.wait;
               p: = bufs(top);
               top: = top-1;
               end request;

           procedure release (p: bufptr);
               top: = top+1;
               bufs(top): = p;
               waiting.signal;
               end release;
       top:= N;
       do i:= 1 to N;   /* create buffer instances */
           bufs(i): = buffer.create; end;
       end allocator;
```

with existing languages. One specific application of resources is to describe the interface to machine devices. This is, we feel, a feasibl and valuable way to isolate machine dependent components from other modules in a system. We have also introduced the scope phrase, capabilities, and pointers to provide flexible access control.

Elsewhere we analyze the relation of our language features to the other three goals [9]. We briefly summarize our results here. Throughout this paper we have respeatedly referred to the problem of data integrity. The semantic rules governing scope of access and the use of capabilities and pointers are specifically concerned with insuring that only one process at a time can ever access any variable. As long as programs do not escape from our language and violate its semantics, we have shown that data integrity is insured.

As we have described the problem, security has two aspects: data safety and absence of deadlock. The safety problem [4] is concerned with deciding what blocks can access each program variable. An exact solution requires knowledge of the execution flow of a program and is therefore unattainable in general. In [9], however, we show how to determine the potential access of each block at compile time. By potential access we mean those variables a program would access if it took every possible execution path.

As with the safety problem, an exact determination of whether or not a program is free of mutual blocking is in general undecidable. It is possible, however, to model any program using our language features, monitor its execution, and detect a deadlock if one occurs.

No language can both make it impossible to deadlock programs and allow programs to control scheduling (via waits and signals in resources). The best that can be hoped is that deadlock can be detected and guidelines for its avoidance can be enumerated.

The final goal, program verification, is the one we are furthest from achieving. The _parallel_ phrase adds complexity to any proof because it adds parallel activity. Much work remains to be done here. Our consolation is that the same is true for all non-trivial languages.

No language proposal can or will be accepted until it has stood the test of extensive use. A necessary prelude is its implementation. This is one of our anticipated future tasks.

8.0   BIBLIOGRAPHY

1. Brinch Hansen,P. The programming language Concurrent Pascal.
        IEEE Transactions on Software Engineering Vol. SE-1,
        No. 2, June 1975, 199-207.

2. Brinch Hansen,P. The Solo operating system: a Concurrent
        Pascal program. Software Practices and Experience 6
        (1976), 141-149.

3. Courtois,P.J.,Heymans,F., and Parnas,D.L. Concurrent control
        with readers and writers. Comm. ACM 14,10 (Oct. 1971),
        667-668.

4. Harrison,M.A.,Ruzzo,W.L., and Ullman,J.D. Protection in
        operating systems. Comm. ACM 19,8 (August 1976),461-471.

5. Hoare,C.A.R. Monitors: an operating system structuring concept.
        Comm. ACM 17,10 (October 1974), 549-557.

6. Holt,R.C. Some deadlock properties of computer systems.
        Computing Surveys Vol. 4, No. 3, (September 1972),
        179-196.

7. Howard, J.H. Proving monitors. Comm. ACM 19,5 (May 1976),
        273-285.

8. Lampson,B.W., and Sturgis,H.E. Reflections on operating
        systems design. Comm. ACM 19,5 (May 1976), 273-279.

9. McGraw,J.R. Representing process interaction in a programming
        language. Ph.D. Thesis, Department of Computer
        Science, Cornell University (in preparation).

10. Shaw, A.C. et. al. A multiprogramming nucleus with dynamic
        resource facilities. Software Practices and Experience
        Vol. 5, 1975, 245-267.

11. Silberschatz,A.,Kieburtz,R.B., and Bernstein,A.
Extending Concurrent Pascal to allow dynamic resource
management. Technical Report #53, Department of
Computer Science, State University of New York at
Stony Brook, June 1976.

12. Wirth,N. The programming language Pascal. Acta Informatica,
Vol. 1, 1971, 35-63.

13. Wirth,N. Modula: A language for modular multiprogramming.
Technical Report #18, Institut für Informatik, ETH,
March 1976.

14. Wirth,N. The use of Modula and Design and implementation
of Modula. Technical Report #19, Institut für
Informatik, ETH, June 1976.

15. Wulf, W.A. el. al. Hydra: the kernal of a multiprocessor operating
system. Comm. ACM 17,6 (June 1974), 337-345.

SEPARATE DEFINITION AND COMPILATION

IN LIS AND ITS IMPLEMENTATION

Jean D. Ichbiah - Guy Ferran

Compagnie Internationale pour l'Informatique
CII - Honeywell Bull
Louveciennes - FRANCE

1. INTRODUCTION

This paper presents the language entities introduced in the
LIS language for separate definition and compilation {1,2}. Instantiation and visibility rules are then described. Finally, the
main functions of the separate compilation system which manages
the compilation units are reviewed.

Separate compilation in LIS is an evolution from the earlier
proposal in the SUE language {3}. The main differences are in
terms of the facilities offered for modularization-partitions,
and in the explicit designation of the compilation units.

2. THE LANGUAGE ENTITIES

The LIS language offers two forms of conceptual units : partitions and segments.

Partitions are the abstraction for packages. Each partition
contains a set of data items, data types and subprograms which
are semantically interrelated. Segments are subprograms which
are meant to be separately compiled.

Partitions and segments are conceptual units. In any of them we may distinguish two parts :

(a) a part which may be shown (exported) to other units : the DATA part,

(b) a part which will remain hidden for other units : the PROGRAM part.

The LIS language permits a separate compilation of these two parts. As a consequence we can distinguish four types of compilation units :

- data   partitions
- program partitions
- data   segments
- program segments

Both data partitions and data segments are called visibility units since they represent the units which may be made visible (exported) to other modules.

3. PARTITION EXAMPLE

The example given below shows how a package used for table handling could be written as a partition.

The data partition contains all the information needed by a user. Thus he would need to know what ELEMENTs are ; similarly he would need to know the names of the actions INITIALIZE, INSERT and RETRIEVE, the names of their parameters, their type and mode (value, result or both).

Specifications of the actions of the package naturally belong to its visible part, i.e. to the data partition.

The program partition contains the bodies of the subprograms INITIALIZE, INSERT and RETRIEVE. It also contains declarations of local entities : the type CELL, the constant MAX and the array A. Finally it may contain local actions such as INTERNAL_ HOUSEKEEPING.

```
TABLE_HANDLING : Partition ;
```

```
Data Partition TABLE_HANDLING ;
    Type ELEMENT = ...
    INITIALIZE : Action ;
    INSERT    : Action (E : In ELEMENT) ;
    RETRIEVE  : Action (E : Out ELEMENT) ;
    $ Specifications of initialize, insert and retrieve $
End ;
```

```
Program Partition TABLE_HANDLING ;
    Type CELL = ...
    MAX : Constant INTEGER == ...
    A   : Array (I..MAX) Of CELL ;
    INTERNAL_HOUSEKEEPING : Action ;

    Program INTERNAL_HOUSEKEEPING ;
        ...
    End ;

    Program INITIALIZE ;
        ...
    End ;

    Program INSERT ;
        ...
    End ;

    Program RETRIEVE ;
        ...
    End ;
End ;
```

It is important to note that the source <u>text</u> of the program partition need not be provided to a user of the table handling package (all he will need is the object module). This is made possible by the fact that the data partition and the program partition are two separate texts which are separately compiled.

Hiding the program partition is important if we want to retain the ability to substitute a given realization of the specifications by a later one, possibly using a different principle. In such situations we do not want to be bound by "implicit" specifications which the user would have derived from reading the text of the actions and which he would have used in his application.

This ability of hiding the parts which are not exported is one of the differences of the LIS partitions with alternate proposals : Modula modules {4}, Clu clusters {5}, Alphard forms {6}.

4. DECLARATIONS AND INSTANTIATION MODEL

Both partitions and segments are declared in data segments.

<u>Example</u>

```
Data Segment A ;
    GRAPHS, GEOMETRY, ALGEBRA : Partition ;
    B, C : Segment Action (U : In BOOLEAN) ;
End ;
```

```
Data Segment B ;
    TOPOLOGY, WATERCOLORS, STRUCTURES : Partition ;
    D, E : Segment Action ;
End ;
```

```
Data Segment C ;
    WOODWORK, TABLE_HANDLING : Partition ;
    F    : Segment Action (V : Out INTEGER) ;
    G, H : Segment Action ;
End ;
```

Instances of segments and partitions are created on a stack. Segments are instantiated when they are called. Partitions are instantiated when their declaration is elaborated. As a consequence, when a segment is called, its instance is created together with the instances of the partitions declared in the segment.

In the above example, the call of the segment A will result in the instances of A, GRAPHS, GEOMETRY and ALGEBRA. If A then calls C the stack should be as follows :

```
                    ...
  ┌─────────────────────────────┐
  │                             │
  ├─────────────────────────────┤
  │ instance of A               │ ⎫
  ├─────────────────────────────┤ │
  │ instance of GRAPHS          │ │  result of the
  ├─────────────────────────────┤ ⎬  activation of A
  │ instance of GEOMETRY        │ │
  ├─────────────────────────────┤ │
  │ instance of ALGEBRA         │ ⎭
  ├═════════════════════════════┤
  │ instance of C               │ ⎫
  ├─────────────────────────────┤ │  result of the
  │ instance of TABLE_HANDLING  │ ⎬  activation of C
  ├─────────────────────────────┤ │
  │ instance of WOODWORK        │ ⎭
  └─────────────────────────────┘
```

5. VISIBILITY

Visibility defines the set of names which are accessible at various program points. Different rules are used in LIS for stating visibility between modules or within a given module. This distinction is related to that existing between "programming in the large and in the small" {7}.

(a) Between modules

Visibility has to be stated explicitly through a context
specification. In other words, a module should state explicitly which partitions and segments are imported. In the
example below, for instance, the program partition TABLE_
HANDLING sees the data partitions GRAPHS, WOODWORK, TABLE_
HANDLING. On the other hand, it does not see the data partitions GEOMETRY and ALGEBRA nor the data segments A and C although these will exist on the stack when one of the TABLE_
HANDLING actions is called.

```
Use Data GRAPHS, WOODWORK, TABLE_HANDLING ;
Program Partition TABLE_HANDLING ;

   ...

End ;
```

(b) Within a module

The visibility follows rules similar to those of block structure.

The justification for these two different rules is as follows.
Within a small size module, block structure is an acceptable visibility model. Indeed, the problems with globals only become severe with large size programs. The latter will however be split
into several compilation units and visibility will then be stated
explicitly.

For reasons of scale it does not appear desirable to permit
the specification of "small" entities such as variables in a context specification, since this could result in long import lists,
difficult to understand and to maintain.

We should expect programs to be structured in such a way that entities which are semantically related and hence likely to be imported at the same time are grouped together. Hence only names of partitions and segments can appear in a context specification.

6. THE SEPARATE COMPILATION SYSTEM

Traditional compilers have no memory from one compilation to the next. However, if a compiler is to permit separate compilation and do type checking across modules, its normal input will have to consist of :

(1) the text of the compilation unit to be compiled,

(2) a separate compilation file containing information on previously treated compilation units belonging to the same program family.

The separate compilation file of the LIS compiler contains on one hand general information and on the other hand one subfile per compilation unit.

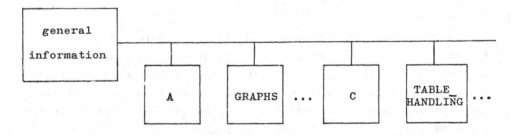

The separate compilation system is the part of the compiler which manages these files. It will be mainly concerned by the compilation of data partitions and segments and by the treatment of context specifications.

For each data partition or segment, the separate compilation system produces a subfile containing :

(a) a relocatable form of the symbol table associated with the compilation unit,

(b) the initialization code, if any, corresponding to the data items declared in the unit.

The need for symbol table relocation comes from the fact that there may be references from the symbol table of one unit to the other. This arises, for instance, if a data item is declared in a given partition as being of a type defined in another partition.

During the analysis of a context specification, the separate compilation system will load and relocate the symbol tables of the units indicated in the context. Thus the treatment of :

USE DATA GRAPHS, WOODWORK, TABLE_HANDLING ;

will result in loading and relocating the symbol tables of GRAPHS, WOODWORK and TABLE_HANDLING.

In addition, if compiling a program unit (i.e. either a program partition or a program segment), the code file will be initialized with the initialization code produced for the corresponding data partition or segment.

The separate compilation system is also responsible for several checking functions :

(1) <u>Incomplete contexts</u>

Will be detected when data items of a symbol table are found to refer to a symbol table not provided in the context specification. Depending on the case, these will be either repaired or signaled by compiler warnings.

(2) <u>Unique visibility</u>

A context specification will only be correct if each identifier declared in one of the units specified is declared in just that unit.

(3) <u>Need for recompilations</u>

If the name of a partition or segment P appears in the context of another partition or segment Q, then the recompilation of P causes the subfile produced by a previous compilation of Q to become obsolete. The use of obsolete units is detected by the separate compilation systems. It also provides information on the subsequent recompilations which become necessary after a given recompilation. These checks use comparisons of compilation dates recorded in the separate compilation file.

In general, the separate compilation system has the ability to produce displays of global information concerning a program family.

7. CONCLUSION

Separate compilation has its justification in practical ressons : in large projects it would not be reasonable to recompile the complete system for each modification. Nor would it be reasonable to have every member of a programming project have access to all other program parts.

The facilities provided in the LIS language for separate definition and compilation show that it can be achieved at a reasonable cost. Moreover the availability of the separate compilation system permits type checking to be achieved across separately compiled modules.

REFERENCES

{ 1 } Ichbiah, J.D., Rissen, J.P., Heliard, J.C., Cousot, P.,
       "The System Implementation Language LIS"
       CII Technical Report 4549 E1/EN - December 1974

{ 2 } Ichbiah, J.D., Cousot, P.,
       "Visibility and Separate compilations"
       IFIP WG2.4 M.O.L. Bulletin - 4 - May 1974

{ 3 } Clark, B.L., Horning, J.J.,
       "The system language for Project SUE"
       Sigplan Notices - Vol. 8 - Number 2 - February 1973 - 28-34

{ 4 } Wirth, N.,
       "Modula : a language for modular multiprogramming"
       Institut für Informatik - Report 18 - ETH Zürich - March 1976

{ 5 } Liskov, B.,
       "A note on Clu"
       Mac-TR - M.I.T. - June 1975

{ 6 } Wulf, W.A., London, R.L., Show, M.,
       "Abstraction and verification in Alphard"
       Carnegie Mellon Technical Report - February 1975

{ 7 } De Remer, F., Kron, H.H.,
       "Programming in the large versus programming in the small"
       IEEE Transactions on Software Engineering - SE-2, 2 - June
       1976 - pp 80-86

REQUIREMENTS FOR REAL-TIME LANGUAGES

Timothy A. Dreisbach

Larry Weissman

Intermetrics, Inc.
701 Concord Avenue
Cambridge, Massachusetts   02138

Abstract

"Real-time systems" is an all-encompassing term that includes systems
from many diverse application areas. A common property of these systems
is that they contain processing that must be completed under critical
time constraints. The language requirements for real-time systems differ
more in degree than in nature from the requirements for other systems.
This paper discusses five categories of requirements at a fairly general
level and describes specific requirements in each of the areas. The five
categories are reliability, maintainability, power, efficiency, and
portability. Requirements which differ significantly in degree for real-
time systems, and language capabilities and features to meet those requirements are discussed. The paper does not propose specific features
for the "ideal" real-time language, but points out the areas of concern.

This work was supported by Contract F19628-76-C-0225, Electronic
Systems Division, U. S. Air Force Systems Command.

1.0 INTRODUCTION

"Real-time systems" is an all-encompassing term that includes systems
from many diverse application areas. A common property of these systems
is that they contain processing that must be completed under critical time
constraints. In general these time constraints are relatively short (e.g.,
less than a minute), thus precluding such systems as payroll programs with
critical but large time constraints.

The language requirements for real-time systems differ more in degree
than in nature from the requirements for other systems. For example, the
following five categories of language requirements apply to real-time
systems as well as many other systems: reliability, maintainability, power,
efficiency, and portability. The difference with real-time systems, however,
is in the relative importance of the requirements, the degree to which each
has to be satisfied, and the consequences of not satisfying a requirement.

In the past, the major emphasis for real time systems was placed on
efficiency and this was used to justify the exclusive use of assembly language for real-time systems. The deficiencies of assembly language, however,
are apparent when it comes to meeting the other requirements, especially
reliability. With hardware getting faster and compilation techniques getting
better, the use of high-order languages for real-time systems is gaining
acceptance. In fact, given that the critical time constraints can be met,
reliability becomes a much more important requirement than efficiency.

Section 2 of this paper discusses each of the five categories of
requirements at a fairly general level and describes specific requirements
in each of the areas.

Section 3 then selects those requirements which differ significantly
in degree for real-time systems. For each requirement, language capabilities and features to meet the requirement are discussed.

Discussing real-time language requirements and capabilities is not a
straightforward task. It is not possible to state, for example, that a
given capability is an absolute requirement for real-time and languages
not possessing that capability are unsuitable for real-time processing

(i.e., it may be possible to realize the capability in another way). Thus, the requirements and capabilities discussed in this section are those that are considered extremely desirable for real-time processing but need not be considered absolutely essential.

It should be emphasized that the requirements and capabilities discussed are not necessarily the most important ones for a real-time language, but rather the ones that differ significantly from other applications. For example, language masterability is an extremely important requirement in the category of reliability but no more so for real-time systems than for other systems. Consequently it is not included in the section on real-time specific requirements.

2.0 GENERAL REQUIREMENTS FOR REAL-TIME LANGUAGES

2.1 Reliability

Reliability is an especially important requirement for real-time systems because of the nature of many real-time applications (e.g., process control, weapon systems). As Brian Randell has noted, "Reliability is not an add-on feature." Consequently, requirements must be placed on programming languages to support the production of reliable software.

2.1.1 Masterability

One important requirement is language masterability. The programming language is a tool with which the programmer solves the problem at hand. Thus, his full effort should be devoted to understanding the problem to be solved and not to understanding the tool [Hoare 1974]. Properties of a language that contribute to its masterability are simplicity, naturalness, uniformity of features, implementation independence, completeness of definition, and the availability of effective documentation.

2.1.2 Understandability

Another important requirement is that the language support the writing of understandable programs. Understandability is important to reliability throughout the entire life-cycle of the software system. Programs that are clear and understandable are easier to debug, validate, and maintain. All the language properties that contribute to masterability also contribute to understandability. In addition, structuring features including functional and data abstraction also contribute to understandability.

2.1.3 Error Handling

Another important requirement for reliability is error prevention and detection. Language capabilities that support this are strong typing, useful redundancy, and explicitness (e.g., lack of defaults and implicit conversions).

Related to this requirement is the handling of exceptional conditions. As Hoare has pointed out, "It is quite unacceptable for a real-time program in the middle of its operation to suddenly give up, however polite the excuse" [Hoare 1975]. Consequently, facilities must be provided in the language to enable all errors and exceptional conditions to be handled by the program.

2.1.4 Implementation Correctness

A final reliability requirement is that the language implementation be correct. All errors should be due to programming errors at the source language level and not due to incorrect machine code generated by the compiler.

2.2 Maintainability

Maintainability refers to the ability to make changes to a program, both to fix errors and to support changing requirements of the program. In order to be able to make changes to a program, it is obviously necessary to understand the program. Thus all the language capabilities that support understandability, as previously discussed, also are applicable to maintainability. Understandability is especially important since frequently the person responsible for maintaining the program is different from the person who originally wrote it.

In addition, structuring capabilities that support modularity and locality are important for maintainability. A problem with making changes to a program is the need to ensure that the change does precisely what it is intended to do without affecting other portions of the system. The better structured and localized a program is, the smaller the probability that a change will adversely affect unrelated portions of the system.

2.3 Power

In order for a language to be suitable for real-time systems, it must be powerful enough to conveniently handle the processing requirements of the system.

2.3.1 Sequential Computational Ability

One class of processing requirements includes the ability to handle
sequential computation. The language features needed to support this
requirement include control structures and data structures such as those
found in general purpose programming languages. Sometimes a case is made
for some "real-time specific" data types such as fixed point, matrix, and
vector. The need for these, however, is highly dependent on the application
area and is not intrinsic to the real-time nature of the system.

2.3.2 Parallel Computational Ability

Another class of requirements includes parallel processing capabilities. Many real-time systems conceptually can be thought of as several
tasks operating in parallel with some degree of interaction. Language
features that support parallelism enable the expression of programs that
implement the system to follow closely the conceptualization of the system.
In addition to features that support the existence of parallel tasks,
features are also needed to control their interaction reliably.

2.3.3 Machine-Dependent Capability

An important aspect of the language power required for real-time
systems is support of full use of the system hardware. Past attempts at
general purpose high-order language design, having machine-independence as
a goal, have not incorporated machine-dependent capabilities as an integral and uniform part of the languages. The fact that these have not been
provided, even though needed, is a major reason for the predominance of
assembly-language software in real-time systems [Wirth 1976].

An important reason for providing machine-dependent capabilities is
that in many real-time systems, specific hardware (such as peripheral
devices) is used having features especially designed for the particular
application (or class of applications). The programming language must
provide a means for accessing and using these special features. Machine-
dependent capabilities are also a means of achieving efficiency in that
programmers, having explicit control of storage layouts and instruction
sequences, can take maximum advantage of the hardware.

2.4 Efficiency

Although it is generally agreed that real-time software must be efficient, there has been a great deal of debate as to the relative importance of efficiency when compared with the requirements for reliability and maintainability. An ideal solution is to (1) provide software that is efficient enough to meet the time and space constraints of doing the job, (2) strive toward reliability and maintainability as long as the essential efficiency is provided, and (3) provide additional efficiency only when it will not compromise the reliability and maintainability achieved in (2).

The problem faced by the language designer is that the "essential level" of efficiency can vary greatly, depending on the application requirements and the available hardware. The best he can do is (1) provide features that contribute to efficiency (and not provide features contributing to inefficiency) whenever there is no conflict with the other language requirements, and (2) attempt to minimize the number of basically-subjective trade-offs made between these requirements.

Machine-dependent capabilities can be used to achieve efficiency, as described above. In addition, a language can provide machine-independent "optimizer hooks", i.e., features that provide additional information that can be used by a "smart" compiler for optimization and that enable a programmer to specify time-space trade-offs. However, language features that require a smart compiler in order to achieve an efficient implementation should be avoided. Also to be avoided are features that have, independent of a compiler's cleverness, relatively high time or space costs and ones that require a non-trivial amount of run-time support.

2.5 Portability

There are at least two advantages in having computer software that can be transported from one set of hardware to another. First, capabilities developed in one project can be transferred to another project, even with different equipment, and second, software lifetimes can be increased by carrying software from one machine generation to the next within the same installation [Tinman 1976]. The transportation of software not only has the potential for reduced costs, but also for increased reliability which would result naturally from the increased use of the same programs. There are several language requirements that are related to portability:

2.5.1 Machine and Implementation Independence

It must be possible to implement the language for a variety of target
computers, and these implementations must be consistent with one another.
Thus, the language design should avoid features that require the capabilities
of any specific computer family for achieving a "reasonable" implementation.
The specification of the language must explicitly indicate all places where
machine and implementation dependencies are not avoided (such as the actual
precision of floating-point numbers). It is also desirable to specify
these dependencies in as independent (i.e., parameterized) a manner as
possible. In other words, when dependencies cannot be realistically avoided,
the goal should be to make such dependencies highly visible, so that their
effect will not "cause any surprises" when a program is transported to
another implementation.

2.5.2 Encapsulation of Machine-Dependencies

The previous section discussed the desirability of achieving, to the
extent it is possible, machine-independence of language features. However,
we have also noted that languages for real-time systems must provide the
applications programmer with direct access to specific machine capabilities.
Clearly the use of such capabilities will make real-time software machine-
dependent. Just as machine-dependent portions of a language should be
explicitly specified, so should machine-dependent portions of an applications program. Thus the language should provide a mechanism to insure
that machine-dependent data and instructions are encapsulated for explicit
designation. When transporting a program, only those designated portions
should need to be rewritten.

2.5.3 Re-Usability

Another goal often mentioned for real-time software is that programs
developed for one system should be applicable to several other systems.
Transportation of software from one system to another usually requires that
the program provide a "general-case" solution to the problem at hand. It
would be desirable to have the necessary generality of the solution built
into the program during its initial development, but achieving this is not
a function of the language design. However, by requiring explicit interface definitions and features to support readability (as previously discussed), a language can at least assist in the development of re-usable
software, and can aid potential re-users of the software, who must understand it in order to evaluate its applicability.

3.0 SPECIFIC REQUIREMENTS FOR REAL-TIME LANGUAGES

3.1 Parallelism

The concept of parallelism is intrinsic to the nature of most real-time systems. This is the case because (1) various components of the system may have possibly-independent time-critical deadlines and (2) various peripheral devices may require immediate servicing.

Language features that support parallelism can not only contribute to the understandability and reliability of the programs produced, but can also facilitate actual parallel execution when a suitable hardware configuration is available.

Language features are needed to specify the creation (and termination) of parallel tasks and also the interaction among the parallel tasks. As Hoare has noted, however, "Methods of building parallelism into a high level language are a lively topic for ongoing research at the present time" [Hoare 1975]. Nonetheless, there are certain characteristics that the parallelism features must provide for real-time systems.

One important characteristic that must be present is that parallel tasks be independent except for explicitly specified interactions. Thus, implicit inheritance of global variables by a parallel task is clearly inappropriate. Shared variables must be explicitly declared and accessed as such. Two possible mechanisms for this are critical regions and monitors. This characteristic is extremely important for reliability as well as understandability.

In addition to shared variables, features for synchronization among parallel processes are also required. The ability is needed for a process to delay itself if a particular condition is not currently satisfied. Similarly, the ability is needed for a process to indicate the fulfillment of a condition so that a delayed process may continue its execution.

Hardware interrupts from peripheral devices are conceptually a synchronization indication from a hardware process to a software process (i.e., an indication of the fulfillment of a condition). With a small amount of run-time support, this hardware-software synchronization can be unified with the software-software synchronization facilities of the language, thus eliminating the need for an explicit interrupt handling mechanism.

A final constraint that may be appropriate for real-time systems regards the creation and deletion of parallel process. Hoare feels that "The dynamic creation and deletion of processes is ill-advised. There should be a fixed number of processes; and when a process has nothing to do, it should simply wait for its next task" [Hoare 1975]. The question of dynamic vs. static creation of processes is really a time-space trade-off. Eliminating the ability to create processes dynamically in the language removes the system implementor's ability to make the trade-off himself. This is too restrictive for real-time systems.

3.2 Exception Handling

Exception-handling facilities are extremely important in a language for real-time systems. It is absolutely unacceptable for an error to cause a real-time system to lose control or terminate abnormally. The real-time system itself should decide whether an error can be corrected adequately and if not provide an appropriate recovery action.

It should be noted that by exception handling, we are referring strictly to error handling. More general definitions of exceptions have been proposed [e.g., Goodenough 1975] that attempt to unify the mechanisms for dealing with errors and other "exceptional" conditions. Such an approach clearly includes the needed facilities for real-time error-handling but may provide more than is actually required for real-time systems.

Hardware interrupts can also be treated by the exception handling mechanism. However, there are conceptually different classes of hardware interrupts. As mentioned in the previous section, hardware interrupts from peripheral devices are conceptually a synchronization indication between parallel (asynchronous) tasks, and should be handled by the synchronization facilities of the language. Error interrupts (e.g., overflow) on the other hand are conceptually synchronous in that a given instruction stream has committed an error which causes invocation of an error handler.

Language facilities are needed for specifying error-handling routines for all classes of errors that can occur. The mechanism must provide the handler with sufficient information (e.g., in the form of parameters) for the handler to diagnose the situation correctly. The handler should have the following options after completing its execution: (1) resume the routine that caused the error and allow it to retry to operation causing the error, (2) resume the routine that caused the error immediately after

the operation causing the error, (3) abort the routine that caused the
error and pass control to an appropriate recovery point. Cases (1) and (2)
generally would be used when the handler is able to correct the error,
whereas case (3) would be used when the error is uncorrectable.

3.3 Efficiency

Although efficiency should be an important consideration in any programming effort, it is especially crucial for real-time software. The
programmer must insure that the system (1) meets the critical time constraints of the application, (2) can be implemented within the size constraints of the hardware, and (3) has a time and space margin of safety so
that system enhancements are possible during its period of use. The ease
with which this can be achieved is significantly affected by the design of
the programming language. Real-time languages should avoid features that
contribute to inefficiency or that place a heavy burden on an implementation
in order to achieve efficiency. Desirable features are ones which aid
in the generation of efficient object code and ones which allow the program
to resolve explicitly efficiency trade-offs such as time versus space.

3.3.1 Efficient Storage Allocation

An important design issue related to software efficiency is that of
storage allocation strategies. Under a static strategy, the allocation and
storage layout for all program data is determined prior to the program's
execution. The same storage can be allocated, and used safely, for the
local data belonging to two or more blocks or procedures whenever their
activation periods are mutually disjoint. In addition, a static strategy
implies minimal overhead on procedure invocations, and increased reliability
since potential storage overflows can be detected at compile-time.

The disadvantage of static storage is that it is allocated throughout
the execution, even when large portions may not be needed or used. Various
dynamic allocation strategies alleviate this problem by allocating and
deallocating storage as it is needed during the execution. For example,
local procedure data can be allocated on a stack when a procedure is invoked
and deallocated upon the procedure's return. The price for this more
efficient use of memory is run-time storage management and more complex
data accessing through a static chain or display. However, it is a price
that must be paid if recursive procedures are desired in the language.

Other dynamic allocation strategies can be even more costly. For example, heap storage used for linked data structures is not automatically deallocated and requires periodic garbage collection. Another example is the requirement for cactus stacks when separate processes are permitted to reference the same automatic variables. General cactus stacks can add a great deal of run-time overhead since most hardware offers little direct support, although there are some notable exceptions [Cleary 1969]. Most real-time systems do not require the power of these dynamic strategies, and certainly cannot afford the additional costs.

3.3.2 Machine-Dependencies for Efficiency

A strong argument for assembly language programming is that it allows the program to take full advantage of the hardware capabilities. Thus the user has direct control over the efficiency of his data representations and instruction sequences. However, in recent years the ability of high-order language compilers to provide approximately the same level of efficiency has been demonstrated [Intermetrics 1975]. Features in these languages have been designed to reduce the need for machine-dependent constructs. For example, discriminated union and, on a more general level, block structure provide high-level, reliable means for achieving the efficiency of data overlays on the same physical storage.

In spite of these advances in high-order language design, there are still many cases where direct access to the machine is desired. For example, the program may be able to make assumptions that, for special cases, permit highly-specialized packing of data or optimization of control. While not generally condoning such practices (because of the potential impact on reliability, maintainability, and transportability), the language must permit them for applications having extremely critical time or space constraints.

3.3.3 Optimizer "Hooks" and User Controls for Efficiency

A language should not require the use of a smart (and therefore complex) compiler in order to generate efficient code. Often features can be incorporated into a language to provide a compiler with optimization information that the compiler itself could only obtain with great difficulty, if at all. For example, one can require explicit specification of numeric ranges, thereby allowing the compiler to determine efficient physical representations. Another example is requiring that the need for re-entrancy in a procedure be explicitly declared.

Other language features can be incorporated to give the user some control over his program's efficiency. For example, a machine-independent packing specification can be used to determine the time/space trade-off to be made between compact data representations and minimal data access times. Another example is the ability to specify whether the code for a procedure is to be closed and accessed from every invocation point, or openly regenerated at each of those points.

3.3.4 Avoiding Inefficiency

There are many features that, by their very nature, imply relatively high run-time costs and therefore should be avoided by the language designer. For example, dynamically-varying array sizes require costly storage allocation strategies as have been discussed previously. Even the requirement that the maximum size be fixed during the initial allocation does not eliminate the need for dope vectors and run-time address computations. Another area of run-time overhead is that involving checking. While desirable for reasons of reliability, the costs of such features can sometimes be prohibitive. A partial solution is to perform as many of the checks as possible at compile-time. This increases both efficiency and reliability at run-time, and in many cases can be accomplished without sacrificing necessary computational power. A third area to be avoided encompasses features that require extensive run-time support. A minimal amount of support must be provided for "administrative" purposes, especially if the system includes parallel processes. However, extensive manipulation of files and peripheral devices, complex scheduling algorithms, sophisticated data management, and so on, are highly dependent upon the particular application. They are best "tailored" to meet the needs of a given system by that system's software and not by the supporting high-order language. However, this does not prevent the sharing of the same routine if it is applicable to more than one system.

3.4 Machine Independence and Machine-Dependent Capabilities

Although machine independence is a desired goal for real-time software, the widely divergent set of hardware designs makes its complete achievement virtually impossible. The best that can be done is to indicate explicitly all such dependencies as a part of the language specification. This includes both machine dependencies like integer range variations due to differing word sizes and implementation dependencies such as the number of allowable nesting levels. Often the dependency specification can be done using parameters in a uniform machine-independent manner.

Many real-time systems require the introduction of machine-dependencies
so that the software can take advantage of specialized hardware. This is
not only for reasons of efficiency, as we have discussed previously, but
also because of application-dependent computational requirements such as
the control of peripheral devices. Thus the supporting high-order language
must provide machine-dependent capabilities. However, it should provide
such capabilities in a machine-independent fashion that is consistent with
the overall language design. For example, machine-dependent data types
may vary from one implementation to another, but the rules for handling
them should be consistent with those for other types. Similarly, direct
code procedures should have a parameter mechanism that is both syntactically
and semantically consistent (although not necessarily identical) with the
mechanism for machine-independent procedures.

It is important that the language design makes the use of machine-
dependent features explicit in an applications program. Machine-dependent
data should be clearly labeled as such. Direct code should be encapsulated
into explicitly-designated segments similar to BEGIN blocks or procedures
(which may be either closed or opened inline). Again, the machine-
dependent mechanisms should be as machine-independent as possible. For
example, using parameters to machine-dependent procedures should not require
that the programmer understand the general parameter storage layouts for
a particular implementation. Nor should the rules constrain every implementation to use the same parameter organization. Instead, the programmer
should be permitted to specify the layouts himself through a machine-
dependent structuring mechanism.

By following the above approach of indicating explicitly all machine
and implementation dependencies, program transportation can be accomplished
reliably. The only constraint on the program is that:
> "(1) it violates none of the clearly defined resource constraints
>   of either implementation, [and]
> (2) all program modules containing machine code have been
>   replaced by modules having the same effect on the other
>   machine" [Hoare 1975].

4.0 SUMMARY

In this paper we have attempted to identify those programming language requirements that are particularly important in real-time software. Types of language capabilities and features satisfying these requirements have been discussed. However, many unsolved problems remain; our main goal was not to propose specific features for the "ideal" real-time language but to point out the areas of concern. There are many language features that satisfy a given requirement, but in doing so conflict with other requirements. It is difficult for the designer of a language intended for differing real-time systems to determine the appropriate trade-offs between conflicting requirements. Proper trade-off determination is often highly dependent on the specific applications and is influenced by both the system's functional requirements and the underlying hardware. High-order languages must be designed so that the implementor of each system is given the maximum flexibility in specifying his own requirement trade-offs.

5.0   REFERENCES

[Cleary 1969]

   Cleary, J.G.   "Process Handling on Burroughs B6500," in the Proceedings
      of the Fourth Australian Computer Conference, 1969.

[Goodenough 1975]

   Goodenough, J.B.   "Exception Handling: Issues and a Proposed Notation,"
      CACM 18, 12, 1975.

[Hoare 1974]

   Hoare, C.A.R.   "Hints on Programming Language Design," in Computer
      Systems Reliability, Infotech State of the Art Report, No. 20, 1974.

[Hoare 1975]

   Hoare, C.A.R.   "Hints on the Design of a Programming Language for Real-
      Time Command and Control," in Implementation Languages for Real-
      Time Systems, U. S. Army European Research Office Tech. Report
      No. ERO-2-75, Vol. 2, 1975.

[Intermetrics 1975]

   "On the Performance of the HAL/S-FC Compiler," Intermetrics, Inc.,
      Report IR-162, 1975.

[Tinman 1976]

   "Requirements for High Order Computer Programming Languages: 'Tinman'",
      Department of Defense, 1976.

[Wirth 1976]

   Wirth, N. "MODULA: A Language for Modular Multiprogramming," Institut
      fur Informatik Report No. 18, Eidgenossische Technische Hochschule,
      Zurich, 1976.

Remarks on the Impact of Program Verification on Language Design

Ralph L. London[*]

USC Information Sciences Institute

Several members of the Program Committee of the Workshop asked me to elaborate on some remarks I made at the Symposium on the Impact of Research on Software Technology, in Durham, North Carolina, in mid-July, 1976. My main observation is that in the "Tinman" there seems to be little concern for verification. To be sure, there is the suggestion that assertions be provided at various points in the program so that a program can be shown to satisfy these assertions. However, the impact of program verification on language design is significantly deeper than just providing assertion statements. Perhaps the best way to illustrate this viewpoint is to discuss experiences from two language designs in which I am a participant. These examples are intended to be suggestive and indicative of the kinds of influences that seem important and that have been helpful; there is no intent that they be exhaustive, final, or definitive.

The two programming languages of interest here are Euclid [Lampson77] and Alphard [Wulf76a,b, Shaw76b]. Both of these language designs have as one of their important goals verifiability of the resulting programs. Naturally, additional goals and numerous other concerns exert major influences on these languages. Nevertheless, it has been both surprising and extremely pleasing to observe the degree to which these

----

[*] Supported by the Defense Advanced Research Projects Agency Contract DAHC-15-72-C-0308. The views expressed are those of the author.

concerns have reinforced each other. A brief glimpse into the interactions starts with Euclid.

The Euclid language, drawing heavily on Pascal [Jensen74] and deliberately restricted to current knowledge of programming languages and compilers, is intended for the expression of system programs which are to be verified. Both the language and its compiler are given part of the task of producing a correct program and of verifying its correctness. For example, although global variables are permitted, they must be explicitly listed when used in a procedure (or a module). This explicit listing means that no reader of a program need do computing or complex searching to determine the global variables. One class of readers in particular, human or mechanical verifiers, has this information readily available for use. Furthermore, the language is able to guarantee that two identifiers in the same scope can never refer to the same variable, i.e., there is no aliasing. All of this – by deliberate design – meshes well with a new, easily explained proof rule for verifying procedure definitions and calls [London77, Guttag77]. The proof rule, developed for Euclid from several existing proof rules, captures exactly the full Euclid procedure definition and call mechanism and also removes restrictions and known problems with other proof rules. In a very real sense, the Euclid design is one of adding restrictions and the enforcing mechanisms to meet a desired level of program understandability and verification capability.

The use and verification of pointers in Euclid is made easier than in other languages by allowing each dynamic variable to be assigned to a language construct, the *collection*, and guaranteeing that two pointers into different collections can never refer to the same variable. Thus assertions need not be invented and verified to obtain this guarantee; instead it is all part of the language.

When possible, the above guarantees are provided by extensive compile-time checks. If the compiler is unable to complete a check, it generates *legality assertions* for the verifier to establish. Verification concepts are thereby used to complement other mechanisms. Further discussion of verification influences in the design of Euclid may be found in [Popek77].

The Alphard language is a new language design rather than one starting from an exisiting language. The effort focuses simultaneously on issues of programming structure (methodology) and verification. The abstraction mechanism of Alphard, the *form*, encapsulates a set of related function definitions and associated data descriptions, allowing a programmer to reveal the behavior of an abstraction to other users while hiding information and protecting details of the concrete implementation.

This explicit distinction between the abstract behavior of a data abstraction and the concrete program that happens to implement that behavior provides an ideal setting in which to apply Hoare's techniques for proving the correctness of data representations [Hoare72]. In the Alphard adaptation one shows that the concrete representation is adequate to represent the abstract objects, that it is initialized properly, and that each operator provided on the abstract objects both preserves the integrity of the representation and does what it is claimed to do (in terms of both the abstract behavior and the concrete procedure that actually implements the operator).

The verification techniques and the methodology decisions both require providing specifications of the abstract objects and the related operations. They also need conditions describing the concrete objects and operations, invariants holding over all operations, and a representation function giving the relation between concrete and abstract objects. All of this information, made an integral part of a form definition, was originally included for verification reasons. Its presence, however, has directed attention toward things which, on methodological grounds, ought to be of concern. The verification technique exposed the need for certain language features, which at best were viewed as conveniences and at worst would have been missed completely on the basis of methodological or language considerations alone.

Methodology concerns have, in turn, also benefited verification. The entire form concept, for example, was introduced for methodological reasons. It is this factorization and isolation, however, which appears to make either hand or mechanical verification feasible. Similarly the notion of *generators*, which permits hiding certain details of iteration, was introduced on methodological grounds, but is also simplifying the verification of many loops. Loop control using generators is implicit rather than explicit, and therefore a single verification of that loop control suffices for all of its invocations.

An important part of language design is knowing what should be left out. During the Alphard design, constructs were repeatedly proposed which either gave difficulty in formulating the needed proof rules or which looked suspect on methodological grounds. Usually such a problem signalled an unforeseen problem in the other domain. For example, an early version of the iteration statement was much more elaborate than the one currently adopted [Wulf76c]. Nevertheless, it seemed plausible on methodological grounds. Its verification, however, was a horror to behold. Subsequently it became apparent that the complexity of its verification was symptomatic of a difficulty which any programmer would have in attempting to understand the statement or its use.

Numerous example forms, and programs using these forms, have been designed and verified [Wulf76a,b, Shaw76a,b, London76]. The proofs are modular, reflecting the structure of the programs. In addition, the lengths of the proofs are within reasonable limits and indeed quite encouraging. Most importantly, when modifications have been made to a program, corresponding modifications needed in the proof have been nearly always easy to identify and to complete, without the need to redo the entire proof. If the implementation of an abstraction is changed, but not the specifications, then all programs using the abstraction and all verifications of those uses are also unchanged.

There are no panaceas to be derived from the above summary of some of the impacts of verification on programming language design and in the expression of quality programs. A useful approach, however, in both Euclid and Alphard was to ask questions such as the following:

- How, for a proposed language, would one specify and then verify the behavior of a program which uses a feature or, even more importantly, a set of interacting features?

- What might be the proof rules for proposed constructs?

- Can the language provide assistance to the verification by guaranteeing certain desired states (rather than requiring that these states be verified)?

These sorts of questions provide an important and rather objective way to evaluate a language design, an observation already made by Dijkstra [Dijkstra75a].

There are examples of other languages whose designs have been influenced by verification concerns generally, or by considerations of appropriate axiomatic definitions or other semantic definitions in particular. Among the better known are Pascal, Concurrent Pascal [Brinch Hansen75], PL/CS [Conway76], Clu [Liskov77], Gypsy [Ambler77], and although not a language, Dijkstra's guarded commands [Dijkstra75b]. One may also classify languages according to their concern for verification in a slightly different way. Was verification an important goal, was it influential in the design, was it neutral and essentially of no concern, or was there, in retrospect, what seems to be a "deliberate attempt to subvert" or "a desire to remove any possibility" of verification?

As several people have noted, the best time to be concerned with verifying a program is at the earliest possible time in the life of that program. An unnecessarily challenging task can easily be created by suddenly requiring that an extant program be verified. While the choice of language in which a program is written is not of primary concern, obviously some languages lend themselves to verification better than others. Since Tinman is to be a new language in which presumably the best of existing technology is to be exploited, it seems appropriate that the design of the language consider the desirability of verified Tinman programs. Indeed, the language design should contribute actively to that goal, one which is extremely often consistent with other goals.

Language design is currently an art and clearly involves many competing factors. The design of useful, verifiable languages is no less an art, but some experience does exist. It would be unfortunate if that experience were not at least considered in the Tinman endeavor. In summary, let verification influences be consciously omitted from Tinman but not accidentally overlooked.

References

[Ambler77] Ambler, A. L., D. I. Good, J. C. Browne, W. F. Burger, R. M. Cohen, C. G. Hoch, and R. E. Wells, "Gypsy: A Language for Specification and Implementation of Verifiable Programs," *Proceedings of Language Design for Reliable Software*, 1977 (to appear).

[Brinch Hansen75] Brinch Hansen, P., "The Programming Language Concurrent Pascal," *IEEE Transactions on Software Engineering*, Vol. SE-1, No. 2, June 1975, pp. 199-207.

[Conway76] Conway, R., "PL/CS--A Highly Disciplined Subset of PL/C," *SIGPLAN Notices*, Vol. 11, No. 12, December 1976, pp. 21-24. Also *Cornell University Technical Report TR76-273*, March 1976.

[Dijkstra75a] Dijkstra, E. W., "Correctness Concerns and, Among Other Reasons, Why They Are Resented," *Proceedings of the International Conference on Reliable Software*, 1975, pp. 546-550. Also *SIGPLAN Notices*, Vol. 10, No. 6, June 1975.

[Dijkstra75b] Dijkstra, E. W., "Guarded Commands, Nondeterminacy and Formal Derivation of Programs," *Communications of ACM*, Vol. 18, No. 8, August 1975, pp. 453-457.

[Guttag77] Guttag, J. V., J. J. Horning, and R. L. London, *A Proof Rule for Euclid Procedures*, 1977 (submitted for publication).

[Hoare72] Hoare, C.A.R., "Proof of Correctness of Data Representations," *Acta Informatica*, Vol. 1, No. 4, 1972, pp. 271-281.

[Jensen74] Jensen, K., and N. Wirth, *PASCAL User Manual and Report*, Lecture Notes in Computer Science, Vol. 18, G. Goos and J. Hartmanis, (eds.), Springer-Verlag, 1974.

[Lampson77] Lampson, B. W., J. J. Horning, R. L. London, J. G. Mitchell, and G. J. Popek, "Report on the Programming Language Euclid," *SIGPLAN Notices*, 1977 (to appear).

[Liskov77] Liskov, B., A. Snyder, R. Atkinson, and C. Shaffert, "Abstraction Mechanisms in Clu," *Proceedings of Language Design for Reliable Software*, 1977 (to appear). Also *MIT Computation Structures Group Memo 144*, October 1976.

[London76] London, R. L., M. Shaw, and W. A. Wulf, *Abstraction and Verification in Alphard: A Symbol Table Example*, Carnegie-Mellon University and USC Information Sciences Institute Technical Reports, 1976.

[London77] London, R. L., J. V. Guttag, J. J. Horning, B. W. Lampson, J. G. Mitchell, and G. J. Popek, *Proof Rules for the Programming Language Euclid*, 1977.

[Popek77] Popek, G. J., J. J. Horning, B. W. Lampson, R. L. London, and J. G. Mitchell, "Some Design Issues in Euclid" (working title), *Proceedings of Language Design for Reliable Software*, 1977 (to appear).

[Shaw76a] Shaw, M., "Abstraction and Verification in Alphard: Design and Verification of a Tree Handler," *Proceedings of Fifth Texas Conference on Computing Systems*, 1976, pp. 86-94. Also Carnegie-Mellon University Technical Report, 1976.

[Shaw76b] Shaw, M., W. A. Wulf, and R. L. London, *Abstraction and Verification in Alphard: Iteration and Generators*, Carnegie-Mellon University and USC Information Sciences Institute Technical Reports, 1976. Also *Communications of ACM* (to appear).

[Wulf76a] Wulf, W. A., R. L. London, and M. Shaw, *Abstraction and Verification in Alphard: Introduction to Language and Methodology*, Carnegie-Mellon University and USC Information Sciences Institute Technical Reports, 1976.

[Wulf76b]   Wulf, W. A., R. L. London, and M. Shaw, "An Introduction to the Construction and Verification of Alphard Programs," *IEEE Transactions on Software Engineering*, Vol. SE-2, No. 4, December 1976, pp. 253-265.

[Wulf76c]   Wulf, W. A.,   M. Shaw,   and   R. L. London,   "Achieving   Quality Software: Reflections on the Aims and Objectives of Alphard," *Computer Science Research Review 1975-76*, Carnegie-Mellon University, pp. 7-15.

TARGET COMPUTER INDEPENDENT OPTIMIZATION
PROCEDURES FOR METACOMPILERS

by
Paul M. Cohen
Defense Communications Engineering Center
1860 Wiehle Avenue
Reston, Virginia 22090

1. INTRODUCTION

Efficient use, by several computers, of a common high order language may be accomplished with cross-compiling techniques and a metacompiler which permits the development of the several compilers from a single computer program. Methods exist [1,2,3] for developing such a metacompiler in two parts which are referred to, respectively, as the front end program and the back end program. Front end programs are "almost" identical for each compiler implementation, but separate back end programs must be developed, either in a common programming language or in a special interpretive language.

Obviously, the more compiling tasks that can be placed in the front end, the less reprogramming that has to be accomplished to develop additional compilers for additional target computers. Optimization can be treated as one such task by describing algorithms generically and modularly developing them to operate on an intermediate level language representation of the source program. Optimization techniques have been used in studies of efficient high order languages for communications processing, and have been implemented, within a front end metacompiler program, so that they map a quadruple table representation of a source language program into itself.

The following types of optimizations have been implemented by the above method:

*   Code motion to minimize store and load instructions

*   Evaluation of literal expressions

*   Elimination of common subexpressions

*   Minimization of the number of registers, the amount of temporary storage, and the stack length in use at any one time.

* Utilization of commutativity to affect one or
  more of the above optimizations

* Short circuit evaluation of Boolean "AND" and "OR"

* Elimination of Boolean "NOT" (De Morgan's Theorem).

As a by-product of front end optimization the following
tasks occur which simplify the back end program:

* Interpretation of variable "TYPE" information so that
  back end program deals with a "TYPE"-less language

* Transformation of control structures, such as
  "IF-THEN-ELSE", into simpler "GOTO" operations.

Study has shown that these techniques can be used to build a
single front end which can drive code for a wide variety of
architectures, from a simple computer with a one address
instruction, a single accumulator and indirect addressing, to one
with many multi-purpose registers, and to one performing
arithmetic on a push down stack. These techniques should be
considered in the developing a family of cross compilers for the
emerging DoD common language.

2. TEST IMPLEMENTATION.

The Generic Optimization described in this paper has been
demonstrated on an experimental metacompiler called FLAG
(Flexible Language Generator), which has been developed at the
Defense Communications Engineering Center (DCEC) as part of a
project to develop a Communications Oriented Language. The FLAG
system is built around a two part metacompiler which operates in
the following manner: In the first part the source language
inputs are translated into a common language which is in the form
of a quadruple table. In the second part the common language is
compiled into assembler language code. The metacompiler is
designed to compile under the control of an input data set which
defines both the high order language and the target computer.
The inputs to the first part include a parametric description of
each source language operator. These parameters are entered into
translation tables which control translation into the common
language. The inputs to the second part are a code skeleton for
each common language operator and instructions to operate on the
skeletal code. These instructions are in the form of an
interpretive program to translate skeletal code into assembler
language code. The output of this metacompiler is an assembler
language-like listing.

323

Techniques similar to those used by FLAG are being used by the avionics industry to develop software for on-board aircraft computers.

3. OPTIMIZATION PROCEDURES

The following is a set of examples to illustrate the target computer independent optimization which is possible with a compiler that is organized as described above. The examples use PL/I as a source language and illustrate the optimization by a sequence of three tables as follows:

TABLE A -- The basic quadruple table representation of the source language statements.

TABLE B -- The quadruple table after optimization.

TABLE C -- A more readable representation of Table B.

3.1 EXAMPLE 1, ARITHMETIC STATEMENT OPTMIZATION

In Example 1, the infix minus operator compiles, in some computers, more efficiently when the right argument is compiled before the left argument. Thus quadruples are permuted to accomplish this translation. The order to perform this motion is parametrically entered into the attributes assigned to the real and integer infix minus operators.

The expression, -3, is evaluated and identified as C(01$.

Following the customary defaults (integer variables start with I, J, K, L, M, or N), the first statement is in integer arithmetic, and the second in real arithmetic. These default attributes of the variables are, in Table A, associated with the variables as indicated by the flags, ">" and ">1", for integer and real, respectively. In Table B, the arithmetic operators are each identified as integer or real and the identifiers can be considered typeless.

3.2 EXAMPLE 2, COMMON SUBEXPRESSION OPTIMIZATION

In Example 2, two common subexpressions are recognized and saved as T)02 and T)03. The final time each is used it is flagged with "=". The identifiers, T)02 and T)03 can represent either a temporary storage location or a multi-purpose register, depending upon the target computer. Thus the information in Table B cues the reuse of such resources.

In the last "+(R)" quadruple, X and Y have been permuted to facilitate subsequent STORE-LOAD sequence optimization. The conditions under which to perform such permutation are parametrically controlled and are a function of the target computer.

3.3 EXAMPLE 3, SHORT CIRCUIT BOOLEAN EXPRESSION

Example 3 shows the quadruple table representation of an IF-THEN-ELSE construct. The quadruple contains precedence level information for each Boolean operator. This precedence is ordered by, first, the parentheses level of the operator, and, second, the usual precedence order, NOT, AND, OR. In the absence of any NOT operators, the following algorithm can be used to map the construct into a short circuit representation:

An OR is mapped into a JUMP-TRUE to the subsequent AND of lower precedence, or to the THEN clause. An AND is mapped into a JUMP-FALSE to the subsequent OR of lower precedence, or to the END (of the THEN clause). The THEN is mapped into a JUMP-FALSE to the END (of the THEN clause). During each sequential search for a jump address, the precedence level of the AND, OR being mapped is dynamically lowered to the level of any AND, OR operator (of lower level) through which it passes.

Note that in Example 3, a distinction is made between an integer and a real comparison.

3.4 EXAMPLE 4. DE MORGAN'S THEOREM

In practice, Example 3 is treated as a special case of the following algorithm which implements De Morgan's Theorem concurrently with short circuiting as follows:

Define NOT-OR, NOT-AND, NOT-THEN, as the OR, AND, THEN, operators immediately preceded by an odd number of NOT operators. This forms a class of six operators to be mapped by the algorithm: OR, AND, NOT-OR, NOT-AND, THEN, NOT-THEN. Each operator in this class is mapped into a "mapped instruction" to the subsequent "jump destination" of lower precedence according to the following table. The "jump destination" is controlled by a negation counter, NEG, which is inverted each time the sequential search for a "jump destination" passes through a NOT (of lower precedence). Also, the precedence level of the operator being mapped is dynamically lowered to the level of any operator (of lower precedence) of the class through which it passes:

OPERATOR	MAPPED INSTRUCTION	JUMP DESTINATION NEG=0	NEG=1
OR	JUMP-TRUE	AND THEN	OR END
AND	JUMP-FALSE	OR END	AND THEN
NOT-OR	JUMP-FALSE	AND THEN	OR END
NOT-AND	JUMP-TRUE	OR END	AND THEN
THEN	JUMP-FALSE	END	
NOT-THEN	JUMP-TRUE	END	

Example 4A and Example 4B show Boolean equivalents of the statement in Example 3 as processed by this algorithm.

4.   EFFECT OF DIFFERENT ARCHITECTURES

Compilers for a variety of architectures can be driven from the same front end compiler program. Example 5 and Example 6 illustrate code generated for two hypothetical computers, one with multi-purpose accumulators and one with a Polish organization.

5.   CONCLUSIONS

The DoD1 language effort will result in a language being developed for many target machines, some of which will not support resident compilers. Techniques such as those presented in this paper can be perfected to reduce the cost and time involved in developing efficient DoD1 compilers for such machines. Thus these compilers should be organized to include target computer independent optimization proceedures.

REFERENCES

[1]   P. M. Cohen and W. O. Felsman, "Meta-Compiler Use in Machine Design," Proc, IEEE Symposium on Programming and Machine Organization (April 1971)pp 1-15.

[2]   IBM-FSD, Owego, N.Y., 73-M68-002, "Common Intermediate Language Compiler," F. Bostrom, D. Foreman, L. Haibt, 1973.

[3]   DCEC TN 17-75, "The Use of a Communications Oriented Language Within a Software Engineering System," P. M. Cohen, April 1975.

```
/*                 EXAMPLE 1                  */
/*                                            */
/*              CODE MOTION                   */
/*  EVALUATION OF LITERAL EXPRESSION          */
/*                 AND                        */
/*            TYPE-LESS LANGUAGE              */
/*                                            */
  I=-3*J1-K1*K2;
  Y=R*S-((A*B-C*D)-P*R);
```

TABLE A

-		3$	T)02
*	T)02	J1>	T)03
*	K1>	K2>	T)04
-	T)03	T)04	T)05
=	I>	T)05	I>
;			I>
*	R>1	S>1	T)07
*	A>1	B>1	T)08
*	C>1	D>1	T)09
-	T)08	T)09	T)10
*	P>1	R>1	T)11
-	T)10	T)11	T)12
-	T)07	T)12	T)13
=	Y>1	T)13	Y>1
;			Y>1

TABLE B

*	K1	K2	T)04=
*	C(01$	J1	T)03=
-	T)03=	T)04=	I
;			I
*(R)	C	D	T)09=
*(R)	P	R	T)11=
*(R)	A	B	T)12=
-(R)	T)12=	T)09=	T)12=
-(R)	T)12=	T)11=	T)12=
*(R)	R	S	T)07=
-(R)	T)07=	T)12=	Y
;		K	Y

TABLE C

0	T)01	=	K1	*	K2
1	T)02	=	C(01$	*	J1
2	I	=	T)02	-	T)01
3	T)01	=	C	*	D
4	T)02	=	P	*	R
5	T)03	=	A	*	B
6	T)03	=	T)03	-	T)01
7	T)03	=	T)03	-	T)02
8	T)01	=	R	*	S
9	Y	=	T)01	-	T)03
10	C(01	GEN -		3	
		END	0		

327

```
/*              EXAMPLE 2                */
/*                                       */
/*           ELIMINATION OF              */
/*      COMMON SUBEXPRESSIONS            */
/*      REGISTER MINIMIZATION            */
/*        AND COMMUTATIVITY              */
/*                                       */
W=A+B+C+D;
X=E*(A+B);
Y=(A+B+C)-F;
Z=E*(A+B)+Y;
```

TABLE A

+	A>1	B>1	T)02
+	T)02	C>1	T)03
+	T)03	D>1	T)04
=	W>1	T)04	W>1
;			W>1
+	A>1	B>1	T)06
*	E>1	T)06	T)07
=	X>1	T)07	X>1
;			X>1
+	A>1	B>1	T)09
+	T)09	C>1	T)10
−	T)10	F>1	T)11
=	Y>1	T)11	Y>1
;			Y>1
+	A>1	B>1	T)13
*	E>1	T)13	T)14
+	T)14	Y>1	T)15
=	Z>1	T)15	Z>1
;			Z>1

TABLE B

+(R)	A	B	T)02==
+(R)	T)02==	C	T)03==
+(R)	T)03==	D	W
;			W
*(R)	E	T)02=	X
;			X
−(R)	T)03=	F	Y
;			Y
+(R)	Y	X	Z
;		K	Z

TABLE C

0	T)01	=	A	+	B
1	T)02	=	T)01	+	C
2	W	=	T)02	+	D
3	X	=	E	*	T)01
4	Y	=	T)02	−	F
5	Z	=	Y	+	X
		END	0		

```
/*                 EXAMPLE 3                  */
/*                                            */
/* SHORT CIRCUIT BOOLEAN EVALUATION  */
/*                AND                         */
/*    SIMPLIFY CONTROL STRUCTURES    */
/*                                            */
 IF A NE 0 OR B NE 0 OR (I EQ 0 AND J EQ 0 AND X EQ 0)
                                      THEN K=1;
                                      ELSE K=0;
```

TABLE A

IF			T)02
NE	A>1	0$	T)03
OR	T)03		C(11H
NE	B>1	0$	T)04
OR	T)04		C(11H
EQ	I>	0$	T)05
AND	T)05		C(22H
EQ	J>	0$	T)06
AND	T)06		C(22H
EQ	X>1	0$	T)07
THEN	T)07		T)07
=	K>	1$	K>
;			K>
ENDTHEN			
ELSE			T)09
=	K>	0$	K>
;			K>
ENDELSE			

TABLE B

IF			T)02=
NE(R)	A	0$	T)03=
JT)	105THEN	101A	C(11H
NE(R)	B	0$	T)04=
JT)	105THEN	102A	C(11H
EQ	I	0$	T)05=
JF)	105END	103A	C(22H
EQ	J	0$	T)06=
JF)	105END	104A	C(22H
EQ(R)	X	0$	T)07=
JF)	105END	105THEN	T)07=
=	K	1$	K
;			K
ENDTHEN			
ELSE			T)09=
=	K	0$	K
;			K
ENDELSE			

TABLE C

0	101I	IS	A	NOT EQL	0$
1		JUMP	-TRUE	105THEN	
2	: : : :				
2	101A	IS	B	NOT EQL	0$
3		JUMP	-TRUE	105THEN	
4	: : : :				
4	102A	DOES	I	EQUAL	0$
5		JUMP	-FALSE	105END	
6	: : : :				
6	103A	DOES	J	EQUAL	0$
7		JUMP	-FALSE	105END	
8	: : : :				
8	104A	DOES	X	EQUAL	0$
9		JUMP	-FALSE	105END	
10	: : : :				
10	105THEN				
10	K	=	1$		
11		JUMP	105ELSE		
12	: : : :				
12	105END				
12	K	=	0$		
13	: : : :				
13	105ELSE				
		END	0		

```
/*              EXAMPLE 4A                 */
/*                                         */
/*          DE MORGAN'S THEOREM            */
/*                                         */
IF NOT(A EQ 0 AND B EQ 0 AND NOT(I EQ 0 AND J EQ 0 AND X EQ 0))
                                          THEN K=1;
                                          ELSE K=0;
```

TABLE A

IF			T)02
EQ	A>1	0$	T)03
AND	T)03		C(22H
EQ	B>1	0$	T)04
AND	T)04		C(22H
EQ	I>	0$	T)05
AND	T)05		C(32H
EQ	J>	0$	T)06
AND	T)06		C(32H
EQ	X>1	0$	T)07
NOT		T)07	C(23H
NOT		C(23H	C(13H
THEN	C(13H		C(13H
=	K>	1$	K>
;			K>
ENDTHEN			
ELSE			T)09
=	K>	0$	K>
;			K>
ENDELSE			

TABLE B

IF			T)02=
EQ(R)	A	0$	T)03=
JF)	105THEN	101A	C(22H
EQ(R)	B	0$	T)04=
JF)	105THEN	102A	C(22H
EQ	I	0$	T)05=
JF)	105END	103A	C(32H
EQ	J	0$	T)06=
JF)	105END	104A	C(32H
EQ(R)	X	0$	T)07=
NOT		T)07=	C(23H
NOT		C(23H	C(13H
JF)	105END	105THEN	C(13H
=	K	1$	K
;			K
ENDTHEN			
ELSE			T)09=
=	K	0$	K
;			K
ENDELSE			

TABLE C

0	101I	DOES	A	EQUAL	0$
1		JUMP	-FALSE	105THEN	
2	: : : :				
2	101A	DOES	B	EQUAL	0$
3		JUMP	-FALSE	105THEN	
4	: : : :				
4	102A	DOES	I	EQUAL	0$
5		JUMP	-FALSE	105END	
6	: : : :				
6	103A	DOES	J	EQUAL	0$
7		JUMP	-FALSE	105END	
8	: : : :				
8	104A	DOES	X	EQUAL	0$
9		JUMP	-FALSE	105END	
10	: : : :				
10	105THEN				
10	K	=	1$		
11		JUMP	105ELSE		
12	: : : :				
12	105END				
12	K	=	0$		
13	: : : :				
13	105ELSE				
		END	0		

```
/*              EXAMPLE 4B              */
/*                                      */
/*      DE MORGAN'S THEOREM             */
/*                                      */
IF NOT(A EQ 0 AND B EQ 0 AND (I NE 0 OR J NE 0 OR X NE 0))
                                        THEN K=1;
                                        ELSE K=0;
```

TABLE A

IF			T)02
EQ	A>1	0$	T)03
AND	T)03		C(22H
EQ	B>1	0$	T)04
AND	T)04		C(22H
NE	I>	0$	T)05
OR	T)05		C(31H
NE	J>	0$	T)06
OR	T)06		C(31H
NE	X>1	0$	T)07
NOT		T)07	C(13H
THEN	C(13H		C(13H
=	K>	1$	K>
;			K>
ENDTHEN			
ELSE			T)09
=	K>	0$	K>
;			K>
ENDELSE			

TABLE B

IF			T)02=
EQ(R)	A	0$	T)03=
JF)	105THEN	101A	C(22H
EQ(R)	B	0$	T)04=
JF)	105THEN	102A	C(22H
NE	I	0$	T)05=
JT)	105END	103A	C(31H
NE	J	0$	T)06=
JT)	105END	104A	C(31H
NE(R)	X	0$	T)07=
NOT		T)07=	C(13H
JT)	105END	105THEN	C(13H
=	K	1$	K
;			K
ENDTHEN			
ELSE			T)09=
=	K	0$	K
;			K
ENDELSE			

TABLE C

0	101I	DOES	A	EQUAL	0$
1		JUMP	-FALSE	105THEN	
2	::::				
2	101A	DOES	B	EQUAL	0$
3		JUMP	-FALSE	105THEN	
4	::::				
4	102A	IS	I	NOT EQL	0$
5		JUMP	-TRUE	105END	
6	::::				
6	103A	IS	J	NOT EQL	0$
7		JUMP	-TRUE	105END	
8	::::				
8	104A	IS	X	NOT EQL	0$
9		JUMP	-TRUE	105END	
10	::::				
10	105THEN				
10	K	=	1$		
11		JUMP	105ELSE		
12	::::				
12	105END				
12	K	=	0$		
13	::::				
13	105ELSE				
		END	0		

```
/*              EXAMPLE 5                */
/*                                       */
/*      DIFFERENT ARCHITECTURES          */
/*              FROM                     */
/*         SAME FRONT END                */
/*                                       */
/*   MULTI-ACCUMULATOR ORGANIZATION      */
/*                                       */
Z=A*B-C*C;


  0      101I    LDF        A        T)01
  1              MPF        B        T)01
  2              LDF        C        T)02
  3              MPF        C        T)02
  4              SBF      T)02       T)01
  5              SDF        Z        T)01
```

```
/*              EXAMPLE 6                */
/*                                       */
/*      DIFFERENT ARCHITECTURES          */
/*              FROM                     */
/*         SAME FRONT END                */
/*                                       */
/*      POLISH ORGANIZATION              */
/*                                       */
Z=A*B-C*C;


  0      101I               A
  1                         B
  2                   *
  3                         C
  4                   @SQ@
  5                   -
  6                         Z
  7                   =
  8                   T)01
            END      0
```

THE NEED FOR
OPTIMIZATION STANDARDS

John B. Goodenough

1021-13.1
September 1976

Prepared for presentation at the Workshop
on the DoD Common Language,
Cornell University,
September 30 - October 1, 1976

Prepared under
U. S. Army Contract DAAB07-75-C-0373

SofTech, Inc.
460 Totten Pond Road
Waltham, MA 02154

THE NEED FOR OPTIMIZATION STANDARDS

Summary

The premise of this paper is that in writing programs for military systems, programming style is often strongly affected by a compiler's optimization behavior. For example, in the SAM-D project (see [1]), early deliveries of a JOVIAL J3 compiler did not optimize common sub-expressions. SAM-D programmers asserted that the programs written to compensate for this lack of optimization were less readable, under-standable, and maintainable than those written later for an optimizing version of the compiler. They asserted, moreover, that in their opinion, the most significant effect of optimization was to permit more readable programs to be written. This assertion has been further studied and verified in [1]. Similar findings have been noted in [2], [3], and [4]. Consequently, the principal point I wish to make is this:

- HOL Standards must address the effect of optimizations on programming style -- Unless compiler optimization behavior is standardized across implementations, the impact on coding, training, and maintenance will be similar to that of programming in different dialects of the "same" language, because programmers will adapt their programming style to conform to the opti-mization behavior of different compiler implementations.

In the remainder of the paper, I will:

- present some examples supporting this conclusion by illustrating the style of optimization standards that should be applied to the DoD Common Language;
- discuss briefly the interaction between language design decisions and optimization standards;
- note some possible effects of optimization standards on compiler procurement procedures; and
- conclude with a brief analysis of the impact of these ideas on Common Language requirements as expressed in the TINMAN [5] document.

1. Examples of Possible Optimization Specifications

The intent of the proposed optimization standards is to encourage programmers to express programs clearly by letting them know when different ways of phrasing an algorithm will and will not have an impact on object code efficiency. Instead of saying "Don't worry about efficiency," the idea is to use a programmer's concerns for efficiency as an incentive to write clearer programs.

The proposed optimization standards are of two kinds. The first states that certain alternate ways of expressing a computation will always yield the same object code. The second states that certain object code efficiencies will be attained if a program is expressed in particular ways.

As examples of optimization standards of the first kind, consider the following possible specifications:

1) the object code generated for the THEN and ELSE branches of a conditional statement will not change if the controlling predicate is negated and the THEN and ELSE branches are interchanged. (Some compilers perform only a limited common subexpression analysis which leads to THEN branches being better optimized than ELSE branches).

2) If X is a variable declared to have values greater than or equal to zero, then identical object code will be generated regardless of whether a programmer writes:

IF X $\neq$ 0 THEN

or

IF X > 0 THEN

3) If the only assignment to DD is in the following set of statements (where F is an array and DD is a local variable):

DD = F(I);
M(DD) = G(I);
N(DD) = H(I);

then the code generated will be the same even if the following had been written instead:

M(F(I)) = G(I);
N(F(I)) = H(I);

(Note that this implies the compiler must perform a dead variable analysis, but this optimization technique is not specifically required. Instead, the optimization's effect on source language style is specified.)

338

4) Either of the following forms will produce the same object code when X and Y are variables:

> IF X > 0
> THEN Y = Y + X;

or

> IF X > 0
> THEN Y = X + Y;

(Note that this implies that comutativity of addition will be recognized by the optimizer.)

5) Given either of these data declarations:

> DCL 1 X,
>   2 X1 FIXED BIN,
>   2 X2 FIXED BIN,
>   2 X3 FIXED BIN;

or

> DCL X(3) FIXED BIN;

a reference to element X2, for example, will produce the same code as a reference to element X(2).

6) Given the following data declaration (which declares RECNUM to be a signed seven bit value packed in the left half of a word, and RECFIL to be a signed seven bit value packed in the right half of the same word):

> TABLE RECTAB () 1; BEGIN
>   ITEM RECNUM S 7 (0, 0);
>   ITEM RECFIL S 7 (8, 0);
>   END;

then the contiguous assignment statements:

> RECNUM := 0;
> RECFIL := 32;

will generate the same object code as if RECTAB were overlaid with a signed fifteen bit integer value to which the value 32 was assigned. (Note that requiring this sort of optimization eliminates one of the needs for overlay statements.)

7) In the following conditional statement, the computations establishing the addressability of X(I, J) will be performed only once (if neither I or J are assigned to in the THEN and ELSE branches), and the instruction actually assigning to X(I, J) will appear only once:

```
IF ...
    THEN DO;
        . . .
        X(I, J) = ... ;
        END;
    ELSE DO;
        . . .
        X(I, J) = ... ;
        END;
```

This implies the programmer need not create a
temporary variable simply to ensure addressing
calculations are performed only once, e.g., the
programmer need not write:

```
IF ...
    THEN DO;
        . . .
        TEMP  = ... ;
        END;
    ELSE DO;
        . . .
        TEMP = ... ;
        END;
    X(I, J) = TEMP;
```

The second kind of optimization constraint states, in effect, that
certain seemingly inefficient methods of expressing algorithms will not
actually result in inefficient code. For example, the following constraints
might be imposed:

1)   In the following construct (assuming short-circuited
      evaluation of Boolean expressions), code to test the
      value of A will not be generated in the IF statement:
```
DO WHILE A AND B;
    . . .
END;
IF NOT A THEN ...
```

2)   In a loop of the following form, the loop control predi-
      cate will not be evaluated the first time:
```
TIME = TIME_DUE(I);
DO WHILE(TIME = TIME_DUE(I));
    . . .
END;
```

3)   In the following computations, only one division instruc-
      tion will be executed, where A, B, C, and D are integer
      variables:
```
D = B/A;
C = B mod A;
```

Clearly, a great many such directives must be developed for
a given language. Moreover, the directives cannot appeal to specific
examples, such as I have done, but rather must describe the class of
constructs covered by a directive. Having such directives will make
a compiler implementer's job easier at least in that he will be more
certain of what optimizations he is required to implement. In addition,
acceptance tests for evaluating whether a compiler satisfies optimization requirements can be more accurately and fairly specified.

Clearly, deciding on exactly what optimization constraints
should be imposed on a given language is a complex task affected by
what features the language supports, decisions about what kind of programming style should be encouraged (or supported) by the optimization standards, and the impact of required optimizations on compiler
development schedules and costs. Nonetheless, developing such standards
must be an integral part of the DoD Common Language effort if the benefits of having such a language are to be fully realized.

2.   The Impact of Optimization Standards on Language Design

It is not infrequently the case that language design decisions
are based on optimization considerations, e.g., a particular feature
may be included in a language because otherwise, optimization would
be too difficult. Alternatively, a feature may be excluded (to simplify
a language) on the assumption that compilers can implement compensating optimizations. For example, the decision to exclude conditional
expressions from PL/I means that programmers cannot write such
statements as:

        X(I, J) = IF ... THEN A ELSE B;
        CALL F(IF ... THEN A ELSE B, ...);
but instead must write:
        IF ... THEN X(I, J) = A; ELSE X(I, J) = B;
        IF ... THEN CALL F(A, ...);
            ELSE CALL F(B, ...);

The impact of this language design decision on object code efficiency will be negligible if all compilers for the language are required to support optimizations compensating for the lack of conditional expressions. (Note that as example 7 in the previous section showed, these optimizations should be supported even if a language has conditional expressions.)

Currently, the optimization issues motivating some language design decisions are never documented in a language specification. Consequently, later compiler implementations may not conform to the language designers' assumptions. Alternatively, optimization issues are not given sufficient consideration in language design so that compiler implementation costs escalate when requirements for highly efficient code exist.

3.   Impact of Optimization Standards on Compiler Procurement

The principal impact of the optimization standards concept on compiler procurements is that initial deliveries of compilers must conform to the standard as well as final deliveries. This does not necessarily imply that all optimizations implemented in the final delivery must also be supported by the initial delivery, but it does imply that optimizations made available in later compiler deliveries must not impact programming style in using the later compiler versions. For example, if invariant computations inside loop bodies are computed once outside the loop in later compiler deliveries, then they must also be removed in the initial delivery, since depending on whether this optimization is or is not performed, programmers may write their loops differently. On the other hand, optimizations which cannot be controlled through appropriate use of the source language can be phased in with later deliveries. For example, removing addressing computations from loop bodies might be an optimization provided by later compilers for languages that provide an HOL programmer with no way of removing these computations from the loop by rephrasing his source program. In short, unless an optimization standard applies to <u>all</u>

deliveries of a compiler, its purpose will be defeated. Programmers who become accustomed to optimization behavior of early compiler deliveries seldom change their programming style when later deliveries become available.

This probably implies that early compiler deliveries will have to produce more highly optimized code than is currently the practice, and, of course, this probably implies that the first delivery of a compiler will be later than would be the case if the optimization standards were not applied to all deliveries. This may be an unacceptable impact of optimization standards, unless they are carefully chosen to minimize their impact on early compiler deliveries. Whether or not this is possible remains to be seen.

It should be noted, that providing optimizations not required by an optimization standard is as dangerous as providing superset implementations of a language's syntax and semantics. Of course, this means merely that if the initial optimization standard is discovered to forbid desirable optimizations, then it should be changed and <u>all</u> compilers updated to conform to the new standard. In any event, the concept of an optimization standard does imply that some feasible optimizations may never be performed by any compiler implementation (just as some feasible language constructs may never be supported by any language implementation conforming to the TINMAN; see requirement L1, "No Superset Implementations").

4. Impact on TINMAN requirements

Optimization has not traditionally been considered to fall within the domain of language standardization activities. But in military programming, at least, the performance semantics of a language/translator is as important as its conventional (i. e. , logical) semantics. The impact of compiler optimization behavior on programming style is sufficiently great* that optimization standards are as necessary to achieve the benefits of language standardization as traditional syntactic and semantic standards.

*Military programmers <u>do</u> look at compiler output and experiment with different source language programming styles to ensure efficient code is produced. Such experimentation is encouraged by contracts that limit the amount of system code that can be implemented in assembly language.

In keeping with the traditional view that optimization falls outside the domain of standardization, the TINMAN does not address the need for optimization standards, and in fact, is in some conflict with the concept. In particular, L1 states that "library definition optimizations which are translator-unique" are allowed, and I5 states, "There will be no prohibition on a translator incorporating specialized optimizations for particular extensions. Programs using the extension will be translatable by any compiler for the language, but not necessarily with the same object code efficiency." The notion of translator-unique optimizations, however, is potentially in conflict with the idea of optimization standards. It may be that this requirement should be rephrased to state that optimization standards will be defined for standard library definitions (see M6), and these standards must be satisfied by translators that implement the library definitions directly. This is not an entirely satisfactory solution, because if a translator does not directly support some library-defined extensions, these extensions may be implemented so inefficiently that programmers will be unable to use them. In effect, the use of the standard extensions will become translator dependent for all practical purposes. The net effect also may be to motivate a somewhat more complex base language than I5 implies is desirable, simply to ensure that frequently used extensions have standard performance semantics over all implementations.

The notion of optimization standards seems consistent, however, with the comment in J1, "Language features will result in special efficient object code when their full generality is not used. A large number of special cases should compile efficiently." To ensure that this requirement is satisfied over all implementations, something similar to optimization standards need to be imposed.

5. Recommendation

In view of the arguments presented here, the following recommendation is proposed:

The DoD Common Language design effort should devise
preliminary performance standards for the language as
well as syntactic and semantic standards.

Even if complete performance standards are not produced by the initial
design efforts, the design documents should address optimization issues
that affect language design decisions, so appropriate performance
standards can be developed when the language design is finalized.

REFERENCES

1.   Goodenough, J. B. An Exploratory Study of Reasons for HOL
      Object Code Efficiency, R&D Tech. Rep. ECOM-75-0373-F,
      U. S. Army Electronics Command, Fort Monmouth, New Jersey,
      07703, August 1976. (AD-A029 664/0).

2.   Martin, F. H. On the Performance of the HAL/S-FC Compiler.
      Intermetrics, Inc., Cambridge, Mass., N76-15796, Oct. 1975.

3.   Parlett, B. N. and Wang, Y. The influence of the compiler or
      the cost of mathematical software -- in particular on the cost
      of triangular factorization. ACM Trans. on Math. Software 1,
      1 (March 1975), 35-46.

4.   Kernighan, B. W. and Plauger, P. J. The Elements of Pro-
      gramming Style. McGraw-Hill, New York, 1974.

5.   Fisher, D. A. A Common Programming Language for the
      Department of Defense -- Background and Technical Require-
      ments. Institute for Defense Analyses, Arlington, VA, Paper
      P-1191, June 1976.

A REMINDER FOR LANGUAGE DESIGNERS

By

Frederic Richard *
Henry F. Ledgard *

COINS Technical Report 76-3
(Revised August 1976)

Keywords: language design, programming languages, readibility,
          program validation, program maintenance.
CR Categories: 4.2, 4.22.

* Computer and Information Science Department,
  University Of Massachusetts,
  Amherst, Massachusetts 01002, USA.

This work was supported by the U.S. Army Reseach Office.

Abstract:

Current programming languages offer limited support in the development and maintenance of programs. These languages do not always account for the human limitations of their users. Notably, few languages really promote ease of readability. This paper suggests nine design principles for the development of readable high level languages. Each principle is backed up by a discussion and several examples. Among the issues discussed are the limitation of the overall complexity, the design of function and procedure facilities, the design of data type facilities, and the correspondence between syntax and semantics.

Introduction.

This paper stems from the difficulties we have had while
experimenting with current programming languages. To implement
real problems, no current programming language offers clean
solutions. Too often, the structure of the problem must be
twisted to the structure of the language.

We believe there is a need for a new general purpose, procedure
oriented programming language. This UTOPIA 84 (Knuth 74) should
not only be designed to enable the programmer to devise clear data
structures and algorithms. It should also provide assistance to the
user in the development of large programs, their verification and
their maintenance. For this purpose, the readability of a language
(i.e. human appreciation) is far more important that its writability
(i.e. translation from precise implementation specifications).

In this paper we suggest nine language design principles for
UTOPIA 84. These principles (see Table 1) are based in part on the
works of Dijkstra (68), Gannon and Horning (75), Hoare (72), Knuth
(67), Ledgard and Marcotty (75), Weinberg (75), Wirth (74), and
Wulf and Shaw (73). No attempt is made to address the whole language
design area. Little consideration is given to writability and
efficiency of implementation. We believe that these goals have
received too much attention in the past.

There is no formal justification for any of our principles. Each
principle is supported by a short discussion and several examples
borrowed from languages in widespread use: Algol 60 (Naur 63),
COBOL (Murach 71), FORTRAN (X3J3 66), PL/1 (ECMA/ANSI 74), PASCAL
(Jensen and Wirth 74), and SIMULA 67 (CDC 71).

1. A language should be limited in complexity and size.

2. A single concept should have a single form.

3. Simple features make simple languages.

4. Functions should emulate their mathematical analogue.

5. A clear distinction should be made between functions and procedures.

6. Multiple data types should be supported.

7. Similar features should have similar forms.

8. Distinct features should have distinct forms.

9. Remember the reader.

```
------------------------------------
TABLE 1: Nine Design Principles.
------------------------------------
```

1. A language should be limited in complexity and size.

Over the past few years, there has been an almost unabated tendency for languages to get larger and larger. In an effort to provide more powerful and more varied features to satisfy more users, the complexity of many languages has markedly increased. We believe this has been a mistake. Our own limitations as users, implementors, and designers call for limitations on the complexity and size of our tools.

It is easy to point out the problems of undue complexity during design and implementation. For the language designer, the evaluation of design alternatives are difficult because of the frequent interplay with other constructs within the hosting language. Formal definitions become increasingly intricate, documentation is harder to prepare and read, and inconsistencies may easily be overlooked. For compiler writers, the production of a clean, reliable, and well human-engineered implementation requires more and more work. There is no perfect language design and the more complex the language, the more difficult it is to offer the user a clean and consistent programming system.

Users pay an even higher price for undue complexity. Learning is slow, and programming often cannot proceed without constant references to the manual. Any inconsistencies take more time to learn and more energy to live with. Most of all, the user may encounter great difficulties in understanding the underlying structure of the language. Mastery and proficiency come only when the user develops a comprehensive internal model of the language. The selection of useful constructs, cleanliness of use, and understanding of error diagnostics proceed far more quickly when the user understands the language in its entirety.

Subsetting, i.e. partitioning a language into semi-independent modules, has often been presented as a practical remedy to large size. There are, however, numerous drawbacks. The user facing a new problem may wonder whether the subset he has mastered is adequate, or whether he should learn a larger subset. Programs may inadvertently activate unknown features and cause confusion. Furthermore, subsetting is of little help in reading programs written by other users, where knowledge of the whole language may be needed. Lastly, there does not seem to exist any good method for partitioning a language in a way acceptable by all users.

Admittedly, the complexity and the size of a language depend mainly on its intended application. When the size is too small, the language primitives are overloaded and the complexity in usage becomes unnecessarily high. When the size is too large, the language often offers more than is necessary, and the user is easily confused. There are few major programming languages that do not in fact suffer from undue size and complexity. The many duplicate forms and the report writer feature of COBOL are questionnable. As a teaching language, PASCAL is too complex. The case against PL/I is obvious.

In summary, programmers should not be slowed in their problem solving activities by the complexity, the size, and the unknown subtleties of their tools. Our own human limitations as users, implementers, and designers call for languages that are limited in complexity and size, and designed to be well implemented.

2. A single concept should have a single form.

Providing more than one form to denote a concept always increases
the size of a language. The additional complexity introduced by
such features should be carefully weighed against their usefulness.

Consider, for instance, the simple PL/I aggregate declaration
in Figure 2.1 and the rather large number of subscripted qualified
names that can be used to denote the same component of the aggregate. A similar declaration and the unique denotation of the same
element, expressed in PASCAL, are given in Figure 2.2. In comparison, the complexity of multiple PL/I denotations is difficult to
justify

COBOL provides a further example of questionnable duplicate
forms. Figure 2.3 shows two different sequences of arithmetic
statements. Both perform the same computations. Further,each sequence is perfectly homogeneous to the eye. But when both notations are combined as in the third sequence of Figure 2.3, we see
the problem more clearly. The symmetry of like operations is not
brought at as in the above examples. A designer may prefer the concise, mathematical notation of the first sequence, or the English
like notation of the second sequence. In any case, it would be
simpler to retain a single notation in the language.

There are some situations where a duplication of forms yields
great convenience without adding much to the overall complexity.
For instance, fully qualified names for aggregates are often
cumbersome to read and to write, especially when the same element
is referenced often over a span of text. PL/I provides numerous

Declaration

```
DECLARE  1 A (10,12),
              2 B (5),
                  3 C (7),
                  3 D;
```

Fully qualified names

```
A(9,11)      .B(4)        .C(7)
A(9)         .B(11,4)     .C(7)
A(9)         .B(11)       .C(4,7)
A            .B(9,11,4).C(7)
A            .B(9,11)     .C(4,7)
A            .B(9)        .C(11,4,7)
A            .B           .C(9,11,4,7)
A(9,11)      .B           .C(4,7)
A(9)         .B           .C(11,4,7)
A(9,11,4,7).B          .C
```

Partially qualified names
(in some contexts only)

```
B(9,11,4)  .C(7)
           C(9,11,4,7)
B(9,11)    .C(4,7)
B(9)       .C(11,4,7)
B(9,11,4,7).C
```

```
-------------------------------------------
Figure 2.1 : Multiple Denotations of a
             PL/I Structure Element.
-------------------------------------------
```

Declaration
        A: array [1..10,1..12] of
             record
                  B: array [1..5] of
                       record
                            C: array [1..7] of integer;
                            D: integer
                       end
        end

Complete denotation

    A[9,11].B[4].C[7]

Legal abbreviations

    with A[9,11]
          do   ...   B[4].C[7] ...

    with A[9,11].B[4]
          do   ...   C[7] ...

    Figure 2.2 : Legal Denotations for a
                 PASCAL Record Element.

Use of the COMPUTE verb

```
COMPUTE   TOTAL-HOURS    = OVERTIME-HOURS + REGULAR-HOURS.
COMPUTE   NUM-ON-PAYROLL = NUM-EMPLOYEES - NUM-ON-VACATION
                                         - NUM-ON-LEAVE.
COMPUTE   GROSS-PAY      = TOTAL-HOURS * WAGE.
COMPUTE   AVG-HOURS      = TOTAL-HOURS / NUM-ON-PAYROLL.
```

Use of arithmetic verbs

```
ADD   OVERTIME-HOURS TO REGULAR-HOURS
      GIVING TOTAL-HOURS.
SUBTRACT NUM-ON-VACATION, NUM-ON-LEAVE FROM NUM-EMPLOYEES
      GIVING NUM-ON-PAYROLL.
MULTIPLY TOTAL-HOURS BY WAGE
      GIVING GROSS-PAY.
DIVIDE   NUM-ON-PAYROLL INTO TOTAL-HOURS
      GIVING AVG-HOURS.
```

Mixing the two forms

```
COMPUTE  TOTAL-HOURS = OVERTIME-HOURS + REGULAR-HOURS.
SUBTRACT NUM-ON-VACATION, NUM-ON-LEAVE FROM NUM-EMPLOYEES
      GIVING NUM-ON-PAYROLL.
COMPUTE  GROSS-PAY   = TOTAL-HOURS * WAGE.
DIVIDE   NUM-ON-PAYROLL INTO TOTAL-HOURS
      GIVING AVG-HOURS.
```

```
---------------------------------------------
```
Figure 2.3 : Duplicate Features in COBOL.
```
---------------------------------------------
```

abbreviations (see Figure 2.1), but their legal use depends on the denotations for the other variables of the program. On the other hand, the PASCAL <u>with</u> statement (see Figure 2.2) clearly identifies abbreviated denotations over a precise span of text.

Consider also Figure 2.4, which illustrates a typical use of the PASCAL <u>case</u> statement, along with an equivalent compound <u>if</u>-statement (in fact, the <u>case</u> statement is undefined when the value of the selection expression does not fall among the alternatives specified; an <u>otherwise</u> clause would be welcome). The <u>case</u> statement avoids a clumsy nesting of <u>if</u>'s and is easier to read. Unfortunately, the PASCAl <u>case</u> statement is much too limited. A recent proposal for a more powerful <u>case</u> statement (Weinberg, Geller and Plum 75) seems promising. However, the additional complexity of this proposal remains to be investigated.

Providing multiple forms for a single concept generally makes a language more difficult to learn, use, and read. Alternate forms should be introduced only to promote readability, and only when they do so, without creating an undue increase of the complexity.

356

Sample PASCAL IF Statement

```
     if command = insert then insertlines(currentposition)
else If command = delete then deletelines(currentposition,
                                            linecount)
else if command = print then printlines (currentposition,
                                            linecount)
else if command = search then
                        begin
                           searchstring(currentposition,
                             string,stringfound,newposition);
                           if stringfound
                              then currentposition := newposition
                        end
```

Sample PASCAL CASE Statement

```
case command of

    insert:  insertlines(currentposition);
    delete:  deletelines(currentposition,linecount);
    print:   printlines (currentposition,linecount);
    search:  begin
                searchstring(currentposition,string,
                             stringfound,newposition);
                if stringfound
                   then currentposition := newposition
             end
end
```

```
----------------------------------------------------
Figure 2.4: Alternate PASCAL Control Structures.
----------------------------------------------------
```

3. Simple features make simple languages.

It would be too simplistic to characterize the complexity of a language only by its size. Each construct has an inherent complexity as well as an interplay with other features.

A designer should be especially careful of features with a highly dynamic behavior. Consider the Algol 60 call-by-name feature: it is a powerful feature, not too difficult to learn (in the following discussion, we will ignore a possible clash of identifiers with call-by-name parameters. A call-by-name parameter can have a complex run-time behavior not reflected by its written representation. For example, "Jensen's device" (Figure 3) has been used to promote call-by-name parameters (Knuth 67). When considered alone, the declaration of the procedure SIGMA looks innocent indeed. The invocation of SIGMA seems natural because of its analogy with a classical mathematical notation. However, when the procedure declaration and its invocation are examined together, it takes some effort to realize that SIGMA is activated N+1 times to compute the double sum of the elements of an N*L array. Note that neither the declaration or the invocation of SIGMA 'explains' Jensen's device. Furthermore, if more descriptive names had replaced L, N, and A, the similarity with mathematics would no longer appear. This is a sufficient reason to question the usefulness of call-by-name parameters. A language designer should be very cautious of clever examples. They usually promote features of greater complexity than the eye can meet.

```
begin
      integer array  A [1:N, 1:L];
      integer  I, J;
      integer  GRANDTOTAL;
                    .
                    .
                    .

integer procedure SIGMA (K, LOW, HIGH, TERM );
              value LOW, HIGH;
              integer K, LOW, HIGH, TERM;
              begin
                  integer SUM;
                  SUM := 0 ;
                  for K := LOW step 1 until HIGH
                      do SUM := SUM + TERM ;
                  SIGMA := SUM
              end
          .
          .
          .

      GRANDTOTAL := SIGMA(I, 1, N, SIGMA(J,1,L,A[I,J]) );
          .
          .
          .

end
```

              Figure 3 : Jensen's Device is used to sum
                       the elements of an N x L array.

A further illustration is provided by our friend the <u>goto</u> statement. Its basic mechanism is simple to explain, but its interplay with other features leads to significant problems. Arbitrary branching usually requires that some variables be given definite values on entry or exit. These associations, however, are not explicit in the program text. A cleaner solution is offered by the basic one-in one-out control structures (see Ledgard and Marcotty 75). The advantage of one-in, one-out control structures is not only the explicit mention of the conditions upon which the control flow is modified, but also a clean behavior when combined together or with other features of the language.

A similar issue concerns the introduction of pointers in a high level language. Recursive data structures (Hoare 75) are an adequate substitute in most cases. They simplify program reading and specification by replacing pointer manipulations with logical operations on structures (note that PL/I provides a similar hiding mechanism).

In summary, the simplicity of a language relies as much in the number and the simplicity of basic features as in the simplicity of their interaction. The art of language design is to achieve a tolerable balance.

4. Functions should emulate their mathematical analogue.

Function and procedure facilities are the basic tools for program decomposition. They provide the operational abstractions necessary to manage complex problems. The usefulness of these abstraction tools is so important that they demand a careful design.

In most procedural languages, an analogy is made with conventional mathematics. Expressions in programming languages are meant to be read as expressions in mathematics. The invocation of functions within expressions hides irrelevant computational details and, most importantly, facilitates the of new operational abstractions. Accordingly, our understanding of function facilities in programming languages is based on our mathematical background. In mathematics, a function is a mapping from a set of values to a set of values. In programming languages, a function is understood as an algorithmic transformation from input values to a single output value.

In most programming languages, there appear a number of discrepancies from the simple mathematical analogue. In particular, assignments in function declarations may cause side-effects. For example, consider the well-known Algol 60 program (Knuth 67) of Figure 4.1. Since the variable GLOBAL is modified within the body of the function SUCCESSOR, this program will print _false_ rather than _true_ (the Algol 60 Report leaves the order of evaluation of expressions undefined; however, the Report does not forbid modifications of globals in functions; consequently, the output of Figure 4.1 will be _false_ or _true_ depending on the implementation).

```
begin
      integer GLOBAL;

      integer procedure SUCCESSOR (FORMALPARM);
                         value FORMALPARM;
                         integer FORMALPARM;
                         begin
                            SUCCESSOR := FORMALPARM + 1;
                            GLOBAL := SUCCESSOR
                         end;

      GLOBAL := 0;
      print( (GLOBAL + SUCCESSOR(GLOBAL))
                = (SUCCESSOR(GLOBAL) + GLOBAL)  )
end
```

Figure 4.1: Modification of a global variable
            in an Algol 60 function.

Even the access to a global variable within a function declaration may cause a loss of transparency in an expression. In the example of Figure 4.2, the global variable INCREMENT is modified between two invocations of INCREASE. The meaning of INCREASE is thus dynamically modified and, although the two invocations are identical, different results will be produced.

Another discrepancy occurs when parameters of a function are modified within the function declaration. In the well-known example (Weil 65) of Figure 4.3, the function INCREMENT BY NAME is evaluated twice during the invocation of ADD BY NAME. Since INCREMENT BY NAME modifies its parameter, successive evaluations do not yield the same result.

Many other languages also allow side-effects in function invocations. For easier validation and better readability, we recommend that functions be implemented according to the simple model discussed earlier. In particular, all parameters should be considered as input values that are "evaluated" upon invocation. No assignment should be performed on parameters within functions. If references to global are allowed, the function declaration should at least contain mention of this fact in its header.

Designing functions from a simple mathematical model implies strong restrictions on their use. However, the very nature of these restrictions forces the programmer to devise clear solutions and enables the program reader to rely on a transparent notation for expressions.

```
begin
      integer INCREMENT;
      integer procedure INCREASE (BASE);
                        integer BASE; value BASE;
                        INCREASE := BASE + INCREMENT;


      INCREMENT := 1;
      print( INCREASE(1) );

      INCREMENT := 100;
      print( INCREASE(1) )
end
```

Figure 4.2: Modification of a function through
           a Global Variable in Algol 60.

```
begin
      integer innocent;

      integer procedure INCREMENT BY NAME (corrupt);
                        integer corrupt;
                        begin
                              corrupt := corrupt + 1;
                              INCREMENT BY NAME := corrupt
                        end;

      integer procedure ADD BY NAME (evil);
                        integer evil;
                        ADD BY NAME := evil + evil;

      innocent := 1;
      print( ADD BY NAME( INCREMENT BY NAME(innocent) ) );
      print( innocent )
end
```

Figure 4.3: Algol 60 call-by-name parameters.

---

5. A clear distinction should be made between functions and
   procedures.

Many abstractions encountered in programming cannot be programmed with functions. An operation may contain inherent side effects,
invoke input-output, create or update a structure, or modify the
run-time environment. It would be misleading to extend the simple
model of functions to these abstractions for, unlike the analogue
of function invocations with mathematical expressions, the procedure invocation is the analogue of a statement.

The main conceptual difference between procedures and functions
is that modifications of the execution environment are allowed in
procedures. In most languages, global variables may be referenced
and modified in procedures. Before further discussing the issue of
global variables, it must be pointed out that, in some cases, the
use of globals results from poor language design. Consider a state
transition table, a keyword mapping table, or any kind of unvarying
information whose lookup is limited to one module. To represent
such a constant object in some languages (e.g. PASCAL), a variable
must be declared and initialized outside of the module where it is
used, i.e. it must be global. A more natural solution would be to
have local, stuctured constants.

Since modification of the execution environment is the
essence of a procedure, problems of poor readability and
difficult validation that were eliminated for functions must be re-
examined. The design of a procedure facility should minimize these
problems (see Gannon and Horning 75). In the first place, a complete

specification of interfaces should be required (Wulf and Shaw 73, Deremer and Kron 76). The procedure header should indicate which parameters are input values, output results, and updated variables, as shown in Figure 5.1. The language processor should make sure that each parameter is used properly according to the header specification. Thus, efficient parameter passing modes can be generated by the compiler. The procedure invocation (CALL statement or procedure statement) should contain similar information as illustrated in Figure 5.2.

As to global variables accessed in procedures, they should be regarded as "implicit" parameters. Their use may increase the conciseness of procedure invocations and thus improve readability. The procedure header, however, should explicitly mention all global variables that are referenced or updated (see Figure 5.1).

The basic design of function and procedure facilities we have presented may appear very restricted. Indeed, there are attractive extensions like polymorphic procedures or procedures with functional parameters whose arguments are variable in number and type (e.g. see Gries and Gehani 76). However, the effect of such extensions on readability and ease of validation should be carefully assessed before their introduction in a language.

```
procedure SWAP (input I, J: integer);

    updated var
                A: array [1..MAX_ELEMENTS] of integer;
    var
                TEMP: integer;

    begin
            TEMP := A[I];
            A[I] := A[J];
            A[J] := TEMP;
    end
```

Figure 5.1: Complete Specification of Interfaces
          in Procedure Declaration.

```
        .
        .
        .
parse_if_statement( input current_pos,
                    output parse_error, subtree, new_pos);

if parse_error = serious
    then recover_statement(update current_pos,
                           output fatal_error);
        .
        .
        .
```

Figure 5.2: Specification of Actual Parameters in
          Procedure Invocations.
---

6. Multiple data types should be supported.

A data type is usually defined as a distinguished set of values and associated operators. Since all programming languages are designed to manipulate some kind of data, they all provide one or more data types.

So called "typeless" languages are indeed a contradiction in terms. In LISP (Weissman 67) and GEDANKEN (Reynolds 70), values may be atoms, integers, reals or booleans. However, no declaration can restrict the range of values taken by identifiers. A true "unitype" language is BLISS (Wulf, Russel, and Habermann 71). BLISS provides only one basic type, namely bit patterns, to represent all quantities.

Although the above languages have been widely accepted, we find them difficult to read, mainly because the interpretation of identifiers cannot be derived from their declaration or from the context in which they are used. We believe that the association of a name with a specific data type should be made explicit. At the same time, a language should offer a sufficient number of basic data types (e.g. boolean, character, integer, real) and structuring mechanisms (e.g. array, string, record) to avoid obscure programming.

Another problem with many current programming languages is implicit type coercion. Implicit type coercion often makes program validation and modification hazardous. We believe that there should be no automatic type conversion in a language, except, perhaps, from integer to real or from subrange to scalar. Other conversions should be specified by the programmer using built-in functions.

Providing multiple basic data types and structuring facilities may appear sufficient. However, we believe that the programmer should be allowed to define his own data types to adapt the language to an application. There are two separate aspects to the notion of a data type "extension": abstraction and implementation.

From the abstraction point of view, the programmer defines a new type by naming a set of objects and operators relevant to the application. For instance, the (limited) type definition facility of PASCAL offers the possibility to declare and name "new" classes of objects(Figure 6.1). Such a declaration helps clarifying the meaning of values that a variable of this type can assume.

The implementation aspect of a new data type consists in programming the representation and operators of this new type. The implementation is usually performed in terms of previously defined types and operators. For instance, Figure 6.2 shows the definition of the type "stack of integers" using the class facility of SIMULA 67.

What constitutes a good mechanism for a full data type facility is still being explored (e.g. see Conference On Data Abstraction 76). Some combination of the PASCAL and SIMULA facilities, where the exchange of information between a data type definition and its use would be tightly controlled, would provide great convenience (see Koster 76).

There are advantages to multiple data types other than abstraction and readability. First, a strict notion of type allows an extensive type checking to be performed at compile time. Being able to put more confidence in a syntactically correct program is

Type
```
        commandtype = (insert,delete,search,invalidcommand);

        tokentype   = (keyword,identifier,constant,
                        specialsymbol, unrecognizable);

        constanttype = (integerconst,realconst,string);
```

Figure 6.1: Sample PASCAL scalar type declarations.

```
class  stack ( maximumsize );
       integer maximumsize;

       comment This class defines the type stack of integers;


       begin
           integer array store [1:maximumsize];

           integer topindex, maxstorage;

           boolean procedure empty;
                   empty := (topindex ≼ 1);

           boolean procedure full;
                   full := (topindex = maxstorage);

           integer procedure top;
                   top := store[topindex];

           procedure push (token);
                   integer token;
                   begin
                       topindex := topindex + 1;
                       store[topindex] := token;
                   end;

           procedure pop (token);
                   name token;
                   integer token;
                   begin
                       token := store[topindex];
                       topindex := topindex - 1;
                   end;


           comment stack initialization at creation time;

           topindex := 0;
           maxstorage := maximumsize

       end class stack;
```

Figure 6.2: Declaration of the Class "Stack
           of Integers" in SIMULA 67.
----

important when maintaining it. Second, since axiomatic definitions of types can be produced, validation of programs can be accomplished more rigorously (see Guttag 76).

7. Similar features should have similar forms.

Syntax has often been compared to the icing that covers a cake. Of course, if the cake is stale, the icing will little improve it. But if the cake is fine, the taster will soon associate its flavor with its appearance. In programming languages, a concept and its external representation are often taken synonymously. For example, we often use the terms "if-statement" and "while-statement" rather than the terms "selection control structure" and "iteration control structure". The association between concepts and their representation is an important human factor in the design of a programming language. To benefit from such associations and promote readability, similar syntactic forms should be used for similar features.

Our first example deals with the concept of declarations and their syntactic forms. A sample of possible PL/I declarations appears in Figure 7.1a. The syntax of these declarations is somewhat confusing. The variable declarations and procedure declarations do not follow a similar scheme. In the variable declarations, the LIKE attribute provides the aggregate PURCHASE with the same structure as SALE, although this is not so obvious at first glance. A structure itself is indicated only by an integer before the major component name. The amount of information provided by each declaration is not identical, mainly because of default attributes. In the procedure header, the declaration of formal parameters takes two steps.

In comparison, the PASCAL declarations of Figure 7.1b. are

(a) PL/I

```
DECLARE  INDEX FIXED;

DCL  1 SALE,
         2 DATE,
             3 YEAR CHAR(2),
             3 MONTH CHARACTER(3),
             3 DAY CHAR(2),
         2 TRANSACTION,
             3 (ITEM,QUANTITY) FIXED (7,0),
             3 PRICE,
             3 TAX FIXED;

DECLARE 1 PURCHASE LIKE SALE;

UPDATE_STOCKS : PROC (ARTICLE,AMOUNT);
              DCL  (ARTICLE,AMOUNT) FIXED (7,0);
```

(b) PASCAL

```
type operation =
         record
            date: record
                    year:  array [1..2] of char;
                    month: array [1..3] of char;
                    day:   array [1..2] of char
                  end;
            transaction:
                  record
                    item,
                    quantity: integer;
                    price:    integer;
                    tax:      integer
                  end
         end;


var  index:    integer;
     sale:     operation;
     purchase: operation;


procedure updatestock (article, amount: integer);
```

Figure 7.1: PL/I and PASCAL declarations.
---

longer, but clearer. A similar scheme is used for type declarations, variable declarations, and procedure declarations. Notably, the declarations of a structures variable and of an integer variable follow the same scheme.

As a second example, consider the syntax of PASCAL control structures (without the goto). Some disparity in the form of control stuctures can be noticed. The case and end keywords of a case statement (see Figure 2.5) clearly delimit this construct in the program text; conversely, the if statement is not bracketted in a similar fashion (Figure 7.2). A more important discrepancy also appears. Whereas a list of statements can be used in a repeat...until construct, the if, case, and while constructs may only accomodate a single statement. To include a sequence of instructions in an if or a case statement, a clumsy begin...end bracketting pair must be added. Since control structures form a class of features, the same syntactic scheme should apply for all of them. Accordingly, examples of a modified PASCAL syntax are shown in Figure 7.3.

A discussion of statement lists cannot omit the "missing semicolon" problem . The use of a separator in statement lists needlessly singles out the last statement, which does not have an ending punctuation mark. This rule is difficult to learn and remember (see Gannon and Horning 75). Conversely, the use of a statement terminator provides a more natural rule for all statements (see Figure 7.3).

Similar forms for similar features can greatly reduce the conceptual complexity of a programming language. The likeness of forms

```
if  (linecount = maxlineperpage)
      then
            begin
                  pagecount := pagecount + 1;
                  newpage(printfile);
                  printheader(printfile, pagecount, date);
                  linecount := 1;
            end
      else
            linecount := linecount + 1
```

Figure 7.2: A sample PASCAL if statement.

```
(a)     if (line_count = max_line_per_page)
            then
                page_count := page_count + 1;
                new_page(print_file);
                print_header(print_file, page_count, date);
                line_count := 1;
            else
                line_count := line_count + 1;
        endif;



(b)     while  (input_char in digits)  do

            number := number*10 + int_value(input_char);
            read(input_char);

        endwhile;



(c)     repeat

            digit := digit + 1;
            one_tenth := number div 10;
            decimal_digit := number - 10*one_tenth;
            number := one_tenth;

        until  (number = 0);



(d)     case  command  of

            insert: insertlines(current_position);

            delete: deletelines(current_position, line_count);

            print:  printlines(current_position, line_count);

            search: searchstring(current_position, string,
                                 string_found, new_position);
                    if string_found
                        then current_position := new_position;
                    endif;
        endcase;
```

Figure 7.3: Control Structures with Full Bracketing.

----

indicates to the user the likeness of contents. These associations should be carefully designed, for even a single anomaly can confuse the user.

8. Distinct features should have distinct forms.

The association between concepts and their representation
supports the use of similar forms for similar features. Recipro-
cally, it is important not to give rise to misleading associations.
Distinct concepts should be emphasized by distinct syntactic forms.

The formal parameters and the local variables of a procedure
form distinct conceptual categories. In FORTRAN and PL/I (see
Figure 8.1), formal parameters appear in the procedure heading, but
their declaration is made along with the declarations of local
variables. On the other hand, this distinction is well made in
ALGOL 60. The declaration of formal parameters are located in the
module header. However, some confusion remains because a formal
parameter may occur up to three times in the header (e.g. LOWBOUND
and UPPERBOUND in Figure 8.1). A better solution is offered in
PASCAL where the declarations of formal parameters are grouped in
the procedure header.

The declarations of variables and the sequence of operations
performed upon these variables represent distinct concepts. In
COBOL, this distinction is made by using DATA and PROCEDURE
DIVISION's. On the other hand, PL/I allows declarations to be
located anywhere in a procedure. A similar objection can be made
against the FORMAT statement in FORTRAN. FORMAT statements are
not executable and they seriously slow down program reading when
located among executable statements.

In the previous section, we proposed a full bracketting for
control structures. Of course, these control structures differ in

some manner, for they are not duplicate features. Unfortunately,
this difference is not generally emphasized enough. In PASCAL, the
end keyword is the closing bracket of too many constructs, e.g.
blocks, compound statements, and case statements. Readers can easily be confused by the "matching end" problem. Distinct constructs
should have distinct pairs of brackets. Preferably, the two brackets should be short and have the same length; but most of all,
they should be readable. For this reason, fi, esac, elihw, or
nigeb are not acceptable. In this paper (see Figure 7.3), we used
endif, endcase, endwhile, and end, but we are not
fully satisfied with them.

Similarly, some languages use the "+" symbol to denote addition, set union, and boolean OR. This can lead to obscure constructs, because the exact interpretation of a single "+" must be
derived from the type of its operands. Using "+", "U", and "OR"
surely adds to readability. The programmer, not the designer
should be responsible for any possible operator overloading.
However, the character sets used in current programming
languages are limited, and it might still be necessary
to associate two different meanings with a single token. This
should only be allowed where the the contexts for each interpretation are so different that no confusion arises.

Transparency can be obtained by combining similar forms for
similar features and distinct forms for distinct features. Thus,
the similarities and differences of basic concepts are easily
apparent to the user, who can rapidly learn to recognize the
various forms in programs.

FORTRAN

```
SUBROUTINE PLOT(LOW, UPPER, CURVE)
    REAL LOW
    DIMENSION LINE(120)
    ...
```

PL/I

```
PLOT_CURVE: PROCEDURE(LOW_BOUND, UPPER_BOUND, CURVE);
    DCL (LOW_BOUND, UPPER_BOUND) FLOAT;
    DCL CURVE  ENTRY (FLOAT) RETURNS FLOAT;
    DCL LINE (120)
    ...
```

Algol 60

```
procedure PLOTCURVE( LOWBOUND, UPPERBOUND, CURVE);
            value LOWBOUND, UPPERBOUND;
            real  LOWBOUND, UPPERBOUND;
            real procedure CURVE;
begin
    integer array LINE [1:120];
    ...
```

PASCAL

```
procedure PLOTCURVE( LOWBOUND, UPPERBOUND: real;
                     function CURVE: real      );

    var LINE: array [1..120] of integer;
    ...
```

Figure 8.1: Formal Parameters and Local
        Variables for a plotting routine.
---

9. Remember the reader.

Once a program written, it will be read many times by its author
or other programmers. It is thus important that the program
listing clearly convey all information necessary to the reader.

The overall structure of a program and the basic organization
of modules are the outlines on which a program reader establishes
his understanding. Consider the task of reading a PASCAL or Algol 60
program you have never seen before. First, you will probably inspect
the global declarations. Then, you will turn the pages to the end of
the listing to find the body of a program. However, further examination of the variable declarations is needed to grasp important
details of the program body. Much back and forth page flipping
will occur before the first level of the program is understood.
For each successive level, the same process is repeated, but with
more difficulty, because the boundaries of each module are less
apparent.

In general, the top-down development of a program exhibits the
overall structure of a tree. Reading and understanding such a program is simplified if the program were presented in top-down
fashion. To achieve top-down readability, the program listing should
represent a breadth first traversal of the program tree. Thus, the
program reader is led step by step through the successive levels of
the program with minimum effort. As mentionned above, PASCAL and
Algol 60 do not allow such a presentation. In FORTRAN, the programmer can choose the textual order of his modules, but no relative
position is enforced. PL/I allows any combination of the Algol 60

and FORTRAN schemes.

The program code alone is usually inadequate to explain all of a program. Additional information must be provided by the programmer, e.g. the meaning of important variables, the description of algorithms, the peculiarities of a run-time environment, and references to existing documentation, etc. To promote this pratice, a language should offer easy and secure documentation tools.

Provision for long names, along with a "break" character (e.g. the "_" in "CURRENT_POSITION"), represents an incentive to imbed documentation in the code. Possible break characters are the hyphen (COBOL) and the underscore (PL/I). The Algol 60 and FORTRAN convention where blanks may be interspersed arbitrarily in identifiers (e.g. ADD BY NAME in Figure 5.1) is not recommended, for various occurences of an identifier may look quite different.

More comprehensive documentation is usually given in comments. The following kinds of information are provided in comments:

a) General information: e.g. program purpose, modification record, references to external documentation, and run-time requirements.

b) Module summary: e.g. specification of the local computations, input and output domains, and algorithm used.

c) Statement grouping: e.g. identification or paraphrase of a group of statements to highlight their logical content as a unit.

d) Statement support: e.g. emphasis of a crucial step, assertions, and precise meaning of constant and variables.

Unfortunately, most languages do not provide adequate comment facilities. In COBOL,general information is given in the

IDENTIFICATION DIVISION and in the ENVIRONMENT DIVISION, but the remaining types of comments are not distinguished and must be made on a line by line basis. PL/I and PASCAL offer a single parenthetic scheme which does not distinguish between the various types of documentation. There is little need to mention the highly complex rules for Algol 60 comments and their mediocre readability.

In our opinion, a single comment scheme is rarely sufficient to encompass all possibilities of the above classification and, at the same time, to emphasize their differences. On one hand, general information and module summaries appear usually in dense blocks at the beginning of programs and modules: a simple parenthetic scheme allowed only in module headers is needed to accomodate the type of documentation. On the other hand, statement grouping and statement support comments are usually short. A line oriented comment scheme would be more appropriate for this type of comment. One such scheme might be the use of a distinguished token, say "/*", to begin the comment anywhere on a line; a comment would be implicitly terminated by the end of the line. Specific designs could introduce additional schemes, e.g. assertion comment.

In summary, a programming language should offer easy and secure documentation tools to help the programmer produce readable listings. Indeed, the top-down listing feature and viable comment schemes do not appear easy to devise and require further study. But their usefulness makes it an important topic for careful design.

Parting Comments.

UTOPIA 84 is still a long way off. The selection of the primitives of a language and the elaboration of data type facilities are important issues that we barely touched upon. Moreover, the design of a comfortable operating environment, including input/output primitives, and the quality of an implementation have a serious effect on the acceptance of a language.

Through the design principles presented in this paper we have tried to emphasize that all consequences of a design decision should be evaluated. Each design decision should promote ease of learning, program validation, and program maintenance. We cannot underestimate the use of formal definitions in the language design cycle, for they should provide useful indications on the simplicity and clarity of the result. Above all, the designer should strive to keep a language small, consistent, and readable.

A note on implementation must be made. Although we have given little consideration to efficiency of implementation, we doubt that any of our recommandations would lead to high inefficiency. Even so, if one considers the actual cost of software development and maintenance, a sensible gain in readability justifies some loss of efficiency.

In parting, we must admit that some notions used in this paper, like readability, remain purely subjective. Language designers may be easily misled if they keep to their own notions. They must listen to the users and interpret their complaints. After all, users remain the ultimate judges in language design.

Acknowledgments.

We are grateful to Michael Marcotty for his helpful comments on the drafts of this paper. We also would like to thank Andrew Singer, Louis Chmura, Caxton Foster, and Amos Gileadi for fruitful discussions.

REFERENCES:

CDC 71
    Control Data Corporation. Simula Reference Manual.
    Publication No 602348000 (1971).

CONFERENCE ON DATA ABSTRACTION 76
    Conference on Data: Abstraction, Definition, and Structure.
    March 22-24, Salt Lake City, Utah. Sigplan Notices, Vol 11,
    Special Issue (April 1976),pp.1-190.

DEREMER AND KRON 76
    DeRemer, F., and Kron, H. Programming-in-the-large versus
    Programming-in-the-small. IEEE Transactions on Software
    Engineering, Vol SE-2, No 2 (June 1976), pp.80-86.

DIJKSTRA 68
    Dijkstra, E.W. Goto Statement Considered Harmful. Comm.
    of the ACM, Vol 11, No 3 (March 1968) pp.147-148.

ECMA/ANSI 74
    European Computer Manufacturers and American National
    Standards Institute. PL/I. ECMA/TC10/ANSI.X3J3. BASIS 1-12
    (July 1974).

GANNON AND HORNING 75
    Gannon, J.D., and Horning, J.J. Language Design for
    Programming Reliability. IEEE Transactions on Software
    Engineering Vol SE-1, No 2 (June 1975) pp.179-191.

GRIES AND GEHANI 76
    Gries,D., and Gehani, N. Some Ideas on Data Types in
    High Level Languages. Conference on Data: Abstraction,
    Definition and Structure. Sigplan Notices, Vol 11, Special
    Issue (April 1976), p.120.

GUTTAG 76
    Guttag, J. Abstract Data Types and the Development of
    Data Structures. Conference on Data: Abstraction, Definition
    and Structure. Siplan Notices, Vol 11, Special Issue (April
    1976), p.72.

HOARE 72
    Hoare, C.A.R. Hints on Programming Language Design.
    Computer Science Department. Stanford University.
    Tech. Rep. STAN-CS-74-403 (December 1973) pp.1-32.

HOARE 75
    Hoare, C.A.R. Recursive Data Structures. International
    Journal of Computer and Information Sciences, Vol 4,
    No 2 (1975) pp.105-132.

JENSEN AND WIRTH 74
    Jensen, K., and Wirth, N. PASCAL User Manual and Report.
    Lectures Notes in Computer Science NO 18, Springer Verlag
    (1974).

KNUTH 67
    Knuth, D.E. The Remaining Trouble Spots in Algol 60.
    Comm. of the ACM, Vol 10, No 10 (October 1967) pp.611-618.

KNUTH 74
    Knuth, D.E. Stuctured Programming with Go To Statements.
    Computing Surveys, Vol 6, No 4 (December 1974) pp.261-302.

KOSTER 76
    Koster,C.H.A. Visibility and Types. Conference on Data:
    Abstraction, Definition, and Structure. Sigplan Notices, Vol 11,
    Special Issue (April 1976), pp.179-190.

LEDGARD AND MARCOTTY 75
    Ledgard, H.F., and Marcotty, M. A Genealogy of Control
    Structures. Comm. of the ACM, Vol 18, No 11 (November
    1975) pp.629-639.

MURACH 71
    Murach, M. Standard COBOL. SRA (1971)

NAUR 63
    Naur, P. (Editor) Revised Report on the Algorithmic Language
    Algol 60. Comm. of the ACM, vol 6, No 1 (January 1963) pp.1-17.

REYNOLDS 70
    Reynolds, J.C. GEDANKEN: A Simple Typeless Language Based
    on the Principle of Completeness and the Reference Concept.
    Comm. of the ACM, Vol 13, No 5 (May 1970) pp.308-319.

WEIL 65
    Weil, R.L. Jr. Testing the Understanding of the Difference
    between Call by Name and Call by Value in Algol 60. Comm.
    of the ACM, Vol 8, No 6 (June 1965) p378.

WEINBERG, GELLER AND PLUM 75
    Weinberg, G.M., Geller, D.P., and Plum, T.W-S. IF-THEN-ELSE
    Considered Harmful. Sigplan Notices, Vol 10, No 8 (August 1975)
    pp.34-44.

WEISSMAN 67
    Weissman, C. Lisp 1.5 Primer. Dickenson Publishing Company
    (1967).

WIRTH 74
    Wirth, N. On the Design of Programming Languages. Information
    Processing 74. North Holland Publishing Company (1974)
    pp.386-393.

WULF, RUSSEL AND HABERMANN 71
    Wulf, W.A., Russel, D.B., and Habermann, A.N. BLISS: a
    Language for Systems Programming. Comm. of the ACM, Vol 14,
    No 12 (December 1971) pp.780-790.

WULF AND SHAW 73
    Wulf, W., and Shaw, M. Global Variables Considered Harmful.
    Sigplan Notices, Vol 8, No 2 (February 1973) pp.28-34.

X3J3 76
    American National Standards Committee X3J3. Draft proposed
    ANS FORTRAN. Sigplan Notices, Vol 11, No 3 (March 1976).

The Tinman and Communications Applications*
--- ------- --- ---------------- -------------

Prepared for the Workshop on the

Design and Implementation of Programming Languages

Cornell University

September 30 and October 1, 1976

Arthur Evans Jr. and C. Robert Morgan

Bolt Beranek and Newman Inc.

50 Moulton Street

Cambridge MA   02138

September 29, 1976

ABSTRACT

The design of a programming language is based largely on criteria
derived from the needs of its intended users.   These criteria
depend strongly on the applications area for which the language is
intended. In designing a Communications Oriented Language (COL),
we have been influenced by forces somewhat at variance from those
which have influenced the Tinman.   We have thus designed a
language which, although conforming in many ways to the Tinman,
also differs from it in some significant ways. We discuss first
the philosophy that has governed our design, with particular
emphasis on ways in which our goals differ from those of the
Tinman.   We then illustrate how such differences have led to
features in the COL that are at variance with the Tinman criteria.

* This work was supported by the Defense Communications Agency
under contract no. DCA100-76-C-0051.

The Tinman and the COL

INTRODUCTION

We have been involved in the design of a Communications Oriented Language (COL) to meet the needs of the Defense Communications Agency. We produced first a preliminary design of a proposed COL, this design being documented in [1]. We are presently involved in refinement of the language design, as well as investigation of the suitability of the language for compilation.

During the course of our original design, we were aware of the Woodenman document, and we have been aware of the Tinman during our more recent design efforts. Although the ideas presented in these documents have significantly influenced our thinking in many areas, we have not felt constrained by them; we have, in fact, differed from them in some non-trivial ways. This paper presents those of our design goals that differ from those of the Tinman, along with a comparison of these goals with those stated in the Tinman.

THE COL'S DESIGN GOALS

The first and foremost goal in the design of the COL has been that it be a useful tool for the programmer involved in a communications application. Primary requirements for communications applications are efficiency of the compiled code and portability, in that order. (A program is "portable" if it can be easily transfered from one object computer to another.) We feel that the sine

---

[1] "Development of a Communications Oriented Language", Arthur Evans Jr. and C. Robert Morgan, Bolt Beranek and Newman Inc., BBN Report No. 3261, 20 March 76. This document is available on the ARPANET as [BBNE]<EVANS>COL.MANUAL .

The Tinman and the COL

qua non of COL design is that it be possible, at least locally, to produce programs that make maximally effective use of the hardware resources. Portability runs a close second in importance, but we have found that it is not possible to maximize both simultaneously. Thus in all cases where we have had to choose, we have opted to maximize efficiency. Where possible we have sought portability; where it had to be sacrificed, we have specified language features that make conspicuous the non-portable machine-dependent parts of programs. Thus we require that inclusion of a machine-dependent feature be preceded by a warning flag that alerts both the compiler and the most casual reader of the code. For example, the programmer can override the compiler's type-checking mechanism, but it is easy to see when this is being done. Contrast the FORTRAN approach in which it is done by an EQUIVALENCE statement, probably in a remote part of the program text.

Maintenance of programs is a significant part of the cost of a large programming project, and we have kept this factor in mind. We have worked towards making the COL easy to read as well as easy to write, since it is usually the case that someone other than the original programmer is responsible for maintenance and later changes.

Other goals of the COL design are completely consistent with goals of the Tinman.

THE TINMAN'S GOALS

The Tinman Report, Chapter III, presents the General Goals that led to the specific Needed Characteristics spelled out in

The Tinman and the COL

detail in Chapter IV. We now examine those Tinman goals which differ in any important way from those of the COL.

COST

The important fact with respect to cost is that, in the areas of interest to the DoD in general and to DCA, the cost of development of a language and of implementation of a really high quality compiler is small compared to the cost of the software to be written in the language. Thus it is totally appropriate to specify a language which requires a very complex and costly compiler.

As a closely related point, cost of compilation is small compared to cost of running. Given the need for run-time efficiency which we feel to be so important in the COL, we require an optimizing compiler that emits truly high quality code. (The rationale for this conclusion is presented later.) The high cost of operation of such a compiler is acceptable.

RELIABILITY

We emphatically concur with the Tinman -- if it doesn't work in all situations it is useless. The problem with this goal is to find features to put into the language to help meet it. This matter is receiving much more attention from us now than it did in our initial design. Features that improve readability help, since a program that can be read and understood by another has a better chance of being correct in its more subtle applications.

The Tinman and the COL

TRAINING, ACCEPTABILITY

Although we do not disagree with these goals, they have not been important ones for us. Each programmer must be indoctrinated and trained in a new language only once; he then lives with it for a long time. Thus convenience of use and readability have been more important to us than ease of learning. On the other hand, we have tried not to introduce change just for the sake of change. Where a construct of an existing language was as good as a new one, we have tended to select the former.

TRANSPORTABILITY

This has to do with moving a program written for one machine to another machine. Although we agree that this goal is an important one, we feel that it conflicts frequently with the need for efficiency in the object code. In such conflicts, we have tended to opt for object code efficiency. Thus, for example, we permit machine-level code in the COL, as well as other machine-dependent features. However, we have designed the language so that the use of any machine-dependent feature is immediately obvious to the most casual reader of the program. Further, the compilation listing will flag in a conspicuous manner all such machine dependencies.

READABILITY/WRITABILITY

The Tinman states (page 13), "Readability is more important to the DoD than writability." We concur fully with this excellent point. (Note that features that help readability assist in attaining such other goals as maintainability and reliability.) The

The Tinman and the COL

Tinman again says it well: "The program is written once, but may have to be read dozens of times over a period of years for verification, modification, etc." We would add one further point: Since the readers will almost invariably be people other than the writers (who will be unavailable for consultation), they must depend solely on what has been written.

EFFICIENCY

Here we are concerned with efficiency of the object code, since we have already made clear that efficiency of the compilation process is not an important issue. For various reasons, run-time efficiency is much more important in communications applications than in other application areas within the DoD. As this point is perhaps not obvious, we give it further attention. We consider first efficiency of space in the object code and then efficiency of time. The difficult problem in communications applications is that each of these must be maximized simultaneously.

A communication program frequently runs in a mini-computer, with there being many identical instances of the computer. (For example, a communications net may have hundreds of identical nodes.) Although it is true as the Tinman suggests (page 14) that the cost of adding more memory or a faster processor is a small part of the total cost of a large procurement, the existence of 100 or more installations changes the economics of the situation. There is a further point. Mini-computers used for communications applications are frequently built around an architecture that is inherently incapable of expansion beyond a certain point. For

The Tinman and the COL

example, there is no simple way to expand to more than 32,768 memory locations if the addressing path is only 15 bits wide. (Paging schemes are not simple.)

Efficiency of execution time is particularly important in communications applications, at least in selected parts of the program. Often the throughput of an entire application is critically dependent on the efficiency of a single piece of code. An example might be the code that actually sends the formatted message over the communication channel. It is appropriate to give the job of coding this section to the most skilled member of the programming team, since every improvement made in this part of the code is mirrored directly in the performance of the entire project. This programmer, presumably an expert in the details of the architecture of the object computer, must be able to specify an exact sequence of machine instructions. That is, the programming must be done in assembler or equivalent. In the COL we have opted for an equivalent. Although the programmer can specify the exact machine instructions he wants, this specification uses the usual COL syntax rather than a syntax such as assembler.

Note that really high quality time efficiency is needed in only a small part of the program, while in most applications space efficiency is important throughout. Thus in most of the code it is appropriate to select a compiler option that tends to optimize space usage at the expense of running time. (Doubling the execution time of perhaps 80% or 90% of the code would have a negligible effect on the throughput of the entire application.) Thus one needs compiler options to control what is to be optimized.

The Tinman and the COL

Clearly, the code emitted by the COL compiler must be of high quality indeed. The Tinman report points out quite accurately (page 15) that HOLs are suspect in many circles because of the notoriously low quality of the output of many compilers. However, it goes on to point out that most compilers have been written with tight budgets, since the cost of compiler construction is often perceived as being important. We have said already and feel it worth repeating that the cost of the software written in the COL will exceed by orders of magnitude the cost of the most sophisticated possible compiler. It is thus appropriate to specify (as we have) that the compiler be of extremely high quality, pushing right to the state of the art in optimizing compilers.

The final question relates to that art: Is it in fact possible to produce a compiler as good as we want? We have no doubt that it is possible. Consider BLISS/11, a compiler for the BLISS language that cross compiles from the PDP-10 to the PDP-11. The output of that compiler is of extremely high quality indeed, comparing favorably with that of most programmers. Although it is true that a highly skilled programmer can do better if he makes a concerted effort, that observation misses the point. First, most programmers on the kind of project we are concerned with are not "highly skilled"; and second, even the most skilled programmer does not work to the same high standards all the time. In particular, while careful optimization may well be part of the first writing of the program, subsequent revisions and repairs will surely not be optimized with as much care. The advantage of the compiler is that all its output is of the same high quality. Once the cost is paid for development of high quality optimizing

The Tinman and the COL

algorithms (and we again admit that the cost is indeed high), the advantages continue to accrue. The compiler does not have "off days", as even the best programmer does.

This whole topic is extremely important and deserves a summary. Since communications applications have unusually stringent demands for object code efficiency both in space and in time, a truly high quality compiler is required. The anticipated usage of the compiler is great enough to justify the large expenditure needed to develop it. Finally, the present state of the compiler building art is such that such a compiler is feasible.

CONCLUSIONS

There is only one significant area in which the goals that have led to the development of the COL differ from those enunciated in Chapter III of the Tinman, and the difference is more in degree of emphasis than a serious difference of opinion. We feel that run-time efficiency is a consideration which overrides almost all other goals. In particular, we have chosen to make significant sacrifices to portability in order to attain it.

Programming Language Design Issues

T.E. Cheatham, Jr.

Center for Research in Computing Technology

Harvard University

September 10, 1976

I. Introduction

In this paper we want to look at several issues in the design of a language like the DoD Common Programming Language. In particular, we want to focus on those issues which arise in considering tools to aid in the process of program development, validation, and maintenance. There are three major points which we would like to make; let us commence by stating them:

> A. Program development, validation, and maintenance should be done on a computer big enough to host a reasonable program development system - an integrated collection of tools to aid in all aspects of the process. The availability of such a system will have a significant impact, particularly on the cost and reliability of program maintenance.

B. Assuming that there is to be a good collection of tools, there are a number of features which a programming language ought to have and others which it ought not to have, based on the fact that we want the tools to be as straightforward to implement and as reliable as possible.

C. There is a great deal more to programming language standardization than providing a syntactic and semantic model.

In the sections which follow we will identify a collection of tools and look at the implication of these in language design in some detail. In the remainder of the introduction we will present a short essay on the programming process in the hope that this will help set the stage for the discussion and argument to follow.

Let us thus consider the "programming process". It commences with some "abstract program" which may occasionally be stated mathematically (as in the case of sorting, parsing, solving a system of linear equations, and the like), but more often cannot (as in the case of such procedures as payroll, inventory, MIS and satellite tracking). In any event, the abstract program is "understood" by humans to constitute an algorithm at some level of specification. Given the initial "abstract program," the programming process involves making <u>choices</u>:

> * dividing the program into modules and sub-modules,
>
> * choosing representations for the data objects, and
>
> * choosing representations for the operations or transactions.

This making of choices should be done at several levels of abstraction, as suggested by the principles of structured programming.

The <u>goals</u> of such choices are always to preserve functionality, often to reduce the cost of the program, and hopefully to maintain clarity. The <u>domain</u> of choice is some inventory of possiblities which strongly depend upon the language and system used and the experience and skill of the programmer. The <u>bases</u> for making a choice are <u>facts</u> or <u>predicates</u> which enable a given choice. We might obtain these facts in several different ways; for example:

> 1. They are inherent in the program and we must maintain functionality.
>
> 2. They are deduced -- e.g. we note that some array is sorted at some point and take advantage of that fact.

3. We decide arbitrarily -- e.g. we decide that
an identifier will be less than 30 characters
long, or we decide that some array will be sorted
at some point.

We here propose a need for dramatic departure from current
programming practice: we suggest that these facts are every
bit as much a part of the final "program" as is, for
example, some machine instruction occurring in a run time
load module. In the sections which follow we present
arguments which speak to the advantages to be gained by
treating these facts as an integral part of the program.

A dual problem to that of making choices is that of
optimization of some extant program. By optimization we
mean doing some activity in a less costly way or not doing
some thing because we know we do not need to. There are the
"usual" kinds of optimization, including common
subexpression elimination, register allocation, and
retrieval of storage from "dead" variables. There are also
a number of "high level" optimizations which might be
considered, including recursion removal, program
simplification, loop fusion, loop cleavage, and loop
reduction. But again, optimizing transformations are
enabled by facts (or predicates) about the program.

There are a number of ways in which the computer itself

can be of considerable aid in the programming process. One obvious example is that of providing a compiler for a good high level programming language. However there are a number of other tools which can also be of significant aid; we shall look at these in detail presently. We will assume that such an integrated collection of tools will exist, and that the tools will be hosted by what we shall term a Program Development System (PDS). We assume that the program and its documentation will be in machine readible form from the earliest stages of sketching the functions and inter-relationships of modules through the stages of refinement and selection of representations for data and operations which ultimately result in a production-quality program.

Obviously a PDS cannot be available on every computer in the DoD; some are simply not large enough to host such a system. However it is now very well established that we need not use the ultimate host computer to develop programs to be run on it - there are now dozens of compilers running on large computers and producing code for small computers. With the development of a new programming language we have the opportunity to do things right, and to insure that a rich collection of tools be provided to aid the programming process.

For many programs, the initial development of the

program represents only a small fraction of its overall cost, the major cost element being the maintenance of the program, adapting it to new needs, to accommodate equipment changes, and so on. In most programming environments the maintenance function is carried out with very poor tools and is often largely a matter of patch and paste. The availability of a PDS with its rich collection of tools, would permit the maintenance activity to be carried out in an environment in which the complete history of the program's development would be available to aid in making and validating the changes required. We suggest that this would have a very significant impact on the cost and reliability of program maintenance.

We end our philosophical excursion with the following point.

Considering the implications of the PDS and various tools on the design of the programming language they support is critical. The DoD Common Programming Language must be part of a _system_, and not just be a language, if it is to have real impact on the cost of developing and maintaining embedded computer systems.

II. Language Processing and Analysis Tools

In this section we want to identify and discuss a collection of language processing and program analysis tools. We will look at the implications of these tools on language design in later sections. In some cases the tools are quite standard and are likely available in most installations at the present time. In others, the tools are relatively new or are still to be developed. However, a language like the DoD Common Programming Language will presumably have a significant lifetime and we should certainly try to look a bit into the future and attempt to make the incorporation of the sophisticated tools one can forsee as becoming available in production form in the next decade as easy as possible.

Let us consider some tools (or components) which are primarily concerned with programming language text processing.

A. Text Processing Tools

1. Lexical Analysis and Parsing

There is a lexical analyzer and parser for every programming language and often times several - varying in speed, sophistication of error correction and recovery, and so on.

2. Text Editing

Every modern computing system has a text editor available (and often several). Recently, there have been text editors developed which are specialized to text in a particular programming language in the sense, that they "understand" the language structure and can, for example, insure that program text contains no syntactic errors. We anticipate increasing use of this type of editor.

3. Paragraphing (Pretty Printing)

Many installations now have facilities for taking a program in some form (e.g. text, some internal representation, and so on) and producing a formatted version of that program, using indentation and spacing to emphasize the relationships among the various program parts. This is a very simple kind of tool but it can have a significant impact on the readability of programs, and thus their understanding, validation, and the like.

4. Pre-processing

In the early stages of program development it is often convenient to be able to provide certain constructs in an "abstract" form which possibly cannot actually be executed. Later we replace or "rewrite" these constructs by "refined" versions which can be executed (or further refined). The facility to include such constructs in early versions of a program can have a significant impact on one's ability to understand a program (and to verify its correctness).

B. Program Analysis

There is another collection of tools which have to do primarily with program analysis. Here the range of sophistication is great - and the next five years should see the power of tools available as standard facilities in a PDS increase significantly.

1. Optimization/Program Transformation

At present most program optimization is done by a compiler and is limited to reasonably straightforward techniques for common sub-expression elimination, code movement, dead variable storage retrieval, optimal or near optimal register allocation, and so on. Some work has been reported on more sophisticated techniques (see [8]) and there is presently considerable interest in such higher level optimizations as loop reduction (see [5]), recursion removal back-substitution of procedures, program simplification (see [9]), and so on. The next five years should see some such techniques available on a production basis.

2. Fault Detection

Most compilers have some modest facilities for fault detection - for example insuring that the data types of arguments to a procedure are compatible with those declared for the parameters, verifying that (constant) selectors are acceptable for the data objects selected upon, and so on. Again, we anticipate that current work, for example, on symbolic evaluation of programs (see [1]), will result in considerably more sophisticated fault detection facilities being readily available within a few years.

3. Cost Analysis

At the present time the facilities available for cost analysis of programs are rather crude. The usual facility basically permits one to insert probes into a program in order to gather statistics about the number of times certain operations are performed when the program is confronted with test data. There has been some work reported on analytic tools which attempt to develop "cost expressions" - expressions involving various branching probability distributions and object sizes as parameters - and which represent the "cost" of a program as a function of some assumed costs of basic operations and the relevant parameters. It seems clear that such tools will grow considerably in sophistication over the next few years.

4. Program Synthesis

There have, of course, been program synthesizers (generators) for such common tasks as sorting, merging, and report generation for many years. Recently work on automatic or semi-automatic selection of data representations has been reported (see [6,7]). There is also work on the generation of complete programs for such applications as inventory control, accounting systems, and so on currently under way (see [3]).

5. Program Verification

For several years program verification - the automatic or semi-automatic derivation of a mathematical proof that a program correctly computes what it is supposed to compute has been considered as a possible alternative to the usual methods of validation which simply show that for some representative collection of input data, the program does indeed do what is intended. Recently the sophistication of mechanical program verification has moved from the "toy" stage to that of actually being able to prove the correctness of some complex real-world programs (see [4]), and significant progress is probably to be expected in the next few years.

6. Interpreters

It is often very convenient to be able to execute a program without having to "compile" it, that is, to execute the program interpretively. Among other advantages, the fact that the program being executed is in a form which can directly be correlated to the program text, considerably enhances communication between the execution monitor and the programmer. Also it is much easier to insert probes, trap the program at various points, and so on if the program is executed interpretively.

7 Compiling (Code Generation)

Clearly there will be a number of compilers available for the DoD Common Programming Language, compiling code appropriate for a variety of computers and run-time systems. A point we would like to make here is that with an appropriate set of tools integrated into a PDS, compiling becomes an activity which is invoked once a program is debugged and high level optimizations performed. It is not an activity necessary for the program to run at all, but merely a tool to enhance its efficiency or transport it to an operational environment.

Having identified an inventory of tools for aiding in various aspects of program development, validation, and maintenance, let us now consider the implications of these tools on the programming language for which they are

intended to be used and in which they will presumably be
written. In the next section we will consider the
implications of those tools primarily concerned with program
text processing. The following section will discuss the
basic requirements for the analysis tools and be followed by
a section discussing the language implications of these.

III. Some Implications of Program Text Processing Tools

We divide our discussion into four parts, corresponding
to the four topics mentioned above.

A. Lexical Analysis and Parsing

Given the present state of the theory and practice of
compiling, we can draw some obvious conclusions about the
syntactic specification of a programming language. First,
it is surely now classical to consider the syntactic
specification of a language in two stages - one to describe
the structure of lexemes (identifiers, constants, and the
like) and one to describe the higher level constructs of the
language in terms of its terminal symbols (e.g. BEGIN, DCL,
and so on) and lexemes. Surely the appropriate mechanism
for the specification of lexemes is (the equivalent of) a
finite state automaton (which has the advantage of
specifying both the generation and recognition of lexemes).
For describing the syntactic structure of the language a

context free grammar is clearly appropriate. One would hope that the CFG were so constrained as to be guaranteed to describe an unambiguous language for which some mechanically generated parser with no backtracking and fixed look-ahead would be appropriate (e.g. LALR(1)).

What is perhaps not so obvious is that the syntactic specification of the language should include a specification of the internal representation of a program to be produced by the parser in addition to its text representation. That is, nearly all the tools cited above need to deal with some internal representation of a program; in the interests of commonality we argue that a standard internal representation for programs should therefore be specified.

One particularly appealing representation is to represent constants and identifiers by pointers to or indexes of entries in appropriate constant tables and a symbol table, and to represent each expression as a function applied to its arguments very much in the manner of LISP internal representations. We emphasize that we are not proposing that every implementation employ the same detailed storage structures; we are proposing that the attributes of, for example, symbol table entries, and the means of denoting access to these attributes be standardized.

Given that the internal representation is to be a part of the specification of the language, we note that a good device for specifying both external and internal representations is an "augmented grammar", in which each rule describing some external construct is augmented by a specification of the internal representation of that construct.

B. Text Editing

A text editor which is "smart" about the structure* of a program is usually implemented as a "bridge" between the internal and external representations of text. That is, it usually follows the internal representation, "pretty-printing" constructs to be seen by the user and parsing the constructs the user submits.

The kind of thing which makes a "smart" editor difficult to construct is the use of excessive syntactic constraint in the programming language being edited. An example which has been particularly painful in the editor with which we are most familiar (for the ECL language, see [2]), is that declarations in the language were constrained to have the form of a key word (DECL) followed by an

---

*For example it would permit one to move the cursor from statement to statement, into and out of block levels, and so on, as well as providing search patters which were composed of expressions including formal parameter positions.

identifier (or list of identifiers) followed by a colon followed by other constructs not relevant to the present point. By insisting that the variables being declared be identifiers, we precluded a search pattern of the form

DECL ?X: FOO...

trying to search for all instances of some identifier being declared to be a FOO because ?X (? being a prefix operator) was not acceptable syntactically.

One conclusion is that an editor should be designed before the grammar is cast in concrete; another is that constraints on programming constructs are probably much better dealt with by processors which inspect some program in order to guarantee the absence of certain constructs unacceptable at some stage rather than by the grammar itself.

C. Paragraphing

The basic mechanism for paragraphing is to "walk" over some internal representation of the program and produce a text stream with the spacing and indentation desired. There have been general purpose (table driven) paragraphers constructed which have the power to handle the formatting of most any programming language. Further, the tables can be derived from quite readable specifications of the formatting, usually keyed to the various internal constructs which can occur. Our point is that including a specification of the resulting format for paragraphed programs is quite within the state-of-the-art and might want to be considered as part of the "standard specification" for the language.

D. Pre-processing

The basic idea behind most pre-processors is to permit the programmer to employ certain high level constructs not provided for in the base language and to later replace these by the appropriate base language constructs before further processing (like source-source transformation, compiling, and so on). What is required is the ability to extend the syntax of the language to permit the new constructs to be written and to provide a mechanism for recognizing and replacing the extended constructs. Because of the difficulties of modifying extant compilers, most pre-processors have been implemented by using a new parser* for the extended language and some ad hoc program to do the transformation, resulting in a text stream which can then be

----

*Some pre-processors have been implemented as string processors, but providing a grammar and parser for the extended language and doing the transformations on an internal representation permits a much more sophisticated and reliable pre-processor.

handled by the usual compiler.

It is our contention that language extensions for providing new constructs can in most cases be accomodated by a parser which can handle new infix, prefix, and matchfix** operators and which permits new terminal symbols to be defined having the parse properties of standard terminals in the language (e.g. FOR\EACH might have the same parse properties as FOR, providing a new syntactic form for iterations). (Such a parser is quite within the state-of-the-art and can be highly efficient as well.)

Of course providing the user the ability to define new operators alarms some who fear that thereby programs will become unreadable (or, better put, more easily mis-read). However this problem is surely susceptible to administrative control (e.g. restricting the ability to add new operators to some "systems group", etc.), and the appeal of having a single parser is very strong. Also, if we insist on employing functional form for the extended or abstract operations, their readability and appeal may be reduced considerably.

**A "matchfix" operator is a pair of operators which act like parentheses or brackets and whose interpretation is the "left bracket" operator applied to the arguments. E.g. <*FEE,FOO*> is interpreted as <* applied to FEE and FOO.

We note that, again, the implementation of a pre-processor will often involve the manipulation of a program represented in some internal representation, and the result of pre-processing may well be automatically produced by a paragrapher (pretty-printer). We would also note that certain kinds of pre-processing require understanding of the program in the sense, for example, of knowing the declared data types of variables. Thus such a facility might well want to be combined with various analysis tools whose business it is to "understand" a program.

IV. Basic Requirements for Analysis Tools

Any analysis tool has to "understand" and "reason" about a program in some sense. Obviously the level of the "understanding" varies considerably. For example the classical optimizers have relatively superficial understanding while a program verifier has a relatively sophisticated understanding and a symbolic evaluator in some sense "understands completely". Independent of the level of understanding, there are three basic components which any analysis tool must have - a flow graph for the program, an environment description, and a calculus for reasoning about the facts. Let us discuss these in turn:

A. Flow Graph

A flow graph for a program is essentially a directed graph whose nodes correspond to pieces of the program with no control transfers in or out; the arcs emanating from a node correspond to the possible exits or branches and each may be tagged with the predicate enabling that exit or branch.

B. Environment Description

The content of an environment description varies widely depending upon the kind of analysis tool we have in mind. Basically, however, we must have some table entry for each variable which is declared in the program plus an indication of the set of values that variable takes on various control paths. This indication may be as simple as use/set information and as complicated as expressions describing the value of the quantity as functions of symbolic values of other variables.

C. A Calculus

With some of the simpler analytic tools, such as those for classical optimization, the "reasoning" about the program is relatively straightforward. For example by simply detecting and recording each different possible value for some variable, common sub-expressions can be detected by comparing two expressions into which have been substituted

some distinct representation of the value of each variable
for occurrences of that variable in the appropriate context.
The analysis of dead variables is usually done using boolean
vectors representing use/set information for the collection
of variables. And so on.

However, for the more sophisticated analysis tools, the
reasoning about the program requires a _calculus_ - a
collection of mathematical functions and rules which permit
one to describe and reason about what is happening as a
result of executing the program. For example these
functions would include the usual arithmetic, relational,
and logical operations, plus functions which correspond to
other "programming" operations such as array access,
determining lengths, modes, and other attributes of data
objects, and so on. In addition it may well be convenient
to include such functions as finite sum and product,
functions which define arrays or lists (e.g. that array
whose jth element is $f(j)$, least and greatest functions
(e.g. the least j in $j_1, j_1+1, \ldots$ such that $p(j)$), and so
on. The arguments to these functions would include manifest
constants as well as special "symbolic values" representing
the value of some variable or component in some context.

Given that we can describe the effect of some fragment
of a program via these mathematical functions, reasoning
about them requires a logical calculus - for example the

first order predicate calculus - plus the means for proving theorems within that calculus. Present tools often include rather elaborate facilities for constructing and simplifying symbolic expressions; a great deal of "theorem proving" at the present time is done by simplification of the logical expression to _true_. There is usually in addition some goal/sub-goal mechanism to guide the theorem prover in more difficult cases as well as an ability for the user to add new "axioms" (new knowledge) in a reasonably straightforward way.

V. Some Language Implications

There are several implications on the design and structure of a programming language which is both to host the kinds of analysis tools sketched above and to be the subject of analysis. These derive primarily from a desire to have these tools be straightforward to implement and reliable. In some cases, however, they determine whether some kinds of operations can be performed at all. In any event, they often give rise to a dilemma - we need some feature for purpose P but should reject it for reason R; we shall comment on the resolution of these dilemmas in the section following. We have identified five categories which we discuss in turn.

A. Indeterminacy

It is obviously necessary to permit certain things to be indeterminate until a program or procedure is actually executed; an obvious example is the set of values of input parameters. However, indeterminacy surely blocks the ability of analysis tools to reason about a program and compilers to generate efficient run-time code. The question is where to draw the lines. We argue that the following constraints permit the user reasonable flexibility without too severely hampering analysis:

1. Modes and sizes of data objects should be determinable when an object is declared (i.e. created); they should remain fixed for the lifetime of that object. This is not to say that we should deny, for example, arrays of variable dimension at some level; rather, it says that provisions for objects of varying sizes should not be built in but constructed by extension of the built-in facilities.

2. Values of procedure valued variables should be statically determinable whenever possible. Analysis of programs or procedures which employ unknown procedures is particularly difficult. On the other hand, it is sometimes necessary to write such procedures (e.g. the analysis tools

themselves).

3. A (finite) union-type mode should be employed
whenever   possible   in   the   face   of   mode
indeterminacy   -   and   the   "universal"   mode
(indicating that the actual mode may be anything
at all) should be employed only as a last   resort.
Again it is necessary for certain programs to deal
with (statically) completely indeterminate   modes
but this should be minimized.

B. Control Structures

One of the more difficult things to handle in any kind
of analysis tool is the existence of arbitrary labels and
gotos.   Indeed, given that label valued variables are
permitted, determination of a reasonable flow graph for some
program may be impossible.

The problem is basically this. The central issue in
most any kind of analysis of a program is determining what
happens in loops. That is, we are looking for some property
concerning some quantity (e.g.   the range of some index,
whether or not some pointer can be NIL, whether or not some
variable is used or set, and so on) and at any point in the
program where several paths join, we must essentially take
the union of properties on all input paths. With well
structured   and   nested   loops   this   kind of analysis is

considerably simpler than is the case if we have arbitrary branching. By eliminating gotos in favor of structured loops, conditionals, returns, case statements, and so on, we can eliminate that stage of processing which determines the flow structure and loop nesting - it is manifest by looking at the program. If gotos are permitted, we can, of course, introduce a stage of processing whose business it is to analyze the flow graph and determine the nesting structure. However, if two distinct, non-nested loops each employ some segment of the program, we have the further difficulty of effectively making two copies of the common segment.* The problem is alleviated slightly if gotos are restricted to the same (block) scope, since entry and exit points are then "clean", but the basic problem remains.

On these bases, plus the fact that iteration, recursion, case statements, return, and conditional expressions are sufficient control structures (leaving aside multiprogramming facilities for the moment) and their use tends to lead to well structured programs in the sense that they can be read and understood more readily, we would strongly propose the elimination of gotos from the DoD Common Programming Language.

---

* In the technical jargon of interval analysis flow graphs which lead to this kind of difficulty are termed irreducible.

There is, of course, another side to this coin. That is, at some level gotos are clearly necessary since virtually all modern computers have essentially one control mechanism - the goto. The question is - how far "up" do we let this creep? There are, in fact, good reasons for permitting gotos at some level of use of a higher level language deriving from a desire to optimize certain program constructs by source-to-source transformation. For example, if we wish to eliminate certain recursive constructs in favor of more efficient iterative equivalents, or eliminate the overhead of certain procedure calls it is necessary (at least highly desirable) to employ gotos.

Thus we have a dilemma.

C. Run-time Environment

Since code produced from the DoD Common Programming Language must, in some cases, be run on small computers having virtually no run-time support, it would appear that we cannot permit dependence of code on such run-time facilities as type checking, dynamic storage allocation and retrieval ("garbage collection"), and so on. On the other hand, particularly in the case of the analysis tasks (presumably run only on reasonably large and sophisticated computer systems), there must be such sophisticated run-time facilities available - either provided by the "system" or

425

included as componennts of the tools. It is surely not reasonable to expect that each analysis tool include its own version of these facilities (e.g. a good garbage collector will very likely be written in machine code for some time to come), and thus we have another dilemma.

D. Language Structure

It is possible, in principle, to leave such features as case statements, controlled loops, and the like out of a language because there are "lower level" constructs which are equivalent. Of course no sensible language designer would propose this because of the convenience and structure such higher level constructs lend. We have also noted that certain kinds of program analysis are easier if the analyzer realizes that it has a certain kind of construct (e.g. a controlled loop). Thus, let us assume that such higher level constructs will be built-in. Now there are certain kinds of source-to-source optimizing transformations which, effectively, replace some construct by an equivalent construct at a "lower" level which is more efficient because of certain special case considerations. Examples of this would include replacement of a case statement by a more efficient conditional expression, elimination of some procedure call by substitution of a block equivalent to the procedure body, elimination of some declaration by substitution of the initializing value for occurrences of the variable declared, and so on.

Our concern is that such substitutions be possible, and their possibility basically rests on the ability to model the higher level constructs by lower level constructs. Some specific desiderata are the following:

1. There should be the means to model a procedure application by an equivalent block. Essentially, this block would have declarations for each of the formals, initializing their values to those of the actuals, then declaration* of the result as the value of the body of the procedure and return of that as the value of the block. To do this requires a notion of "parallel" declarations (i.e. normally the declaration of all formals must be completed before any of the declared variables "appear" in the environment); the declaration of the result must, of course, take place in an environment which includes all the formals.

2. In general it should be possible to substitute for any expression (in particular, a variable) any other expression whose value is equivalent. Thus the language should surely permit conditional expressions as both L-values and R-values.

———

*See appendix B for a more detailed discussion of this point.

3. The format of a declaration should include provision for the initializing value of the variable(s) being declared. In general, the binding of actuals to formals should be exactly like the declaration of a local variable, and vice versa.

4. It should be possible to model a case statement by a conditional expression.

5. In general, we should look very carefully at the question of the substitutability of one construct in favor of some other, so that optimization by source-source transformation is not made difficult or impossible.

E. Reasoning About Programs

As we discussed earlier, reasoning about a program in any sophisticated way requires a collection of mathematical functions which describe the values of various quantities at various points in the program in terms of certain symbolic quantities denoting the values of unknowns. The sophistication of the facilities for manipulating these functions (e.g. simplifying them) will be strongly dependent upon the arithmetic, logical, and relational expressions enjoying the usual mathematical algebraic laws of commutativity, associativity, and the like. This will be the case only if the corresponding operators in the programming language enjoy these properties. In the case of integer operations there is probably no issue. However with the floating point operations, the user must clearly have the ability to specify the order of computation if he is to control error propagation. We thus propose that some facility be included in the language to provide the control which must be employed for certain computations. This could take the form of special operators to be used for the critical cases, addition of declarative constructs to the language to permit the programmer to identify critical computations or regions, and so on. We might parenthetically note that forcing the programmer to indicate which computations had a critical order would enhance program documentation.

VI. Resolving the Dilemmas

In the last section we pointed out a number of dilemmas -- features we surely wanted on one account, but whose existence was to be decried on some other account. We must now consider the question of how we can resolve these dilemmas.

The answer is quite simple -- there really are no dilemmas at all. The apparent dilemmas arise from a defect in our view of the programming process and the role of a higher level language and its compiler in that process. That is, the classical view of the programming process entails the preparation of a program in some higher level language, compiling that program to produce load modules with the compiler, and then loading the relevant modules and confronting them with test data. Hopefully, all this is done in the presence of some clever debugging aids which permit us to explore the ramifications of this confrontation in some format more appealing than octal snapshots of some portion of core. The dilemmas arise because we insist on thinking about the high level language and the compiler.

Let us consider an alternative point of view -- one certainly within the current state-of-the-art, and consistent with providing the kind of support we think necessary for the various activities involved in the programming process. We do this by sketching some highlights of an imagined series of sessions with a program development system in the development of some program (perhaps a component of a larger system of programs).

1. The process commences with the programmer choosing some set of (abstract) data types and operations which seem to him to have a natural correspondence with the things which need to be done in the task at hand. He prepares a first draft program in terms of these operations and data

types, perhaps having to inform the parser if he has introduced any new infix or prefix operations to ease his task.

2. The program is input to the PDS via an interactive editor which insures that no syntactic errors occur. (Any which do can be immediately repaired).

3. The programmer now develops procedures and/or rewrites corresponding to each higher level operator in his program. He also chooses concrete data representations for his abstract data objects, insuring that the functionality of the abstract objects is retained in his concrete representations. This might, for example, involve encapsulating the definitions of data objects and including special operators for selection, generation, or assignment to insure that the required behavior was obtained.

At this stage he might also be able to appeal to a tool to aid him in the process of representation selection. Such a tool would, on the basis of program analysis and dialogue with the programmer, choose a representation from its inventory, basing the choice on facts deduced by the analysis or claimed by the programmer. Alternatively, he might be able to procure some general representation from a library (e.g. for sets, matrices, lists, or other standard data objects), deferring until a later stage of development

a more detailed analysis of his particular needs and the
concomitant tailoring of specialized representations which
provide more efficient implementations for his application.

4. The program is then mechanically rewritten to
replace high level constructs by their implementations, this
perhaps taking place in several stages corresponding to the
levels of refinement.

5. At this point the program can be executed. First,
however, the programmer would likely employ a fault detector
tool to identify faults which were certain and/or possible
faults in his program, appealing to the editor to modify his
program to protect against these. He might also employ a
tool which inspected his program and noted the use of
various undesirable (or unacceptable) constructs like gotos,
various kinds of indeterminacies which he might be able to
remove, and so on.

6. He might then confront his program with test data,
running the program interpretively. Alternately, he might
employ a program verifier to verify that the program as a
whole or, perhaps, certain functions of the program would
perform correctly.

7. Given that his program appeared to run correctly,

he might now insert a variety of probes in order to obtain measurements of the cost of various operations and again execute the program interpretively to obtain the measurement data. Alternatively, he might be able to employ a cost analysis tool which could develop cost expressions as functions of various (symbolic) size parameters and the like.

8. Availed of the measurement data or cost expressions, the programmer might well fall back to reconsider certain choices of representation of data or operations on the basis that their relative cost was out of balance. This would be followed by a new cycle of verification and/or test execution.

At this point the program might be analyzed and an inventory of source-to-source transformations applied to enhance its efficiency.

10. Finally any dependence on system features which were not available on the eventual target computer would have to be eliminated. At this point a code generation tool for generating code for the target computer would be invoked to produce an appropriate load module for that computer.

VII. Conclusions

In this paper we have proposed that the DoD Common Programming Language be thought of not just as a language but as the linguistic component of a rich collection of tools hosted by a program development system. We have further proposed that it is particularly important to view a program as _existing at many levels_. Our own experience in using two such program development systems is that these increase the overall programmer productivity quite significantly.

Given that one accepts this thesis, it is our concern that the impact of a system of tools on the language itself be considered very carefully before the language is finalized. There are many subtle interactions between the language and the tools developed to support it; the careful consideration of these interactions for present and future tools should have a high pay off in terms of making them simpler and more reliable.

References

1] Cheatham, T. E. Jr., and Judy A. Townley, "Program Analysis Techniques for Software Reliability," Center for Research in Computing Technology, Harvard University, 1976.

[2] ECL Programmers Manual, Center for Research in Computing Technology, 23-74, Harvard University, December 1974.

[3] Goldberg P.C., "Automatic Programming," in Programming Methodology, vol. 23, Lecture Notes in Computer Science, Springer-Verlag 1975.

[4] Igarashi,S., London, R., Luckham, D., "Automatic Program Verification: A Logical Basis and Its Implementation," ACTA Information, Vol. 4, No. 2., 1975.

[5] Loveman, David B., "Program improvement by source-to-source optimization," JACM 24, 1, January 1977.

[6] Low, J.R., "Automatic Coding: Choice of Data Structures," Dept. of Computer Science, U. Rochester, August 1974.

[7] Rovener, P., "Automatic Representation Selection for Associative Data Structures," Ph.D. Thesis, Center for Research in Computing Technology, Harvard University 1976.

[8] Standish, T. A., Harriman, D., Kibler, D., and Neighbors, J., "The Irvine Program Transformation Catalogue," Dept. Information and Computer Science, U.C. Irvine, January 1976.

[9] Wegbreit, B., "Goal Directed Program Transformation," Xerox Palo Alto Research Center, 1975.

WORKSHOP ON ALTERNATIVES IN THE DESIGN AND IMPLEMENTATION OF A COMMON PROGRAMMING
LANGUAGE FOR EMBEDDED COMPUTER APPLICATIONS

TITLE: Parallel Processing and Modular Software Construction

AUTHOR: K.Jackson, Mindef, Malvern, UK.

INTRODUCTION

The one common denominator in the software for all real time computer systems is that
it consists of a set of co-operating parallel processes. This is true whether the
parallelism is achieved by having many hardware processors or by multiplexing a single
processor among many competing processes (pseudo-parallelism); it is also independent of
the way the pseudo parallelism is achieved eg interrupts, scheduler etc. It is therefor
regretable that in the TINMAN document this topic receives only scant treatment. In fac
only two sub sections (approx. 2½ per cent) of the document are devoted to this topic.

This paper presents an opposite point of view. Starting from the parallel processing
common denominator, the advantages of bringing this out into the open at as early a
possible a stage in the software design are considered. The consequences of this
approach are that the concept of 'the program' disappears and is replaced by a network
of parallel processes and data areas. This enables a different and more flexible approa
to software construction to be adopted. The language implications of this approach are
quite minor but the advantages in terms of software quality and true modularity are very
significant as also are the consequences on ease of management.

PARALLEL PROCESSING

Parallel processing implies that the many processes are running in parallel and that
they are as far as possible unrelated in time. In other words they run asynchronously.
However, since in embedded computer applications all the processes do co-operate to
perform a single overall task, they must, of necessity, intercommunicate.

There are two facets to this intercommuncation. Firstly two communicating processes
must be able to access the data area(s) (although not necessarily at the same time);
secondly a synchronisation mechanism must be provided to allow processes to mutually
exclude and/or cross stimulate each other to ensure orderly intercommunication.

Before considering process intercommunication in a language context it is necessary to
consider how processes are identified within the language. One approach, often used,
is to allow any procedure to become a process. Data communication is then possible
via any data areas that are in scope for any two communicating procedures. This
approach obviously works (more accurately - systems designed by using this approach can
be made to work) but it gives rise to many problems of integration and testing because
of poor modularity. This poor modularity arises because data access far in excess of
the designer's intention is permitted.In normal block structured languages all global
data is available to all processes. In other words the question "how is the access
limited to only that set intended by the designer?" is either (a) never asked or (b)
answered in the negative.

In the view of the author a different approach which rejects the hierarchical block
structured approach at the parallel process network level is preferable. It is
necessary to clearly identify the statements that will be used for a process by some
special syntactic device eg the language word PROCESS. It is also necessary (and
perhaps more important) to force the process to declare explicitly a list of data areas
through which it will communicate with other processes. The compiler can then check
that no access is made to data areas (external to the process) that are not present
on the list. In this way the designer's intentions can be checked by the compiler.
However the consequence of this approach is that the concept of a program as a single

block structured hierarchy containing (at various levels as necessary) many co-operating parallel processes is destroyed together with the concept of (universally accessible) global data. Instead we are left with the program consisting of a network of co-operating parallel processes together with the data areas through which they communicate.

ADVANTAGES OF THE NETWORK APPROACH

The network, being static (on a statement-statement timescale), can then be used as the basis for a modular approach to design implementation and testing. The design is conceived as a network from the earliest possible moment. The network can be expressed in diagramatical notation (eg Phillips network diagram ref 1) to give good design visibility. It is also easy to represent such a network in a data base form for management and project control (eg SDS ref 2). The network clearly identifies the first level of design in terms of modules that can remain visible right through the software production process.

Each module of the network must be described in terms of its purpose (in its context) related to the overall requirement (specification) of the software. In a strongly typed language each data area will have a distinct type and each process will state its communication requirements in terms of these types. Thus the major interfaces of the system are clearly visible and can be expressed:

(a) in the network diagram
(b) in the data base
(c) in the actual program.

Further advantages of this clear modularity become evident in the testing phase. Each process can be individually tested by setting it up with a suitable set of data areas (ie exactly that set which it specifies internally). The process is then unable to distinguish this test environment from any operational environment. Thus it is easier to organise the testing (test processes communicate with the process under test only through the same well defined interface) and it is easier to specify the test and to check for both compliance (when running the test) and exhaustiveness (when vetting the specification).

The aspect of process synchronisation in a system can also be handled in a tidy and modular manner using this approach. The problem of real time interactions and the consequent need for a synchronisation mechanism is concentrated on the access to the intercommunicating data areas made by the parallel asynchronous processes of the network. By adopting the concept of the <u>access procedure</u>, all direct access to the data areas and consequently all use of synchronisation mechanisms can be encapsulated. The access procedures for the data areas thus form a convenient and sensible unit of design, implementation and testing, which collectively provide a level of abstraction that provides a reliable means of communication between processes. This leaves the processes themselves as single sequential processes that need take no special precaution to handle parallelism and asynchronism.

The final advantage of this approach that is worth mentioning here is the promise of re-usable software modules. Because of the well defined external data interface of each process, it follows that any process will work in any context so long as its data environment is set up correctly. This fact has already been used in the testing strategy outlined above but it does mean that processes can be put into a library and fetched for any number of different systems. This re-usability will be further enhanced if, from the inception of the use of the approach suggested here, designers are encouraged to achieve modularity of function within a process.

LANGUAGE AND IMPLEMENTATION IMPLICATIONS

The major implication on language design brought about by the adoption of this approach is the need to reject conventional notions of "the program" and of "global data" The compiler is never concerned with complete programs but always with modules which can be located within the network of processes and intercommunication data areas. The major syntactic units are processes and intercommunication data areas. When compiling a process the compiler must be able to obtain the specification for all the data area types in the external communication data list of the process. This may be obtained by reading the specifications before reading the process statements and may be done manually or preferably by an automatic file search triggered by the external communication list. However it is done, it is essential that the data areas are defined beforehand and the specification marked in a distinctive manner within the language to tell the compiler to remember the specification in the file.

The access procedure concept can be neatly incorporated into the language by encapsulating the access procedures with the data areas they manipulate. The system designer is effectively defining a set of ways of accessing or using a particular data area by defining access procedures. This can be extended in scope by introducing a protection mechanism used to limit access to only one of many sets of access procedures and data fields. Thus a designer could decide all possible combinations of access rights and then allocate each process one set for each data area in its external list. With this information represented in language terms the compiler can control access according to the rules laid down by the designer.

An important consequence of this approach is the ability to construct systems from a set of processes and data areas after compilation. At compile time there is no information available or necessary about the actual network that the processes and data areas being compiled will be used to create. Indeed one of the most important aspects of this approach is that an infinite number of networks can be constructed from the pre-compiled modules. The method of constructing a network merely requires the specification of each process together with a set of data areas which satisfy the external data requirements of the process. It is vitally important that full type checking can be carried out at this stage. This imposes a requirement on the compiler to record the external data requirements of each process and also the type of each data area used in the network. It is convenient to refer to these processes and data areas used to construct networks as System Elements.

MASCOT AND MORAL

The concepts that have been described above are derived from two projects at the Royal Signals and Radar Establishment. In this section a brief description of each project together with a status report of each will be given.

Work started on MASCOT in 1972 with the aim of identifying a Modular Approach to Software Construction Operation and Test (hence the acronym)(Refs 3, 4, 5, 6, 7, 8). It has resulted in a well disciplined and formalised method of dealing with the interconnection and inter-communication between parallel processes (called activities). This work suggested the network approach outlined earlier in the paper and some basic modules have been defined which are independent even after compilation (ie System Elements). Mascot system elements are:

(a) Root Procedures - procedures that define the data processing actions of activities The root procedure has parameters that define the total external data communication of the root procedure and hence of the activity or activities it supports. Root procedures can not be called in the normal manner but can only be executed when they are made into activities (see below).

(b) Channel - A generic class (containing any number of individual types) of intercommunication data areas used exclusively for producer/consumer (message passing etc) interactions between activities.

(c) Pool - A generic class (containing any number of individual types) of intercommunication data areas used to hold non transient or reference data (data base). The important distinction between channels and pools is that reading data from a pool does not disturb that data in any way (ie it is not consumed).

(d) Interrupt Channels - A special class of intercommunication data area used to communicate between an activity (software) and a hardware device of some kind.

These modules may be connected together to construct subsystems containing a network with one or more activities. The subsystem can then be started or stopped and the total system consists of a set of subsystems. Thus the system can evolve gradually by subsystem substitution.

This construction facility is supported by a small software 'kernel' which provides a basic set of synchronisation primitives that can be used within access procedures to ensure an orderly and sustained flow of data through the system. Synchronisation is based upon a synchronisation device called a 'controlqueue' with four operations on it:

JOIN
LEAVE } to achieve mutual exclusion (similar to Dijkstra P and V)

WAIT   an activity can call wait (if it has already JOINed the queue) and th s
        stop any further processing until it receives an explicit software stimulus
        from another activity

STIM   this primitive is the means of applying a software stimulus

An important aspect of the kernel is that this control queue synchronising device has been applied within the interrupt handling area. An activity can WAIT for the arrival of an interrupt and the interrupt itself is transformed into a STIM. Associated with the WAIT INTERRUPT is a data transfer which always takes place between the call and control being returned to the caller.   This WAIT INTERRUPT primitive, which has been implemented on computers with a wide range of interrupt and input/output architectures, leads to a rudimentary form of processor independent input/output.

At present there are seven implementations of the Mascot kernel. Some have been built on host operating systems. All of them allow software to be expressed as a network of activities, channels, pools and interrupts. The bare machine implementations allow the flexible construction and evolution of the software by subsystem substitution. Mascot is actually language independent. The present implementations allow user programs to be written in Coral 66 (six implementations) or Algol 68R (one implementation).

Over the past two years Mascot has been used on three internal projects (all using Algol 68R) and the resulting programmer productivity and ease of system integration has been remarkable. For example one system with a total size of 180K bytes was produced in 4 man months. These internal projects have crystallised methodologies for the design, implementation, testing and documentation of software using MASCOT together with suggestions concerning the management and quality assurance of such software (refs 6,7). Mascot with Coral 66 is currently being used on two defence projects by UK contractors. Reactions to the new approach have changed from highly sceptical to fully converted over a period of 2 to 3 months at the start of each project.

Our experience with the use of both Coral 66 and Algol 68R with Mascot suggested that to make Mascot really easy to use and thereby further improve speed of system production a language specifically tailored to Mascot was worth investigation. It was decided, because of the large investment in Coral 66 within the UK, that the language should be built upon Coral 66. This has been achieved by designing the language so that it can be translated fully automatically into standard Coral 66. The resulting language is called MORAL.

MORAL is an acronym for Mascot Oriented Reliable Applications Language. (refs 8,9). The language is specifically tailored towards the Mascot approach containing language words like ROOT PROCEDURE, CHANNEL, POOL AND INTERRUPT and also containing all the Mascot kernel primitives as statements of the language. In addition it contains some constructs that are aimed at further reinforcing the form of modularity which Mascot demands with the objective of improving the reliability of the software thus produced.

Moral allows the definition of new user types and full compile time checking of the use of these types. Of particular interest in this paper is the GROUP definition which is the construct used to specify channels, pools and interrupts. Consider the group definition in figure 1.

This particular group definition defines a new user type called CHARCHAN and further the language word CHANNEL indicates that this is a special user type belonging to the generic class of CHANNEL and it should therefore be remembered in the appropriate file(s). Within the group the fields are listed in four sets demarked by the language word LOCK. The first set containing three INTEGER constants are freely accessible. The second set contains two CONTROL QUEUES, two INTEGER pointers and an ARRAY of CHAR. These fields constitute control variables and the buffer of the channel and therefore access should be carefully controlled. In this case the designer has decided that these fields should be completely inaccessible from outside the channel. He represents this decision by the language word LOCK followed by an empty list of keys that will open the lock. The third set consists of a single field that is a procedure. This is an access procedure for the channel used by producer activities to send messages (in this case consisting of a single character) into the channel. The field is LOCKed but the lock can be opened by the key 'producer'. The final field of the group is a procedure used for receiving messages from the channel and its lock can be opened by the key 'consumer'.

Each instance of a group has the option of selecting one of the set of keys which defines a mode of access. Thus for example a ROOT PROCEDURE which might be used to take characters from one CHARCHAN and copy them into two other CHARCHANs would be specified as follows:

```
ROOT PROCEDURE duplicate (REF CHARCHAN  input (consumer),
                                        output 1 (producer)
                                        output 2 (producer));


BEGIN CHAR ch;
      DO [input ].receive (ch);
         [output 1] .send (ch);
         [output 2] .send (ch)
      ENDLOOP
END;
```

Thus because of the lock and key mechanism, duplicate may only call the procedure 'receive' to access the CHARCHAN 'input' and the procedure 'send' to access the CHARCHAN 'output 1' and 'output 2'. Use of any other fields except of course the three unlocked constants would cause a compilation failure.

The procedures within the group can access any fields of the group by naming them directly. The compiler (or translater) must include an extra parameter in each procedure to indicate to which particular instance of the variables any call refers. This extra parameter is automatically supplied with the call of the procedure. The information is easily obtained because the instance of the group must be mentioned(and possibly dereferenced) in order to select the access procedure field (see body of 'duplicate' above).

The parameters of the root procedure are used by the compiler to obtain the specification of the appropriate set of channels, pools and interrupts from the filing system. The keys specified are used to select the appropriate accessible fields of each instance. An important aspect of this selection is the selection of the access procedures which the root procedure requires. This information is stored in the filing system as control data for the linking process so that the root procedure can be linked to the code of the access procedures it requires during the process of making the root procedure into a System Element.

ubsystems are formed from system elements by a command called FORM. An example of
his command is:

```
ORM triplicated expansion =
                expand (in, trans 1, dictionary),
                duplicate (trans 1, trans 2, out 1),
                duplicate (trans 2, out 2, out 3);
```

his generates a subsystem called 'triplicated expansion' containing three activities.
ach activity is specified by naming the root procedure and supplying an appropriate
et of actual parameters to satisfy the formal parameter requirements of the root.
ORM first checks that all the root procedures and the parameters are contained in the
ystem Element File (SEF). Then it must <u>check</u> that the actual parameters types do match
he formal parameter specification. This implies that the SEF must contain the compile
ime information derived from the CHANNEL, POOL and INTERRUPT type specifications and
rom the ROOT PROCEDURE parameter lists. This method of constructing software enables
oftware modularity to be maintained through all stages of software construction. The
rocess of generating System Elements is completely unaware of the way in which the
odules involved will be connected together: it is only concerned with establishing
he rules which will govern the eventual connection ie the 'plugs and sockets' compati-
ility between ROOT PROCEDURES and CHANNELS, POOLS and INTERRUPTS. The FORMing of
ubsystems is the only place where actual interconnections are specified. In the
onventional approach to software construction the actual interconnections are present
n the source text and carried right through. Thus the MASCOT approach has significant
dvantages over the conventional approach in the areas of software maintainance and
eusability of System Elements where some existing modules must be used and combined
ith some new ones.

he present status of the MORAL project is that a preliminary language specification has
een prepared (after several iterations); a free standing translator has been written
nd is currently undergoing evaluation and assessment. After this period a further
teration on the language specification and translator strategy will take place followed
y the integration of the translator into a fully comprehensive and (hopefully) well
ngineered Mascot system. This system will be used for 'software prototype' projects
here the software will be produced first and used to decide what hardware configuration
s required. Then the software will be transferred keeping the structure intact on to
he target machine(s).

TATE OF THE ART

 paper by Clark et al (reference 10) has criticised Tinman's predecessor Woodenman in
uch the same vein as this paper. In particular they identify four areas where the
eport is deficient (these are still deficient in Tinman): modular construction of
rograms, handling of machine dependencies, parallel processing and exception handling.
hey go on to highlight the advantages that could be obtained by incorporating these
oncepts into a language for real time systems and then point out that such a
anguage is beyond the current state of the art. With the exclusion of exception
andling, MASCOT and MORAL go a long way towards providing a viable product satisfying
hese requirements. Although it is not claimed that these products provide the ultimate
n perfection it is suggested that they have been used sufficiently widely to be worthy
f consideration as a state of the art input to the HOL being devised by the Department
f Defense.

REFERENCES

1   C S E Phillips "Networks for Real Time Programming", British Computer Journal,
     May 1967.

2   F R Albrow   "The Pilot SDS" RRE Newsletter and Research Review 1975.

3   K Jackson, Gp Capt H R Simpson, "MASCOT - A modular approach to software
     construction operation and test" RRE Tech Note 778, October 1975.

4   K Jackson, C I Moir, "Parallel Processing in Software and Hardware - the
     MASCOT approach" 1975 Sagamore Computer Conference on Parallel Processing.

5   K Jackson, "Modularity in Real Time Computer Systems" IFAC/IFIP Workshop on
     Real Time Programming, Boston, Mass. 1975

6   K Jackson, "Software Structure", Proceedings of Colloquium on Quality Assurance
     of Software, February 1976.

7   K Jackson, Fl.Lt J A Cloke "A Mascot Software Standard" Unpublished.

8   K Jackson, H F Harte, "The Achievement of well structured software in Real
     Time Systems" IFAC/IFIP Workshop in Real Time Programming, IRIA France 1976.

9   Software Sciences Ltd "A description of the Programming Language MORAL"
     Unpublished.

10   D D Clark, M M Hammond, J B Dennis, B H Liskov, M D Schroeder, "Appraisal of
     the Woodenman and Recommended Plan for DOD High Order Language Development"
     Research and Consultancy Incorporated, October 1975.

```
CHANNEL TYPE CHARCHAN =
GROUP
        CONST INTEGER size:=16,maxpointer:=15, inc modulus:=31;

    LOCK:
        CONTROLQ inq,outq;
        INTEGER inpoint, outpoint;
        ARRAY(O TO maxpointer)CHAR buffer

    LOCK producer;
        PROCEDURE send(CHAR ch);
        BEGIN
            JOIN inq;
                WHILE inpoint=outpoint DO WAIT inq
                    THEN
                            buffer(inpointMASKmaxpointer):=ch;
                            inpoint:=(inpoint+1)MASKincmodulus;
                            STIM outq
                ENDLOOP;
            LEAVE inq
        ENDsend

    LOCK consumer;
        PROCEDURE receive(REF CHAR ch);
        BEGIN
            JOIN outq;
                WHILE (inpoint-outpoint)MASK incmodulus =size DO WAIT outq
                    THEN
                            [ch]:=buffer(outpointMASKmaxpointer);
                            outpoint:=(outpoint+1)MASKincmodulus;
                            STIM inq
                ENDLOOP;
            LEAVE outq
        ENDreceive
    UNLOCK
ENDGROUP;
```

Figure 1. Example of a CHANNEL Group Definition.

After-dinner speech
J. J. Horning

Just after dinner on the first evening of the workshop,
a tall, gaunt, bearded man rose quietly and moved toward the front of the hall. He
looked tired and worn, as though exhausted by his long, arduous journey from the
north the night before. As he turned to speak, a hush fell upon the room, and with
soft and solemn voice he began ....

"Fourscore and seven weeks ago
ARPA brought forth upon this community a new Specification,
conceived in desperation, and dedicated to the proposition
that all embedded computer applications are equal.
Now we are engaged in a great verbal war,
testing whether that Specification, or any specification so conceived and so
dedicated, can long be endured.
We are met on a great Battlefield of that war.
We have come to dedicate a Proceedings of that Battle,
as a final resting place for those Papers
that here gave their Ideas that that Specification might live.
It is altogether fitting and proper that we should do this.
But, in a larger sense,
we cannot dedicate - we cannot authorize - we cannot enforce - this Specification.
The brave men, military and civilian, who funded this Specification,
have authorized it far above our poor power to add or subtract.
The world will little note, nor long remember, what we say here,
but it can never forget what they did elsewhere.
It is for us the experts, rather,
to be dedicated here to the unfinished work
which they who fought here have thus far so nobly advanced.
It is rather for us to be here dedicated to the great task remaining before us,
- that from these honored papers we take increased devotion to that cause
    for which they gave the last full measure of devotion
- that we here highly resolve that these papers shall not have been
    written in vain
- that this Specification, under DoD, shall have a new birth of reason
- and that programming
    of common problems,
    by common programmers,
    in common languages,
    shall not perish from the earth."

APPENDIX

Department of Defense
Requirements For High Order
Computer Programming Languages

Tinman
Needed Characteristics

June 1976

Needed Characteristics

The set of characteristics prescribed below represent a synthesis of the requirements submitted by the Military Departments and are intended to be consistent with the general goals of Section III, to be self-consistent, and to be achievable with existing computer software and hardware technology. The needed characteristics are the requirements to be satisfied by an existing, modified or new language which is selected as a Common HOL. They prescribe capabilities and properties which a common DoD language should possess but are not intended to impose any particular language features or mechanization of those capabilities. The header of each item gives a general description of the needed language characteristic while the subsequent paragraph(s) of its body provide clarification, discuss some of the implications and problems, provide the rationale behind its inclusion, and/or further detail the requirement. The entire text and not just the headers constitute the requirements.

The large number of characteristics reflects an attempt at thoroughness in dealing with the relevant issues. Similarly, the length of the discussion for many items reflects the need to resolve the ambiguities, examine the implications, and demonstrate the feasibility of the compendious statement introducing that characteristic. Because the characteristics address issues in the design, implementation, and use of the language and properties of the resulting product, there should be no correlation between the number of characteristics discussed here and the number of features in a language which satisifes these characteristics. Many of the characteristics will influence the choice of many features, and every feature will be influenced by many of the needed characteristics. Good language design is a unification process. Any language which satisfies these characteristics must be smaller and simpler than the set of issues underlying its choice.

The material reported in the last three sections (K,L,M) was generated by the Services at the same time as the technical characteristics, but is concerned with translators, support software, documentation, training, standards, application libraries, management policy, and procurement practices for the common language and its use. These issues are important. While mistakes and oversights in the technical characteristics can guarantee failure of the common language effort, success is not guaranteed no matter how technically meritorious the resulting language. Success can only be guaranteed by close attention to a variety of administrative issues, including those considered below.

Several of these issues, including those of implementation, documentation, and support will either directly or indirectly affect the acceptability of candidate languages. As with the needed technical characteristics for the common language, the issues raised here are often not resolved at the most detailed level. Until more detailed characteristics of the language come into focus there is no rationale with which to resolve all these issues in detail.

A. DATA AND TYPES
1. Typed Language
2. Data Types
3. Precision
4. Fixed Point Numbers
5. Character Data
6. Arrays
7. Records

A1. The language will be typed. The type (or mode) of all variables, components of composite data structures, expressions, operations, and parameters will be determinable at compile time and unalterable at run time. The language will require that the type of each variable, and component of composite data structures be explicitly specified in the source programs.

By the type of a data object is meant the set of objects themselves, the essential properties of those objects and the set of operations which give access to and take advantage of those properties. The author of any correct program in any programming language must, of course, know the types of all data and variables used in his programs. If the program is to be maintainable, modifiable and comprehensible by someone other than its author, the the types of variables, operations, and expressions should be easily determined from the source program. Type specifications in programs provide the redundancy necessary to verify automatically that the programmer has adhered to his own type conventions. Static type definitions also provide information at compile time necessary for production of efficient object code. Compile time determination of types does not preclude the inclusion of language structures for dynamic discrimination among alternative record formats (see A7) or among components of a union type (see E6). Where the subtype or record structure cannot be determined until run time, it should still be fully discriminated in the program text so that all the type checks can be completed at compile time.

A2. The language will provide data types for integer, real (floating point and fixed point), Boolean and character and will provide arrays (i.e., composite data structures with indexable components of homogeneous type) and records (i.e., composite data structures with labeled components of heterogeneous type) as type generators.

These are the common data types and type generators of most programming languages and object machines. They are sufficient, when used with a data definition facility (see E6, D6, and J1), to efficiently mechanize other desired types such as complex or vector.

A3. The source language will require global (to a scope) specification of the precision for floating point arithmetic and will permit precision specification for individual variables. This specification will be interpreted as the maximum precision required by the program logic and the minimum precision to be supported by the object code.

This is a specification of what the program needs, not what the hardware provides. Machine independence, in the use of approximate value numbers (usually with floating point representation), can be achieved only if the user can place constraints on the translator and object machine without forcing a specific mechanization of the arithmetic. Precision specifications, as the minimum supported by the object code, provide all the power and guarantees needed by the programmer without unnecessarily constraining the object machine realization. Precision specifications will not change the type of reals nor the set of applicable operations. Precison specifications apply to arithmetic operations as well as to the data and therefore should be specified once for a designated scope. This permits different precisions to be used in different parts of a program. Specification of the precision will also contribute to the legibility and implementability of programs.

A4. Fixed point numbers will be treated as exact quantities which have a range and a fractional step size which are determined by the user at compile time. Scale factor management will be done by the compiler.

Scaled integers are useful approximations to real numbers when dealing with exact quantity fractional values, when the object machine does not have floating point hardware, and when greater precision is required than is available with the floating point hardware. Integers will also be treated as exact quantities with a step size equal to one.

A5. Character sets will be treated as any other enumeration type.

Like any other data type defined by enumeration (see E6), it should be possible to specify the program literal and order of characters. These properties of the character set would be unalterable at run time. The definition of a character set should reflect on the manner it is used within a program and not necessarily on the print representation a particular physical device associates with a bit pattern at run time. In general, unless all devices use the same character code, run-time translation between character sets will be required. Widely used character sets, such as, USASCII and EBCDIC will be available in a standard library. Note that access to a linear array filled with the characters of an alphabet, A, and indexed by an alphabet, B, will convert strings of characters from B to A.

A6.   The language will require user specification of the number of dimensions, the range of subscript values for each dimension, and the type of each array component. The number of dimensions, the type and the lower subscript bound will be determinable at compile time. The upper subscript bound will be determinable at entry to the array allocation scope.

This is general enough to permit both arrays which can be allocated at compile or load time and arrays which can be allocated at scope entry, but does not permit dynamic change to the size of constructed arrays. It is sufficient to permit allocation of space pools which the user can manage for allocation of more complex data structures including dynamic arrays. The range of subscript values for any given dimension will be a contiguous subsequence of values from an enumeration type (including integers). The preferable lower bound on the subscript range will be the initial element of an enumeration type or zero, because it often contributes to program efficiency and clarity.

A7.   The language will permit records to have alternative structures, each of which is fixed at compile time. The name and type of each record component will be specified by the user at compile time.

This provides all that is safe to use in CMS-2 and JOVIAL OVERLAY and in FORTRAN EQUIVALENCE. It permits hierarchically structured data of heterogeneous type, permits records to have alternative structures as long as each structure is fixed at compile time and the choice is fully discriminated at run time, but it does not permit arbitrary references to memory nor the dropping of type checking when handling overlayed structures. The discrimination condition will not be restricted to a field of the record but should be any expression.

B. OPERATIONS
   1. Assignment and Reference
   2. Equivalence
   3. Relationals
   4. Arithmetic Operations
   5. Truncation and Rounding
   6. Boolean Operations
   7. Scalar Operations
   8. Type Conversion
   9. Changes in Numeric Representation
   10. I/O Operations
   11. Power Set Operations

B1. Assignment and reference operation will be automatically defined for all data types which do not manage their data storage. The assignment operation will permit any value of a given type to be assigned to a variable, array or record component of that type or of a union type containing that type. Reference will retrieve the last assigned value.

The user will be able to declare variables for all data types. Variables are useful only when there are corresponding access and assignment operations. The user will be permitted to define assignment and access operations as part of encapsulated type definitions (see E5). Otherwise, they will be automatically defined for types which do not manage the storage for their data. (See D6 for further discussion).

B2. The source language will have a built-in operation which can be used to compare any two data objects (regardless of type) for identity.

Equivalence is an essential universal operation which should not be subject to restriction on its use. There are many useful equivalence operations for some types and a language definition cannot foresee all these for user defined types. Equivalence meaning logical identity and not bit-by-bit comparison on the internal data representation, however, is required for all data types. Proper semantic interpretation of identity requires that equality and identity be the same for atomic data (i.e., numbers, characters, Boolean values, and types defined by enumeration) and that elements of a disjoint types never be identical. Consequently, its usefulness at run time is restricted to data of the same type or to types with nonempty intersections. For floating point numbers identity will be defined as the same within the specified (minimum) precision.

B3. Relational operations will be automatically defined for numeric data and all types defined by enumeration.

Numbers and types defined by enumeration have an obvious ordering which should be available through relational operations. All six relational operations will be included. It will be possible to inhibit ordering definitions when unordered sets are intended.

B4. The built-in arithmetic operations will include: addition, subtraction, multiplication, division (with a real result), exponentiation, integer division (with integer or fixed point arguments and remainder), and negation.

These are the most widely used numeric operations and are available as hardware operations in most machines. Floating point operations will be precise to at least the specified precision.

B5. Arithmetic and assignment operations on data which are within the range specifications of the program will never truncate the most significant digits of a numeric quantity. Truncation and rounding will always be on the least significant digits and will never be implicit for integers and fixed point numbers. Implicit rounding beyond the specified precision will be allowed for floating point numbers.

These requirements seem obvious, particularly for floating point numbers and yet many of our existing languages truncate the most significant mantissa digits in some mixed and floating point operations.

B6. The built-in Boolean operations will include "and," " "or, " "not, " and "nor." The operations "and" and "or" on scalars will be evaluated in short circuit mode.

Short circuit mode as used here is a semantic rather than an implementation distinction and means that "and" and "or" are in fact control operations which do not evaluate side effects of their second argument if the value of the first argument is "false" or "true, " respectively. Short circuit evaluation has no disadvantages over the corresponding computational operations, sometimes produces faster executing code in languages where the user can rely on the short circuit execution, and improves the clarity and maintainability of programs by permitting expressions such as, "i<=7 & A[i] >x" which could be erroneous were short circuit execution not intended. Note that the equivalence and nonequivalence operations (see B2) are the same as logical equivalence and exclusive-or respectively.

B7. The source language will permit scalar operations and assignment on conformable arrays and will permit data transfers between records or arrays of identical logical structure.

Conformability will require exactly the same number of components (although a scalar can be considered compatible with any array) and one for one compatibility in type.   Correspondence will be by position in similarly shaped arrays.   In many situations component by component operations are done on array elements.   In fact, a primary reason for having arrays is to permit large numbers of similarly treated objects to have a uniform notation.   Operations on data aggregates available directly in the source language hide the details of the sequencing and thereby, simplify the program and make more optimizations available.   In addition, they permit simultaneous execution on machines with parallel processing hardware.   Although component by component operations will be available for built-in composite data structures which are used to define application-oriented structures, that capability will not be automatically inherited by defined data structures. A matrix might be defined using an array, but it will not inherit the array operations automatically. Multiplication for matrices would, for example, be unnatural, confusing and inconvenient if the product operator for matrices were interpreted as a component by component operation instead of cross product of corresponding row and column vectors.   Component by component operations also allow operations on character strings represented as vectors of characters and allow efficient Boolean vector operations.

Transfers between arrays or records of identical logical structure are necessary to permit efficient run time conversion from one object representation to another, as might be done when data is packed to reduce peripheral storage requirements and I/O transfer times but need to be unpacked locally to minimize processing costs.

B8.   There will be no implicit type conversions but no conversion operation will be required when the type of an actual parameter is a constituent of a union type which is the formal parameter. The language will provide explicit conversions operations among integer, fixed point and floating point data, between the object representation of numbers and their representations as characters, and between fixed point scale factors.

Implicit type conversions which represent changes in the value of data items without an explicit indicator in the program, are not only error prone but can result in unexpected run time overhead.

B9. Explicit conversion operations will not be required between numerical ranges. There will be a run time exception condition when any integer or fixed point value is truncated.

Because ranges do not form closed systems, range validation is not possible at compile time (e.g., "I:=I+1" may be a range error). At best, the compiler might point out likely range errors. (This requirement is optional for hardware installations which do not have overflow detection).

B10. The base language will provide operations allowing programs to interact with files, channels or devices including terminals. These operations will permit sending and receiving both data and control information, will enable programs to dynamically assign and reassign I/O devices, will provide user control for exception conditions, and will not be installation dependent.

Whether the referenced "files" are real or virtual and whether they are hardware devices, I/O channels or logical files depends on the object machine configuration and on the details of its operating system if present. But in any programming system I/O operations ultimately reduce to sending or receiving data and/or control information to a file or to a device controller. These can be made accessible in a HOL in an abstract form through a small set of generic I/O operations (like "read" and "write," with appropriate device and exception parameters). Note that devices and files are similar in many respects to types, so additional language features may not be required to satisfy this requirement. This requirement, in conjunction with requirement E1, permits user definition of unique equipment and its associated I/O operations as data types within the syntactic and semantic framework provided by the generic operations.

B11. The language will provide operations on data types defined as power sets of enumeration types (see E6). These operations will include union, intersection, difference, complement, and an element predicate.

As with any data type, power sets will be useful only if there are operations which can create, select and interrogate them. Note that this provides only a very special class of sets but one which is very useful for computations on sets of indicators, flags, and similar devices in monitoring and control applications. More general sets if desired, must be defined using the type definition facilities.

C. EXPRESSIONS AND PARAMETERS

1. Side Effects
2. Operand Structure
3. Expressions Permitted
4. Constant Expressions
5. Consistent Parameter Rules
6. Type Agreement in Parameters
7. Formal Parameter Kinds
8. Formal Parameter Specifications
9. Variable Numbers of Parameters

C1. Side effects which are dependent on the evaluation order among the arguments of an expression will be evaluated left-to-right.

This is a semantic restriction on the evaluation order of arguments to expressions. It provides an explicit rule (i.e., left-to-right) for order of argument evaluation, but allows the implementations to alter the actual order in any way which does not change the effect. This provides the user with a simple rule for determining the effects of interactions among argument evaluations without imposing a strict rule on compilers which are sophisticated enough to detect potential side-effects and optimize through reordering of arguments when the evaluation order does not affect the result. Control operations (e.g., conditional and iterative control structures), of course, must be exceptions to this general rule since control operations are in fact those operations which specify the sequencing and evaluation rules for their arguments.

C2. Which parts of an expression constitute the operands to each operation within that expression should be obvious to the reader. There will be few levels of operator hierarchy and they will be widely recognized.

Care must be taken to ensure that the operator/operand structure of expressions is not psychologically ambiguous (i.e., to guarantee that the parse implemented by the language is the same as intended by the programmer and understood by those reading the program). This kind of problem can be minimized by having few precedence levels and parsing rules by allowing explicit parentheses to specify the intended execution order, and by requiring explicit parentheses when the execution order is of significance to the result within the same precedence level (e.g., "X divided by Y divided by Z" and "X divided by Y multiplied by Z"). The user will not be able to define new operator precedence rules nor change the precedence of existing operators.

C3. Expressions of a given type will be permitted anywhere in source programs where both constants and references to variables of that type are allowed.

This is an example of not imposing arbitrary restrictions and special case rules on the user of the source language. Special mention is made here only because so many languages do restrict the form of expressions. FORTRAN, for example, has a list of seven different syntactic forms for subscript expressions, instead of allowing all forms of arithmetic expressions.

C4. Constant expressions will be allowed in programs anywhere constants are allowed, and constant expressions will be evaluated before run time.

The ability to write constant expressions in programs has proven valuable in languages with this capability, particularly with regard to program readability and in avoiding programmer error in externally evaluating and transcribing constant expressions. They are most often used in declarations. There is no need, however, that constant expressions impose run time costs for their evaluation. They can be evaluated once at compile time or if this is inconvenient because of incompatibilities between the host and object machines, the compiler can generate code for their evaluation at load time. In any case, the resulting value should be the same (at least within the stated precision) regardless of the object machine (see D2). Allowing constant expressions in place of constants can improve the clarity, correctness and maintainability of programs and does not impose any run time costs.

C5. There will be a consistent set of rules applicable to all parameters, whether they be for procedures, for types for exception handing, for parallel processes, for declarations, or for built-in operators. There will be no special operations (e.g., array substructuring) applicable only to parameters. Uniformity and consistency contributes to ease of learning,

implementing and using a language; allows the user to concentrate on the programming task instead of the language; and leads to more readable, understandable, and predictable programs.

C6. Formal and actual parameters will always agree in type. The number of dimensions for array parameters will be determinable at compile time. The size and subscript range for array parameters need not be determinable at compile time, but can be passed as part of the parameter.

Type transfers hidden in procedure calls with incompatible formal and actual parameters whether intentional or accidental have long been a source of program errors and of programs which are difficult to maintain. On the other hand, there is no reason why the subscript ranges for arrays cannot be passed as part of the arguments. Some notations permit such parameters to be implicit on the call side. Formal parameters of a union type will be considered conformable to actual parameters of any of the component types.

C7. There will be only four classes of formal parameters. For data there will be those which act as constants representing the actual parameter value at the time of call, and those which rename the actual parameter which must be a variable. In addition, there will be a formal parameter class for specifying the control action when exception conditions occur and a class for procedure parameters.

The first class of data parameter acts as a constant within the procedure body and cannot be assigned to nor changed during the procedures execution; its corresponding actual parameter may be any legal expression of the desired type and will be evaluated once at the time of call. The second class of data parameter renames the actual parameter which must be a variable, the address of the actual parameter variable will be determined by (or at) the time of call and unalterable during execution of the procedure, and assignment (or reference) to the formal parameter name will assign (or access) the variable which is the actual parameter. These are the only two widely used parameter passing mechanisms for data and the many alternatives (at least 10 have been suggested) add complexity and cost to a language without sufficiently increasing the clarity or power. A language with exception handling capability must have a way to pass control and related data through procedure call interfaces. Exception handling control parameters will be specified on the call side only when needed. Actual procedure parameters will be restricted to those of similar (explicit or implicit) specification parts.

C8. Specification of the type, range, precision, dimension, scale and format of parameters will be optional in the procedure declaration. None of them will be alterable at run time.

Optional formal parameter specification permits the writing of generic procedures which are instantiated at compile time by the characteristics of their actual parameters. It eliminates the need for compile time "type" parameters. This generic procedure capability, for example, allows the definition of stacks and queues and their associated operations on data of any given type without knowing the data type when the operations are defined.

C9. There will be provision for variable numbers of arguments, but in such cases all but a constant number of them must be of the same type. Whether a routine can have a variable number of arguments must be determinable from its description and the number of arguments for any call will be determinable at compile time.

There are many useful purposes for procedures with variable numbers of arguments. These include intrinsic functions such as "print," generalizations of operations which are both commutative and associative such as "max" and "min," and repetitive application of the same binary operation such as the Lisp "list" operation. The use of variable number of argument operations need not and will not cause relaxation of any compile time checks, require use of multiple entry procedures allow the number of actual parameters to vary at run time, nor require special calling mechanisms. If the parameters which can vary are limited to a program specified type treated as any other argument on the call side and as elements of an array within the procedure definition, full type checking can be done at compile time. There will be not prohibition on writing a special case of a procedure for a particular number of arguments.

D. VARIABLES, LITERALS AND CONSTANTS
1. Constant Value Identifiers
2. Numeric Literals
3. Initial Values of Variables
4. Numeric Range and Step Size
5. Variable Types
6. Pointer Variables

D1. The user will have the ability to associate constant values of any type with identifiers.

The use of identifiers to represent constant values has often made programs more readable, more easily modifiable and less prone to error when the value of a constant is changed. Associating constant values with an identifier is preferable to assigning the value to a variable because it is then clearly marked in the program as a constant, can be automatically checked for unintentional changes, and often can have a more efficient object representation.

D2. The language will provide a syntax and a consistent interpretation for constants of built-in data types. Numeric constants will have the same value (within the specified precision) in both programs and data (input or output).

Literals are needed for all atomic data types and should be provided as part of the language definition for built-in types. Regardless of the source of the data and regardless of the object machine the value of constants should be the same. For integers it should be exact and for reals it should be the same within the specified precision. Compiler writers, however, would disagree. They object to this requirement on two grounds: that it is too costly if the host and object machines are different and that it is unnecessary if they are the same. In fact, all costs are at compile time and must be insignificant compared to the life time costs resulting from object cope containing the wrong constant values. As for being unnecessary, there have been all too many cases of different values from program and data literals on the same machine because the compile time and run time conversion packages were different and imprecise.

D3. The language will permit the user to specify the initial values of individual variables as part of their declaration. Such variables will be initialized at the time of their apparent allocation (i.e., at entry to allocation scope). There will be no default initial values.

The ability to initialize variables at the time of their allocation will contribute to program clarity, but a requirement to do so would be an arbitrary and sometimes costly decision to the user. Default initial values on the other hand, contribute to neither program clarity nor correctness and can be even more costly at run time. It is usually a programming error if a variable is accessed before it is initialized. It is desirable that the translator give a warning when a path between the declaration and use of a variable omits initialization. Whether a variable will be assigned is in general an unsolvable problem, but it is sometimes determinable whether assignments occur on potential paths. In the case of arrays, it it possible at compile time only to determine that some components (but not necessarily which) have been initialized. There will be provision (at user option) for run time testing for initialization.

D4. The source language will require its users to specify individually the range of all numeric variables and the step size for fixed point variables. The range specifications will be interpreted as the maximal specifications will be interpreted as the maximal range of values which will be assigned to a variable and the minimal range which must be supported by the object code. Range and step size specifications will not be interpreted as defining new types.

Range specifications are a special form of assertion. They aid in understanding and determining the correctness of programs. They can also be used as additional information by the compiler in deciding what storage and allocation to use (e.g., half words might be more efficient for integers in the range 0 to 1000). Range specifications also offer the opportunity for the translator to insert range tests automatically for run time or debug time validation of the program logic. With the ranges of variables specified in the program, it becomes possible to perform many subscript bounds checks at compile time. These bounds, checks, however, can be only as valid as the range specifications which cannot in general be validated at compile time. Range specifications on approximate valued variables (usually with floating point implemetation) also offer the possibility of their implementation using fixed point hardware.

D5. The range of values which can be associated with a variable, array, or record component will be any built-in type, any defined type or a contiguous subsequence of any enumeration type.

There should not be any arbitrary restrictions on the structure of data. This permits arrays to be components of records or arrays and permits records to be components of arrays.

D6. The language will provide a pointer mechanism which can be used to build data with shared and/or recursive substructure. The pointer property will only affect the use of variables (including array and record components) of some data types. Pointer variables will be as safe in their use as are any other variables.

Assignment to a pointer variable will mean that the variable's name is to act as an additional label (or reference) on the datum being assigned. Assignment to a nonpointer variable will mean that the variable's name it to label a copy of the object being assigned. For data without alterable component structure or alterable component values, there is no functional difference between reference to multiple copies and multiple references to a single copy. Consequently, pointer/nonpointer will be a property only of variables for composite types and of composite array and record components Because the pointer/nonpointer property applies to all variables of a given type, it will be specified as part of the type definition. The use of pointers will be kept safe by prohibiting pointers to data structures whose allocation scope is narrower than that of the pointer variable.

Such a restriction is easily enforced at compile time using hierarchical scope rules providing there is no way to dynamically create new instances of the data type. In the latter case, the dynamically created data can be allocated with full safety using a (user or library defined) space pool which is either local (i.e., own) or global to the type definition. If variables of a type do not have the pointer property then dynamic storage allocation would be required for assignment unless their size is constant and known at the time of variable allocation. Thus, the nonpointer property will be permitted only for types (a) whose data have a structure and size which is constant in the type definition or (b) which manage the storage for their data as part of the type definition. Because pointers are often less expensive at run time than nonpointers and are subject to fewer restrictions, the specification of the nonpointer property will be explicit in programs (this is similar to the Algol-60 issue concerning the explicit specification of "value" (i.e., nonpointer) and "name" (i.e. pointer). The need for pointers is obvious in building data structures with shared or recursive substructures; such as, directed graphs, stacks, queues, and list structures. Providing pointers as absolute address types, however, produces gaps in the type checking and scope mechanisms. Type and access restricted pointers will provide the power of general pointers without their undesirable characteristics.

E. DEFINITION FACILITIES
1. User Definitions Possible
2. Consistent Use of Types
3. No Default Declarations
4. Can Extend Existing Operators
5. Type Definitions
6. Data Defining Mechanisms
7. No Free Union or Subset Types
8. Type Initialization

E1. The user of the language will be able to define new data types and operations within programs.

The number of specialized capabilities needed for a common language is large and diverse. In many cases, there is no consensus as to the form these capabilities should take in a programming language. The operational requirements dictating specific specialized language capabilities are volatile and future needs cannot always be foreseen. No language can make available all the features useful to the broad spectrum of military applications, anticipate future applications and requirements or even provide a universally "best" capability in support of a single application area. A common language needs capability for growth. It should contain all the power necessary to satisfy all the applications and the ability to specialize that power to the particular application task. A language with defining facilities for data and operations often makes it possible to add new application-oriented structures and to use new programming techniques and mechanisms through descriptions written entirely within the language. Definitions will have the appearance and costs of features which are built into the language while actually being catalogued accessible application packages. The operation definition facility will include the ability to define new infix operators (but see H2 for restrictions). No programming language can be all things to all people, but a language with data and operation definition facilities can be adapted to meet changing requirements in a variety of areas.

The ability to define data and operations is well within the state of the art. Operation definition facilities in the form of subroutines have been available in all general purpose programming languages since at least the time of early FORTRANs. Data definition facilities have been available in a variety of programming languages for almost 10 years and reached their peak with a large number of extensible languages(Stephen A. Schuman (Ed.) Proceedings of the International Symposium on Extensible Languages, SIGPLAN Notices, Vol. 6, No. 12, December 1971. Also, C. Christensen and C.J. Shaw (Ed.), Proceedings of the Extensible Language Symposium, SIGPLAN Notices 4, August 1969.) (over 30) in 1968 and shortly thereafter. A trend toward more abstract and less machine-oriented data specification mechanisms has appeared more recently in PASCAL(Niklaus Wirth, "An Assessment of the Programming Language PASCAL, "Proceedings of the International Conference on Reliable Software 21-23 April 1973, p. 23-30). Data type definitions, with operations and data defined together, are used in several languages including SIMULA-67(Jacob Palme, "SIMULA as a Tool for Extensible Program Products, "SIGPLAN Notices, Vol. 9, No. 4, February 1974). On the other hand, there is currently much ferment as to what is the proper function and form of data type definitions.

E2. The "use" of defined types will be indistinguishable from built-in types.

Whether a type is built-in or defined within the base will not be determinable from its syntactic and semantic properties. There will be no ad hoc special cases nor inconsistent rules to interfere with and complicate learning, using and implementing the language. If built-in features and user defined data structures and operations are treated in the same way throughout the language so that the base language, standard application libraries and application programs are treated in a uniform manner by the user and by the translator, then these distinctions will grow dim to everyone's advantage. When the language contains all the essential power, when few can tell the difference between the base language and library definitions, and when the introduction of new data types and routines does not impact the compiler and the language standards, then there is little incentive to proliferate languages. Similarly, if typed definitions are processed entirely at compile time and the language allows full program specification of the internal representation, there need be no penalty in run time efficiency for using defined types.

E3. Each program component will be defined in the base language, in a library, or in the program. There will be no default declarations.

As programmers, we should not expect the translator to write our programs for us (at least in the immediate future). If we somehow know that the translator's default convention is compatible with our needs for the case at hand we should still document the choice so others can understand and maintain our programs. Neither should we be able to delay definitions (possibly forget them) until they cause trouble in the operational system. This is a special case of requirement I1.

E4. The user will be able, within the source language, to extend existing operators to new data types.

When an operation is an abstraction of an existing operation for a new type or is a generalization of an existing operation, it is inconvenient, confusing and misleading to use any but the existing operator symbol or function named. The translator will not assume that commutativity of bulit-in operations is preserved by extensions, and any assumptions about the associativity of built-in or extended operations will be ignored by the translator when explicit parentheses are provided in an expression.

E5. Type definitions in the source language will permit definition of both the class of data objects comprising the type and the set of operations applicable to that class. A defined type will not automatically inherit the operations of the data with which it is represented.

Types define abstract data objects with special properties. The data objects are given a representation in terms of existing data structures, but they are of little value until operations are available to take advantage of their special properties. When one obtains access to a type, he needs its operations as well as its data. Numeric data is needed in many applications but is of little value to any without arithmetic operations. The definable operations will include constructors, selectors, predicates, and type conversions.

E6. The data objects comprising a defined type will be definable by enumeration of their literal names, as Cartesian products of existing types (i.e., as array and record classes), by discriminated union (i.e., as the union of disjoint types) and as the power set of an enumeration type. These definitions will be processed entirely at compile time.

The above list comprises a currently known set of useful definitional mechanisms for data types which do not require run time support, as do garbage collection and dynamic storage allocation. In conjunction with pointers (see D6), they provide many of the mechanisms necessary to define recursive data structures and efficient sparse data structures.

E7. Type definitions by free union (i.e., union of non-disjoint types) and subsetting are not desired.

Free union adds no new power not provided by discriminated union, but does require giving up the security of types in return for programmer freedom. Range and subset specifications on variables are useful documentation and debugging aids, but will not be construed as types. Subsets do not introduce new properties or operations not available to the superset and often do not form a closed system under the superset operations. Unlike types, membership in subsets can be determined only at run time.

E8. When defining a type, the user will be able to specify the initialization and finalization procedures for the type and the actions to be taken at the time of allocation and deallocation of variables of that type.

It is often necessary to do bookkeeping or to take other special action when variables of a given type are allocated or deallocated. The language will not limit the class of definable types by withholding the ability to define those actions. Initialization might take place once when the type is allocated (i.e., in its allocation scope) and would be used to set up the procedures and initialize the variables which are local to the type definition. These operations will be definable in the encapsulation housing the rest of the type definition.

F. SCOPES AND LIBRARIES
   1. Separate Allocation and Access Allowed
   2. Limiting Access Scope
   3. Compile Time Scope Determination
   4. Libraries Available
   5. Library Contents
   6. Libraries and Compools Indistinguishable
   7. Standard Library Definitions

F1.   The language will allow the user to distinguish between scope of allocation and scope of access.

The scope of allocation or lifetime of a program structure is that region of the program for which the object representation of the structure should be present. The allocation scope defines the program scope for which own variables of the structure must be maintained and identifies the time for initialization of the structure. The access scope defines the regions of the program in which the allocated structure is accessible to the program and will never be wider than the allocation scope.   In some cases the user may desire that each use of a defined program structure be independent (i.e., the allocation and accessing scopes would be identical).   In other cases, the various accessing scopes might share a common allocation of the structure.

F2.   The ability to limit the access to separately defined structures will be available both where the structure is defined and where it is used.   It will be possible to associate new local names with separately defined program components.

Limited access specified in a type definition is necessary to guarantee that changes to data representations and to management routines which purportedly do not affect the calling programs are in fact safe. By rigorously controlling the set of operations applicable to a defined type, the type definition guarantees that no external use of the type can accidentally or intentionally use hidden nonessential properties of the type.   Renaming separately defined programming components is necessary to avoid naming conflicts when they are used.

Limited access on the call side provides a high degree of safety and eliminates nonessential naming conflicts without limiting the degree of accessibility which can be built into programs.   The alternative notion, that all declarations which are external to a program segment should have the same scope, is inconvenient and costly in creating large systems which are composed from many subsystems because it forces global access scopes and the attendant naming conflicts on subsystems not using the defined items.

F3.   The scope of identifiers will be wholly determined at compile time.

Identifiers will be declared at the beginning of their scope and multiple use of variable names will not be allowed in the same scope.   Except as otherwise explicitly specified in programs, access scopes will be lexically embedded with the most local definition applying when the same identifier appears at several levels. The language will use the above lexically embedded scope rules for declarations and other definitions of identifiers to make them easy to recognize and to avoid errors and ambiguities from multiple use of identifiers in a single scope.

F4.   A variety of application-oriented data and operations will be available in libraries and easily accessible in the language.

A simple base alone is not sufficient for a common language.   Even though in theory such a language provides the necessary power and the capability for specialization to particular applications, the users of the language cannot be expected to develop and support common libraries under individual projects There will be broad support for libraries common to users of well recognized application areas.   Application libraries will be developed as early as possible.

F5.   Program components not defined within the current program and not in the base language will be maintained in compile time accessible libraries. The libraries will be capable of holding anything definable in the language and will not exclude routines whose bodies are written in other source languages.

The usefulness of a language derives primarily from the existence and accessibility of specialized application-oriented data and operations.   Whether a library should contain source or object code is a question of implementation efficiency and should not be specified in the definition of the source language, but the source language description will always be available.   It should be remembered, however, that interfaces cannot be validated at program assembly time without some equivalent of their source language interface specifications, that object modules are machine-dependent and, therefore, not portable, that source code is often more compact than object code, and that compilers for simple languages can sometimes compile faster than a loader can load from relocatable object programs. Library routines written on other languages will not be prohibited provided the foreign routine has object code compatible with the calling mechanisms used in the Common HOL and providing sufficient header information (e.g., parameter types, form and number) is given with the routine in Common HOL form to permit the required compile time checks at the interface.

F6. Libraries and Compools will be indistinguishable. They will be capable of holding anything definable in the language, and it will be possible to associate them with any level of programming activity from systems through projects to individual programs. There will be many specialized compools or libraries any user specified subset of which is immediately accessible from a given program.

Compools have proven very useful in organizing and controlling shared data structures and shared routines. A similar mechanism will be available to manage and control access to related library definitions.

F7. The source language will contain standard machine independent interfaces to machine dependent capabilities, including peripheral equipment and special hardware.

The convenience, ease of use and savings in production and maintenance costs resulting from using high order languages come from being able to use specialized capabilities without building them from scratch. Thus, it is essential that high level capabilities be supplied with the language. The idea is not to provide all the many special cases in the language, but to provide a few general case . hich will cover the special cases.

There is currently little agreement on standard operating system, I/O, or file system interfaces. This does not preclude support of one or more forms for the near term. For the present the important thing is that one be chosen and made available as a standard supported library definition which the user can use with confidence.

G. CONTROL STRUCTURES

G1. The language will provide structured control mechanisms for sequential, conditional, iterative, and recursive control. It will also provide control structures for (pseudo) parallel processing, exception handling and asynchronous interrupt handling.

These mechanisms, hopefully, provide a spanning set of control structures. The most appropriate operations in several of these areas is an open question. For the present, the choice will be a spanning set of composable control primitives each of which is easily mapped onto object machines and which does not impose run time charges when it is not used. Whether parallel processing is real (i.e., by multiprocessing) or is synthesized on a single sequential processor, is determined by the object machine, but if programs are written as if there is true parallel processing (and no assumption about the relative speeds of the processors) then the same results will be obtained independent of the object environment.

It is desirable that the number of primitive control structures in the language be minimized, not by reducing the power of the language, but by selecting a small set of composable primitives which can be used to easily build other desired control mechanisms within programs. This means that the capabilities of control mechanisms must be separable so that the user need not pay either program clarity or implementation costs for undesired specialized capabilities. By these criteria, the Algol-60 "FOR" would be undesirable because it imposes the use of a loop control variable, requires that there be a single terminal condition and that the condition be tested before each iteration. Consequently, "FOR" cannot be composed to build other useful iterative control structures (e.g., FORTRAN "DO"). The ability to compose control structures does not imply an ability to define new control operations and such an ability to define new control operations, and such an ability is in conflict with the limited parameter passing mechanisms of C7.

G2. The source language will provide a "GO TO" operation applicable to program labels within its most local scope of definition.

The "GO TO" is a machine level capability which is still needed to fill in any gaps which might remain in the choice of structured control primitives, to provide compatibility for translitterating programs written in older languages, and because of the wide familiarity of current practitioners with its use. The language should not, however, impose unnecessary costs for its presence. The "GO TO" will be limited to explicitly specified program labels at the same scope level. Neither should the language provide specialized facilities which encourage its use in dangerous and confusing ways. Switches, designational expressions, label variables, label parameters and numeric labels are not desired. Switches here refer to the unrestricted switches which are generalizations of the "GO TO" and not to case statements which are a general form for conditionals(see G3). This requirements should not be interpreted to conflict with the specialized form of control transfer provided by the exception handling control structure of G7.

G3.   The conditional control structures will be fully partitioned and will permit selection among alternative computations based on the value of a Boolean expression, on the subtype of a value from a discriminated union, or on a computed choice among labeled alternatives.

The conditional control operations will be fully partitioned (e.g., an "ELSE" clause must follow each "IF THEN") so the choice is clear and explicit in each case. There will be some general form of conditional which allows an arbitrary computation to determine the selected situation (e.g., Zahn's device(Donald E. Knuth, "Structured Programming with go to Statements," ACM Computer Surveys, Vol. 6, No. 4, December 1974) provides a good solution to the general problem). Special mechanisms are also needed for the more common cases of the Boolean expression (e.g., "IF THEN ELSE") and for value or type discrimination (e.g., "CASE" on one of a set of values or subtype of a union).

G4.   The iterative control structure will permit the termination condition to appear anywhere in the loop, will require control variables t be local to the iterative control, will allow entry only at the head of the loop, and will not impose excessive overhead in clarity or run the execution costs for common special case termination conditions (e.g., fixed number of iterations or elements of an array exhausted).

In its most general form, a programmed loop is executed repetitively until some computed predicate becomes true. There may be more than one terminating predicate, and they might appear anywhere in the loop. Specialized control structures (e.g., "WHILE DO") have been used for the common situation in which the

termination conditions precedes each iteration. The most common case is
termination after a fixed number of iterations and a specialized control structure
should be provided for that purpose (e.g., FORTRAN "DO" or Algol-60 "FOR"). A
problem which arises in many programming languages is that loop control variables
are global to the iterative control and thus, will have a value after loop termination,
but that value is usually an accident of the implementation. Specifying the meaning of
control variables after loop termination in the language definition resolves the
ambiguity but must be an arbitrary decision which will not aide program clarity or
correctness, and may interfere with the generation of efficient object code. Loop
control variables are by definition variables used to control the repetitive execution
of a programmed loop and as such will be local to the loop body, but at loop
termination it will be possible to pass their value (or any other computed value) out of
the loop, conveniently and efficiently.

G5. Recursive as well as nonrecursive routines will be available in the
source language. It will not be possible to define procedures within the body
of a recursive procedure.

Recursion is desirable in many applications because it contributes directly to
their elegance and clairty and simplifies proof procedures. Indirectly, it contributes
to the reliability and maintainability of some programs. Recursion is required in
order to avoid unnecessarily opaque, complex and confusing programs when
operating on recursive data structures. Recursion has not been widely used in DoD
software because many programming languages do not provide recursion,
practitioners are not familiar with its use, and users fear that its run time costs are to
high. Of these, only the run time costs would justify its exclusion from the language.

A major run time cost often attributed to recursion is the need for the
presence of a set of "display" registers which are used to keep track of the
addresses of the various levels of lexically imbedded environments and which must
be managed and updated at run time. The display, however, is necessary only in
programs in which routines access variables which are global to their own definition,
but local to a more global recursive procedure. This possibility can easily be
removed by prohibiting the definition of procedures within the body of a recursive
procedure. The utility of such a combination of capabilities is very questionable, and
this single restriction will eliminate all added execution costs for nonrecursive
procedures in programs which contain recursive procedures.

As with any other facility of the language, routines should be implemented in
the most efficient manner consistent with their use and the language should be
designed so that efficient implementations are possible. In particular, the most
possible regardless of whether the language or even the program contains recursive

procedures. When any routine makes a procedure call as its last operation before exit (and this is quite common for recursive routines) the implementation might use the same data area for both routines, and do a jump to the head of the called procedure thereby saving much of the overhead of a procedure call and eliminating a return. The choice between recursive and nonrecursive routines involves trade-offs. Recursive routines can aid program clarity when operating on recursive data, but can detract from clarity when operating on iterative data. They can increase execution time when procedure call overhead is greater than loop overhead and can decrease execution times when loop overhead is the more expensive. Finally, program storage for recursive routines is often only a small fraction of that for a corresponding iterative procedure, but the data storage requirements are often much larger because of the simultaneous presence of several activations of the same procedure.

> G6. The source language will provide a parallel processing capability. This capability should include the ability to create and terminate (possibly pseudo) parallel processes and for these processes to gain exclusive use of resources during specified portions of their execution.

A parallel processing capability is essential in embedded computer applications. Programs must send data to, receive data from, and control many devices which are operating in parallel. Multiprogramming (a form of pseudo paralell processing) is necessary so that many programs within a system can meet their differing real time constraints. The parallel processing capability will minimally provide the ability to define and call parallel processing and the ability to gain exclusive use of system resources in the form of data structures, devices and pseudo devices. This latter ability satisfies one of the two needs for synchronization of parallel processes. The other is required in conjunction with real time constraints (see G8).

The parallel processing capability will be defined as true parallel (as opposed to coroutine) primitives, but with the understanding that in most implementations the object computer will have fewer processors (usually one) than the number of parallel paths specified in a program. Interleaved execution in the implementation may be required.

The parallel processing features of the language should be selected to eliminate any unnecessary overhead associated with their use. The costs of parallel processes are primarily in run time storage management. As with recursive routines most accessing and storage management problems can be eliminated by prohibiting complex interactions with other language facilities where the combination has little if any utility. In particular, it will not be possible to define a parallel routine within the body of a recursive routine and it will not be possible to define any routine including parallel routines within the body of those parallel routines which can have multiple simultaneous activations. If the language permits several simultaneous activations of a given parallel process then it might require the user to give a upper bound on the number which can exist simultaneously. The latter requirement is reasonable for parallel processes because it is information known by the programmer and necessary to the maintainer, because parallel processes cannot normally be stacked, and because it is necessary for the compilation of efficient programs.

G7. The exception handing control structure will permit the user to cause transfer of control and data for any error or exception situation which might occur in a program.

It is essential in many aplications that there be no program halts beyond the user's control. The user must be able to specify the action to be taken on any exception situation which might occur within his program. The exception handling mechanism will be parameterized so data can be passed to the recovery point. Exception situations might include arithmetic overflow, exhaustion of available space, hardware errors, any user defined exceptions and any run time detected programming error.

The user will be able to write programs which can get out of an arbitrary nest of control and intercept it at any embedding level desired. The exception handling mechanism will permit the user to specify the action to be taken upon the occurrence of a designated exception within any given access scope of the program. The transfers of control will, at the users option, be either forward in the program (but never to a narrower scope of access or out of a procedure) or out of the current procedure through its dynamic (i.e., calling structure. The latter form requires an exception handling formal parameter class (see C7).

G8. There will be source language features which permit delay on any control path until some specified time or situation has occurred, which permit specification of the relative priorities among parallel control paths, which give access to real time clocks, which permit asynchronous hardware interrupts to be treated as any other exception situation.

When parallel or pseudo parallel paths appear in a program it must be possible to specify their relative priorities and to synchronize their executions. Synchronization can be done either through exclusive access to data (see G6) or through delays terminated by designated situations occurring within the program.

These situations should include the elapse of program specified time intervals, occurrence of hardware interrupts and those designated in the program. There will be no implicit evaluation of program determined situations. Time delays will be program specifiable for both real and simulated times.

H. SYNTAX AND COMMENT CONVENTIONS

1. General Characteristics
2. No Syntax Extensions
3. Source Character Set
4. Identifiers and Literals
5. Lexical Units and Lines
6. Key Words
7. Comment Conventions
8. Unmatched Parentheses
9. Uniform Referent Notation
10. Consistency of Meaning

H1.   The source language will be free format with an explicit statement delimiter, will allow the use of mnemonically significant identifiers, will be based on conventional forms, will have a simple uniform and easily parsed grammar, will not provide unique notations for special cases, will not permit abbreviation of identifiers or key words, and will be syntactically unambiguous.

Clarity and readability of programs will be the primary criteria for selecting a syntax.   Each of the above points can contribute to program clarity.   The use of free format, mnemonic identifiers and conventional forms allows the programmer to use notations which have their familiar meanings to put down his ideas and intentions in the order and form that humans think about them, and to transfer skills he already has to the solution of the problem at hand.   A simple uniform language reduces the number of cases which must be dealt with by anyone using the language.   If programs are difficult for the translator to parse they will be difficult for people. Similar things should use the same notations with the special case processing reserved for the translator and object machine.   The purpose of mnemonic identifiers and key words is to be informative and increase the distance between lexical units of programs.   This does not prevent the use of short identifiers and short key words.

H2.   The user will not be able to modify the source language syntax. Specifically, he will not be able to modify operator hierarchies, introduce new precedence rules, define new key word forms or define new infix operator precedences.

If the user can change the syntax of the language, then he can change the basic character and understanding of the language.   The distinction between semantic extensions and syntactic extensions is similar to that between being able to coin new words in English or being able to move to another natural language. Coining words requires learning those new meanings before they can be used, but at the same time increases the power the language for some application areas. Changing the grammar, (e.g., Franglais, the use of French grammar with interspersed English words) however, undermines the basic understanding of the language itself, changes the mode of expression, and removes the commonalities which obtain between various specializations of the language. Growth of a language through definition of new data and operations and the introduction of new words and symbols to identify them is desirable, but there should be no provision for changing the grammatical rules of the language. This requirement does not conflict with E4 and does not preclude associating new meanings with existing infix operators.

H3. The syntax of source language programs will be composable from a character set suitable for publication purposes, but no feature of the language will be inaccessible using the 64 character ASCII subset.

A common language should use notations and a character set convenient for communicating algorithms, programs, and programming techniques among its users. On the other hand, the language should not require special equipment (e.g., card readers and printers) for its use. The use of the 64 character ASCII subset will make the language compatible with the federal information processing standard 64 character set, FIPS-1, which has been adopted by the U.S.A. Standard code for Information Interchange (USASCII). The language definition will specify the translation from the publication language into the restricted character set.

H4. The language definition will provide the formation rules for identifiers and literals. These will include literals for numbers and character strings and a break character for use internal to identifiers and literals.

Lexical units of the language should be defined in a simple uniform and easily understood manner. Some possible break characters are the space(W. Dijkstra, coding examples in Chapter I, "Notes in Structured Programming," in Structured Programming by O.-J. Dahl, E. W. Dijkstra and C.A.R. Moore, Academic Press, 1972. & Thomas A. Standish, "A Structured Program to Play Tic-Tac-Toe," notes for Information and Computer Science 3 course at Univ. of California-Irvine, October 1974) (i.e., any number of spaces or end-of-line), the underline and the tilde. The space cannot be used if identifiers and user defined infix operators are lexically indistinguishable, but in such a case the formal grammar for the language would be ambiguous (see H1). A literal break character contributes to the readability of programs and makes the entry of long literals less error prone. With a space as a break character one can enter multipart (i.e., more than one lexical unit) identifiers such as "REAL TIME CLOCK" or long literals, such as, "3.14159 26535 89793." Use of a break can also be used to guarantee that missing quote brackets on character literals do not cause errors which propagate beyond the net end-of-line. the language should require separate quoting of each line of a long literal: "This is a long" "literal string".

H5. There will be no continuation of lexical units across lines, but there will be a way to include object characters such as end-of-line in literal strings.

Many elementary input errors arise at the end of lines. Programs are input on line oriented media but the concept of end-of-line is foreign to free format text. Most of the error prone aspects of end-of-line can be eliminated by not allowing lexical units to continue over lines. The sometimes undesirable effects of this restriction can be avoided by permitting identifiers and literals to be composed from more than one lexical unit (see H4) and by evaluating constant expressions at compile time (see C4).

H6. Key words will be reserved, will be very few in number, will be informative, and will not be usable in contexts where an identifier can be used.

By key words of the language are meant those symbols and strings which have special meaning in the syntax of programs. They introduce special syntactic forms such as are used for control structures and declarations or the are used as infix operators, or as some form of parenthesis. Key words will be reserved, that is unusable as identifiers, to avoid confusion and ambiguity. Key words will be few in number because each new key word introduces another case in the parsing rules and thereby adds to complexity in understanding the language, and because large numbers of key words inconvenience and complicate the programmer's task of choosing informative identifiers. Key words should be concise, but being information is more important than being short. A major exception is the key word introducing a comment; it is the comment and not its key word which should do the informing. Finally, there will be no place in a source language program in which a key word can be used in place of an identifier. That is, functional form operations and special data items built into the language or accessible as a standard extension will not be treated as key words but will be treated as any other identifier.

H7. The source language will have a single uniform comment convention. Comments will be easily distinguishable from code, will be introduced by a single (or possibly two) language defined characters, will permit any combination of characters to appear, will be able to appear anywhere reasonable in programs, will automatically terminate at end-of-line if not otherwise terminated, and will not prohibit automatic reformatting of programs.

These are all obvious points which will encourage the use of comments in programs and avoid their error prone features in some existing languages. Comments anywhere reasonable in a program will not be taken to mean that they can appear internal to a lexical unit, such as, an identifier, key word, or between the opening and closing brackets of a character string. One comment convention which nearly meets these criteria is to have a special quote character which begins comments and with either the quote or an end-of-line ending each comment. This allows both embedded and line-oriented comments.

H8. The language will not permit unmatched parentheses of any kind.

Some programming languages permit closing parentheses to be omitted. If, for example, a program contained more "BEGINs" than "ENDs" the translator might insert enough "ENDs" at the end of the program to make up the difference. This makes programs easier to write because it sometimes saves writing several "ENDs" at the end of programs and because it eliminates all syntax errors for missing "ENDs." Failure to require proper parentheses matching makes it more difficult to write correct programs. Good programming practice requires that matching parentheses be included in programs whether or not they are required by the language. Unfortunately, if they are not required by the language then there can be no syntax check to discover where errors were made. The language will require full parentheses matching. This does not preclude syntactic features such as "case x of s1, s2...sn end case" in which "end" is paired with a key word other than "begin." Nor does it alone prohibit open forms such as "if-then-else-."

H9. There will be a uniform referent notation.

The distinction between function calls and data reference is one of representation, not of use. Thus, there will be no language imposed syntactic distinction between function calls and data selection. If, for example, a computed function is replaced by a lookup table there should be no need to change the calling program. This does not preclude the inclusion of more than one referent notation.

H10.   No language defined symbols appearing in the same context will have essentially different meanings.

This contributes to the clarity and uniformity of programs, protects against psychological ambiguity and avoids some error prone features of extant languages. In particular, this would exclude the use of = to imply both assignment and equality, would exclude conventions implying that parenthesized parameters have special semantics (as with PL/1 subroutines), and would exclude the use of an assignment operator for other than assignment (e.g., left hand side function calls).   It would not, however, require different operator symbols for integer, real or even matrix arithmetic since these are in fact special cases of the same abstract operations and would allow the use of generic functions applicable to several data types.

I. DEFAULTS, CONDITIONAL COMPILATION AND LANGUAGE RESTRICTIONS
  1. No Defaults in Program Logic
  2. Object Representation Specifications Optional
  3. Compile Time Variables
  4. Conditional Compilation
  5. Simple Base Language
  6. Translator Restrictions
  7. Object Machine Restrictions

I1.   There will be no defaults in programs which affect the program logic. That is, decisions which affect program logic will be made either irrevocably when the language is defined or explicitly in each program.

The only alternative is implementation dependent defaults with the translator determining the meaning of programs.   What a program does, should be determinable from the program and the defining documentation for the programming language.   This does not require that binding of all program properties be local to each use.   Quite the contrary, it would, for example, allow automatic definition of assignment for all variables or global specification of precision.   What it does require is that each decision be explicit: in the language definition, global to some scope, or local to each use.   Omission of any selection which affects the program logic will be treated as an error by the translator.

I2.   Defaults will be provided for special capabilities affecting only object representation and other properties which the programmer does not know or care about.   Such defaults will always mean that the programmer does not care which choice is made.   The programmer will be able to override these defaults when necessary.

The language should be oriented to provide a high degree of management control and visibility to programs and toward self-documenting programs with the programmer required to make his decisions explicit.   On the other hand, the programmer should not be forced to overspecify his programs and thereby cloud their logic, unnecessarily eliminate opportunities for optimization, and misrepresent arbitrary choices as essential to the program logic.   Defaults will be allowed, in fact, encouraged in don't care situations.   Such defaults will include data representations (see J4), open vs. closed subroutine calls (see J5), and reentrant vs. nonreentrant code generation.

I3.   The user will be able to associate compile time variables with programs. These will include variables which specify the object computer model and other aspects of the object machine configuration.

When a language has different host and object machines and when its compilers can produce code for several configurations of a given machine, the programmer should be able to specify the intended object machine configuration. The user should have control over the compile time variables used in his program. Typically they would be associated with the object computer model, the memory size, special hardware options, the operating system if present, peripheral equipment or other aspects of the object machine configuration. Compile time variables will be set outside the program, but available for interrogation within the program (see I4 and C4).

I4.   The source language will permit the use of conditional statements (e.g., case statements) dependent on the object environment and other compile time variables.   In such cases the conditional will be evaluated at compile time and only the selected path will be compiled.

An environmental inquiry capability permits the writing of common programs and procedures which are specialized at compile time by the translator as a function of the intended object machine configuration or of other compile time variables (see I3).   This requirement is a special case of evaluation of constant expressions at compile time (see C4).   It provides a general purpose capability for conditional compilation.

I5.   The source language will contain a simple clearly identifiable base or kernel which houses all the power of the language.   To the extent possible, the base will be minimal with each feature providing a single unique capablity not otherwise duplicated in the base.   The choice of the base will not detract from the efficiency, safety, or understandability of the language.

The capabilities available in any language can be partitioned into two groups, those which are definable within the base and those which provide an essential primitive capability of the language.   The smaller and simpler the base the easier the language will be to learn and use.   A clearly delineated base with features not in the base defined in terms of the base, will improve the ease and efficiency of learning, implementing and maintaining the language.   Only the base need be implemented to make the full source language capability available.

Base features will provide relatively low level general purpose capabilities not yet specialized for particular applications. There will be no prohibition on a translator incorporating speciaized optimizations for particular extensions. Any extension provided by a translator will, however, be definable within the base language using the built-in definition facilities. Thus, programs using the extension will be translatable by any compiler for the language but not necessarily with the same object efficiency.

16. Language restrictions which are dependent only on the translator and not on the object machine will be specified explicitly in the language definition.

Limits on the number of array dimensions, the length of identifiers, the number of nested parentheses levels in expressions, or the number of identifiers in programs are determined by the translator and not by the object machine. Ideally, the limits should be set so high that no program (save the most abrasive) encounters the limits. In each case, however: (a) some limit must be set, (b) whatever the limit, it will impose on some and therefore must be known by the users of the translator, (c) letting each translator set its own limits means that programs will not be portable, (d) setting the limits very high requires that the translator be hosted only on large machines and (e) quite low limits do not impose significantly on either the power of the language or the readability of programs. Thus, the limits should be set as part of the language definition. They should be small enough that they do not dominate the compiler and large enough that they do not interfere with the usefulness of the language. If they were set at say the 99 percent level based on statistics from existing DoD computer programs the limits might be a few hundred for numbers of identifiers and less than ten in the other cases mentioned above.

17. Language restrictions which are inherently dependent only on the object environment will not be built into the language definition or any translator.

Limits on the amount of run time storage, access to specialized peripheral equipments, use of special hardware capabilities and access to real time clocks are dependent on the object machine and configuration. The translator will report when a program exceeds the resources or capabilities of the intended object machine but will not build in arbitrary limits of its own.

J. EFFICIENT OBJECT REPRESENTATIONS AND MACHINE DEPENDENCIES
1. Efficient Object Code
2. Optimizations Do Not Change Program Effect
3. Machine Language Insertions
4. Object Representation Specifications
5. Open and Closed Routine Calls

J1. The language and its translators will not impose run time costs for unneeded or unused generality. They will be capable of producing efficient code for all programs.

The base language and library definitions might contain features and capabilities which are not needed by everyone, or at least, not be everyone all the time. The language should not force programs to require greater generality than they need. When a program does not use a feature or capability it should pay no run time cost for the feature being in the language or library. When the full generality of a feature is not used, only the necessary (reduced) cost should be paid. Where possible, language features (such as, automatic and dynamic array allocation, process scheduling, file management and I/O buffering) which require run time support packages should be provided as standard library definitions and not as part of the base language. The user will not have to pay time and space for support packages he does not use. Neither will there be automatic movement of programs or data between main store and backing shore which is not under program control (unless the object machine has virtual memory with underlying management beyond the control of all its users). Language features will result in special efficient object codes when their full generality is not used. A large number of special cases should compile efficiently. For example, a program doing numerical calculations on unsubscripted real variables should produce code no worse than FORTRAN. Parameter passing for single argument routines might be implemented much less expensively than multiple argument routines.

One way to reduce costs for unneeded capabilities is to have a base language whose data structures and operations provide a single capability which is composable and has a straight-forward implementation in the object code of conventional architecture machines. If the base language components are easily composable they can be used to construct the specialized structures needed by specific applications, if they are simple and provide a single capability they will not force the use of unneeded capabilities in order to obtain needed capabilities, and if they are compatible with the features normally found in sequential uniprocessor digital computers with random access memory they will have near minimum or at least low cost implementation on many object machines.

J2. Any optimizations performed by the translator will not change the effect of the program.

More simply, the translator cannot give up program reliability and correctness, regardless of the excuse. Note that for most programming languages there are few known safe optimizations and many unsafe ones. The number of applicable safe optimizations can be increased by making more information available to the compiler and by choosing language constructs which allow safe optimizations. This requirement allows optimization by code motion providing that motion does not change the effect of the program.

J3. The source language will provide encapsulated access to machine dependent hardware facilities including machine language code insertions.

It is difficult to be enthusiastic about machine language insertions. They defeat the purpose of machine independence constrain the implementation techniques complicate the diagnostics, impair the safety of type checking, and detract from the reliability, readability, and modifiability of programs. The use of machine language insertions is particularly dangerous in multiprogramming applications because they impair the ability to exclude, "a priori," a large class of time-dependent bugs. Rigid enforcement of scope rules by the compiler in real time applications is a powerful tool to ensure that one sequential process will not interfere with others in an uncontrolled fashion. Similarly, when several independent programs are executed in an interleaved fashion, the correct execution of each may depend on the others not having improperly used machine language insertions.

Unfortunately machine language insertions are necessary for interfacing special purpose devices, for accessing special purpose hardware capabilities, and for certain code optimizations on time critical paths. Here we have an example of Dijkstra's dilemma in which the mismatch between high level language programming and the underlying hardware is unacceptable and there is no feasible way to reject the hardware. The only remaining alternative is to "continue bit pushing in the old way, with all the known ill effects." Those ill effects can, however, be constrained to the smallest possible perimeter in practice if not in theory. The ability to enter machine language should not be used as an excuse to exclude otherwise needed facilities from the HOL; the abstract description of programs in the HOL should not require the use of machine language insertions. The semantics of machine language insertions will be determinable from the HOL definition and the object machine description alone and not dependent on the translator characteristics Machine language insertions will be encapsulated so they can be easily recognized and so that it is clear which variables and program identifiers are accessed within the insertion. The machine language insertions will be permitted only within the body of compile time conditional statements (see I4) which depend on the object machine configuration (see I3). They will not be allowed interspersed with executable statements of the source language.

J4. It will be possible within the source language to specify the object presentation of composite data structures. These descriptions will be optional and encapsulated and will be distinct from the logical description. The user will be able to specify the time/space trade-off to the translator. If not specified, the object representation will be optimal as determined by the translator.

It is often necessary to give detailed specifications of the object data representations to obtain maximum density for large data files to meet format requirements imposed by the hardware of peripheral equipment, to allow special optimizations on time critical paths, or to ensure compatibility when transferring data between machines.

It will be possible to specify the order of the fields, the width of fields, the presence of don't care fields, and the position of word boundaries. It will be possible to associate source language identifiers (data or program) with special machine addresses. The use of machine dependent characteristics of the object representation will be restricted as with machine dependent code (see J3). When multiple fields per word are specified the compiler may have to generate some form of shift and mask operations for source program references and assignments to those variables (i.e., fields). As with machine-language insertions, object data specifications should be used sparingly and the language features for their use must be Spartan, nor grandiose.

If the object representation of a composite data object is not specified in the source program, there will be no specific default guaranteed by the translator. The translator might, for example, attempt to minimize access time and/or memory space in determining the object representation. It might, depending on the object machine characteristics, assign variables and fields of records to full words, but assign array elements to the smallest of bits, bytes, half words, words or exact multiple words permitted by the logical description.

J5. The programmer will be able to specify whether calls on a routine are to have an open or closed implementation. An open and a closed routine of the same description will have identical semantics.

The use of inline open procedures can reduce the run time execution costs significantly in some cases. There are the obvious advantages in eliminating the parameter passing, in avoiding the saving of return marks, and in not having to pass arguments to and from the routine. A less obvious, but often more important advantage in saving run time costs is the ability to execute constant portions of routines at compile time and, thereby, eliminate time and space for those portions of the procedure body at run time. Open routine capability is especially important for machine language insertions.

The distinction between open and closed implementation of a routine is an efficiency consideration and should not affect the function of the routine. Thus, an open routine will differ from a syntax macro in that (a) its global environment is that of its definition and not that of its call and (b) multiple occurrences of a formal value (i.e., read only) parameter in the body have the same value. If a routine is not specified as either open or closed the choice will be optimal as determined by the translator.

K. PROGRAM ENVIRONMENT
   1. Operating System Not Required
   2. Program Assembly
   3. Software Development Tools
   4. Translator Options
   5. Assertions and Other Optional Specifications

K1. The language will not require that the object machine have an operating system. When the object machine does have an operating system or executive program, the hardware/operating system combination will be interpreted as defining an abstract machine which acts as the object machine for the translator.

A language definition cannot dictate the architecture of existing object machines whether defined entirely in hardware or in a hardware/software combination. It can provide a source language representation of all the needed capabilities and attempt to choose these so they have an obvious and efficient translation in the object machines.

K2. The language will support the integration of separately written modules into an operational program.

Separately written modules in the form of routines and type definitions are necessary for the management of large software efforts and for effective use of libraries. The user will be able to cause anything in any accessible library to be inserted into his program. This is a requirement for separate definition but not necessarily for separate compilation. The decision as to whether separately defined program modules are to be maintained in source or object language form is a question of implementation efficiency, will be a local management option and will not be imposed by the language definition. The trade-offs involved are complicated by other requirements for type checking of parameters (see C6), for open subroutines (see J5), for efficient object representations (see J1), and for constant expression evaluation at compile time (see C4). In general, separate compilation increases the difficulty and expense of the interface validations needed for program safety and reliability and detracts from object program efficiency by removing many of the optimizations otherwise possible at the interfaces, but at the same time it reduces the cost and complexity of compilation.

K3. A family of programming tools and aids in the form of support packages including linkers, loaders and debugging systems will be made available with the language and its translators. There will be a consistent easily used user interface for these tools.

The time has passed in which a programming language can be considered in isolation from its programming environment. The availability of programming tools which need not be developed and/or supported by individual projects is a major factor in the acceptability of a language. There is no need to restrict the kinds or form of support software available in the programming environment, and continued development of new tools should be encouraged and made available in a competitive market. It is, however, desirable that tools be developed in their own source language to simplify their portability and maintainability.

K4. A variety of useful options to aid generation, test, documentation and modification of programs will be provided as support software available with the language or as translator options. As a minimum these will include program editing, post- mortem analysis and diagnostics, program reformating for standard indentations, and cross-reference generation.

There will be special facilities to aid the generation, test, documentation and modification of programs. The "best" set of capabilities and their proper form is not currently known. Since nonstandard translator options and availability of nonstandard software tools and aids do not adversely affect software commonality, the language definition and standards will not dictate arbitrary choices. Instead, the development of language associated tools and aids will be encouraged within the constraint of implementing and supporting the source language as defined. Tools and debugging aids will be source language oriented.

Some of the translator options which have been suggested and may be useful include the following. Code might be compiled for assertions which would give run time warnings when the value of the assertion predicate is false. It might provide run time tracing of specified program variables. Dimensional analysis might be done on units of measure specifications. Special optimizations might be invoked. There might be capability for timing analysis and gathering run time statistics. There might be translator supplied feedback to provide management visibility regarding progress and conformity with local conventions. The user might be able to inhibit code generation. There might be facilities for compiling program patches and for controlling access to language features. The translator might provide a listing of the number of instructions generated against corresponding source inputs and/or an estimate of their execution times. It might provide a variety of listing options.

K5. The source language will permit inclusion of assertions, assumptions, axiomatic definitions of data types, debugging specifications;, and units of measures in programs. Because many assertional methods are not yet powerful enough for practical use, nor sufficiently well developed for standardization, they will have the status of comments.

There are many opinions on the desirability, usefulness, and proper form for each of these specifications. Better program documentation is needed and specifications of these kinds may help. Specifications also introduce the possibility of automated testing, run time verification of predicates, formal program proofs, and dimensional analysis. The language will not prohibit inclusion of these forms of specification if and when they become available for practical use in programs. Assertions, assumptions, axiomatic definitions and units of measure in source language programs should be enclosed in special brackets and should be treated as interpreted comments -- comments which are delimited by special comment brackets and which may be interpreted during translation or debugging to provide units analysis, verification of assertions and assumptions, etc.--but whose interpretation would be optional to translator implementations.

L. TRANSLATORS
1. No Superset Implementations
2. No Subset Implementations
3. Low-Cost Translation
4. Many Object Machines
5. Self-Hosting Not Required
6. Translator Checking Required
7. Diagnostic Messages
8. Translator Internal Structure
9. Self-Implementable Language

L1. No implementation of the language will contain source language features which are not defined in the language standard. Any interpretation of a language feature not explicitly permitted by the language definition will be forbidden.

This guarantees that use of programs and software subsystems will not be restricted to a particular site by virtue of using their unique version of the language. It also represents a commitment to freezing the source language, inhibiting innovations and growth in the form of the source language, and confining the base language to the current state of the art in return for stability, wider applicability of software tools, reusable software, greater software visibility, and increased payoff for tool building efforts. It does not, however, disallow library definition optimizations which are translator unique.

L2. Every translator for the language will implement the entire base language. There will be no subset implementations of the base language.

If individual compilers implement only a subset of the language, the there is no chance for software commonality. If a translator does not implement the entire language, it cannot give its users access to standard supported libraries or to application programs implemented on some other translator. Requiring that the full language be implemented will be expensive only if the base language is large, complex, and nonuniform. The intended source language product from this effort is a small simple uniform base language with the specialized features, support packages, and complex features relegated to library routines not requiring direct translator support. If simple low cost translators are not feasible for the selected language, then the language is too large and complex to be standardized and the goal of language commonality will not be achievable.

L3. The translator will minimize compile time costs. A goal of any translator for the language will be low cost translation.

Where practical and beneficial the user will have control over the level of optimization applied to his programs. The programmer will have control over the tradeoffs between compile time and run time costs. The desire for small efficient translators which can be hosted by machines with limited size and capability should influence the design of the base language against inclusion of unnecessary features and towards systematic treatment of features which are included. The goal will be effective use of the available machines both in object execution and translation and not maximal speed of translation.

Translation costs depend not only on the compiler but the language design. Both the translator and the language design will emphasize low cost translation, but in an environment of large and long-lived software products this will be secondary to requirements for reliability and maintainability. Language features will be chosen to ensure that they do not impose costs for unneeded generality and that needed capabilities can be translated into efficient object representations. This means that the inherent costs of specific language features is the context of the total language must be understood by the designers, implementers and users of the language. One consequence should be that trivial programs compile and run in trivial time. On the other hand, significant optimization is not expected from a minimal cost translator.

L4. Translators will be able to produce code for a variety of object machines. The machine independent parts of translators might be built independent of the code generators.

There is currently no common widely used computer in the DoD. There are at least 250 different models of commercial machines in use in DoD with many more specialized machines. A common language must be applicable to a wide variety of models and sizes of machines. Translators might be written so they can produce object code for several machines. This reduces the proliferation of translators and makes the full power of an existing translator available at the cost of producing an additional code generator.

L5. The translator need not be able to run on all the object machines. Self-hosting is not required, but is often desirable.

The DoD operational programming environment includes many small machines which are unable to support adequately the design, documentation, test, and debugging aids necessary for the development of timely, reliable or efficient software. Large machine users should not be penalized for the restrictions of small machines when a common language is used. On the other hand, the size of machines which can host translators should be kept as small as possible by avoiding unnecessary generality in the language.

L6. The translator will do full syntax checking, will check all operations and parameters for type compatibility and will verify that all language imposed semantic restrictions on the source programs are met. It will not automatically correct errors detected at compile time.

The purpose of source language redundancy and avoidance of error prone language features is reliability. The price is paid in programmer inconvenience in having to specify his intent in greater detail. The payoff comes when the translator checks that the source program is internally consistent and adheres to its authors' stated intentions. There is a clear trade-off between error avoidance and programming ease; surveys conducted in the Services show that the programmers as well as managers will opt for error avoidance over ease when given the choice. The same choice is dictated by the need for well documented maintainable software.

L7. The translator will produce compile time explanatory diagnostic error and warning messages. A suggested set of error and warning situations will be provided as part of the language definition.

The translator will attempt to provide the maximal useful feedback to its user. Diagnostic messages will not be coded but will be explanatory and in source language terms. Translators will continue processing and checking after errors have been found but should be careful not to generate erroneous messages because of translator confusion. The translator will always produce correct code; when source programs errors are encountered by the translator or referenced program structures omitted, the compiler will produce code to cause a run time exception condition upon any attempt to execute those parts of the program. Warnings will be generated when a source language construct is exceptionally expensive to implement on the specified object machine. A suggested set of diagnostic messages provided as part of the language definition contributes to commonality in the implementation and use of the language. The discipline of designing diagnostic messages keyed to the design may also uncover pitfalls in the language design and thereby contribute to a more precise and better understood language description.

L8. The characteristics of translator implementations will not be dictated by the language definition or standards.

The adoption of a common language is a commitment to the current state of the art for programming language design for some duration. It does not, however, prevent access to new software and hardware technology, new techniques and new management strategies which do not impact the source language definition. In particular, innovation should be encouraged in the development of translators for a common language providing they implement exactly the source language as defined. Translators like all computer programs should be written in expectation of change.

L9. Translators for the language will be written in their own source language.

There will be at least one implementation of the translator in its own language which does all parsing and compile-time checking and produces an output suitable for easy translation to specific object machines. If the language is well-defined and uniform in structure, a self-description will contribute to understanding of the language. The availability of the machine independent portion of a translator will make the full power of the language available to any object machine at the cost of producing an additional code generator (whose cost may be high) and it reduces the likelihood of incompatible implementations. Translators written in their own source language are automatically available on any of their object machines providing the object machine has sufficient resources to support a compiler.

M. LANGUAGE DEFINITION, STANDARDS AND CONTROL
1. Existing Language Features Only
2. Unambiguous Definition
3. Language Documentation Required
4. Control Agent Required
5. Support Agent Required
6. Library Standards and Support Required

M1. The language will be composed from features which are within the state of the art and any design or redesign which is necessary to achieve the needed characteristics will be conducted as an engineering design effort and not as a research project.

The adoption of a common language can be successful only if it makes available a modern programming language compatible with the latest software technology and is compatible with "best" current programming practice but the design and implementation of the language should not require additional research or require use of untried ideas. State-of-the-art cannot, however, be taken to mean that a feature has been incorporated in an operational DoD language and used for an extended period, or DoD will be forever tied to the technology of FORTRAN-like languages; but there must be some assurances through analysis and use that its benefits and deficiencies are known. The larger and more complex the structure, the more analysis and use that should be required. Language design should parallel other engineering design efforts in that it is a task of consolidation and not innovation. The language designer should be familiar with the many choices in semantic and syntactic features of language and should strive to compose the best of these into a consistent structure congruous with the needed characteristics. The language should be composed from known semantic features and familiar notations, but the use of proven feature should not necessarily impose that notation. The language must not just be a combination of existing features which satisfy the individual requirements but must be held together by a consistent and uniform structure which acts to minimize the number of concepts, consolidates divergent features and simplifies the whole.

M2. The semantics of the language will be defined unambiguously and clearly. To the extent a formal definition assists in attaining these objectives, the language's semantics will be specified formally.

A complete and unambiguous definition of a common language is essential. Otherwise each translator will resolve the ambiguities and fill in the gaps in its own unique way. There are currently a variety of methods for formal specification of programming language semantics but it remains a major effort to produce a rigorous formal description and the resulting products are of questionable practical value. The real value in attempting a formal definition is that it reveals incomplete and ambiguous specifications. An attempt will be made to provide a formal definition of any language selected but success in that effort should not be requisite to its selection. Formal specification of the language might take the form of an axiomatic definition, use of the Vienna Definition Language, or use of some other formal semantic system.

M3. The user documentation of the language will be complete and will include both a tutorial introductory description and a formal in-depth description. The language will be defined as if it were the machine level language of an abstract digital computer.

The language should be intuitively correct and easily learned and understood by its potential users. The language definition might include an Algol-60 like description(P. Naur (Ed.), "Revised Report on the Algorithmic Language Algol-60," Communication of the A.C.M. Vol.6, No. 1, January 1963, p. 1-17.) with the source language syntax given in BNF or some other easily understood metalanguage and the corresponding semantics given in English. As with the descriptions of digital computer hardware, the semantics and syntax of each feature must be defined precisely and unambiguously. The action of any legal program will be determinable from the program and the language description alone. Any computation which can be described in the language will ultimately draw only on capabilities which are built into the language. No characteristics of the source language will be dependent on the idiosyncrasies of its translators.

The language documentation will include syntax, semantics and examples of each language construct, listings of all key words and language defined defaults. Examples shall be included to show the intended use of language features and to illustrate proper use of the language. Particularly expensive and inexpensive constructs will be pointed out. Each document will identify its purpose and prerequisites for its use.

M4. The language will be configuration managed throughout its total life cycle and will be controlled at the DoD level to ensure that there is only one version of the source language and that all translators conform to that standard.

Without controls a hopefully common language may become another umbrella under which new languages proliferate while retaining the same name. All compilers will be tested and certified for conformity to the standard specification and freedom from known errors prior to their release for use in production projects. The language manager will be on the OSD staff, but a group within the Military Departments or Agencies might act as the executive agent. A configuration control board will be instituted with user representation and chaired by a member of the OSD staff.

M5. There will be identified support agent(s) responsible for maintaining the translators and for associated design, development, debugging and maintenance aids.

Language commonality is an essential step in achieving software commonality, but the real benefits accrue when projects and contractors can draw on existing software with assurance that it will be supported, when systems can build from off the shelf components or at least with common tools, and when efforts can be spent to expand existing capabilities rather than building from scratch. Support of common widely used tools and aids should be provided independent of projects if common software is to be widely used. Support should be on a DoD-wide basis with final responsibility resting with a stable group or groups of qualified in-house personnel.

M6. There will be standards and support agents for common libraries including application-oriented libraries.

In a given application of a programming language three levels of the system must be learned and used: the base language, the standard library definitions used in that application area, and the local application programs. Users are responsible for the local application programs and local definitions but not for the language and its libraries which are used by many projects and sites. A principal user might act as agent for an entire application area.

Vol. 49: Interactive Systems. Proceedings 1976. Edited by A. Blaser and C. Hackl. VI, 380 pages. 1976.

Vol. 50: A. C. Hartmann, A Concurrent Pascal Compiler for Mini-computers. VI, 119 pages. 1977.

Vol. 51: B. S. Garbow, Matrix Eigensystem Routines – Eispack Guide Extension. VIII, 343 pages. 1977.

Vol. 52: Automata, Languages and Programming. Fourth Colloquium, University of Turku, July 1977. Edited by A. Salomaa and M. Steinby. X, 569 pages. 1977.

Vol. 53: Mathematical Foundations of Computer Science. Proceedings 1977. Edited by J. Gruska. XII, 608 pages. 1977.

Vol. 54: Design and Implementation of Programming Languages. Proceedings 1976. Edited by J. H. Williams and D. A. Fisher. X, 496 pages. 1977.

This series aims to report new developments in computer science research and teaching – quickly, informally and at a high level. The type of material considered for publication includes:

1. Preliminary drafts of original papers and monographs
2. Lectures on a new field, or presenting a new angle on a classical field
3. Seminar work-outs
4. Reports of meetings, provided they are
   a) of exceptional interest and
   b) devoted to a single topic.

Texts which are out of print but still in demand may also be considered if they fall within these categories.

The timeliness of a manuscript is more important than its form, which may be unfinished or tentative. Thus, in some instances, proofs may be merely outlined and results presented which have been or will later be published elsewhere. If possible, a subject index should be included. Publication of Lecture Notes is intended as a service to the international computer science community, in that a commercial publisher, Springer-Verlag, can offer a wider distribution to documents which would otherwise have a restricted readership. Once published and copyrighted, they can be documented in the scientific literature.

Manuscripts

Manuscripts should comprise not less than 100 and preferably not more than 500 pages.
They are reproduced by a photographic process and therefore must be typed with extreme care. Symbols not on the typewriter should be inserted by hand in indelible black ink. Corrections to the typescript should be made by pasting the amended text over the old one, or by obliterating errors with white correcting fluid. Authors receive 75 free copies and are free to use the material in other publications. The typescript is reduced slightly in size during reproduction; best results will not be obtained unless the text on any one page is kept within the overall limit of 18 x 26.5 cm (7 x 10½ inches). The publishers will be pleased to supply on request special stationery with the typing area outlined.
Manuscripts in English, German or French should be sent to Prof. G. Goos, Institut für Informatik, Universität Karlsruhe, Zirkel 2, 7500 Karlsruhe/Germany, Prof. J. Hartmanis, Cornell University, Dept. of Computer-Science, Ithaca, NY/USA 14850, or directly to Springer-Verlag Heidelberg.

Springer-Verlag, Heidelberger Platz 3, D-1000 Berlin 33
Springer-Verlag, Neuenheimer Landstraße 28–30, D-6900 Heidelberg 1
Springer-Verlag, 175 Fifth Avenue, New York, NY 10010/USA

ISBN 3-540-08360-X
ISBN 0-387-08360-X